Governing Fables

Learning from Public Sector Narratives

A volume in
Research in Public Management
Lawrence R. Jones, *Series Editor*

Research in Public Management

Lawrence R. Jones
Series Editor

Governing Fables

Learning from Public Sector Narratives

Sandford Borins

University of Toronto

INFORMATION AGE PUBLISHING, INC.
Charlotte, NC • www.infoagepub.com

Library of Congress Cataloging-in-Publication Data

Borins, Sandford F., 1949-
Governing fables : learning from public sector narratives / Sandford
Borins.
    p. cm. – (Research in public management)
Includes bibliographical references.
ISBN 978-1-61735-490-8 (pbk.) – ISBN 978-1-61735-491-5 (hardcover) –
ISBN 978-1-61735-492-2 (e-book)
1. Narrative inquiry (Research method) 2. Public administration–United
States. 3. Public administration–Great Britain. 4. Organizational
change–United States. 5. Organizational change–Great Britain. I. Title.
H61.295.B67 2011
351.41–dc23

                                                    2011020338

Copyright © 2011 Information Age Publishing Inc.

Printed in the United States of America

For Beth Herst

Contents

Preface

An exploding Google count, from 16 million in 2007 to 50 million currently, makes it official. Narrative has become a buzzword. For those who study narrative, that is both good news and bad. Good, because attention is unquestionably being paid. Bad, because as the term grows ever more inescapable, it is losing both precision and meaning. Within popular culture, a narrative now is a rationale, an explanation, a justification. It is what wins an election, accounts for a catastrophe (economic or otherwise), sells a product, builds a brand. It is a story with intent. In its fullest conception, however, narrative denotes something more: a distinctive means of ordering experience; a particular mode of perceiving, representing, and communicating events; a way of structuring meaning in time.

Well in advance of narrative becoming a buzzword, there was an explosion of interest in narrative in the academic world. Originally, it was a field reserved for a small and specialized group of literary or film scholars known as narratologists. This interest is now shared across an expanding range of disciplines: cognitive science, artificial intelligence, evolutionary biology and psychology, anthropology, medicine, and law. Unlike the other disciplines, however, public management has been reluctant to embrace narrative, either as a research methodology or the subject of research. Therefore, my fundamental reason for writing this book is to encourage public management to take the narrative turn.

It is the understanding of narrative as a distinctive means of ordering experience that inspires *Governing Fables*. And it is for this reason that the

Governing Fables: Learning from Public Sector Narratives, pages xi–xii
Copyright © 2011 by Information Age Publishing
xi

book addresses itself to both academics and practitioners in public management. Within the public management domain, we must all deal in narratives: political, institutional, personal, pedagogic, or methodological. They are the implicit structures that govern what we do, how we perceive it, and how we communicate it to others. When we gain "narrative competence," we gain awareness of and perhaps mastery over the stories that shape our worlds. At the very least, we gain an understanding of the complex mechanisms at work in the narrative structures we are continually encountering and creating.

This book is offered as an example of a practice, not a manifesto. The analysis does not focus on single narratives looked at it isolation, but rather identifies a large enough range of narratives to establish genres, and then elucidates their common elements. More specifically, it focuses on authored narratives about public management produced in the UK and the United States in the last fifty years. Linking questions of narrative form to managerial content, *Governing Fables* discovers fundamental lessons about narrative and management. The most fundamental might well be the essential relationship between the two. That is the story at the heart of this book.

Acknowledgements

This book has been a long time in the making. It had its origins in the courses on narrative and management that I have taught over the last 2 decades at the Schulich School of Business at York University, the Department of Management at the University of Toronto at Scarborough, and the University of Toronto's Rotman School of Management. The courses have evolved over the years in terms of the increasing use of narratological concepts as a foundation, the expanding role I have given to student participation and presentations, and the continual updating of the set of movies, novels, and plays used. I have often assigned term papers requiring students to choose a text not discussed in class and analyze it, and these term papers have often brought to my attention works worthy of analysis. My University of Toronto at Scarborough colleagues Andrew Stark and Chandran Mylvaganam have occasionally given this course. Thus, the contributions of my colleagues and my students have influenced my thinking about public management narratives, and hence this book.

Research support for the book, as well as some teaching release time, was provided by a grant from the Social Sciences and Humanities Research Council of Canada. The two anonymous reviewers of my proposal also provided valuable suggestions.

A number of research assistants over the years have helped me with the choice of texts and the gathering of secondary materials. The assistants include Grace Bhesania, Ahsan Nanji, Eliza Jiang Chen, Laura Sampson, Kenneth Lee, and Kaylee Chretien. I very much appreciate their help.

Governing Fables: Learning from Public Sector Narratives, pages xiii–xiv
Copyright © 2011 by Information Age Publishing

I have sent portions of the manuscript to colleagues with relevant expertise or to creators whose narratives I have discussed, and have wherever possible incorporated their suggestions. They include Irv Ash, David Brown, D. Graham Burnett, Bob Costrell, Michael Dobbs, Dan Lang, Dennis Littky, Jonathan Lynn, Janet Morgan, Chris Mullin, Peter Russell, and John Stockwell. Prof. Lawrence Jones, editor of the Research in Public Administration series at Information Age Publishing, was very supportive of the project and made many helpful suggestions. Jowenne Herrera designed the cover and Natalie Neill provided the index. George Johnson, president and publisher of IAP, and Sarah Williams, production manager, brought the book to fruition.

My greatest debt of gratitude goes to my wife, Dr. Beth Herst. Her support went far beyond the expected, but always appreciated, spousal encouragement. As a literary scholar and playwright in her own right, she was deeply involved in the project in many ways, including pointing me toward narratological theory, watching and reading many texts, and sharing with me her reactions, and extensively revising the manuscript. So, for her support and participation in this project, I dedicate the book to her, with respect, appreciation, and love.

1

Narrative as Object and Method of Study

Introducing Narrative into Public Management

Once upon a time, the study of narrative was an activity reserved for the literary scholars known as narratologists. Entrenched behind ramparts of specialist terminology, frequently absorbed in abstruse theoretical skirmishes, their claims for the universal and timeless nature of their subject matter went largely unnoticed. That was then. The past two decades have seen an explosion of scholarly interest in narrative, whether understood simply as storytelling or more formally as the action of ordering, representing, and communicating a constructed sequence of events. It is an interest shared across an expanding range of disciplines: cognitive science, artificial intelligence, evolutionary biology and psychology, anthropology, law, and medicine. And its influence extends to popular discourse too. At time of writing, "narrative" boasts a Google count of 50 million, up sharply from 16 million in November 2007.

The pervasiveness of this narrative interest should not surprise us. More and more, the narrative impulse is being understood to be embedded deep in the developmental history of our species, a universal "category of human endeavor and experience" (Gottschall & Wilson, 2005), essential

Governing Fables: Learning from Public Sector Narratives, pages 1–26
Copyright © 2011 by Information Age Publishing
All rights of reproduction in any form reserved.

1

to our survival and evolution. Disciplines such as cognitive science, artificial intelligence, evolutionary biology and psychology, and linguistics posit a fundamental link between narrative and the management of complexity in acquiring, storing, and exchanging information. Narrative, in this view, is nothing less than the mark of that "cognitive fluidity" that enabled our Homo sapiens ancestors to enact a "cultural big bang" some 30,000 to 60,000 years ago, an evolutionary tipping point that saw the emergence of representational art, complex tool technology, long-range trade, and the rise of religion (Slingerland, 2008). Nor have we as a species outgrown our need for stories. They remain our primary means of making sense of experience, of creating meaning for ourselves and the world around us.[1]

The literature on narrative tends to abound in universalizing statements like these. But if we shift our gaze from the general to the specific, the narrative imperative appears no less pervasive. Consider the contemporary public sector and its range of actors (or protagonists). Now consider the innumerable stories these protagonists generate, communicate, and enact.

Every political party consciously creates a narrative of recent history to validate its claim to govern. Election campaigns are increasingly structured around "the story." How that story will be defined becomes the paramount strategic decision. And because rival parties' narratives are necessarily in conflict, engaging with (and disrupting) opposing stories becomes a priority. Party leaders also fashion personal biographical narratives that root their leadership capabilities in their life histories. Barack Obama's *Dreams from My Father* and *The Audacity of Hope* are perhaps the most striking example of the importance such personal stories now possess. Clearly, for large sections of the electorate, it was the explanatory, persuasive, and inspirational character of the candidate's story, the coherence of his narrative, far more than specific policies, that mattered.

Narrative is equally inseparable from policy and planning, which invariably require stories of origins (how a particular policy developed), as well as predictive narratives of future interactions between environmental forces and departmental commitments. In controversial policy areas, such as the debate over public health insurance in the United States, proponents of alternative approaches invariably employ personal narratives about representative individuals to dramatize the benefits of their proposed solutions ("happy endings") and the ineffectiveness or worse of their opponents' programs ("scare stories"). Much of the so-called public debate over the issue then becomes a matter of dueling stories.

In a political culture that places heavy emphasis on performance and public accountability, failures are bound to occur, and they must be explained. And here too stories become central. These explanatory institutional narratives, often embodied in the reports of blue ribbon panels or special investigators, provide sequence and locate agency, culminating in an attribution of responsibility. They function, to use the popular term, as a means of effecting "closure," an attempt to guarantee that this particular story will not be repeated.

Narrative functions even (or especially) at the purely personal level of the individual public sector career. When public servants apply for promotion, they must not only document their credentials but also generate a coherent narrative of their employment history and its meaning and why it has uniquely prepared them for the challenges of the new position they seek. Perhaps even more than most professions, public service demands a personal story—a work narrative—that can accommodate the complex interactions and competing claims of ambition, loyalty, discretion, commitment, service, politics, and governance.

The point I'm making is simple: if narratives so pervade the public sector, skill at engaging with, creating, and communicating compelling stories must be considered essential for both politicians and public servants. Similarly, if narratives are such a universal and compelling means of creating meaning and engaging an audience, they should be an essential way of communicating management concepts and skills.

There is an extensive and growing literature on "management and narrative." Little of it, however, discusses how to create and communicate effective narratives. Most of it deals with how to use narratives to communicate *other* management concepts and skills. This literature encompasses a variety of forms, including prescriptive guides for using extracts or "clips" for teaching purposes, articles espousing the research and pedagogical benefits of narratives, books of so-called lessons for managers drawn from an array of narrative sources as disparate as Shakespeare and Winnie the Pooh, as well as studies of the fictional depiction of public servants, politicians, and other public sector agents and organizations across a variety of forms— novels, dramas, films, and television.

A detailed survey of this literature will be provided below. The point I would make here is that, with notable exceptions, all these studies tend to suffer from at least three significant limitations. There is a general lack of any rigorous, or even systematic, selection criteria to justify the choice of narratives analyzed. And this initial omission is compounded by an equal lack of a clearly defined analytic methodology capable of addressing issues of narrative form as well as content. Failing to address issues of narrative form, this literature provides no insight into what makes the narratives it studies effective and, therefore, how practitioners could create persuasive narratives of their own. The result, especially in the lessons' literature, too often amounts to little more than a superficial reframing of characters and actions in the service of a random assortment of self-evident "insights."

This book hopes to do better. It takes as its point of departure (and its goal) a practice I call "narrative competence." The idea has its roots both in my own teaching and research experience, and the highly suggestive work now being done on the functional value of narrative—the evolutionary advantages it confers—which I cited briefly at the outset.

Some intellectual autobiography—my personal narrative—is necessary here. I began using fictional narratives to illustrate principles of public administration for students two decades ago with episodes of the British television series *Yes Minister* and *Yes Prime Minister*. The effectiveness of that modest beginning (and a concurrent research project on the role of public choice theory in the conceptualization of the television series [Borins, 1988]) encouraged me to develop a course on management and narrative that I have taught in updated versions most years since.

During this time, while I focused my research on new public management, innovation, and information technology, I became increasingly aware of the importance of narrative modes (histories, case studies, profiles of leaders) as methodologies in all these areas, and also as aspects of my research subjects themselves. The successful implementation of an innovation, as well as its subsequent replication, to take just one example, can depend in great measure on the stories innovators tell, the narratives they author (Borins, 2011; Denning, 2001). Growing in tandem with this personal narrative awareness was the inescapable knowledge of the changing world in which public sector managers were working. My research on information technology, in particular, revealed the paradox of an information-rich environment that was often communication and knowledge poor. It is a world, moreover, in which traditional organizational structures are being challenged, collaboration is the new norm, and intellectual and professional flexibility is a necessity (Borins et al., 2007).

It was at this juncture that I became aware of theories of narrative's relationship to "the evolved architecture of the human brain" (Slingerland, 2008), in particular, the importance of narrative to the management of both information and change. And it was then that I understood that it was not merely the content of the narratives I was teaching, but the experience of engaging critically with narrative itself, that was of value. So "narrative competence" was born, out of a conviction that managers who train themselves as conscious decoders of narrative structures also train themselves as meaning makers across the spectrum of their personal and professional experiences. In the new public service environment, such training has become essential.

At this point, an obvious objection arises. Granting this value to narrative competence, why choose one particular set of narratives over another for its exercise? The benefit of the practice, presumably, is independent of the specific texts engaged with. And that is true. This book could read with equal advantage texts by Stendhal or Scorsese. My choice, narratives of public sector agents and institutions produced in English during the last 50 years, reflects a doubled ambition. The chapters that follow will seek to model narrative competence through close analysis of stories that possess an intrinsic relevance for public sector managers by reason of their settings and content. These include American narratives of educational transformation; British narratives of politicians and senior bureaucrats; and American narratives of electoral politics, political management, and decision making by juries and in national defense. (These subgenres have been defined according to national and institutional setting rather than theme.) The goal, again, is double: to hone skills for managers as consumers and creators of complex and changing professional narratives *and* to provide context-specific insights for *public sector* managers in key areas of public sector activity.

This doubled ambition demands a doubled methodology drawing from both narratology and social science theory. The pitfall here is the easy assumption that the former speaks only to issues of narrative form, the latter only to those of (public sector) content. The challenge is to question wherever possible the interactions between the two.

Three Core Narratological Concepts

As I quickly discovered when I began my research, the field of narratology presents a daunting prospect to an outsider seeking entry. Decades of internal warfare between schools, ideologies, methods, and terminologies have generated a discourse so contested and so opaque as to appear, to the uninitiated at least, like a secret code. Even the noun itself is unstable. One of the most frequently cited dictionaries of narratology offers three significantly differing definitions (Prince, 2003).

Drawing on the work of the Dutch scholar Mieke Bal, in particular the revised edition of her influential book *Narratology: An Introduction to the Study of Narrative* (1985, rev. 1997), I take narratology to refer to the study of communications structured as a sequence of meaningfully related events, with "related" carrying the double sense of linked and retold.[2] And it is from my reading of Bal that I derive the three core narratological concepts that inform my engagement with public management narratives (stories both within and about public management).

Mieke Bal's work stands firmly within the Structuralist tradition of literary studies. From a 21st-century perspective, my choice may seem belated. Aren't we all post-Post-Structuralists now? Bal herself directly addresses the issue of the continuing relevance of her methodology throughout her revised edition, positioning her work beside more recent theories and schools. The practice she advocates is presented as an approach to the "cultural mode of expression" she calls "narrativity" (Bal, 1997, p. 222), a tool that "provides focus to the expectations with which readers process narrative" (1997, p. xv). In Bal's revised formulation, this tool is never intended to be exhaustive, nor does she consider it in any way inimical to the deconstructionist forms of critical engagement that have since become dominant among literary scholars. Simply put, what Bal's work offers is a means of identifying structural features that define narrative texts. What makes this particularly valuable for other disciplines seeking to engage with "narrativity" is her interest in nonliterary and nontextual narratives across the range of cultural production.

From Bal, I have directly adapted two core concepts: the distinction between fable and narrative and the idea of narrative polyphony (literally multivocality). Both require some explanation. At the center of Bal's method is a three-part distinction between "fabula," "story," and "text." These are, for her, the three essential components of a narrative, regardless of medium. "Text" refers to the "finite, structured whole composed of language signs," the words on the page, the marks on the canvas, the succession of images on the film. "Fabula" denotes "the material or content that is worked into a story," the basic story matter: its character types, actions, plots, settings, and themes. "Story" is the specific instantiation of the fabula, its unique rendering by a particular agent or agents (Bal, 1997, pp. 5–7).

Bal repeatedly stresses that all three levels interact continuously to create the narrativity effect, yet for my purposes it is the distinction between fabula and story that is crucial. To mark this distance from Bal, and in the hopes of making the terminology more intuitively transparent, I have renamed the concepts "fable" and "narrative." The meanings, however, remain essentially the same: fable connotes the informing story structures; narrative the specific mediations that relate those structures to each other and to the reader/viewer/audience. To quote Bal (1997, p. 6), it is "the difference between the sequence of events and the way in which those events are presented."

As Bal's analysis makes clear, that way is never uniform. Narratives are always multiple in their strategies, with numerous different narrating voices and viewpoints embedded within them; some explicit, others almost subliminal. Without importing the highly complex typologies Bal employs to categorize these narrative effects, I have adopted the phrase "narrative polyphony" to denote this crucial dimension of a narrative. The value of the term, for me, is the emphasis it places on a careful consideration of the many "voices" that speak through a narrative and the interplay of points of view they inevitably set in motion. While Bal's focus is on the multiplication of *intra*narrative voices, the constant layering, shifting, and embedding of points of view, time frames, and voices that a single narrative typically activates, I extend the concept outwards to encompass *inter*narrative polyphony as well; that is, the interplay between multiple narratives (re)telling a single fable.

The standard storytelling convention of the nineteenth century (the great age of the realist novel)—the omniscient narrator who sees into the minds of all the characters and is aware of all the events in the story, present and to come, and who often bestows on all characters and events a particular bias or perspective—was a way of reducing narrative polyphony. Twentieth-century developments—an increasing use of first-person or multiple narrative perspectives, experimentation with unreliable or misleading narrators, narratives enacting the process of consciousness itself—have, in contrast, enhanced polyphony. We will see occasional texts presented by an omniscient narrator, but far more of the more recent approaches.

The final narratological concept that informs my analysis, that of dominant and counter-fables, looks back beyond Bal to her acknowledged forebear, the Russian Formalist Vladimir Propp. In his *Morphology of the Folk Tale*, first published in Russian in 1928 and widely read in English translation in the 1960s, Propp (1968) used 100 Russian folk tales to identify inductively a set of 31 fundamental structural elements; that is, recurring constituent elements operating at the level of the fable (or fabula). While Propp's work had its critics, this model of a typology of recurring characters, functions, and actions has been widely adopted. We might be more familiar with it in its popular-culture manifestation of movie genres and genre-specific plot lines and character types identified by movie critics and film studies scholars: the lone gunman and the Western fable of inevitable violent confrontation; the cynical detective in his film noir plot of dangerous women and inescapable corruption (Hayward, 2006, pp. 185–188; McKee 1997, pp. 79–99).[3] In these schemas, little attention is paid to the political or managerial films that will be discussed in this book.

My analysis does not aspire to either the exhaustiveness or the formulaic rigidity of the tradition associated with Propp. It has been inspired, however, by the notion of dominant forms emerging within a particular genre of fable, and no less by the counter-fables these tend to produce, narratives that parody, invert, distort, or subvert the familiar formal structures of a given archetype. The counter-fable may be embedded within the dominant fable itself or exist as a retelling of it. It is a concept that both overlaps with, and folds back into, that of internarrative polyphony and serves to address precisely the phenomenon that first motivated my own "narrative turn": the recurring structures that I observed in public administration narratives and my desire to account for them more fully.

The Basic Fables

As mentioned above with reference to both Propp and film scholars, fables are discovered by induction from actual texts rather than deduction from first principles. But it may be more useful to begin by presenting the basic structure of a fable as if it were derived from first principles, even though its discovery was clearly the result of studying many narratives.

Public sector narratives concern both public sector organizations and individuals within those organizations. To hold the audience's attention, creators of narratives always focus on individual protagonists, whether actual or imagined. In that, narratives differ from MBA or MPA cases, which are frequently about organizational processes or strategic choices and have no protagonists. The protagonists' fortunes are tied more or less closely to those of their organization; more closely if they are its leaders, less closely if they are middle managers or frontline workers. Also, to hold their audiences' attention, creators of narratives make sure that the organizations chronicled are facing some sort of conflict or challenge. A narrative about a well-performing organization that attempts to perform a little better will not interest an audience. Organizations may respond to their challenges either with renewal or decline. Similarly, the challenge to an individual can be thought of as one of personal growth, so an individual who in some way helps an organization respond to a challenge receives extrinsic rewards (money, reputation), as well as the more intrinsic ones of capability and self-esteem.

These axes of organizational and individual outcomes lead to a four-quadrant classification, as seen in Table 1.1. This classification differs from the critical literature (e.g., McKee, 1997), which either conflates or does not distinguish between outcomes for the organization and outcomes for the protagonist. Reading from the upper left, the two diagonal elements

TABLE 1.1   Categorizing the Fables

	Personal growth of the protagonist	Personal decline of the protagonist
Organizational renewal	Heroic	Sacrificial, Retributive
Organizational decline	Ironic	Tragic, Satirical

are likely most familiar. In the heroic fable, a leader enables an organization to overcome or defeat a challenge and thereby renew itself, and the leader is rewarded both intrinsically and extrinsically. Heroic leadership is the stock-in-trade of many business books, from Peters and Waterman's (1982) classic *In Search of Excellence* to the present.

The opposite of the heroic fable is the tragic or satirical fable. In it, the organization declines as a result of the weaknesses of its leader or leaders. The fable may be tragic if the outcome is the result of a protagonist's fatal flaw, or it may be satirical if the leader has few redeeming virtues, with the narrative mode shifting to anger and/or contemptuous amusement.

The off-diagonal fables occur somewhat less frequently. In the upper right, a sacrificial fable would involve organizational renewal due to action by a protagonist that leads to his or her own decline or even demise. Perhaps the story is of a whistleblower whose revelations lead to the renewal of an organization, but who personally suffers and is never compensated for the damage to her career. A retributive tale involves an organization overthrowing a misguided leader and, through this purge, setting the stage for its own renewal. In the lower left, the ironic fable concerns an individual growing within the context of an organizational decline. An example is the story of an individual who rises to the top of a corrupt organization by embracing and excelling in its culture. While the individual has been successful, the narrative is telling us that, if such a person is the sort of leader that organization throws up, then the organization will ultimately fail. A second version of the fable would be a kind of *bildungsroman,* in which the protagonist is a person early in her career, who grows by learning from the decline of an organization with which she is temporarily associated. The organization may fail, but she has the benefit of her experience and will carry its lessons to other, more hopeful settings.

If a narrative has one protagonist and a simple structure, it will fit neatly into one of the four categories. But if it has multiple protagonists and if outcomes are debatable, in the sense that the audience may reasonably question whether an individual has grown or been corrupted (or both), or whether an organization has experienced a renewal or is in decline, then it may fit in several of the categories.

I will apply this categorization to the various genres that will be discussed in the book. For a certain genre, most texts might fit into one category, and this would be regarded as the dominant fable. We would expect to find counter-fables either concentrated in one or scattered in three of the other categories. This will be illustrated in the chapters that follow.

Organizing my analysis around the concept of "dominant fables" necessitates some attempt, at least, to account for their dominance. And it is here that social science comes to the aid of narratology. Drawing on concepts such as public choice theory and on models of decision making, goal setting, and small-group processes, I will seek to relate the narratives' formal issues to their institutional settings and the "real world" issues they address. These concepts can help in understanding and predicting organizational renewal and decline. For narratives that seek to go beyond obvious extrinsic indicators of personal growth, by engaging with characters' interior lives, I will also make use of Erik Erikson's eight-stage model of ego development—a narrative structure for understanding the human life cycle in terms of the classic Freudian polarities of love and work. The model, which might be unfamiliar to readers, is discussed in more detail after the literature review.

There is a clear challenge here: to prevent the two forms of analysis—the narratological and the social scientific—from running on parallel tracks. Yet it is precisely my conviction that the two domains do meet and interact in illuminating ways in my chosen narratives that animates this project. I will, therefore, be looking to social science in general, and public management in particular, to root the narratological issues I explore in a particular set of interpretive possibilities. By repeatedly questioning why *these* aspects of narrative competence are central to *these* institutional settings and stories—why, for example, the question of the problematized hero features so prominently in narratives of educational reform—I hope to go beyond the sort of prescriptive platitudes familiar from too many "lessons from literature" management books, lessons that habitually ignore both form and context. If my ambitions are realized, this book will offer academics and practitioners a different point of view—an enlarged awareness—from which to engage in and with the storytelling, which is, I believe, an inescapable part of all our lives, professional and personal.

Literature Review

The current literature on management and narrative breaks down into a number of largely unrelated subfields. These include guides for using extracts from (specific) novels or movies in the management classroom; prescriptive articles promoting the use of narratives (in general) for management teaching and/or research; books of management "lessons" drawn from a particular author or fictional work (usually film); and research concerning the image of public servants, entrepreneurs, or corporate executives in contemporary narratives, guides for how individual managers can employ simple narratives as a management tool, and studies using narratives generated by subjects as a research methodology. As disparate as these subgenres are, they share certain limitations: lack of focus and methodological rigor, as well as a less-than-sophisticated understanding of narrative as a form. There are notable exceptions, of course, but the underlying problem appears to be lack of narrative competence in the readings being proposed. Too often the very structures and mechanisms that make narrative so valuable, and so challenging, as a "mode of knowledge" (Prince, 2003, p. 60), are overlooked or rather, looked through, in order to extract the character, plot point, or action that become the sum total of their meaning. The effect of this literature is to flatten and reduce the narrative being studied, and the experience of engaging with it, in a way that calls into question the value of the project itself. One can't help wondering: Is that really all there is?

"Clips" and "Profs"

The popularity of the guides to using narrative extracts in the classroom is easy to account for: the approach works as a welcome variation of the teaching routine, connecting the syllabus to the larger culture in a way that students appreciate and respond to. As technology has facilitated the practice, with the advent first of VCRs, then DVDs, and now YouTube-ready "smart" classrooms, more academics have incorporated "clips" into their pedagogy. It is worth noting that while the guides first tended to propose written narratives (chiefly novels) as source material (Holzer, Morris, & Ludwin, 1979; Puffer, 1991), film and television now predominate—a means of establishing pop culture credibility with students whose media literacy, or at least media immersion, invariably outpaces the professor's own. Political science students, for example, are generally delighted to encounter the concept of the marginal or swing voter through scenes from the American television drama *The West Wing*. And I have had personal experience of the effectiveness of *Yes Minister* to illustrate topics in political-bureaucratic relations, and of political advertisements and satires posted on YouTube to illustrate political communications.

But it is equally worth noting that this approach is fundamentally anti-narrative, in the sense that it has very little to do with the cumulative experience of engaging with a complex narrative structure as a structure. And this is clearly not its goal. Works are "clipped" for their usefulness in illustrating external concepts or issues, and the handbooks themselves are often emphatically prescriptive regarding which clips to select and the principles they are meant to illuminate. The relation of the extracted part to the narrative whole is of no interest here, nor are formal ambiguities, thematic tensions, or alternative readings. What it seeks to do, the "clips" approach can do very well: locating highly effective supplementary or illustrative material to be linked to teaching points. And scholars like Joseph Champoux have introduced a welcome measure of rigor to the genre by publishing handbooks that focus on the use of film to teach specific concepts in both organizational behavior and strategic management (2001a, 2001b). Yet clips, by definition, do not tell the whole narrative story.

Tales, but Not Telling

A more expansive use of narrative would seem to inform a considerable number of academic articles written in the past four decades proposing fiction as a source of insight for students of public management (Alvarez & Merchan, 1992; Cohen, 1998; Czarniawska-Joerges & Guillet de Montoux, 1994; Dubnick, 2000; Goodsell & Murray, 1995; Illiash, 2004; Jurkiewicz & Giacalone 2000; Kroll, 1995; McSwite, 2002; Phillips, 1995; Waldo, 1968). These are, in effect, manifestos for a new area of scholarship. They make their arguments in general terms, with little reference to specific fictional works, and it is not always clear whether the narrative benefits they claim are envisioned for teaching, for research, or for both. More importantly, the foundation of these claims rests almost exclusively on aspects of narrative content—on the tale but not the telling—and still less on the mechanisms of decoding, interpretation, engagement, and distancing that such telling depends upon and deploys. For these scholars, what distinguishes fictional narratives as an object of study is the "thickness" (to borrow the anthropologists' term) of their human interest, the specificity and vividness with which they evoke character and setting, and the interactions between the two. Unlike even the best-written management case study, fictional narrative can encompass the inner life of its agents, the unconscious motivations, conflicting impulses, and deliberate self-deceptions that shape their actions and reactions. And narrative can turn its scrutiny to institutions and organizations as well as individuals, evoking the particularities of setting, culture, and era and their effects on those constrained by them.

These are all, undoubtedly, important aspects of the fictional narrative enterprise. And this understanding of what narrative offers a reader clearly recognizes the cumulative nature of the reading experience, something the clips approach discounts entirely. Yet by focusing so completely on issues of content, the narrative advocates are, paradoxically, diminishing what they seek to defend. Here, too, there is little interest in the mechanisms that generate the narrative effects that are being mined; no sense of the transactional nature of the reading or viewing process, no reflection on the positions and interactions of author, reader, narrator, character, point of view, and medium. Narrative as a mode of knowing and telling is elided in favor of narrative as showing.

What's Wrong with These Pictures?

The self-limiting nature of a methodology that conceives narrative primarily in terms of content can be seen by looking briefly at the scholarly literature on images of politicians and public servants in fictional narratives in the United States. The most detailed study undertook a content analysis of 9,588 characters in 1,234 prime-time American television shows between 1955 and 1999 (Lichter, Lichter, & Amundson, 2000). The large dataset allowed the authors to track changes over time while also identifying broad trends. They found, unsurprisingly, what they characterized as consistently negative images of politicians throughout the period, with bureaucrats sharing that fate by the 1990s. A follow-up study for the period 1999–2001 (Center for Media and Public Affairs, 2002) found a surprising reversal in the images of both groups, which the authors largely attribute to both the presence and influence of *The West Wing*. A more impressionistic study of American movies of the eighties and nineties (Holzer & Slater, 1995) identified equally negative characterizations perpetuating familiar images of corruption and inefficiency. For the authors, this was a matter of serious concern, undermining public confidence in the institutions and agents of governance, and ultimately making it difficult for the public sector to recruit (Holzer, 1997). Lee and Paddock (2001), while agreeing with the overall negative trend, nevertheless identified twenty instances of contemporary movies in which at least some politicians and civil servants were portrayed in a positive light. And a more recent study (Pautz & Roselle, 2009) looked at the top ten grossing American films annually from 1992 to 2006 and found, rather paradoxically, that while government was generally portrayed as incompetent, malevolent, or inefficient, individual civil servants were generally portrayed sympathetically.

These studies were born out of a particular historical moment and likely share a common if unacknowledged motivation. In an era of "government is the problem" political pronouncements and increasingly beleaguered public services, the urge to catalogue the extent of the crisis of (mis)perception is entirely understandable. The defensive impulse clearly takes precedence. But the focus on "images," and the potential implications for real-world practice and practitioners, left these studies with little attention for the narratological questions their own methodology raised. Chief among these were issues of the complex and far-from-unidirectional relationship between fictional narrative and social context, the near impossibility of establishing definitively the *effect* on contemporary opinion of particular narrative constructs, however popular or widely viewed, and the importance of genre conventions and formulas (e.g., the heroic individual versus the repressive institution) for commercially oriented television and film production. The moment that produced these studies has passed. Major new challenges facing national governments, from homeland security to economic recovery, as well as in public perceptions and political ideologies have moved public management scholarship beyond its defensive mode. We have new stories now.

Do What I Say (Not How I Read)

If the "images of" literature focused on issues of portrayal and perception, the "lessons from" books make practice their concern. Here, too, content is sovereign, and anecdotal character analysis is the primary critical tool. While ingenious authors have located management lessons in an improbable range of source material, including ancient military history (Attila the Hun, Genghis Khan), Scripture (Moses, Jesus), fairy tales (Goldilocks) and children's fiction (Winnie the Pooh), I will limit my discussion to eight prescriptive works drawing on contemporary fictional narratives (novels, plays, movies) and whose similar titles make the nature of their enterprise clear. Four nearly contemporary books on fiction for managers (*Fictions of Business: Insights on Management from Great Literature*, Brawer, 1998; *Questions of Character: Illuminating the Heart of Leadership through Literature*, Badaracco, 2006; *Movies to Manage By: Lessons in Leadership from Great Movies*, Clemens & Wolff, 1999; and *Movies for Leaders: Management Lessons from All-time Great Movies*, Higgins & Streigel, 1999) and four nearly contemporary books on Shakespeare for the same readership offer a fair sample of the best of this "lessons from" school (*Shakespeare in Charge: The Bard's Guide to Leading and Succeeding on the Business Stage*, Augustine & Adelman, 1999; *Shakespeare on Management: Leadership Lessons for Today's Managers*, Corrigan, 1999; *Shakespeare on Management: Wise Business Counsel from the Bard*, Shafritz, 1999; and *Power Plays: Shakespeare's Lessons in Leadership and Management*, Whitney & Packer, 2000).

There is a common format to these works. Chapters offer a summary of the fictional source, followed by analysis of one or more characters. These are then compared with a contemporary business leader or figure whom the author has encountered in the course of his or her career. Finally, the "lessons" are elucidated and delivered. This form of argument proves surprisingly similar to the homiletic structure of a traditional sermon, with the difference that a preacher would be more likely to turn to Scripture for exemplars and warnings than to movies, novels, or plays. A thoughtful author drawing on extensive professional experience can nonetheless use this form to provide an insightful personal perspective.

There are, however, limitations built into the model. The first, and in some ways the most fundamental, is the disjunction of contexts. The fictional sources are generally so far removed in culture, setting, era, and ethos from contemporary American business that the attempt to draw parallels can seem unintentionally comic. The speech that Shakespeare *imagined* Henry V making on the eve of the Battle of Agincourt is undoubtedly a sterling example of inspirational rhetoric. (As beloved as the speech is by the writers in this genre, they tend to overlook the fact that there is virtually no historical basis for anything any character says in any of Shakespeare's so-called history plays.) But is it really the best model for IT executives on the eve of release 2.0? In some cases, the pairings can seem downright unfortunate. Higgins and Streigel's (1999, pp. 69–90) discussion of the classic Japanese prisoner-of-war film *Bridge on the River Kwai*, a film replete with scenes of brutality, torture, and racial hatred, opens with an analogy of a team of American engineers being loaned to an Asian company for a year. Stretching for the promised "lessons," the analysis yields nostrums that seem both simplistic and self-evident: today's victory might be a stepping stone for tomorrow's defeat; never let them see you sweat; practice what you preach. This structural incongruity extends to the dramatic stakes involved. And it is here that the nature of the target audience—contemporary private sector managers—is most significant. The fictional sources, generally chosen for their high levels of drama and conflict, deal with life-and-death decisions far removed from the daily experience of business, however "cutthroat" the competitive context might be. (I do note that alone among the authors being considered, Brawer (1998) draws exclusively on narratives that unfold within market contexts.)

If there are problems with the choice of source material, the use of it can also be questioned. None of these works addresses issues of form at all; nor is there any significant attempt to draw on the extensive critical literature that does. What is more, the approach to character tends to reduce this complex narrative effect to an exercise in unproblematic exemplification.[4]

When confronted with often notoriously ambiguous characterizations, the authors adopt a simplifying and generalizing reading that assumes only a single, uniform, and unvarying response. There are exceptions, of course. Both Badaracco (2006, pp. 11–28) and Brawer (1999, pp. 74–85), in their discussions of Arthur Miller's Willy Loman (*Death of a Salesman,* 1949) do explore his status as a victim of capitalism. Given their designated readership, however, it is not surprising that both prefer his prescriptive value as a casualty of his own unrealistic and unexamined ambitions.

Finally, there is the issue of selection criteria, or rather their absence. The authors' choice of source material seems based solely on personal interest or professional experience. The resulting books tend to lack any compelling thematic structure or analytic through-line. They read more as collections of essays or cases than as sustained studies, with little or no connections made between the component parts. Again, there are honorable exceptions. Brawer (1999), whose career was as a senior manager and CEO of Maidenform, had a strong interest in marketing, and selected source narratives dealing with its related issues (*Death of a Salesman*; David Mamet's *Glengarry Glen Ross,* 1984). Badaracco (2006) structured his book loosely around the stages of a manager's career, with narratives related to setting goals and finding mentors featuring in the early chapters, and narratives analyzed in terms of performance standards and success in the later. Yet even here it is difficult to escape the sense of improbable comparisons straining under a prescriptive weight they cannot always bear.

Simple Stories, Big Returns

A number of authors have developed the idea that the telling of simple stories can be an effective management tool. They include Armstrong (1992), Denning (2005, 2007), Ganz (2008), and Simmons (2001, 2007). Their work has a number of points in common. First and foremost, the narratives they advocate are short oral stories, no longer than a minute or two, told by managers to their co-workers, in effect vignettes or anecdotes. They are predominantly (Ganz being the exception) directed at private sector rather than public sector managers, though they often use examples taken from the public sector. Each of the authors has developed a set of different types of stories for different purposes. Ganz has three: a "story of self" that relates an individual's life experiences to her calling, a "story of us" that attempts to define an organization or community on the basis of shared experiences, and a "story of now" that sets forth an agenda for that organization or community to achieve some sort of change now. Denning has eight: stories to persuade the audience to implement new ideas, stories to communicate who the teller is, stories to build trust in the teller's company, stories to instill organizational values, stories to encourage people to work collaboratively, stories to share knowledge within an organization, stories to neutralize gossip and rumor, and stories to lead people into the future.

These authors are primarily management consultants or teachers. The claim of validity for their methods—the effectiveness of the use of stories—is based on their own personal experience or their casual observation of the effectiveness or ineffectiveness of historical models. For example, Denning's transformative personal experience was as a middle manager in the World Bank, where he discovered that the use of stories illustrating successful knowledge sharing initiatives in the mid-1990s helped persuade the organization to embrace knowledge management relatively early in the history of the Internet. The historical models used include an analysis of Al Gore's unsuccessful campaign for the presidency and his greater success as critic of global warming (Denning, 2007, pp. 3–20), Shakespeare's imagined speech by Henry V at Agincourt (Ganz, 2008) and Winston Churchill's addresses at the outset of World War II (Denning, 2005, pp. 230–232).

The use of storytelling by these authors is subject to similar critiques as the use of narrative content in the previous section. The intended audience is primarily the private sector rather than the public sector manager. The use of narrative involves the telling of simple stories rather than engaging with challenging narratives or attempting to relate narrative form and content. The stories are almost invariably upbeat and heroic, thus failing to recognize complexity and ambiguity. (Put in terms of the fourfold categorization developed in Table 1.1, the stories these authors advocate fall within the upper left quadrant alone). Finally, while personal experience should never be discounted, these authors generalize far beyond their personal experience and present little evidence of the effectiveness of the methods they advocate.

Narrative as Research Methodology

One of the uses of narrative in human sciences such as sociology, social work, and medicine is as a research methodology. Using a deliberately unstructured, open-ended format, researchers invite selected subjects to "tell their stories," which are then transcribed, analyzed, and re-presented by the researchers. It is a method that overlaps with the more traditional case study, yet presumes a much more active and indeed interactive role for the interviewer/author in the narrative she elicits (Reissman, 2008). Three instances of public management scholars, taking what its practitioners refer to as "the narrative turn" are Roe's *Narrative Policy Analysis* (1994),

Maynard-Moody and Musheno's *Cops, Teachers, Counselors: Stories from the Front Lines of Public Service* (2003), Ospina and Dodge's three-part series presenting narrative research methodology in *Public Administration Review* (2005a, 2005b; Dodge, Ospina, & Foldy, 2005), and Ospina and Foldy's subsequent application of this methodology (Foldy, Goldman, & Ospina, 2008; Ospina & Foldy, 2010). This body of research is not about narrative, but rather uses narrative to investigate other topics: for Roe, redefining difficult policy disputes using concepts borrowed from literary theory; for Maynard-Moody and Musheno, understanding the work of frontline public servants, in particular when they "go by the book" and when they exercise discretion on behalf of their clients; and for Ospina and Dodge, a better understanding of collective leadership in social change organizations. A key methodological issue in this type of research is whether to "fracture" narratives by drawing out content that can be compared across narratives or whether to regard the individual narrative as a coherent whole and focus on internal analysis, such as the relationship between its content and structure. I regard this issue as a false dichotomy, and indeed this book incorporates both analysis across narratives, such as the structural analysis of fables and counter-fables within genres, and the analysis of the themes and narrative techniques in the individual texts I discuss. In any event, it is heartening to realize that there are public management scholars who are using narrative as a research methodology, even if their research questions and methodological approaches are different from my own.

Going Public: Waldo and Posner

Rigorous focus on the public sector, of course, is not in itself a guarantee of success in this narrative endeavor. An early attempt at a comprehensive study of public management novels prefigures in many ways the various problems, omissions, and limitations I have been exploring here. Dwight Waldo was one of the foremost public administration scholars of the previous generation. For two decades, he pursued a "hobby" of reading what he called administrative novels. Eventually, the hobby produced a monograph entitled, "The Novelist on Organization and Administration: An Inquiry into the Relationship between Two Worlds" (1968). The monograph splits into two quite separate parts. The first articulates Waldo's motivations and findings. Both anticipate strikingly the "images of" writers' defensive stance some twenty years later. Focusing on administrative novels written in the 1950s and 1960s, and largely excluding both biographical narratives and film from consideration, he took issue with what he saw as the novelists' uninformed and unreflecting criticism. What they lacked, in Waldo's view, was any real understanding of bureaucracy in general, or the roles of middle and upper management in particular. Waldo's critical touchstone was the novelist Saul Bellow's contemporary criticism of fellow novelists for their unthinking denunciations of "modern mass society" and its dehumanizing institutions. Waldo reiterated Bellow's (1965) injunction that the writers "look with their own eyes" and "understand what they are rejecting."

The second half of Waldo's study consisted of a set of 154 short reviews of administrative novels written between the 1930s and 1960s, most in the UK or United States, but also including some Russian and European works in translation. The reviews were prepared by seven research assistants who had worked on the project for some twelve years. Waldo had hoped to generate a thorough classification of the novels in terms of type of organization and administrative issue or theme, as well as an index of relevant passages from them. He never accomplished his grand design, due in part to competing interests, but also to his growing dissatisfaction with the direction the administrative novel as a genre was taking. What was left was the raw material for an analysis that was never undertaken and cannot therefore be fully assessed. Yet, given Waldo's stated interest in issues of typology and indexing, it does not seem unfair to assume that the result would likely have emphasized content analysis over narratological concerns, in ways similar to both the "images of" and "clips from" approaches that would follow.

Twenty years after the publication of Waldo's monograph, the senior appellate judge and law professor Richard Posner published a landmark study of law and literature (1988), which he revised extensively in 1998 and again in 2009. The work stands as a model of scholarship in a cross-disciplinary field pioneered three decades ago by writers from both sides of the divide. It remains an important inspiration for this book. There is a natural affinity between law and narrative, and not only in the obvious sense of court cases and legal incidents inspiring the plots of countless novels, dramas, and films. One of the key aspects of the book's evolution is that, while the title remains unchanged, Posner has shifted his focus from canonical novels alone to narrative, defined more broadly in terms of both creators' choice of media (now including popular films) and forms of legal narrative (now including presentencing statements). For both law and narrative, the interpretive act is central, the constant need to engage with texts and the mechanisms by which they generate meanings. And it is out of this deeper understanding of their connection that Posner's work grows. He brilliantly and consistently demonstrates a doubled critical perspective, reading (and watching) for narrative engagement no less than legal content, while also defining that content broadly and searching it deeply.

Unlike virtually all of the other literature reviewed here, Posner's analysis is structured thematically, unifying his wide-ranging source material and creating a series of juxtapositions that enrich his insights, whether addressing trial narratives (Kafka, *The Trial*; Koestler, *Darkness at Noon*; Dostoevsky, *The Brothers Karamazov*; Dickens, *Bleak House*) or the literature of revenge (*The Iliad, Hamlet, Julius Ceasar*, Kleist's *Michael Koolhaus*, Doctorow's *Ragtime*). Equally valuable is Posner's identification of a structuring dichotomy within his discipline between the spirits of legalism and discretion (formalism versus realism, law versus equity, letter versus spirit). His analysis of literary narratives that enact those dichotomies—Melville's *Billy Budd* and Shakespeare's *Merchant of Venice,* to cite just two—convincingly demonstrates the reciprocal illumination his dual focus can yield.[5] And Posner does not hesitate to draw parallels between issues of narratological and legal practice; for example, exploring the question of intentionalism in its literary and legal manifestations and contrasting the effects of its insistence on elucidating authorial intentions and singular textual meanings. It is a tribute to Posner's commitment to the narrative experience that, as a legal scholar, he accepts the necessity of intentionalism in the interpretation of statutes, but as a reader of narratives, he rejects its reductive tendencies in favor of a whole-hearted embrace of textual ambiguity.

This might suggest that Posner's analysis operates largely at a theoretical level. In fact, he devotes considerable attention to the practical benefits of studying law and literature. Literary accounts of trials provide potential models of courtroom practice, while fictional instances of great advocacy could be inspirational to professional advocates. To this end, in the first and third editions, Posner (1988, pp. 278–287; 2009, pp. 450–455) contrasts Brutus's elegantly rhetorical yet unconvincing funeral oration in *Julius Caesar* with Marc Antony's far more persuasive use of emotion, repetition, and irony. Posner is explicit, too, about his belief that legal writing, whether of briefs or judicial opinions, could only benefit from exposure to narrative models whose concreteness of detail and description he contrasts with the overreliance on euphemism and generalization characterizing contemporary judgments (Posner, 1998, pp. 282–287). Posner's work is so convincing because of his skill not only at telling, but also at showing how the analysis of literature can improve legal practice and scholarship by his thorough and compelling analysis of a wide variety of works.

Ultimately, however, Posner has a larger claim to make. In his second edition, he adds a further, existential argument for engaging with narrative. Following the logic of his critique of Nussbaum (1995) and others who argue for literature as a means of informing moral and political judgments (see note 5), Posner finally contends that we read not for advice but, citing

Nietzsche, to "become what we are," finding in the experience of narrative a source of self-fashioning (1998, pp. 326–332; 2009, pp. 487–488). One need not accept Posner's claim to find in his scholarship, with all its depth, erudition, and insight, a compellingly specific brief for legal practitioners and scholars turning to narrative.

The Life Cycle as Narrative: Erik Erikson's Theory

The narrative advocates we encountered in the literature survey—scholars espousing the virtues of fictional narratives for the study and teaching of public management—base much of their claim for narrative's value on the psychological and situational specificity it offers. This is, the scholars assert, a degree of "human interest" and human insight that social science research or business school cases are unlikely to attain or even attempt. Indeed, the research and cases present decision makers as calmly and unemotionally analyzing alternatives in terms of their organizational impact, while paying little attention to the personal implications of, or emotional influences on, their decisions. But if we want to take a broader perspective, how do we integrate these human factors into the study of public management narratives? More importantly, how can we do this systematically with a method that transcends the anecdotal and addresses the distinctly *public* context of these stories?

There are many possible answers, of course. The one I propose here borrows from the work of the ego psychologist Erik Erikson (1980, 1985). Specifically, I turn back to his model of the life cycle, with its eight consecutive developmental stages, each defined by its characteristic binary crisis. It might seem a curious choice in this emphatically post-Freudian age. Erikson was not only a student of Anna Freud, Sigmund's daughter, but also a self-described heir of the Freudian psychoanalytic tradition, even as he sought to transcend its limitations. In his own theoretical work, Erikson chose to focus on the psychosocial rather than psychosexual basis of personality, shifting his attention from the experiences of patients undergoing psychoanalysis to that of "normal" individuals uninvolved in any treatment process (Roazen, 1976). As the putative discoverer of the "identity crisis," Erikson's influence (both clinical and popular) reached its height in the 1960s and 1970s, when his theories of intergenerational conflict and self-definition as a lifetime project resonated most strongly.

Erikson's interest in conceptualizing the entire life cycle, with an extensive focus on its adult phases, as well as his emphasis on the *public*, social context of ego development, are what make his model so useful for my purposes. In particular, his postulation of the phase of "middle adulthood" as shaped by a conflict between competing impulses of "generativity" and "stagnation" offers a means of addressing the competing themes of ambition, pragmatism, altruism, and professionalism that shape the public actor's narrative. Erikson's model is cumulative in design, the subject's response to each stage's defining conflict influencing the outcome of subsequent developmental phases. While I will focus primarily on a single phase, it is worth noting the "crises" that Erikson identifies as preceding it. These include, for the child's early years, trust versus mistrust, autonomy versus doubt/shame, initiative versus guilt, and industry versus inferiority. Adolescence is famously seen by Erikson as defined by a struggle for identity versus role confusion. Young adulthood posits intimacy and solidarity against isolation. Growing out of this is the middle-aged subject's growing concern with what we would now term his "legacy." To frame the concept narratologically, it is a period of anxiety over the subject's relation to his own life's story (as he imagined it to be, as it has told itself, as it could still be fashioned) and to the narratives of the institutions and individuals who will succeed him. Erikson's eighth and final stage, late adulthood, is also of interest to us, defined by a struggle between integrity—the feeling of having made an important contribution to people, institutions, and causes that matter—and despair at mistaken choices and an unrealizable desire to have lived one's life differently.[6]

I hope my own readings will make plain that I do not propose Erikson's model as any sort of "magic key" to the narratives we will encounter. There are undoubted limitations to it. The theory is self-confessedly normative rather than empirical. For Erikson, each life crisis possesses a clearly desirable outcome, the attainment of which becomes that phase's goal: faith in infancy, identity in adolescence, fidelity in early adulthood, and so on. As Paul Roazen concludes: "It seems clear that [Erikson] has committed himself to a version of the life cycle that is not so much an account of what does happen as an ideal of what he would like to come about" (1976, p. 120). And these goals bear the clear impress of an earlier time and ethos, most notably in their configuration of familial and sexual relationships. Nevertheless, subsequent researchers have operationalized the concept of generativity and used in-depth interviews to measure generativity and determine the factors that account for it (McAdams, 2006, pp. 45–72). What is important and valuable for my project is the thematic concept of public and private motivations, outcomes, and measures in constant tension, of the mature subject's need to accommodate conflicts that are perhaps incapable of complete or unambiguous resolution, either professionally or personally, and of the inextricable connections between the two dimensions. For that is a story we will encounter more than once.

Genres, Dominant Fables, and Counter-Fables: Looking Ahead

In the chapters to come, a number of types of texts are examined, including movies (fictional, documentary, and docudramas), television series, novels, memoirs, and histories. While all are important ways of communicating narratives, and each has particular strengths, I do tend to pay most attention to the visual media: movies and television series. In part, this is a function of their popularity in contemporary society. For example, when a novel is successful, the rights are purchased, and it is adapted to the cinema, and very quickly more people will have seen the movie than read the book. The students to whom I have taught courses on narrative and management are also partial to movies, and, for them, if they enjoyed a movie, they might *then* consult print sources about it, such as those found online, or even the book from which the movie was adapted. The visual and aural components of movies are of deep interest in terms of how they reinforce and communicate plot and character. Thus, to pay considerable attention is not resigning oneself to a dumbed-down culture, but rather a choice for which there is a good scholarly rationale.

The book begins at the front lines of the public sector. While there are relatively few narratives about frontline public servants, one group that has received attention are teachers, in particular those in inner-city schools. This is due to the importance of the educational system in delivering on America's promise of equality of opportunity. Chapter 2 defines the dominant fable of the teacher-hero and illustrates it with a number of "based on a true story" narratives. It then probes the limits of that fable in two ways: exploring how the film presentations choose to differ from the stories of record and presenting a set of counter-fables that subvert or critique it.

Chapter 3 moves from the classrooms and hallways of the American school system to the senior levels of government to analyze British narratives on a classic public administration issue: the relationship between political authority and the career public servant. The focus of the chapter is the landmark television series *Yes Minister,* which effectively defined the form and substance of the governmental fable for 30 years. The chapter places *Yes Minister* within the long tradition of British political narratives, looking closely at both the novelist C. P. Snow and the diarist Richard Crossman (an acknowledged source for *Yes Minister*). It pays particular attention to *Yes Minister*'s espousal of public-choice theory to express the motivations of politicians and public servants and to the importance of language to the series' conception of "closed politics." The chapter also surveys the series' most significant heirs (*A Very British Coup, House of Cards, The Thick of It, The*

Amazing Mrs. Pritchard, In the Loop, The Queen, The Deal, The Special Relationship) as they update its dominant fable for the information age.

Chapter 4 uses the ending of Appeasement (government policy toward Nazi Germany prior to the Second World War) as a heroic British fable centered on Winston Churchill. It analyzes several recent and diverse perspectives on Churchill: Roy Jenkins' (2001) essentially political biography; John Lukacs' (1999) fine-grained account of his leadership of the war cabinet at a critical turning point; a recent attempt to distill his leadership lessons for private sector managers; two BBC docudramas, one about his fight against Appeasement in the thirties and the other about his wartime leadership; and finally Lynne Olson's (2007) history of the other anti-Appeasement dissidents in the Conservative Party. In contrast to the standard heroic image of Churchill, the story that emerges emphasizes his skills in "closed politics." Kazuo Ishiguro's (1989) novel (and the Merchant-Ivory film adaptation) *The Remains of the Day* is a counter-fable to the ending of Appeasement fable, in that it explores the thinking of the supporters of Appeasement and examines the psychological fracture of two characters for whom Appeasement never ended. Finally, the chapter shows the lessons two subsequent political leaders, John F. Kennedy and Tony Blair, learned from the ending of Appeasement.

Chapter 5 addresses American political fables. Unlike their British counterparts, there is no clear dominant fable here, but rather there are three contending fables. Self-interested and corrupt politicians populate a cynical fable, well-intentioned but flawed politicians characterize a fable of compromise, and heroic politicians typify an idealistic and nostalgic fable. A variety of contemporary films are analyzed as representatives of each fable. The chapter concludes with an extended analysis of Aaron Sorkin's landmark television series *The West Wing*, as it draws upon elements of all three fables to create something genuinely new within the tradition of American political narrative.

Chapter 6 uses the Cuban Missile Crisis to engage with the issue of crisis leadership. Here, there is a clear heroic president narrative, first expounded in Robert Kennedy's book *Thirteen Days* (1969) and then elaborated academically in Graham Allison's *Essence of Decision* (1971). The Cuban Missile Crisis has its counter-fables, such as the film *Thirteen Days*, which attempted unsuccessfully to heroicize presidential assistant Kenneth O'Donnell; the satire *Dr. Strangelove*; and most significantly, the recollections of Robert McNamara, presented in his memoir *In Retrospect* (1995) and in Errol Morris's documentary *The Fog of War*. It demonstrates the polyphony achieved by incorporating both McNamara's interpretations of events and Morris's challenges to his interpretations, and poses, in a profound way, the irresolvable issues of wartime leadership.

Chapter 7 continues the theme of public sector decision making, presenting it within a small-group context involving common citizens; namely, jury duty. It focuses on the classic narrative on jury decision making, Reginald Rose's *Twelve Angry Men* (2006). It also compares *Twelve Angry Men* with the most comprehensive report available on the lived experience of serving on a jury in a capital trial, Graham Burnett's *A Trial by Jury* (2001). In both cases, there is a strong focus on leadership, as both works revolve around the fact that despite the egalitarian structure of a jury, informal leaders do emerge and do drive the literally life-and-death decisions twelve ordinary citizens are asked to make.

The final chapter begins by summarizing the patterns of fables and counter-fables for the transformational teachers genre, British politics genre (Chapters 3 and 4), and American politics genre (Chapters 5, 6, and 7). Going beyond the managerial lessons presented in each of the previous chapters, it develops a cumulative model of responsible public sector leadership that is, in effect, the dominant fable for the book. The chapter then returns to the relationship between managerial content and narrative form, showing how polyphonic narrative content can be seen as a reenactment of democracy and outlining a set of considerations for public sector practitioners endeavoring to construct their own narratives. The chapter presents some suggestions for future research, applying the approach developed in this book to the study of narratives regarding both the public and private sectors. The chapter concludes on a personal note, with my own list of the ten narratives discussed in this book that I found most rewarding.

Endnotes

1. Hence, scholars have begun to use the apparatus of cognitive psychology, such as MRIs, to explore how neural pathways are activated when people are exposed to various forms of art or literature (Cohen, 2010).
2. Bal's work has a Google scholar count, at time of writing, of 1,320 citations.
3. In a similar exercise in genre analysis, Moretti (2005, pp. 18–20) identifies 44 genres of British novels written between 1760 and 1900 and demonstrates that each was popular for a finite time period.
4. In her recent study of the impact of Shakespeare on, and appropriation of Shakespeare by, modern culture, Shakespeare scholar Marjorie Garber criticizes the authors mentioned above for their use of Henry V to exemplify the leadership lessons they wish to impart and their unwillingness to engage with the ambiguities of Shakespeare's actual play *Henry V*. For this reason, she does not use "leadership" in the title of her chapter about *Henry V*, but rather "exemplarity" (Garber, 2008, pp. 178–200).

5. Martha Nussbaum, in *Poetic Justice* (1995), makes what appears to be a similar argument; namely, that reading novels can benefit judges by cultivating what she refers to as "imaginative empathy," which will lead them to consider the social and historical context relevant to their decisions. In effect, they would be leaning to the side of the legal antinomies embodied by justice and discretion rather than law and rules. Nussbaum even gives as a paradigmatic example of imaginative empathy an appellate decision written by Posner in a sexual harassment case. Ironically, Posner rejects Nussbaum's argument, in effect accusing her of illustrating her points by choosing a set of contemporary novels whose authors' political views were consistent with her own.

6. Erikson's writing is abstract and at times abstruse. To present his ideas more accessibly in the classroom, I have used the 1975 animated film *Everyone Rides the Carousel*. Produced by animators John and Faith Hubley, with psychologist Kenneth Keniston and his students in a Yale University film seminar, the 72-minute film depicts Erikson's stages and crises by means of short narratives and a montage of visual images: teenagers passing through a hall of mirrors (the identity crisis); repeated versions of a young couple discussing their future together, or apart, each repetition with a different outcome (intimacy versus isolation); and an elderly couple, obviously codependent, bickering in a cafeteria about what to order, oblivious to the line of people growing behind them; and a second elderly couple, still in love, preparing Halloween decorations and, in the evening, opening the door to a tall shrouded stranger, but concluding they are not ready to go with him (integrity versus despair). While viewers clearly benefit from a previous introduction to Erikson's theories, the film communicates the key concepts in an engaging and imaginative way, its allusiveness a useful trigger for further discussion.

Frontline Innovators

Transformational Teachers in America

Dominant and Counter-Narratives of Educational Reform

Education is critical to the story of the American dream, providing the individual's best hope for upward mobility. While preschool programs and elementary schools are essential to lay the foundations of future academic success, high schools are equally important. The last step in the public education system, they impart the skills that make it possible for students to prepare for careers in college or university and for the better future—the happy ending—academic accomplishment can help them secure. At every level, the education system's most critical narratives unfold in the classroom, out of the three-sided relationship of teachers, students, and curriculum.

It is in the inner-city high school where this relationship is most problematic. Students are generally poorly prepared and their attention is frequently elsewhere: working to support their families; sometimes belonging to, or threatened by, gangs; and in some cases choosing violence and drugs as means of rebellion or escape. Even if government is committed to equitable funding for all schools, inner-city schools are disadvantaged

Governing Fables: Learning from Public Sector Narratives, pages 27–61
Copyright © 2011 by Information Age Publishing
27

because of a frequent absence of parental commitment and support and a failing social infrastructure. Finally, the best and most ambitious teachers tend to avoid these schools, leaving them to those who are inexperienced or burned out.

Despite these widely acknowledged difficulties, there are exceptional teachers who, through their Herculean efforts, their innovations, or both, have made considerable progress in advancing inner-city high school students toward academic achievement and the possibility of a better future. The narratives in this chapter, both the entirely fictional and the fact-based, focus on the figure of the transformational teacher. That figure stands at the center of a fable so persistent as to constitute a clearly recognizable formula. It is a formula that is either replicated or resisted by all the narratives we will consider. Either way, its influence seems inescapable.

The fable begins with the arrival of the teacher-hero. He or she is inexperienced, fresh from teacher training or from another career, and is appalled by what the classroom presents: undisciplined and unruly students whose skills are far behind the norm for their age. The first challenge the transformational teacher must overcome is seizing the students' attention and asserting discipline. Commanding attention requires convincing the skeptical and often hostile students that the teacher is "cool" and the subject material interesting and relevant. Asserting discipline demands the physical courage to "get in the students' faces" rather than shrink back. After the class begins to function with some discipline and decorum and the students begin learning, the teacher takes the students out of the classroom to begin imagining new and better possibilities for their futures. The teacher then sets a stretch goal for the class as a group and becomes, in effect, a coach, working with the students to master the curriculum. The new dynamic is usually dramatized through a scene of *quid pro quo*: the teacher promising unlimited commitment and support in return for the intellectual striving the students have never yet put forth.

The narrative makes clear that the personal demands of transformational teaching are heavy. Schools usually do not support innovative curricular ideas such as more relevant books or field trips. Often, the impassioned teacher-hero must pay for them personally, despite his or her low salary, frequently taking on other jobs to do so. The students, surprised and delighted by the teacher's unusual commitment, respond by claiming the teacher's attention outside of class hours—attention that is always willingly and unstintingly given.

The transformational teacher's radically personalized and often unorthodox pedagogy creates a pattern of support and opposition within the world of the school. Generally, support comes from above, either the principal or the school board, who begin to see that the teacher is achieving results and, after a while, provide encouragement and some resources. Opposition comes from fellow instructors, the department head, or perhaps the union representative, all of whom see the transformational teacher as a "rate-buster," working far harder and producing far better results.

The teacher-hero's fable ends with victory. The personal bond with the students is cemented despite or, more often, because of external opposition. The stretch goal is achieved. Success brings public attention and more resources, both from the school administration and often from charitable foundations interested in education. The transformational teacher receives media attention and awards. Often, he or she then moves on, perhaps to disseminate more widely this innovative and successful pedagogy, opening the prospect of many more young lives transformed and redeemed.

This narrative of educational victory, especially as presented in films, is clearly designed to generate a "feel good" response in its audience. As Robert Bulman (2005) argues in his analysis of a wide selection of films dealing with high schools, these films are predicated on a belief that "all [the teachers] need to bring to the classroom is discipline, tough love, high expectations, and a little good old-fashioned middle-class common sense about individual achievement and personal responsibility" (p. 54). This, Bulman feels, reinforces "a likely fantasy of the suburban middle-class audience— a character they can identify with goes into a troubled high school and single-handedly rectifies its problems" (p. 55). These films offer a calculated cocktail of surface realism (the grittiness of the inner-city milieu, the markers of socioeconomic disadvantage, the constant threats of violence) and underlying wish fulfillment that a complex, intractable social issue can be resolved through the heroic dedication of committed individuals. It is a measure of this educational fable's power that representations of it are often incorporated into the curriculum of faculties of education, designed as inspiration for future teachers likely to be confronted with the "real life" issues the films depict.

The films we will be considering that exemplify this dominant fable are all avowedly "based on a true story." Yet it is clear that in their cinematic form, these narratives are not telling the whole story of America's public educational crisis. It is not surprising that a counter-fable has emerged to complicate the picture. This tends to take one of two forms. In the first, the teacher knows what is required to be a transformational hero, but is prevented from fulfilling the role by personal weakness. In the second, the institutional barriers to achieving a transformation are too great to be overcome, and the teacher's heroic efforts prove insufficient, leading to frustration rather than victory.

In this chapter, I will begin by examining three films that are expressions of the dominant fable: *Stand and Deliver* (1989), *Dangerous Minds* (1995), and *Freedom Writers* (2007). In each case, there is considerable documentation in books, articles, and online regarding the "true stories" on which these films are based, and I will use the documentation to probe the weaknesses and internal shortcomings of the fable that informs them. I will then look at five counter-fables—the films *Cheaters* (2000), *Dead Poets Society* (1989), *The History Boys* (2006), *Half Nelson* (2007) and *The Class* (2008)—to see how they challenge, even at times invert, the dominant narrative, particularly in their representation of the teacher-hero. One of the conclusions I reach concerns the failure of the dominant narrative to acknowledge the importance of systemic educational reform to achieve enduring results. Within this context, I will examine a narrative about a transformational principal attempting to turn around a failing high school: the made-for-television film *A Town Torn Apart* (1992).

One of the classic issues in public management is the performance of frontline public servants. In contrast to the negative image much of the public holds of frontline public servants as being unimaginative, lazy, and bureaucratic, these teacher-heroes are ideal public servants: devoted to the public interest, always willing to go the extra mile, innovative, and focused on achieving results that improve the lives and prospects of their students. In *Innovating with Integrity* (Borins, 1998), I argued that these ideal public servants are not a myth. One of the most impressive findings of my research was that almost half of a sample of 217 innovations in state and local government were initiated by frontline workers or middle managers. While there are clear parallels between my empirical findings and the fictional treatment of the protagonists in the dominant fables we will be analyzing, what interests me here are the ways all of the films in this chapter, whether intentionally or not, complicate the idea of the local hero as source of innovative achievement in the complex realm of educational reform.

The Teacher-Hero

Although all three of our dominant fable films achieved a measure of popular success, I begin my analysis with brief plot summaries to highlight their common structural and thematic features. *Stand and Deliver* (1989), the earliest of the three, stands in many ways as the *locus classicus* of the transformational teacher fable. It centers on Jaime Escalante, an experienced Bolivian math teacher who emigrates to the United States; initially he works in the computer industry but soon returns to teaching. He arrives at Garfield High School in East Los Angeles expecting to teach computer science but, in the absence of computers, is assigned a basic mathematics class. The class, mainly Latino, lacks purpose, decorum, and basic skills. Slowly, Escalante begins to assert control and establish limits through a variety of conventional and unconventional means: physical toughness (breaking up a fight), sexual humor, an appeal to a shared ethnic heritage (employing Spanish slang and expounding the mathematical achievements of their Mayan ancestors). The new teacher also cuts a deal with the class leader, giving him a textbook to keep at home to avoid being caught in the supremely "uncool" act of actually completing assignments or studying. In return, the young man is to support Escalante's efforts in class.

After the class becomes focused and productive, Escalante arranges a tour of a computer factory to demonstrate to his students successful professionals in the real world using mathematics in their work. He then sets a stretch goal for the class: they will pass the Advanced Placement calculus exam, a highly unlikely, though not impossible, achievement for students of their educational and socioeconomic background. When the students return in the fall, Escalante distributes contracts in which he agrees to provide extra instruction before and after normal class hours and on weekends. The students must agree to attend the extra classes and do the homework, and their parents must support their children's efforts. Escalante voluntarily takes on this additional (uncompensated) daytime teaching, while at the same time working as an evening ESL instructor. He collapses from the workload, apparently suffering a heart attack. His students persevere, inspired by his sacrifice and commitment. Ultimately, the eighteen students in the calculus class take the AP exam and pass. The scores are challenged by the Educational Testing Service, however, on the grounds that it is unlikely that all candidates from one school, which previously had little experience with the AP program would pass, and that all were making the same mistakes—prima facie evidence of cheating.[1] Despite Escalante's accusation of racism, the ETS requires the class to be retested. The scores on the retest are similar to the original. The movie ends with Escalante walking down a school corridor into the light—in effect, a man of enlightenment—and an accumulating on-screen text showing the increasing number of Garfield students passing the AP calculus exam in subsequent years.

Six years later, *Dangerous Minds* offered a narrative markedly similar in its outlines, though lacking either the defined goals or tangible results of Escalante's story. Here, a female teacher-hero assumes the central role, and her transformative effects are more personal than pedagogical. It is interesting that within Hollywood conventions, the centering of the story around a female protagonist would seem to allow, or perhaps demand, a much greater focus on the emotional relationships between teachers and students and a corresponding deemphasizing of academic achievement. The difference in subject matter being taught, of course, contributes to this, calculus being rather less conducive to dramatic recitations, personal revelations, and emotional epiphanies than English literature.

The film begins in familiar fashion with LouAnne Johnson, a former Marine completing her teacher training, being offered a full-time job teaching English in an Academy program for troubled students at a high school in East Palo Alto, California. (Academy programs are targeted at students with low averages and poor attendance records but whose standardized test scores indicate higher potential. The intervention, supported by federal government grants, involved reducing class size to a maximum of 25, keeping the same classes and teachers in place for the full 3 years of high school, and having teachers provide personal instruction and counseling.) Like Escalante, Johnson is confronted with a classroom of out-of-control Black and Hispanic teenagers, who immediately disparage her in terms of race ("white bread") and gender ("bitch"). To assert authority, she boasts of her Marine background and demonstrates her karate prowess. She also increases her street credibility by exchanging the demure blouses and pearls of her first teaching days for a leather jacket. Likening her combative students to Marine inductees with clean records, she assigns everyone an A, with the challenge of maintaining it. She teaches grammar by parsing sentences such as "We choose to die," and "Never shoot a homeboy." She moves to literature by analyzing the lyrics of Bob Dylan's *Mr. Tambourine Man* and Dylan Thomas's poetry. She provides a number of positive incentives such as a class trip to an amusement park, which she pays for, to celebrate completion of a unit of the curriculum, and a Dylan/Dylan contest to find analogies between the American singer and the Welsh poet. The latter has the benefit of leading her students to use the library and undertake research, and Johnson takes the winning team to an expensive restaurant as a reward, also at her own expense.

Unlike Escalante's program, which aimed to instill a particular educational skillset, many of Johnson's interventions are directed at counseling and problem solving for individual students. She convinces a pregnant student to stay in class rather than transferring to a teen mothers' program and lends $200 to the winner of the Dylan/Dylan contest to cover the cost of a jacket he bought on the street to wear when claiming his reward, trusting to his word for repayment. The transformations this teacher-hero effects are largely in the self-esteem and self-image of her students. They commit themselves less to learning for its own sake than to her as the embodiment of a caring, compassionate, dedicated teacher. Though Johnson's personal life receives little direct attention beyond mention of an earlier divorce, the film clearly implies that her students are her life. Indeed, shocked by the murder of one of her class in a gang shooting, Johnson decides to quit teaching at the end of the academic year. The students, who have bonded with her, implore her to stay, calling her their light and their tambourine man ("You're our teacher, and you got what we need"), and ultimately she relents. The film ends with Johnson, too, walking down a school corridor, in a scene of muted triumph that the teacher who was too good to lose has recognized her proper place.

Freedom Writers (2007) follows the now familiar formula closely, a fact remarked upon in a number of reviews of the film (Dargis, 2007; Groen, 2007). The story begins with a new teacher and a difficult, disadvantaged class. Erin Gruwell's English students at Woodrow Wilson High School in Long Beach, California, are sullen, disrespectful, unengaged, unmotivated, and ranged against each other in ethnic cliques. Her attempts to win the students' attention involve discussing rap as poetry and rearranging the seating plan to break up the ethnic enclaves. Her first breakthrough "teachable moment" comes when she seizes a racist picture of a Black student drawn by a Latino. She departs from her lesson plan and begins to discuss Nazi racism. Finding that only one student is aware of the Holocaust, she refers to the Nazis as a successful gang, capturing the others' attention and demonstrating the issue's relevance. She then moves on to "the line game," asking students to stand on a line to show that they have shared certain experiences. The game begins to resonate as she moves from the everyday (liking a particular television show) to highly sensitive subjects (encountering racism, friends victimized by gang violence). Her next step is to buy the students notebooks and ask them to write about their lives. Facing unwillingness by the school to provide copies of *The Diary of Anne Frank*, Gruwell takes on two part-time jobs. With additional funding available, her first initiative is to take her students to a Holocaust museum and to dinner at an expensive restaurant to meet Holocaust survivors.

Gruwell begins her second year with these students by providing four books she has purchased herself and initiating a "toast for change," statements by the students of personal changes they wish to make. She encourages the students to read Anne Frank's diary as a metaphor for the restrictions on their own lives. She sets a collective stretch goal (though, tellingly, not an academic one); namely, raising funds to sponsor a visit to their class by Miep Gies, the Dutch woman who sheltered Anne Frank. The students are successful at raising the funds necessary to pay for Ms. Gies's trip from Holland, and the visit attracts considerable media attention. After studying the freedom riders of the Civil Rights Movement in the sixties, Gruwell conceives of another stretch goal. The students will become "Freedom Writers," with the goal of publishing a collection of their work. Gruwell's workload—teaching, plus extra hours with the Freedom Writers, plus two part-time jobs—is all-consuming, and her husband decides to leave her. In addition to domestic conflict, she encounters administrative opposition: the principal does not want her to teach the Freedom Writers for a third year, a decision she successfully appeals to the school board. Ultimately, the Freedom Writers' diary is published (Freedom Writers & Gruwell, 1999) and Gruwell moves to California State University at Long Beach to establish a foundation to encourage diffusion of her innovations.

The common elements shared by these films extend to their visual storytelling. All three begin with establishing shots that travel through impoverished neighborhoods to arrive at troubled schools populated by unruly students. The camera then moves to the instructor's classroom and remains there for most of the movie, with the teacher-hero him/herself as its most frequent focus, underscoring the character's structural and thematic centrality. We do not share the teacher's viewpoint (looking outward at the students), but rather are invited to observe his or her actions, reactions, and interactions with varying degrees of intimacy. The stars of *Dangerous Minds* and *Freedom Writers*, Michelle Pfeiffer and Hillary Swank, respectively, are known for their preternaturally beautiful faces. The amount of camera time they are given is hardly surprising on purely aesthetic grounds. In contrast, Edward James Olmos, the star of *Stand and Deliver*, is a proverbial "face made for radio," and the movie takes a different approach, emphasizing his pockmarked face and thinning hair as marks of his "realness" and integrity. His trademark "in your face" pedagogy is replicated cinematically with repeated close-up shots of highly charged teacher-student encounters.

These cinematographic choices reflect one of the dominant fable's deep structures: the assumption of the pivotal function of the heroic individual, the teacher, the spectacle of whose charisma is illuminated and glorified by the camera's gaze. The relative restriction of the setting to that all-important crucible, the classroom, demonstrates a similar insistence on the ultimately local nature of both the educational problem (these students) and the solution (this teacher). Of course, there are cogent dramatic reasons for the choice too. The small, confined space of the classroom increases the dramatic stakes, especially in the early confrontational scenes between the unruly (but always attractive) ethnically diverse teenagers and their impassioned instructors. The kinetic energy of the young people (their expressive body language, their "street" vocabulary, their occasional violent outbursts) are further underscored by a soundtrack full of "their" music: rap, hip-hop.

The hero bias of the dominant fable is demonstrated in other structural and visual choices too (remembering that in the film medium, a visual choice is also a narratological one). Within the world of these films, there are few other important adult figures; parents, administrators, principals, other teachers are all essentially peripheral, with little screen time and none of the charged energy the teacher-hero's scenes possess. The time frame, too, is telescoped in a familiar manner, reducing the teacher's dramatic arc to one or at most two academic years, which seem, in classic film fashion, like a mere matter of days, and involving only a single class of students. (In reality, of course, these were teachers with other classes and responsibilities whose achievements required months of unrelenting plodding, both in the classroom and outside.)

Based on a True Story: Challenging the Dominant Fable

As movie-goers, we are by now sophisticated enough to assume that the medium will impose its conventions even (or perhaps especially) on material "based on a true story," no matter what claims to the contrary appear to be made by the inclusion of this familiar formulation in the opening or closing credits. It comes as no surprise, therefore, when we compare written accounts of the three teachers' experiences with their cinematic treatment that we discover notable omissions and distortions, especially in regard to time frame, the nature of the actual teaching program undertaken, and the heroic isolation of the central figure.

It might not be surprising, but it is significant. For these films have, arguably, created a set of expectations surrounding educational reform narratives, as well as the initiatives whose stories they tell, expectations concerning what is needed, the pace of change, outcomes, and legacies. If policymakers and educational professionals themselves are only too aware of the other narratives this story elides, they must still confront an audience (elected politicians, parents, school communities) predisposed to expect the "Hollywood version" their own stories can rarely supply.

Stand and Deliver enjoyed a relatively modest commercial success, grossing $14 million. Its continuing influence on the genre of the contemporary teacher-hero movie, however, makes it worth spending some time exploring the ways in which the film distorted the real-life hero's experience. Written accounts of Jaime Escalante's teaching at Garfield High School (Jesness, 2002; Matthews, 1988) emphasize a number of important differences from *Stand and Deliver*. First, there is the matter of chronology. Escalante's actual transformation process did not unfold nearly as quickly as the movie's version. He began teaching basic mathematics at Garfield in 1974 and only taught his first calculus class in 1979. His students began taking the AP calculus exam that year, and two of five passed, followed by seven of nine in 1980, fourteen of fifteen in 1981, and all eighteen in 1982, the cohort that was presented in the film. Given this progression, it is surprising that the Educational Testing Service did not challenge Garfield's results on the AP calculus exam before 1982. In no case did students go from basic arithmetic to advanced calculus as rapidly as portrayed in the film. Moreover, the change was much more a team effort than a one-man miracle. Another Hispanic mathematics teacher, Ben Jimenez, was centrally involved, and both teachers had the strong support of Principal Henry Gradillas. The movie downplayed Gradillas's role and omitted Jimenez entirely.

In addition to Escalante's classroom innovations, he also created a finely tuned preparatory system to bolster his efforts. With Gradillas's support, he improved the set of math courses at Garfield leading to AP calculus. To overcome curricular gaps in the junior high schools sending students to Garfield, Gradillas and Escalante encouraged them to offer algebra, and established an intensive summer math program at East Los Angeles College. They also instituted a tutoring program, hiring the better students as teachers. The preparatory system was open enrollment, rather than restricted to those who demonstrated strong aptitude, for Escalante believed that "*ganas*"—desire—was at least as important as innate ability.

Seen from this perspective, Escalante's accomplishments are no less impressive, but they are markedly different in nature, and much more consistent with research findings on the practices of successful innovators (Borins, 2006, pp. 18–26). The movie shows us that Escalante succeeded through charismatic teaching and heroic effort. The facts indicate that while Escalante was a superb instructor, he was also an effective manager. He convinced others, particularly Gradillas and Jimenez, to buy into his vision. He was able to organize a delivery system whose final step was the AP calculus exam. He successfully secured additional funding, both internally and externally, for example, from corporate foundations. And, rather than triumph by charismatic conversion, he relied on patience and planning consistently displayed over a sustained change process that took a decade.

When we consider LouAnne Johnson's own story, as recounted in her book *My Posse Don't Do Homework* (1992), the differences from the narrative *Dangerous Minds* presents are at least as striking and seem to owe much to the generic conventions established by the earlier film. In fact, Johnson's book did not offer a narrative at all, but rather a set of recollections of individual students, with each chapter, as she put it, "a separate 'snapshot'" (p. 1).

The book covers a four-year period when Johnson taught in four different programs: a standard English program, an accelerated English program, the Academy program, and an ESL program. The movie deals only with her role in the Academy program. Some of Johnson's snapshots did find their way into the movie, which then created a dramatic through-line to encompass them. Thus, the Dylan/Dylan contest was invented for the movie. While Johnson mentioned student fights in the book, no student of hers was murdered, nor did she seek to leave teaching because of the violence she encountered. In short, the movie took an appealing, if somewhat disjointed memoir, with no single pedagogical (or dramatic) climax and transformed it into a seamless narrative building to an uplifting, if somewhat generalized, "triumph of the spirit" resolution.

The key episodes of the film *Freedom Writers*—the teachable moment regarding racism, the line game, the visit to the Museum of Tolerance, the meeting with Holocaust survivors, the "toast for change," Erin Gruwell's divorce, and the publication of *The Freedom Writers Diary*—are all consistent with Gruwell's memoir (2007). One minor difference involved telescoping her first two years of teaching into one to simplify the movie's plot. A more significant difference concerns Miep Gies. In the movie, the students raised enough money to bring her from Holland to Long Beach, and some time is spent chronicling their efforts. In fact, the students had no prospect of raising the necessary funds, and Gruwell tells us that an initial appeal to the class and their parents brought in $18 (p. 111). Gruwell's plans were realized because she learned from one of her contacts that Gies was already coming to California to promote a documentary, so all Gruwell had to do was convince her to add the students to her schedule. Gruwell made this clear in her book; she also frankly admits that she decided not to tell the students of Gies's itinerary because "it would mean more to them if they thought they were responsible for her visit" (p. 120). While Gruwell's motivational objective is understandable, this double fictionalization has the effect of magnifying Gruwell's transformative effect on her students and further heroicizing her role.

More fundamentally, in her own narrative, Gruwell details strong entrepreneurial talents in fundraising and dealing with outside stakeholders, as well as an ability to take advantage of connections and of serendipity; again, necessary skills for a successful innovator, but much less cinematically interesting than sheer force of personality in the classroom. Gruwell took her students to see *Schindler's List* and to dinner at a restaurant in geographically nearby but socially distant Newport Beach. Expressions of prejudice at the cinema and restaurant led to an article in the local newspaper. The article was noticed by a college friend of Gruwell's who was ombudsman at the University of California, Irvine. It happened that Thomas Keneally, author of *Schindler's Ark*, was a writer in residence at Irvine. This connection led to a visit to Keneally at Irvine, who then arranged for Gruwell and her students to visit producer Steven Spielberg (Gruwell, 2007, pp. 40–72). One of Gruwell's part-time jobs was as a concierge at the local Marriott hotel. This entitled her to the employees' deep discount rates at Marriott hotels. She then was able to convince management on several occasions to give the entire Freedom Writers group the same price (p. 156). My point here is similar to that regarding Escalante. While Gruwell was undoubtedly inspirational in the classroom, she was also entrepreneurial outside it, and it was this entrepreneurial talent that enabled her to promote the Freedom Writers so effectively.

What emerges clearly from these comparisons is more than further, unnecessary confirmation that Hollywood will have its way. Read as narratives of transformation and innovation, these three instances of the dominant teacher-hero fable falsify by omission, consistently ignoring their protagonists' less heroic and dramatic talents as managers, entrepreneurs, and players of institutional politics, as well as consistently isolating educational transformation from its necessary support base among a wide range of stakeholders within the broader educational system. In the narrative world of the fable, it always comes back to, and down to, that single, charismatic teacher in the classroom. The story begins, and ends, there.

Misreaders, Misleaders, and Self-Defeaters: Subverting the Teacher-Hero

We have already pointed to some possible explanations for the centrality of the teacher-hero to the dominant fable of educational reform. The utility of a heroic fable is evident. Clearly, it is easier to frame a compelling story around the actions and effects of a single extraordinary individual. Incremental processes of change, however innovative, are notoriously difficult to dramatize and tend to fall short on immediate uplift. But the choice also serves to perpetuate the very problems the narratives purport to expose. By focusing so convincingly on the individual who makes a difference, these stories fail to address in any meaningful way the failings of the educational and public policy systems that make these heroic interventions necessary. And there is a further serious drawback to the choice of hero mode: extraordinary teachers are, by definition, rare. The burdens they undertake in fulfilling their transformational role, as all three instances of our dominant fable testify, are almost overwhelming. How many others can be expected to assume the role or prove able to sustain it if they do? The teacher-hero's inspirational epic, precisely because of its heroic dimensions, almost guarantees that replication will be impossible. And, barring the systemic changes that the dominant fable rules out by its very structure, that leaves the inner-city students exactly where they were before—still waiting for a miracle.

There are films that address these issues, films we are calling "counter-fables." Interestingly, all of the ones we will be considering effect their critique of the dominant fable from within its narrative structure. They, too, focus on individual teachers and a single group of students, yet they call into question the possibility of transformation. *Cheaters, Half Nelson, The History Boys* (set in the UK, but highly relevant here), *The Class* (set in Paris), and *Dead Poets Society* explicitly or, in the case of the last movie, inadvertently expose the limits of the teacher's role within a system and culture that seem to make change almost beyond individual reach. These are teachers who fail their students and themselves, and their failures convey a larger indictment of both the fable they tried to inhabit and the institutional structures that make that fable a fairytale.

Cheaters (2000) is arguably the most explicitly subversive of the counter-fables we will consider, and we will spend some time analyzing it. The film was made for HBO television and its provenance is significant. HBO, home of *The Sopranos* and *Six Feet Under*, has made something of a specialty of anatomizing the hypocrisies, falsities, mythologies, and perversions of contemporary American life. The *Cheaters* story, based on events at Chicago's Steinmetz High School in 1995, seems tailor-made for the network. Once again, the movie's opening sequence quickly establishes the socio-economic markers: poor neighborhoods; overcrowded classrooms; unmotivated, violent students; overworked, burnt-out teachers; insufficient resources; rock-bottom expectations. We've been here before. The plot setup is equally familiar. English teacher Jerry Plecki (son of a Polish immigrant family, like many of his students) volunteers yet again to coach the school's team for the Academic Decathlon, a national competition testing multiple fields of academic prowess (chiefly of the memorize-and-regurgitate-quickly variety—a point we will return to later). Steinmetz has a history of placing last and Plecki's colleagues make it clear that no one expects this year to be any different.

The setup seems familiar, and yet there are already intimations of a very different narrative agenda. Plecki, subtly and persuasively embodied by Jeff Daniels, is first seen teaching *Paradise Lost* and expounding on Satan's credo: "Better to reign in Hell than serve in Heaven." It is also clear from comments made by Plecki's most motivated student (who provided an impassioned classroom gloss on Satan's words) that the teacher has already proved his transformational credentials, taking an English class to meet Kurt Vonnegut and inspiring the class of nonperformers actually to read *Slaughterhouse Five*, without in any way altering either the students' or the school's general culture of defeat and failure.

Preparations for the competition begin with the recruitment of the usual team of outcasts, rebels, tough boys, and immigrants. Plecki makes his motivational address, promises his own commitment ("I will never abandon you. And I'll never hang you out to dry"), and exacts a promise of seven extra hours of preparation each school day as well as weekends and holidays. The team rises to the challenge and, after truly heroic efforts of cramming and memorization, places fifth in the Chicago competition, the final spot entitling them to compete at the state level. While this represents the best result ever for Steinmetz, they are far behind Whitney Young High School, winner of the state competition for the last nine years, and a magnet school of middle-class overachievers.[2] It is at this point in the story, with the achievement of a decidedly muted victory, and a team both disillusioned and depressed, that the narrative fully assumes its subversive stance.

While Plecki attempts to rekindle the team's ambition for the state competition, a Steinmetz student learns where the state exams are being stored and sells a copy to a member of the team. What follows are a series of scenes of inverted aspiration and misdirected motivation that are both highly entertaining and deeply disturbing. They hold a particular resonance for any viewer familiar with the conventions of the teacher-hero narrative, conventions being thoroughly reversed here. While the majority of the team members immediately agree to cheat, there is a holdout. Plecki then marshals all of his rhetorical skill and pedagogical conviction to persuade her to join the effort. It is an inspired parody of the "nobody thinks you can do it, but you can because you've got the passion" speech that is part of the teacher-hero's inspirational repertoire. And the satire does not end there. Plecki and the team explicitly address the ways in which the academic competition is weighted against them: the advantages Whitney Young enjoys as, effectively, a private school within the public system and the location where the Decathlon offices have been housed for years.[3] In contrast, the Steinmetz team cannot even get access to their school's single photocopier. Cheating thus becomes, in one team member's view, "the ultimate affirmative action." Or, as another puts it, "Two wrongs make it even."

Clearly, Plecki and his team of underdogs are rebelling against much more than a rigged academic talent show. Indeed, the teacher makes the point that cheating is an essential component of the American dream of success: "Do you think Bill Gates fired the guys who stole Apple's operating system? He probably promoted them." In the national narrative of aspiration, winning justifies the means, and one of the students quotes the quintessential statement of that view, Vince Lombardi's "Winning isn't everything, it's the only thing." It is precisely at this moment, *Cheaters* suggests, that Plecki and his students are truly fulfilling the Decathlon's stated ambition in the promotional video they viewed earlier: "Building skills that work in corporate America." (The fact that none of the team members belong to visible minorities focuses the film's attention on issues of social class and economic disadvantage rather than race. This is in marked contrast to the dominant fable where race is the predominant marker of difference and the largely unexamined context of the students' struggles.)

Having made their choice—and won over the remaining holdout—the team then works feverishly to prepare answers and invent ways of bringing them into the examination room. The montage sequences of cooperative cribbing and ingenious answer smuggling (programming pagers and calculators, inscribing soles of shoes and sticks of gum) again offer an incisive parody of the more familiar "sweat of their brow" scenes of hard work and passion of the dominant fable, complete with blackboards full of notations, all-night sessions of homework, high-fives of triumph, and embraces of mutual support. And the cheating is successful. The Steinmetz team wins the state championship and claims its trophies to the sound of the theme from *Rocky*. Despite Plecki's earlier caution ("The only way we get caught is if we do too well"), however, the team overplays its hand and its improvement in performance is so statistically improbable that there are immediate accusations of cheating. The Decathlon organizers ask the Steinmetz team to submit to retesting. The team debates their dilemma and even watches *Stand and Deliver*—another aspect of the film's parody—as they consider their response. The working-class White students identify strongly with Edward James Olmos' impassioned defense of his students—"It's only because my students have Latino names"—and agree that, like Escalante's AP calculus class, they will be believed guilty of cheating if they consent to a retest. They refuse. The Decathlon organizers revoke their state title, and the Steinmetz team, with the support of the school administration, begins litigation against the competition.

Both local and national media embrace the story and the pressure builds on Plecki and the team. The irony grows as Plecki now struggles to motivate his team to persist in their deception ("This will be the real test of your skills"), even quoting Benjamin Franklin, that paragon of American self-invention: "The only way three people can keep a secret is if two of them are dead. Let's see if we can prove him wrong." By now, moreover, the viewer has likely identified so completely with the students' social grievances and struggles as to be in the uneasy position of "rooting" whole-heartedly for the cheaters to escape detection. Within weeks, however, a Steinmetz student who was dropped from the Decathlon team admits to cheating. The state attorney and the Board of Education launch investigations. There is a sustained interrogation in which each student is questioned separately, in effect a multiperson reenactment of a classic prisoner's dilemma. Filmed in a heightened noir style, it underscores the hypocrisy and bad faith of the lawyers involved. The lawyer wrings a confession from a second team member by playing on their shared Catholic background and the Catholic imperative of confession. Plecki is suspended from teaching (ultimately to be fired), and the students return to their original state of hopeless disengagement.

The team's final scene with Plecki is a bitter inversion of the sort of glorification the dominant fable's noble protagonist receives. No light-filled corridors here. Rather, we see the bleak, windswept Chicago waterfront and a group of outcasts estranged from their school, their community, and even from each other. Plecki, fulfilling the teacher-hero's sacrificial role within a very different context, tells the students to blame him for their crime ("If anyone asks you, tell them I got the tests. Forced you to look at them. Threatened you if you talked."). The students, in turn, present him with a copy of *Paradise Lost,* inscribed to "the best teacher we ever had" and assure him that he "taught us how to survive anything." While Plecki also asserts that he believes things will change because of what they did ("They'll have to justify holding a competition that's not really a competition. They'll have to justify warehousing you, while the chosen few get a quality education."), the film scarcely sustains his note of saddened optimism. The movie concludes with a voice-over by the team's most impassioned member, the young woman who defended Satan's stance in the opening classroom sequence. Like the rest of the team, most of whom end up going to college, she has apparently suffered little or no obvious harm from her career as a cheater and continues to maintain that she (and they) did nothing wrong. She is currently attending university (always a marker of victory in the dominant fable) and even contemplating a career in teaching. The movie's final lines are worth quoting at length:

> I learned more about the way the world really works from my nine months on the Decathlon than most people will learn in a lifetime . . . Don't laugh, but I'm thinking of becoming a teacher. There's no more noble job than shaping young minds. So what would I do if I caught one of my students cheating? I'd turn the little bastard in. But if they can get by me, then I'll know they'll be ready for the real world. I wouldn't have it any other way.

A review of news coverage in both the *Chicago Sun-Times* and the *New York Times* suggests that the writer-director of *Cheaters,* John Stockwell, followed closely actual events at Steinmetz high school (Brown & Rossi, 1995; Johnson, 1995a, 1995b, 2000; Ritter & Sneed, 1995; Rossi, Sneed, & Brown, 1995; Sneed & Rodriguez, 1995). In contrast to the dominant fables we have considered, his faithfulness to "the true story" includes a full acknowledgement of the complexity of motive that drives his teacher-"hero." And the film's own judgment of Plecki's actions, the final status it accords him, remains unsettlingly open. So we learn of a possible earlier cheating episode, of a business failure that has left Plecki deeply embittered. (He attributes it to his inability to pay off the appropriate people.) Even his impassioned attack on the inequities of the various systems arrayed against him and his students is met with a pointed rebuttal by his own mother: "You're not the victim here." Insidiously, the narrative forces the viewer into a position similar to that of its conflicted protagonist, caught between moral absolutes, both self-implicated and disillusioned.

It is a classic example of cognitive dissonance—the tension that results from simultaneously holding two conflicting thoughts—and we have, as viewers, already witnessed Plecki enacting its tensions as he rehearses the arguments he will use to win over the sole member of the team who does not immediately embrace the opportunity to see the Decathlon questions in advance. "I'm a teacher," Plecki begins, speaking directly to the camera and placing the viewer in the position of his soon-to-be-compromised students, "so I'm supposed to spout the same platitudes you've heard a million times before. Cheaters don't prosper. It's not whether you win or lose, it's how you play the game. Well, this may not be approved curriculum, but guess what? Winning does matter. Cheaters do prosper." Interestingly, none of the other students are shown to be in the least conflicted about the (im)morality of the situation. In effect, one gleeful team-member speaks for them all as she seizes the stolen test books: "I am *so* comfortable looking at these." But it is clear that Plecki is not comfortable, however much he rationalizes his own urge finally to join the ranks of the winners: "I'm sure your father came to this country like mine did, thinking that a democracy was a meritocracy." And it is a testament to the skill and subtlety of the film's storytelling that by its end, we too are caught, disgusted by the hypocrisy that greets the team's exposure, sympathetic to the very real grievances Plecki and his students articulate, implicated in the deception we hoped would succeed, yet aware inescapably that Plecki is guilty of a serious moral failure.

To this point, we have been considering *Cheaters* primarily as a highly effective corrective to the narrative omissions, simplifications, and implicit falsities of the dominant fable. It functions equally persuasively as a cautionary tale—almost a case study—of the corrosive effects of frustration and lack of support on the would-be teacher-hero. At a still deeper level, the film calls into question the social context of education in contemporary America and its relation to material success and self-advancement in ways the dominant fable never does. In his first speech to the potential decathlon team members, Plecki makes this plain. Why should they compete, he asks rhetorically, and then answers himself: because it will remove them from the realm of failure, allow them to join the ranks of the entitled. It will do what public education is supposed to do. It will fulfill the American dream and change their lives forever: "Do you want to get into Harvard? You'll get into Harvard. On a full scholarship . . . I just want you to know what it feels like to win. Because once you've had that feeling, you'll never let it go."

Four years later, the English playwright Alan Bennett (2004) addressed similar issues in *The History Boys*, a highly successful production of London's National Theatre, adapted by Bennett for film and released in 2006. A purely fictional story (though partly inspired by Bennett's own experiences "going up" for history at Cambridge), *The History Boys* follows the fortunes of a group of final-year grammar school students in Northern England as they prepare for the Oxford and Cambridge entrance exams. The film is structured around contrasting studies in pedagogy embodied by the anachronistic "General Studies" teacher, Hector, a middle-aged misfit devoted to the literature and values of an earlier era, and Irwin, the "temporary contract teacher" of history hired to give these lower-middle-class boys something of the sophistication, polish, and "edge" their more privileged rivals for Oxbridge possess as a birthright. The movie is set in the 1980s, and the young ambitious Irwin is clearly a voice of Thatcherite pragmatism against Hector's decidedly outmoded liberal humanism.

Anything written by Alan Bennett is, by definition, highly intelligent, and *The History Boys* is no exception. Preserving much of the theatricality of its source, the movie presents possibly the most articulate set of high school students ever to appear on screen, while offering deeply sympathetic portraits of two flawed but devoted teachers. What makes the movie an interesting comparator for *Cheaters* is the very different way it too triangulates issues of pedagogy, class, and morality. As he eviscerates the boys' sample history essays—"Dull. Dull. Abysmally dull. Their sheer competence was staggering"—Irwin plays on their social anxieties to prepare them to abandon any principles of historical truth or accuracy in favor of glib, attention-grabbing inversions of received opinions:

"Bristol welcomes you with open arms. Manchester longs to have you. You can walk into Leeds. But I'm the Fellow of Magdalene College and I've just read 70 papers and they're all saying the same thing and I'm asleep."

"But it's all true."

"What's truth got to do with it? What's truth got to do with anything?"

Hector argues passionately against the speciousness and intellectual bad faith of a method the boys themselves describe as "cheating," though it involves no stealing of exam books or cribbing of answers. For him, it negates the very essence of education: the disinterested acquisition of knowledge for its own sake and for the moral empathy it can engender. The debate climaxes in a shared lesson in which Irwin, Hector, and the boys debate the position to be taken on the Holocaust, should it "come up" on the exam. In the end, the boys adopt Irwin's strategy for success and they do succeed. All are accepted into prestigious colleges on the strength of their iconoclastic originality. Posner, the gay Jewish student who is most closely identified with Hector, summarizes it succinctly: "I was terribly understanding about Hitler. They praised my sense of detachment. Said it was the foundation of writing history." He is awarded a scholarship. The movie ends with a memorial service for Hector, who has died in an accident, and with glimpses of the boys' future lives as adults who have, for the most part, settled for much less than they had once seemed to promise, the Oxbridge exams clearly an "entrance" into a future of compromise.

Our analysis has focused on only one of *The History Boys'* two main narrative strands. But the movie also presents a sustained exploration of an issue never explicitly raised by the dominant fable; namely, the eroticism inherent in the teacher-student relationship. In a poignant scene, both Hector and Irwin admit their attraction to their students, though only Hector transgresses. He fondles the boys when offering them rides home on his motorcycle. Bennett is careful to neuter these episodes as much as possible: Hector never makes advances to boys under the age of 16; his "gropes" are easily fended off; and the boys themselves treat the incidents as pathetic, even comic eccentricities they are quite willing to humor. And, of course, the narrative punishes Hector. He is exposed, humiliated, forced to resign and, finally, killed off. While *Cheaters* does not address the issue directly, it is worth noting that when the Steinmetz Decathlon team's cheating is revealed, the press, Plecki's neighbors, and the Chicago school board officials all immediately assume sexual impropriety between the morally compromised teacher and his charges. I am not suggesting that erotic attraction is a defining feature of the counter-fable. The point I would make is rather that the counter-fable focuses on the human complexity of what we can call the teacher-antihero; the untidy mix of motives, ambitions, frailties, frustrations, and passions that animate him (and it is noteworthy that all the compromised teacher-antiheroes are male). If the dominant fable insists on the sufficiency of the teacher-student relationship to "solve" the educational problem, the counter-fable reveals just how difficult and overdetermined that relationship can be.

The most extreme version of the teacher-antihero we will consider stands at the heart of another, still more recent fictional narrative, the independent American film *Half Nelson*, co-written and directed by 29-year-old filmmaker Ryan Fleck and released in 2006. Here, the central figure is a social studies teacher, Dan Dunne. Young, passionate, willing to engage his inner-city students in sophisticated debates on the dialectics of history as demonstrated by the Civil Rights Movement and the overthrow of the Allende government in Chile, Dunne is also a crack addict who is discovered by one of his students sprawled on the floor with his pipe in a school washroom. The film's focus is the relationship that develops between these two characters, offering deeply moving portraits of two damaged souls against a bleak and perilous urban landscape. In interviews, Fleck himself has played down the specific educational aspects of the film to address it as an allegory of the American left's political failures. Still, it is impossible to watch the movie and not be reminded of the narrative conventions and expectations that the dominant fable has so firmly entrenched. An early scene between Dunne and two women he meets in a bar, and with whom he will soon snort cocaine, plays as a bitter rejection of those conventions and the naïve ideology that underlies them. Dunne explains how "the kids keep me focused," saying, "If you can change one . . ." His barmate completes the sentence for him, "You can change them all." But Dunne rejects that easy assumption: "That's not the point." In a scorching irony, Dunne's special topic with his students is "turning points," yet the movie refuses to offer more than the faintest possibility of one for either Dunne or his student. If the dominant fable insists on the students' ability to transcend their social and economic realities through the dedication of their teacher-hero, *Half Nelson* shows the teacher—sourcing his crack from the protector of the student he befriends—dragged down into the worst aspects of that reality.

In an overwhelmingly positive review of *Half Nelson*, *New York Times* film critic Manohla Dargis (2006) made explicit the nature of the narrative clichés the movie eviscerates: "If "Half Nelson" had four times the budget and half the brains it could easily be cinematic Valium, a palliative about a white teacher who, through pluck and dedication, inspires his nonwhite students to victory, in the classroom or on a sports field." Turning to the 1990 film *Dead Poets Society* is to turn to precisely that sort of Valium. By far the most successful of the movies we are considering (made on a budget of $16 million and ultimately grossing $236 million worldwide), it was one of then-highly popular comedian Robin Williams' first dramatic roles. A fictional story set in 1959 at Welton Academy, an old-money prep school in Vermont, the film is ostensibly a paean to individuality and rebellion against the stultifying Ivy League conformity advocated by an older genera-tion of fathers and headmasters. Williams plays John Keating, an iconoclas-tic former Welton student who returns to teach English. Focusing on his interactions with a single class, Keating embarks on a program of coaching his sensitive young charges in self-expression and (minor) rebellion. He en-courages them to tear pages from their textbooks, introduces romantic po-ets into the curriculum whose verses they declaim while standing on their desks. And he tells them of the underground student society he formed while at Welton, the Dead Poets Society of the movie's title. Inevitably, Keat-ing's approach earns him the devotion of his students and the hostility of the school's hidebound headmaster.

The climax of the narrative comes with the conflict engendered by Keating's teaching in the life of one particularly gifted and sensitive student. Neil Perry would like to study drama, but his authoritarian father insists he become a doctor. Forging his parents' signature on a permission form, Neil auditions for and stars in a production of *A Midsummer Night's Dream*. His father sees the play and, outraged by the spectacle of his son in the role of the fairy Puck, withdraws Neil from Welton to transfer to a military academy. Neil then commits suicide. The school's disapproving headmaster conducts an inquiry, questions Keating's students, concludes that Keating was responsible for Neil's suicide, and fires him. The headmaster then takes over Keating's class and returns to the curriculum against which Keating rebelled. The film ends with Keating beatifically witnessing the students ris-ing on their desks to recite Walt Whitman's poem *Oh Captain! My Captain!* in what is meant to be read as a final gesture of support for their devoted teacher and rebellion against the headmaster and all he represents.

In an article reviewing movies about teachers, Stuart Elliott (1993) re-ferred to *Dead Poets Society* as an "inexplicably popular potboiler." Elliott apt-ly summarizes the verdict of the major critics. They found Tom Schulman's screenplay, which won an Academy Award, formulaic, with the villains—the headmaster and Perry senior—one-dimensional and unbelievable and the outcome of the narrative's conflicts entirely predictable (Canby, 1989; Ebert, 1989; Groen, 1989; James, 1989). They also attacked the movie's in-coherence, noting that while it praised nonconformity, the actions inspired by Keating demonstrated that the students were really as immature as the Welton Academy administration believed them to be (Emerson, 1989).

Roger Ebert wrote: "It is, of course, inevitable that the brilliant teacher will eventually be fired from the school and when his students stood on their desks to protest his dismissal, I was so moved, I wanted to throw up."

And yet, having repeatedly taught the movie to undergraduates, I have been surprised at how favorably they receive it. I've concluded that students are impressed by the charismatic teacher portrayed by Williams and identify with his desire to reject an oppressive academic institution and its hidebound pedagogy in favor of an unexplored but potentially attractive alternative. While the final scene of students standing on their desks moved Ebert (and me) to nausea, it seems to resonate with a generation of undergraduates who are surprisingly not in the least put off by the golden-toned nostalgia with which the film drenches its period details. At the risk of appearing to simplify, or even patronize, perhaps any narrative of rebellion against unsympathetic and rigid adult authority would "play well" to this particular audience.

Unlike the other counter-fables we are considering, *Dead Poets Society* proves to be subversive in spite of itself, the narrative apparently unconscious of the critique it offers of the inadequacy of charisma and devotion alone as agents of educational change. Keating certainly displays many of the by-now familiar virtues of the transformational teacher-hero. He is effective at getting his students' attention and winning them over to an academic and personal vision that stands in opposition to that of their school, their parents, and their class culture. But after the students are ready to follow him, he has nowhere to take them (Clemens & Wolff, 1999, pp. 63–65). In the words of one critic, Robert Heilman (2001, p. 418), "we never do see Keating *teaching* anything . . . [He] is not at all a teacher but a performer." Keating misreads both his students and his institutional context, the students in the juvenile ways they would respond to his message of liberation, and the institution in the repressive way it would react. While the best of the transformational teachers, Escalante and Gruwell, set powerful stretch goals, Keating set no goal at all, a failing made evident (despite all the film's efforts) by the nonsensical emptiness of the students' final gesture. It is a hollow and unearned epiphany that clearly reveals the falsities of the narrative formula the film follows.

An explicit contrast with *Dead Poets Society* leads us to consider Laurent Cantet's recent film *Entre les murs*.

> I didn't want to make a version of *Dead Poets Society*, a film where the teacher is brilliant and heroic and knows everything. I wanted to show a school in all its complexity, where the students don't always learn, and the teachers are not always sure of what they're doing. (Lim, 2008)

French filmmaker Laurent Cantet's comments, made in a 2008 interview with the *New York Times*, are an explicit repudiation of the transformational teacher fable. They explain some of the unsettling power of his award-winning *Entre les murs* and go some length to account for its inclusion in this chapter. (It is the only non-English language narrative we will consider.) In some ways, Cantet's film is the bleakest counter-fable we will encounter. For all his (enormous) moral failings, Dan Dunne, the addict-teacher of *Half Nelson* was clearly a gifted, even brilliant, teacher capable of electrifying his students, a fact which makes his spiraling self-destruction all the more tragic. Cantet's protagonist, in contrast, fails spectacularly to inspire, understand, or even, apparently, to like his students. The resulting classroom breakdown, which ends with a student expelled to protect the teacher's own career, has a painful realism that is no less tragic for being almost entirely unnecessary.

Based on Francois Begaudeau's (2006) best-selling autobiographical novel of the same name, *Entre les murs* (literally, Within the Walls) was both a commercial and critical success, winning the Palme d'Or at the 2008 Cannes Film Festival and enjoying a wide (for a subtitled film) North American release. The creation of the film has its own highly unusual narrative. Begaudeau's novel was very loosely structured, a set of vignettes and reflections derived from a year of teaching grammar and composition to an eighth-grade class. Its episodic and impressionistic form was similar to LouAnne Johnson's *My Posse Don't Do Homework*. What Cantet chose to do with the material, however, produced a movie very different from the glossy and predictable *Dangerous Minds*. The director first drafted the outlines of a screenplay with a strong narrative line, extracting a confrontation between Begaudeau and two students that appears and is resolved early in the book and making it the pivot of the story. Cantet then enlisted Begaudeau himself to play the fictional instructor Monsieur Marin. To cast the film, Cantet recruited a diverse group of high school students (as well as some parents and teachers) from the gritty twentieth *arrondissement* where the film would be set, developing the script with them in weekly workshops. These nonactors were not given written screenplays. Descriptions of situations were provided for which they improvised dialogue. These improvised scenes were filmed with three handheld video cameras, one trained on Begaudeau, another on the students, and a third roaming the classroom set (Lim, 2008). Far from gazing reverently at the spellbinding teacher, Cantet's cameras privilege neither teacher nor student, cutting rapidly between them as the confrontation builds and their relationship deteriorates.

Marin teaches his working-class, immigrant students grammar and composition, a subject fraught with issues of race and class divisions in a country whose linguistic purity is still safeguarded through the pronouncements of the Académie Française. Marin enforces the full formality of official French structure, spelling, and pronunciation. His students speak and prefer the language of the streets. And it is, ironically, Marin's own unthinking use of an offensive colloquialism that will ignite the final crisis. But language is not the only source of tension in the class. Marin, aptly described by one reviewer as "a quietly stubborn, prickly man" (Dargis, 2008), routinely baits and teases his pupils with an insensitivity that seems at times to border on hostility (or even contempt). Nor does Marin put in extra hours or make himself available outside of class in the tradition of the self-sacrificing teacher-hero. His primary innovation is to assign his students the task of writing, and presenting, self-portraits (always a risky venture with adolescents). The approach might seem reminiscent of Erin Gruwell in *Freedom Writers,* but these struggling teens do not leap at the opportunity for self-expression, and Marin offers nothing of the empowering nurturing that Gruwell supplied. In fact, the students are plainly uncomfortable with the assignment, reluctant to expose themselves to a teacher who has failed to win their trust, or even liking.

The students' simmering resentment receives open expression at an evaluation session attended by two student representatives, Esmerelda and Louise, whom Marin has routinely and unrelentingly teased. Contrary to school practice, the girls reveal to their fellow students Marin's evaluations of their performance. Furious at their behavior, Marin accuses them, in class, of behaving "*comme petasses,*" a derogatory slang expression with a sexual connotation. The closest English equivalent would be "like skanks." The girls are infuriated in their turn and the class deeply offended. Marin's blundering attempt to defuse the situation—distinguishing between behaving in a way that will be perceived as *petasse,* and actually being one—is entirely lost on the class. A male student, Suleyman, whom Marin had evaluated as "limited scholastically," enters the argument on the girls' behalf. When he storms from the class, his backpack accidentally injures another student. News of this melee travels round the school and when Marin confronts the two girls again in the schoolyard, a growing student audience watches as he loses control completely.

The (accidental) injury to a student means Marin must file an incident report. He does so, omitting any mention of his own role in inciting the events that led to it. Since Marin's provocative language is common knowledge within the school, the principal coaches Marin in his account of the incident in an attempt to defuse criticism. He then convenes the disciplinary committee, of which Marin himself is a member, and supports Marin's contention to the two parent representatives on the committee that he has no need to recuse himself, since Suleyman was using the classroom argument as a pretext for violence and disrespect. The committee duly votes to expel Suleyman, and the principal announces that he will try immediately to find another school that will take him. Suleyman then drops from the narrative as completely as, we assume, he is dismissed from Marin's mind.

The film ends, as teacher narratives so often do, on the last day of class, but there is no valedictory triumph to be found. Attempting to manufacture some sense of accomplishment, Marin polls his hostile students on what they have learned. One mentions the Pythagorean Theorem, another, the history of the slave trade. Esmerelda remarks that the books Marin assigned are "shit" and that she has learned nothing in class. Marin objects, "You can't spend nine months in school and not learn anything." "I'm the living proof," she replies. But she has, she hisses at him, read *The Republic* on her own, not exactly a book for a *petasse*. Another student, one of the weakest, seeks Marin out after class to say she too has learned nothing and fears she will be shunted off to a vocational school.

It is impossible to imagine a mainstream North American film ending in so desolate a fashion. Even *Half Nelson* found some ground for hope in the delicate friendship formed between Dunne and his pupil. Yet Marin is not a villain. He is misguided, insensitive, and lost control of his class (any instructor's worst nightmare), but was saved from the consequences of his own failings by a bureaucracy bent on protecting its own. Marin, however, genuinely believes in the value of what he teaches and in the importance of what he seeks to do. That he fails so miserably is not only a measure of his own limitations but a realistic reflection of the enormity of the task he faces. That it is the students, much more than he, who suffer for this failure, only deepens the bitterness of their shared story.

Changing the System: Beyond the Classroom Hero

A major thrust of our analysis to this point has been the way in which the dominant fable of the transformative teacher-hero fails to address the numerous critical ways in which even the most dedicated, passionate, innovative individual can be defeated by the weight of the system itself, or its larger social context. The counter-fables we have examined have, often very powerfully, dramatized the extent of that defeat. To anyone familiar with the current state of American educational reform, the narrative obsession with individual teachers constitutes a serious misreading. There are other paths to change, and they are producing results. Unfortunately, there are far fewer popular narratives regarding other types of educational initiatives, the bias being, understandably, toward tales of heroic individual struggle.

This scarcity makes the relatively unknown made-for-television movie *A Town Torn Apart* (1992) worth our consideration here. (I taped the production when it was first telecast. It was not widely noticed at the time, and it is not available on www.amazon.com, a rough indication that it enjoyed little afterlife.)

The movie centers on the real-life figure of Dennis Littky, a PhD in psychology and education who, after having been the principal of an innovative high school on Long Island, moves to rustic New Hampshire. There, almost despite himself, he applies for the position of principal at nearby Winchester High School, an underperforming institution in an economically depressed rural backwater.

In many ways, *A Town Torn Apart* belongs to the dominant fable mode. A brief description of its narrative arc might help make that clear. Taking over at the end of the school year, Littky began reaching out to the school's stakeholders and introducing innovative, highly personal new initiatives. He holds an assembly to ask students and faculty for their ideas, hands out questionnaires to students entering the school, and meets with parents and local businesses. During the summer, he directs a cleanup of the property and hires a student artist to paint a mural in the cafeteria. These visible, physical differences make a strong impression when students return in the fall. A key component of his educational methodology is to challenge students, either individually or in groups, to take on learning projects, some of which include a group of students raising a barn, a weak student reading *A Tale of Two Cities* cover to cover, and a pregnant student conducting a survey of attitudes of Winchester residents toward unwed mothers.

Like the teacher-heroes he closely resembles, this principal-hero soon arouses the opposition of educational traditionalists in Winchester who object to his informal style and the unconventional nature and implicit challenges to authority of some of his projects. Littky also attracts media attention, and it is at this point that the narrative takes a slightly different turn. The news story portrays Littky very much in transformative teacher mode, a savior who has single-handedly turned around a failing school. Far from welcoming the recognition, Littky knows these accolades will arouse still more opposition. And the second half of the movie, which gives rise to its title, chronicles this. Littky's opponents are elected to a majority of positions in the local school board, and summarily dismiss him. Littky litigates to retain his position, and his supporters campaign vigorously in the next election, ultimately regaining control of the board in a landslide. The movie concludes with the students whom the movie chronicled graduating successfully, and Littky staying as principal for a total of 13 years, the recipient of recognition and formal honors.

Two aspects of Littky's narrative stand out immediately. First, managerial issues are not suppressed. As a principal, Littky is a manager who must achieve results through the efforts of the teachers whom he supervises. From the outset, he recognizes the importance of "small-p" politics: improving the physical appearance of the school and reaching out to stakeholders, and the narrative accords these rather mundane transformations full weight. The second difference lies in the importance the narrative places upon a clear innovation; namely, the use of individual or group projects. It appears that this innovation, in particular the nontraditional projects chosen by some students, was the key factor in some parents' opposition to Littky. The expression of this opposition through the political process of the school board led Littky, in self-defense, to engage in the "large-p" politics of litigating against the school board and participating in a campaign to elect board members who would be supportive of his innovation.

The movie was based on Susan Kammeraad-Campbell's book *Doc: The Story of Dennis Littky and his Fight for a Better School*, first published in 1989 and revised in 2005. By and large, the movie follows the book, except that it downplays the extent of Littky's professional obsessiveness, which is entirely comparable to the transformational teachers':

> He lived his life in and through the school. It was all-absorbing all-encompassing. His three-year marriage foundered from neglect. Soon he and his wife amicably agreed to divorce. For Littky it was the beginning of a pattern. He would have many more intense relationships with women, all of which would end after a few years when Dennis' attention flagged in favor of work. He would persist in his unwillingness to make an enduring commitment that included marriage and children. (Kammeraad-Campbell, 2005, pp. 29–30)

Kammeraad-Campbell also quotes the husband of one of the teachers most supportive of Littky: "It's tough working for a fanatic. They expect too much. They eat, sleep, and live for their job and expect you to do the same" (p. 102). Littky confirmed that, writing in one of his weekly memos to faculty, "This school is going to take more of your time than a regular school. It will be a great school, not a regular school" (p. 175). Littky managed the inordinate demands of his job by relegating paperwork, letter writing, and phone calls to evenings and weekends, enabling him to spend much of the regular workweek interacting with faculty and students (p. 140).

The real-life prototype of Winchester (Thayer High School) became a key member in a group of high schools that refer to themselves as the Coalition for Essential Schools (www.essentialschools.org). The schools' common principles include mastery of a limited number of essential skills and areas of knowledge rather than breadth of coverage, personalized teaching and learning, conceptualizing the student as worker rather than passive recipient of instruction, and student demonstration of competence through projects or exhibitions. Schools in this group have frequently been recognized by the Innovations in American Government awards. Thayer High School was recognized for its program to disseminate its innovations through conferences, videos, and broadcasts. Central Park East Secondary School in New York applied the Coalition for Essential Schools model to an urban setting in which most students were from lower-income African American and Latino families; and Rindge School of Technical Arts in Cambridge, Massachusetts, applied the model to vocational education (Borins, 1998, pp. 261–282). These innovations were developed by principals rather than individual teachers, and they faced the same obstacles as Littky: opposition within the educational system to their theories and their loosening of rules and procedures, burnout of participating teachers, and the need for additional resources.

The second edition of *Doc* brings the stories of Dennis Littky and Thayer High School to the present. Littky stayed at Thayer until the end of 1992–1993, then moved to the Annenberg Institute for School Reform at Brown University. He soon reimmersed himself in practice, founding a new public high school, the Metropolitan Regional Career and Technical Center, in Providence and a nonprofit educational reform organization, The Big Picture Company. He has written about his experiences and his program for high schools in *The Big Picture: Education is Everyone's Business* (Littky & Grabelle, 2004). Thayer High School after Littky's departure fared less well. Littky's successor as principal followed the same Coalition for Essential Schools philosophy but, according to Kammeraad-Campbell, teachers, parents, and students "were too tired to go the extra step. They didn't have the leadership or the steam to carry it out" (2005, p. 413). The next principal was less innovatively inclined and the school reverted to a more traditional model. The school lost its accreditation due to deterioration of the physical plant and ultimately closed in 2005.

The Fable Structure of Transformational Teacher Narratives

Unlike some of the narrative sets we will encounter in subsequent chapters, the education narratives we've been considering divide quite neatly between the opposing quadrants of the thematic square introduced in Chapter 1.

TABLE 2.1   Transformational Teacher Narratives

	Personal Growth of Protagonist	Personal Decline of Protagonist
Organizational Renewal	*Stand and Deliver* *Freedom Writers* *A Town Torn Apart* *Dangerous Minds*	
Organizational Decline		*Dead Poets Society* *Half Nelson* *Entre les murs*
	Cheaters (students) *History Boys* (students)	*Cheaters* (Plecki) *History Boys* (Hector)

Table 2.1 shows a simple structure, contrasting instances of a clearly heroic dominant fable with counter-fables that generally represent clear failures. *Stand and Deliver, Freedom Writers,* and *A Town Torn Apart* are all stories of organizational renewal at several levels. The class as a mini-organization performs better: the students learn more, achieve things they never imagined, and their life chances as adults are greatly enhanced. There are also benefits for the entire school and, finally, because the innovations developed by Escalante, Gruwell, and Littky are replicated, benefits for other schools across the country. The stories also involve unmistakable growth for these three protagonists. Escalante and Gruwell transcend classroom teaching, and Littky, leadership of one school, to become nationally and internationally recognized innovators in secondary education. I have set apart *Dangerous Minds* because LouAnne Johnson's accomplishments were more modest. While her class benefited from her transformational teaching, there is no evidence that her school did. She left teaching to become a writer and motivational speaker, but she has had nowhere near the same impact as Escalante, Gruwell, or Littky.

Three of the counter-fables provide a sharp contrast with the structures of the dominant fable. In *Dead Poets Society*, Keating leaves the school with his career a shambles. One of his students has committed suicide and, despite the gesture of rebellion with which the film ends, it is unlikely that he has made any lasting impact on his students' education. Setting the movie in 1959 seems to me a shorthand way of saying that, even if Keating's attempt to enliven the teaching of literature has been crushed at Welton, the academy's rigid discipline will prove inconsistent with the ethos of the sixties. *Half Nelson* leaves the question of Dunne's career and personal life entirely open. While he appears clean shaven and drug free in the final frames, no guarantee is provided that his reformation will last or that he will be able to repair the ruin he has made of his professional life. The final frames of *Entre les murs* show Marin's empty classroom, chairs knocked over, desks askew. Voices of students drift in through the windows, but the sound does not fill the void.

Cheaters and *The History Boys* both communicate more ambiguous messages. The cheating episode clearly does Steinmetz High School no good. In fact, the embarrassment was so great that it has never since fielded an Academic Decathlon team. Like Keating and Dunne, Plecki's educational career is in runs. On the other hand, most of the students on the Decathlon team went on to college, evidence that their involvement in the cheating episode did not hurt their life chances. The narrative actually suggests it might have helped ready them for life in early 21st-century corporate America, a world where, as Plecki says, "cheaters do prosper." In *The History Boys*, Hector is humiliated, forced to resign, and dies in a traffic accident. The students, in contrast, succeed at winning admission to Oxford and Cambridge. The school's reputation also benefits. The movie's final, highly theatrical scene, however, played against the backdrop of the school's memorial service for Hector, undercuts any sense of renewal or celebration. It is a threnody for the values that have died with the erring teacher, as each boy steps out of time to confess the compromised choices, disappointed hopes, and mundane achievements he will go on to experience.

Lessons Learned

Turning back from this structural discussion to the teacher-hero, what are the practical lessons to be gleaned from this set of narratives for practitioners within the domain of public education and, more generally, in other areas of public management? What are the narrative competencies the dominant and counter-fables can impart? Setting aside reservations concerning the cinematic representations of their stories, there is no doubt that Escalante and Gruwell's stories can be a valuable source of insights. To effect transformation, as they did, there is clearly a set of necessary skills that can be identified and acquired. We can itemize them as a series of imperatives, starting with those that pertain to the relationship with students in the classroom, then to the relationship with students and their families outside the classroom, and finally to the educational system outside the classroom.

In the Classroom
- Be cool: Find the skill, attitude, or gimmick that will attract and impress your students.

- Aim high: Set a stretch goal for students, defining it either collectively or individually.
- Redefine yourself: Become the students' coach and enabler, helping them to achieve their goal.
- Be patient: Do not expect your transformation to unfold in movie time. It might take years and a succession of cumulative improvements to attain your goal.

Outside the Classroom
- Connect: Share or learn your students' culture. Reach out to them and their families.
- Sacrifice: Be available outside of class hours and be prepared to give time and attention unstintingly.

In the Educational System
- Market: Publicize your efforts in any way possible to attract outside interest and resources.
- Be savvy: Hone your political skills in anticipating opposition and opponents within your school.
- Diversify: Look for support at higher organizational levels or outside the system.

Itemizing the lessons this way makes clear that, while transformation begins in the classroom, it needs support outside the classroom to flourish. These lessons could be generalized more broadly to any frontline innovator in government. The core of the innovation will involve a changed relationship with clients. But the innovation will require additional research and planning, and it will entail a higher level of service that will go beyond the confines of traditional client relationships, and as a consequence, the innovator must commit additional time and energy. Finally, for the innovation to thrive, support from the organization is required, and that necessarily implicates the innovator in the internal organizational politics of persuasion and marketing, seeking allies at higher levels of the organization or outside, mobilizing resources, and disarming critics (Borins 1998, pp. 66–82).

The lessons we can draw regarding narrative competence stem from both the achievements and limitations of the teacher-hero narrative. All the narratives were effective at quickly establishing context and focusing on the key relationship between teacher and students. These both can be taken as lessons for any creator of a narrative. Quickly and vividly establish the context or setting of the story. Focus on the key interaction of the story. That said, the dominant fables suffered from too excessive a focus on the key interaction, to the extent that the story was told—and sometimes misrepresented—in terms of that interaction. The most egregious instance was *Freedom Writers*'s invention that Erin Gruwell's students raised enough money to bring Miep Gies from Holland to Long Beach. Clinging to that fiction led to the inclusion of scenes of students fundraising and celebrating their success; these, paradoxically, detracted from the key interaction in the classroom. Had the movie been faithful to the actual story, it would have substituted a short scene involving Erin Gruwell finding out about Miep Gies's trip to California and then taking advantage of that information to invite Gies to her classroom. What would have been gained was a greater appreciation of Gruwell's entrepreneurial ability, which is part of a deeper understanding of her success as a transformational teacher.

If the creators of these narratives, however, chose to present a simplistic picture of the teacher-hero, then they still challenge the audience to question both the status of the narrative's hero and the replicability of the actions it depicts. Doesn't the heroism of the transformational teacher undermine his or her personal life?[4] Doesn't this heroism require sustained effort over a longer period of time than the narrative suggests? Doesn't it also require the buttress of organizational and political skills that receive little or no screen time? In some instances, in particular regarding the question of work-life balance, sufficient hints are provided in the film to form a judgment (even if the movie itself refuses to). In other instances, in particular, regarding chronology and organizational politics, the information is not provided. The viewer must therefore develop an instinct for the narrative's omissions and falsifications. This instinct is relevant to the reading or viewing of all heroic managerial narratives, not just those about teachers. This instinct would involve both identifying what seems implausible or exaggerated and looking for information outside the narrative itself that could be brought to bear upon initial instinctive judgments.

While the creators of films in this genre have focused on the figure of the solitary transformational teacher, they have overlooked what is now widespread experimentation in the American public high school system. Consider the following initiatives.

The Coalition for Essential Schools, in which Dennis Littky is an exemplary practitioner, seeks to rebuild public education through personalized teaching and learning, and student demonstration of mastery of skills through projects and exhibitions. The Knowledge is Power program (www .kipp.org) is also a family of charter schools that serves students, the vast majority Black and Latino, underserved by the public school system. Rather than relying on individualized learning through project work, it (in its own words) "relentlessly focuses on high student performance on standardized tests and other objective measures." The Gates Foundation has made high school education in the United States one of its priorities, and it has not taken sides in the rivalry among educational models, but has rather supported an eclectic mix of traditional schools that focus on rigorous preparation for college or work, theme-based schools, and student centered schools (http://www.gatesfoundation.org/UnitedStates/Education/Transforming HighSchools/).

Teach for America sees the essential problem in the inner-city high schools as burned-out and dispirited teachers, and seeks a remedy by recruiting recent university graduates to commit to teaching for two years in the highest-poverty areas. Founded in 1988, in current recessionary times it received 46,000 applications for 4,500 places and has become a key source of teachers for many inner-city schools (Winerip, 2010). It has developed a Teaching as Leadership framework that includes setting ambitious measureable goals for students, maintaining the belief that the goals indeed are achievable, and making stringent demands on both teachers and students to realize them (Foote, 2009, pp. 14–40; www.teachforamerica.org/corps/teaching/teaching_leadership_framework.htm). This framework has considerable similarity with the approach taken by teacher-heroes such as Escalante and Gruwell.

New Leaders for New Schools is a nonprofit organization that sees the crucial failing in the high schools as poor leadership and seeks a remedy by recruiting more effective people for academic leadership roles (most notably principals in urban schools), training them, entering into partnerships with major urban school systems to place them, and establishing a community of practice for the organization and its graduates to continue learning from their experiences (New Leaders for New Schools, 2009; www.nlns.org).

The Coalition for Essential Schools, Knowledge is Power, Gates Foundation, Teach for America, and New Leaders for New Schools are all examples of systemic initiatives intending to do what the heroic teachers were attempting to do single-handedly: develop new teaching philosophies; provide additional resources; bring youth, energy, and idealism into the teaching profession; and bring greater managerial skill and a stronger commitment to change into academic leadership. The Obama Administration's $4.5 billion competitive Race to the Top Fund is an incentive to state governments to enact these practices.

It is truly unfortunate that movies dealing with education, including many of the most recent, have not varied from the transformational teacher model. Alternative narrative approaches could explore the experiences of teachers recruited by Teach for America or principals recruited by New Leaders for New Schools, the evolution of either organization, or the experience of various charter schools. It might be the case that some of these are best presented in documentaries rather than "based on a true story" or fictional narratives.[5] Some of these stories, however, would fit a narrative framework with its conventional demands of human interest, conflict, and resolution. They, too, possess charismatic, dedicated protagonists espousing new educational philosophies and methodologies and facing daunting obstacles that must be overcome to bring these to life. Where screenwriters and their audiences would be most challenged is in coming to grips with the pedagogical and managerial principles informing the innovations, a kind of intellectual exploration movies have not tended to embrace, or to do well when they have. But if it is true, as many literary critics and cultural anthropologists suggest, that the stories we tell determine the possibilities we can imagine, then the urgency of creating new educational fables seems indisputable. It is clear we need new possibilities for our inner-city schools. We need new narratives.

If commercial cinema or independent documentarists do not provide those narratives, then the educational innovators should seek to tell their own stories. We have seen the power of the heroic fable, the compelling drama it can produce, the human interest it supplies. It is a story that, emphatically, sells. Rejecting its conventions entirely seems both difficult and self-defeating. But we have seen, too, the way in which too close an adherence to its forms distorts the realities of processes that are necessarily more gradual, more cumulative, more conceptual, more collaborative and, often, considerably messier than the dominant fable will allow. The answer lies in a calculated exploitation of the narrative conventions coupled with an awareness of both the expectations they engender and the distortions they can produce.[6] What is needed, perhaps, is an explicit redefinition of narrative concepts like "heroism," "success," even "action"; a redefinition that highlights rather than ignores the complex social and institutional contexts within which these real-life dramas unfold. The transformational teacher narrative is itself due for a transformation.

Endnotes

1. A simpler and nonaccusatory explanation of why they were all making the same mistakes is that they had all been taught by the same instructor.
2. Information about Whitney M. Young Magnet High School can be found on its Web site (www.wyoung.org). Its slogan is "where academic excellence is the standard" and the Home page highlights Michelle Obama, a 1981 graduate.

3. Plecki and his students are deeply resentful of Whitney Young's advantages. It is important to note that Young's student body is very diverse (31% Black, 21% Hispanic, 18% Asian, and 30% Caucasian) and, to its credit, when *Cheaters* showed groups of Whitney Young students, for example the Decathlon team, they reflected this diversity. The online comments about *Cheaters* at http://www.imdb.com/title/tt0218094/ contain several from people associated with Whitney Young who were nonetheless resentful at how they felt it was portrayed.

4. Erik Erikson (1985) refers to the development challenge of young adulthood as intimacy versus isolation, and the heroism of the transformational teachers exemplifying the dominant fable tends to require a commitment of time and energy to work that makes intimacy impossible, leading to isolation. Few individuals would or, according to Erikson, should want to make such a sacrifice. This issue is discussed further in Chapter 5 within the context of young aides to politicians.

5. Davis Guggenheim's documentary *Waiting for Superman* was released as this book was being completed. It discusses a number of educational reform initiatives, in particular some successful charter schools. Because these schools are oversubscribed, they choose their students by lottery. The film follows five families that apply and shows the elation of those that are chosen and the disappointment of those that are not.

6. If the narrative is being produced in a visual format, a DVD presentation, accompanied by a Web site, could provide space for supplementary and background material. The provision of such material alongside the narrative, however, does not in my mind justify distortion of the material in the core narrative.

$$3$$

The Ugly Business

British Narratives of Government

A Very British Fable

Sir Humphrey: "He has his own car, nice house in London, place in the country, endless publicity, and a pension for life. What more does he want?"

Bernard: "I think he wants to govern Britain."

Sir Humphrey: "Well, stop him, Bernard."

—*Yes Prime Minister*, "The Ministerial Broadcast"

On February 25, 1980, the first episode of a 30-minute comedy series was aired on British television, introducing an unsuspecting public to characters who would become, for better or worse, lodged in the popular imagination as archetypes of government: the smoothly manipulative high-level civil servant, Sir Humphrey Appleby; the hapless but ambitious minister, Jim Hacker; and the decent, perennially torn Principal Private Secretary, Bernard Woolley, forever shuttling between them.

Governing Fables: Learning from Public Sector Narratives, pages 63–102
Copyright © 2011 by Information Age Publishing

Yes Minister, and its successor *Yes Prime Minister,* would go on to five series, 38 episodes, several stand-alone specials, a number of books, and a 21st-century afterlife as a West End play. It would win a shelf-full of awards, be routinely cited as among the best British comedies of all time, and earn the enthusiastic public endorsement of Prime Minister Margaret Thatcher. It would also influence, directly or indirectly, most fictional narratives about politics or government in Britain for decades to come.

From its first appearance, *Yes Minister* was routinely praised for its topicality. Yet the series' creators, Anthony Jay and Jonathan Lynn, never strove for taken-from-the-headlines immediacy. Their aim was to dramatize the tension at the heart of democratic governance, the battle between what the beleaguered Hacker calls "the political Will and the administrative Won't." It was, they felt, a timeless battle untethered to particular policies, parties, or even nations. In inspired comic form, in episode after episode, they depicted a perpetual struggle between the political impetus for change (however specious and/or self-serving its motivation) and the bureaucratic inertia and self-interest seeking to strangle it at birth.

Though they initially conceived of their work as corrective—according to Jonathan Lynn, "In one sense, we viewed *Yes Minister* and *Yes Prime Minister* as training films for politicians, showing how they do things wrong" (http://www.jonathanlynn.com/tv/yes_minister_series/yes_minister_qa.htm)—Jay and Lynn created something far more profound: a satiric fable that was, in the words of British MP Gerald Kaufman, "chillingly accurate" (quoted at http://www.jonathanlynn.com/tv/yes_minister_series/yes_minister_quotes.htm). It is a fable of politicians and bureaucrats alike seizing the moral low ground; of appearances routinely manipulated to produce a convincing semblance of substance; of compromise, duplicity, and ambition; of government as theatrical performance and public relations sleight-of-hand. It is also, inevitably, a fable about language, its political uses and abuses. Indeed, the series became known for its linguistic inventiveness, particularly the arias of bureaucratic doublespeak, boilerplate, dissimulation, and nonsense delivered with unflappable aplomb—and the occasional pause for breath—by Sir Humphrey.

This chapter will examine the *Yes Minister* fable in detail, locating its origins in a tradition of political narrative that stretches back to the 19th-century novelist Anthony Trollope. It will focus in particular on two mid-20th-century precursors: the novelist and civil servant C. P. Snow and the politician, cabinet minister, and diarist Richard Crossman. Lynn and Jay directly acknowledge Crossman's *Diaries of a Cabinet Minister,* published in three volumes from 1975 to 1977, as a source for their writing. But it is Snow's 1964 novel *Corridors of Power,* with its cast of caballing civil servants, aspiring/conspiring politicians, troublesome backbenchers, vaguely sinister quasi-official American "contacts," and its central plot of a radical defense-policy initiative ending a promising ministerial career that most directly anticipates the fable to come.

As we move from *Yes Minister* to its heirs, we will chart the change in this fable's characteristic mode from the satiric and corrective impulses of Lynn and Jay to the cynical, corrosive depiction of political and bureaucratic wrongdoing typical of series like *House of Cards* (based on the novelist Michael Dobbs's 1989 book of the same name) and *The Thick of It*, creator and director Armando Iannucci's updating of *Yes Minister* for the era of Tony Blair and New Labour. (The series debuted in 2005.) It is a shift encapsulated by the distance between the imperturbable Cabinet Secretary, Sir Humphrey, he of the "I foresee grave unforeseen consequences, Prime Minister," and *The Thick of It*'s Malcolm Tucker, a special advisor ("enforcer") to the Prime Minister, whose profane tirades form a stark contrast to the seasoned bureaucrat's linguistic finesse. Here is Tucker, from the series' first episode, informing the Minister for Social Affairs that he will shortly be voluntarily resigning:

> Look. You're in no position to dish out fucking sarcasm, that's over. You no longer have purchase in the sarcasm world. Get on the phone, tell them that you're jumping before you're pushed, although we were going to push you, but not because of press pressure, but because of your deeply held fucking personal issues, whatever they were. (Iannucci, Armstrong, Blackwell, Martin, & Roche, 2007, p. 8)

Iannucci, like Lynn and Jay, conceived of his award-winning comedy as a dramatization of a "fixed, unimpeachable truth about how we are governed" (Iannucci et al., 2007). But the death struggle is no longer between deferential and utterly unyielding bureaucrats and their self-seeking political "masters." Now those same striving masters are confronted by an army of prime ministerial controllers policing every policy decision and public utterance and terrorized still further by an omnivorous media. Yet there are continuities. The landscape might have shifted since the glory days of Sir Humphrey, ministers might now be ruled by "a centralized bunch of twenty-something policy-wonks and adminolescents at Number Ten, abetted by a gang of political bouncers" (Iannucci et al., 2007, p. x), but what has not changed is the complete irrelevance of political principle, honesty, or loyalty to the business of governance.

In the previous chapter, we saw an increasingly idealized dominant fable (the hero-teacher) give rise to a counter-fable that denies or inverts many of its basic narrative assumptions. Here, as the dominant fable grows increasingly black, an alternative version develops, which does not counter its premises so much as allow for exceptions. Two television series produced some 20 years apart present populist, plain-speaking prime ministers pursuing reformist agendas free of cynicism, self-interest, or corruption. Both figures represent a character entirely absent from the satiric-cynical dominant fable: an incorruptible, uncompromising politician. And both are undone: in one case by the combined machinations of the CIA, the gutter press, and the old-boy network; in the other, by family scandal (her husband's not her own) and backroom influence. While the defeats of *A Very British Coup*'s (1988) Harry Perkins and *The Amazing Mrs. Pritchard*'s (2006) Ros Pritchard are presented as moral victories, the narratives through which they unfold still share many of the dominant assumptions. It is probably more accurate to label them "variant" rather than counter-fables, for they too present the business of government as necessarily inimical to decency, truthfulness, or principle. It might be possible for a Perkins or a Pritchard to view public office as a means of serving the people, but it is impossible, the variant-fable suggests, for them actually to do so. The system will defeat them every time.

The miniseries *A Very British Coup* was based on a novel of the same name published in 1982 by the long-time Labour MP Chris Mullin. Written at a time when Margaret Thatcher's Tory ascendancy was not yet a foregone conclusion, but the Labour party was already splintering from within, the novel presented an apotheosis of old Labour values in the person of Prime Minister Harry Perkins: steelworker, self-described third-generation socialist, committed reformer, dynamic orator, and canny political street fighter, who addresses cabinet colleagues as "comrade" in the thick Northern accent that marks his social and geographic distance from the governing establishment. In his novel, Mullin imagines only defeat for Perkins and the political tradition he so gloriously embodies (the television adaptation is somewhat more ambiguous). What Mullin could not have foreseen was the repudiation of much of that tradition and the triumphant rebirth of the Labour party under a leader dramatically different from Perkins in both substance and style.

This chapter will conclude with a discussion of three fictionalized accounts of that leader, the 2006 feature film *The Queen*, the 2003 made-for-television movie *The Deal*, and the 2010 HBO production *The Special Relationship*. Written by Peter Morgan, an Englishman whose other credits include the stage play and film *Frost/Nixon*, the three films together offer a portrait of Prime Minister Tony Blair that suggests a more ambiguous fable. Our analysis will focus primarily on the two narratives most explicitly concerned with internal British politics: *The Deal*, which chronicles the friend-ship/rivalry of Tony Blair and Gordon Brown as they vie for the leadership of the Labour party in the 1980s; and *The Queen*, which focuses on Tony Blair, in his fourth month in office, dealing with the titanic public response to the death of Princess Diana. But we will consider, too, the final film in the trilogy, which revisits key themes as it explores Blair's changing relation-ship with President Bill Clinton, with the Monica Lewinsky scandal and the NATO campaign in Kosovo as the pivots of the narrative.

Anticipating for a moment the discussion of American narratives of pol-itics and government in Chapter 5, the contrast here is striking. Where the American tradition makes room for (qualified) heroism and optimism—not quite *Mr. Smith Goes to Washington*, perhaps, but at least *The West Wing*'s President Bartlet—the British narratives generally share a deep pessimism, even cynicism. *The Deal* refers to the "ugly business" of politics, a phrase that aptly summarizes the British fable's perspective. At least part of the explanation for the difference in tone and premise must lie in the very different postwar histories of the two countries. For Britain, this has been an era marked by slow reconstruction, weak economic growth, a perpetual balance-of-payments crisis, frequent deficits, and rapidly accumulating pub-lic debt, as well as labor unrest occasionally verging on class warfare, and a long-standing civil war in Northern Ireland accompanied by terrorism at home—all this and the final liquidation of the Empire. And the practice of government in Britain, too, has undergone major transformations that might not, in themselves, be either cause or consequence of the dominant satirical-cynical fable, but are certainly an important concomitant to it.

Closed Politics: C. P. Snow and *Corridors of Power*

Born in 1905, Charles Percival Snow was not, technically, a Victorian. Yet this physicist, civil servant, politician, essayist, public intellectual, coiner of catchphrases, author, and Labour-appointed peer might appear to a 21st-century observer as a throwback: a late avatar of those fearsomely prolific 19th-century men of letters who thought nothing of writing a novel a year while editing magazines, delivering public lectures, travelling unceasingly, and "dining out" unremittingly. He recalls, in fact, the mid-Victorian titan Anthony Trollope, who combined a career as a high-ranking civil servant in the Post Office with an astonishing output of some 40 novels (not counting works of nonfiction, short stories, unproduced plays, and magazine journal-ism). The comparison is an apt one. Snow himself was an ardent admirer of his predecessor, writing a biography of Trollope in which he hails him as "the finest psychologist of all nineteenth-century novelists" and "the wisest human judge of the nineteenth century" (Snow, 1975, pp. 9, 24). Trollope's competition, it should be remembered, included Charles Dickens, William Thackeray, George Eliot, and Henry James.

But the connection goes deeper than artistic admiration. If Snow, who died in 1980, is best remembered now for his 1959 lecture *The Two Cultures and the Scientific Revolution,* he was also the author of a series of 11 novels, collectively titled *Strangers and Brothers,* chronicling life in the upper reaches of Britain's academic, political, and civil service establishments; novels that drew inevitable comparisons to Trollope's own political and clerical tales.[1]

The novel we will be considering, *Corridors of Power,* is the most explicitly political of Snow's linked series, the only one to deal with Westminster and Whitehall, Parliament and the civil service. Among other things, Snow's *Corridors of Power* offers a wonderfully nuanced portrait of the shifting culture within Britain's postwar politics and civil service. Published in 1964, the novel is set some years earlier in the immediate aftermath of the Suez crisis of 1956, and it tells the story of Roger Quaife, newly appointed Defense Minister in a Conservative government uneasily seeking its place in the postwar world order. Quaife, intelligent, principled, and ambitious, is married to a daughter of the old Tory establishment, that gilded country house set whose passing as a political force Snow chronicles with incisive clarity. But Quaife himself is an outsider, "solid provincial middle class" (Snow, 1984, p. 10) as Lewis Eliot, the novel's first-person narrator and an acknowledged portrait of Snow himself has it (Ramanathan, 1978; Snow, P., 1982), and Quaife is treated throughout the narrative as a representative of things to come.

The main engine of *Corridors of Power*'s plot is Quaife's attempt to move Britain's defense policy toward a renunciation of nuclear capability. Commissioning a "white paper"—a preliminary (and nonbinding) statement of policy—and establishing a scientific advisory committee to buttress his initiative, Quaife selects Eliot, a high-ranking civil servant and acquaintance, to serve as the committee's secretary, thus granting Eliot privileged access to the events he relates.[2] As the opposition mounts within Quaife's party, the civil service, the scientific and defense establishments, and Parliament, Quaife and Eliot become increasingly intimate, drawn together by their commitment to nuclear disarmament and by mutual liking and respect. Eliot also becomes privy to Quaife's private predicament: he has been conducting an affair with the wife of a colleague, an indiscretion that increases the vulnerability of his controversial political position. As Quaife himself remarks to Eliot, citing an old Church of England maxim, "You can get away with unorthodox behavior. Or you can get away with unorthodox doctrine. But you can't get away with both of them at the same time" (Snow, 1984, p. 118).

Corridors of Power is a narrative intimately concerned with "closed politics," what Eliot describes in a memorable passage as "a process, not entirely conscious, often mysterious to those taking part in it and sometimes to them above all, which had no name, but which might be labeled the formation, or crystallization, of 'official' opinion" (Snow, 1984, p. 78). It is a process carried on in corridors (literally, a number of key scenes in the novel take place in hallways) and clubs, committee rooms, private offices, country house drawing rooms, and dinner parties—everywhere but Parliament itself. It is the implicit negotiations, the unspoken bargains, tacit maneuverings, and silent recalibration of allegiances that determine policy and launch, or end, careers. And the novel's structure reflects the labyrinthine nature of the process with multiple subplots and a proliferation of characters. (A partial list would include eight ministers and parliamentary secretaries, five senior public servants, five scientists, three backbenchers, a society hostess, five political wives, and an influential industrialist, all with significant speaking parts and considerable backstory.)

The "thickness" of Snow's political description (to borrow the anthropologist's term) means that Quaife himself is often lost to view, a problem compounded by his failure to register convincingly as a character rather than an acutely observed social phenomenon. And Snow ends Quaife's story in a decidedly minor key. The opposition (Labour) motion in Parliament against Quaife's white paper is narrowly defeated, numbers of Conservative backbenchers flout party discipline to vote against the government, Quaife resigns from office, divorces his wife, and leaves politics. Eliot, the career civil servant and part-time novelist, takes early retirement. The novel ends with the narrator and his wife attending yet another Tory dinner party, with Eliot, always the novelistic observer, noting, "It was all still going on, I thought. Going on as, for most of them, it had always been: and as, in their expectations, it always would" (Snow, 1984, p. 276). The sting, of course, lies in the parenthetical "in their expectations."

Despite the title's almost immediate currency as a catchphrase, *Corridors of Power* was not well-received by contemporaries. The novelist Anthony Burgess spoke for many critics when he objected to Snow's "puritanical desire to strip his characters and their environment of everything that does not illuminate the big central theme" (Burgess, 1965, p. 73). Though the novel has its partisans, its fortunes have not improved much in the decades since. (The entire *Strangers and Brothers* series was adapted for television in 1984. It made little impression; certainly nothing comparable to the *Brideshead Revisited* phenomenon of three years earlier. *Strangers and Brothers* was not broadcast in North America.)

There's no doubt that Snow's characters suffer from an abstraction, a sort of narrative bloodlessness, that can make it difficult at times to tell them apart, let alone care what happens to them. Yet as a political fable, even more, as a prescient anticipation of developments to come, *Corridors of Power* has an undeniable claim on our attention. And there are significant narrative pleasures to be derived from it. Snow's incisive portrait of the last days of the old Tory "squirearchy," with its country house weekends and dinner table disloyalties, is both sympathetic and devastating. His evocation of the intangible yet irrevocable workings of "closed politics" remains unmatched in the political narrative tradition. Snow's conception of the "solidly middle class" Quaife as the (Tory) politician of the future is an uncanny anticipation of the triumph of the grocer's daughter from decidedly suburban Grantham who would revolutionize the British Conservative party in the late 1970s. The role of "the Americans" in the defeat of Quaife's initiative—a senior American scientist, acting as a quasi-official representative warns him off amid pressure "wafted over via Washington" (Snow, 1984, p. 177)—register Britain's former-world-power status more effectively than pages of explicit analysis. ("The Americans" will play similar daemon-ex-machina roles to comic effect in numerous episodes of *Yes Minister*. They will feature much more sinisterly in *A Very British Coup* as primary agents of the plot against the embattled Prime Minister Perkins.)

One of the subplots, concerning the rivalry between an old-school permanent secretary (Sir Hector Rose) and a "new man" offers a virtual case study of Britain's changing postwar bureaucracy. Sir Hector Rose, who will retire within the year, is a consummate professional disappointed at not becoming Cabinet Secretary. Rose is elaborately polite to colleagues and deferential to ministers, and has for so long pretended that he was simply carrying out the policies of his political masters that he has come to believe that he personally has no influence on events. His younger colleague (and onetime protégé) Douglas Osbaldiston is more straightforward, occasionally brusque, and less circumspect about acting as a policy entrepreneur. Lewis Eliot comments that Osbaldiston no longer finds it necessary to "chant that he was simply there to carry out the policy of his 'masters.' On the contrary, Douglas found it both necessary and pleasant to produce his own" (Snow, 1984, p. 192). Rose staunchly supports Quaife's disarmament initiative, while Osbaldiston, Quaife's permanent secretary, disagrees with the policy and, though formally committed to implementing it, appears to Rose and Eliot to be undermining it. Eliot and Rose see Osbaldiston's covert opposition as also furthering Osbaldiston's ultimate (and Rose's thwarted) ambition of becoming Cabinet Secretary (Snow, 1984, pp. 192, 250). Osbaldiston clearly has his origins in a civil service increasingly abandoning its traditional role of providing information and nonpartisan policy analysis and faithful implementation of government policy into a self-perpetuating institution whose interests are frequently at odds with those of "the government of the day." Jay and Lynn's Sir Humphrey Appleby thus seems to be an amalgam of the loquaciously polite and seemingly deferential personal style of Hector Rose and the ambition, manipulation, and policy entrepreneurship of Douglas Osbaldiston.

But it is Snow's treatment of language that might be the most significant aspect of *Corridors of Power*. Satire of empty political or bureaucratic rhetoric is not new in the British narrative tradition. It dates back at least as far as the "Circumlocution Office" chapters in Charles Dickens' *Little Dorrit*. And Snow does engage in some of this. Reflecting on the almost indistinguishable parliamentary speeches of opposition and government spokesmen, Eliot comments, "It was a curious abstract language, of which the main feature was the taking of meaning out of words" (Snow, 1984, p. 256). He also introduces the translation trope that will become a structural feature of the verbal comedy of *Yes Minister*. When the compulsively circumspect Hector Rose informs a scientist who will be testifying to Quaife's advisory commission "I'm sure you don't need me to tell you, but there may be mild repercussions," Eliot translates for the bewildered outsider to Whitehall: "He's telling you there's going to be a God-almighty row" (Snow, 1984, p. 124). Lynn and Jay are particularly good at this, wringing maximum comedy from the contrast between official euphemism or political platitudes and actual (often quite brutal) meaning.

Snow is more interested, however, in changing styles of political language and equally, in the changing role of language in politics. Quaife is presented as an unusually gifted political communicator. He is not an orator, Eliot explicitly notes, but rather "effective very much in a style of our time" (Snow, 1984, p. 23). Snow (in the voice of Eliot) devotes considerable analysis to Quaife's verbal mastery, noting in particular his ability to switch between "official language, the cryptic, encyclical language of a Minister of the Crown" and "bursts of calculated candour" (Snow, 1984, pp. 144, 197). We are witnessing here, if not the narrative birth of the sound bite and the spin doctor, then the first sustained exploration of political language as a means of performing authenticity. It is a skill that Peter Morgan's Tony Blair will excel at. Even more interesting is the way that Snow links Quaife's abilities to the modern media. In a lengthy analysis of Quaife's final speech to the House of Commons, Eliot clearly establishes the relationship and explicitly identifies the speaker as a new breed of politician:

> When he got down to the arguments, he was using the idiom of a late-twentieth-century man. He had thrown away the old style of parliamentary

rhetoric altogether . . . [This] was the speech of one used to broadcasting studios, television cameras, the exposure of the machine. He didn't declaim: he spoke about war, weapons, the meaning of a peaceful future, in his own voice. This was how, observers said later, parliamentarians would be speaking in ten years' time. (Snow, 1984, p. 263)

Neither Eliot nor his creator could possibly have anticipated just how all-encompassing "the exposure of the machine" would become in modern political life, yet both clearly register the importance of seeming spontaneity, of the expertly performed deeply personal response, of the ability to appear to abandon calculation while remaining in perfect control of the effect being created. The skills are not enough to save Quaife's initiative, or indeed, his political career. But there seems little doubt that Snow sees the future on his side. We will encounter these rhetorical skills repeatedly in numerous iterations of the dominant fable. They will be wielded most notably by two Labour leaders, one old, one new, one fictional, the other fictionalized.

No, Prime Minister: Richard Crossman and *Diaries of a Cabinet Minister*

In 1975, the government of Labour Prime Minister Harold Wilson went to court to block publication of the recently deceased Richard Crossman's *Diaries of a Cabinet Minister*. No less a figure than the Attorney General claimed Crossman's account of his years as Minister of Housing, Secretary of State for Social Services, and Leader of the House of Commons in the first Wilson government (1964–1970) were covered by official secrecy requirements and could not be made public. He lost.

Accustomed as we are now to the regular appearance of the "candid" political memoirs of recently retired office holders, it can be difficult to understand how much attention Crossman's three massive volumes drew. (The lawsuit helped, of course.) Excerpted in the London *Sunday Times*, widely reviewed, hotly disputed by participants in the events they chronicle—"He didn't get a single fact right," Harold Wilson protested publicly (Theakston, 2003, p. 23)—the *Diaries* appeared to offer something unprecedented: an in-the-moment, unvarnished, insider account of the daily business of government. In an essay published in 1977, the critic Clive James noted, "However unsystematically, in these clotted pages the way of life of the British governing class is being laid out before your eyes, even when the diarist thinks he is talking about something else."

What the diarist thought he was talking about was something quite different. Like C. P. Snow, Crossman looked back to a famous Victorian predecessor.[3] An avid diarist since his first days as a backbencher in 1952, and an experienced newspaper columnist, Crossman saw his diaries as raw material for a sustained analysis of the cabinet government system, a 20th-century version of Walter Bagehot's (2001) classic *The English Constitution* of 1867. Unlike Bagehot, however, who never held elected office, Crossman's projected analysis would be "something of my own, even more from the inside" (Theakston, 2003, p. 30). In fact, Crossman would never write his "modern Bagehot," though he would deliver a series of three lectures at Harvard University in 1970, subsequently published as *The Myths of Cabinet Government* (Crossman, 1972), drawing extensively on his then-unpublished personal materials. Instead, for the rest of his life, cut short by cancer in 1974, Crossman focused on turning his six-year, three-million word stream of consciousness into three publishable, if daunting, volumes, eventually totaling some 2,500 pages.[4]

But Crossman's analytic project was not abandoned, for the diaries themselves are shaped by the thesis he had intended to prove: that the role of cabinet in formulating policy was being eroded by an increasingly dominant prime minister, in effect reducing ministers to a consultative, even purely administrative function. It was a theme he returned to repeatedly, almost obsessively, throughout the diaries. Yet the picture his narrative presents of his own active ministerial role, as well as the vigor and contentiousness of cabinet discussion, belies his contention. The tenacity with which Crossman maintained his thesis, his own diaries' evidence notwithstanding, might have owed something to his growing personal dislike of Harold Wilson.[5] While Crossman initially admired Wilson's resilience and effectiveness as a communicator of government policy, he increasingly came to view him as an opportunist without vision or commitment. By the final volume, Wilson is depicted as conspiratorial and isolated, frightened, unhappy, and unsure of himself (Crossman, 1977, pp. 448, 470). "Has there ever been a British Prime Minister who seemed so unimportant, so insignificant—physically and as a personality?" Crossman asks in dismissive summation (p. 595). The narrative contradiction does not seem to bother him, the all-powerful prime minister who is also insignificant, frightened, and marginalized.

Not surprisingly, Wilson fought back in a lengthy rejoinder published in 1978. Wisely leaving personalities to one side, the former prime minister questioned Crossman's analytic premise, insisting that the late cabinet minister had never adequately understood cabinet government, in particular the limits on the prime minister's ability to supersede or control his cabinet colleagues. Yet Crossman was not wrong about the "presidentialization" of the British cabinet, however tendentious or inaccurate his chronicling of it. There is no doubt that the postwar period saw the gradual disappearance of cabinet as a collegial and socially homogenous body engaged in collective decision making under the direction of a "first among equals." Margaret Thatcher, and Tony Blair after her, would indeed dominate both their cabinets and the policymaking process, shifting the center of power in precisely the way Crossman anticipated. It is a trend that culminates in the much more dominant prime minister of *The Thick of It*, a powerful leader supported by an expanding personal bureaucracy within both Number Ten (as the prime minister's office is known) and Cabinet Office, with key decisions no longer referred to cabinet or cabinet committees, and increasingly tight monitoring (and disciplining) of ministers by Number Ten's legions of enforcers. Crossman might have been wrong about the timing, but he would likely have had little difficulty recognizing the significance of Malcolm Tucker, expletives and all.

Crossman's narrative ambitions were not only to document changes in prime ministerial power. He also saw his diaries as offering "a daily picture of how a Minister of the Wilson government spent his time, exactly what he did in his department, in Cabinet Committee and in Cabinet itself" (Crossman, 1975, p. 12), in effect, a field report in which he would feature as both anthropological subject and observer.[6] It was this aspect of the *Diaries'* narrative that drew the attention of Jay and Lynn and that would provide fodder for their most memorable creation, the devious, obstructive, but always impeccably civil civil servant Sir Humphrey. Crossman's own Whitehall nemesis came in the redoubtable form of Dame Evelyn Sharp, his permanent secretary at the Ministry of Housing. Some of Crossman's conflicts with "the Dame," as he calls her, and other senior bureaucratic staff undoubtedly stemmed from his high-handed, at times contemptuous manner. (His long-time Parliamentary Secretary Tam Dalyell (1989) described him as a notorious interrupter and exploder.) Yet though Crossman was philosophically predisposed to view civil servants as the natural enemies of elected politicians, he grew to admire Dame Evelyn's skill at working Whitehall back channels to attain his department's policy goals: "The Cabinet was effectively rigged," he reports happily of one successful episode, "and this was a tactic which my Dame operates with more skill than anybody else I have ever seen" (Crossman, 1975, p. 441).

It would be a mistake to draw too straight a line from "the Dame" to Sir Humphrey, or from Richard Crossman to Jim Hacker, who seems to owe at least as much to Crossman's highly critical portrait of Wilson. Yet given Lynn and Jay's open acknowledgment of the *Diaries* as a source for *Yes Minister* (it was from Crossman himself that they derived the show's name), it seems clear that they found in the *Diaries* their essential comic structure:

the conflict between the politician and the senior bureaucrat locked in a symbiotic relationship and forever jockeying for the upper hand. They might well have found more specific inspiration as well. Crossman recounts a number of practices that would feature to great comic effect in episodes of *Yes Minister*: misleading memos hidden deep in ministerial red boxes, permanent secretaries coordinating the arguments they would present to their respective ministers, the doctoring of cabinet minutes, the undercutting of outside advisors, even restrictions on which ministers and mandarins would have keys to Number Ten. Just as Crossman struggled to resist the prime ministerial dominance he hypothesized, he also struggled to resist bureaucratic dominance with practices such as reading down to the bottom of the red boxes, making written rather than verbal requests to the civil servants, revising letters written on his behalf until he was satisfied, and visiting the ministry's local offices or clients every Friday—all grist for Jay and Lynn's satiric mill.

In his final days as minister, ill and anticipating the electoral defeat soon to come, Crossman experienced moments of panicked despair.[7] His depression included the probable fate of the thousands of pages he had amassed so painstakingly: "I began to brood...on the fact that this diary I thought of as being enormously important to future historians will probably be regarded as the dull detailed history of the last days of the British *ancien regime*" (1977, p. 76). As with so much else, Crossman was only partly right. Few people care to wade through his volumes now. Yet his insights, observations, and revelations did find an enduring if unlikely afterlife in a television series now widely hailed as a classic of British comedy.

"A Loose Confederation of Warring Tribes": *Yes Minister* and the Dominant Fable

Watching episodes of *Yes Minister*, relishing the verbal inventiveness, the tight comic plotting, the skillful balancing of satire and farce, the note-perfect performances of the three lead actors, it is easy to overlook the specific theoretical grounding of the series' "timeless" comic premise. Yet *Yes Minister* is, among other things, a sustained application of public-choice theory to late-20th-century British politics. Co-creator Antony Jay has explicitly acknowledged his debt to the model, developed in the 1960s and 1970s by conservative American economists, which posits that public sector actors pursue personal self-interest just as aggressively as those in the private sector. Politicians compete for power, rather than profit and market share, with election manifestos and government policies the means to that end. Bureaucrats seek to maximize the budget and powers of the agencies they manage, thereby enhancing their own income, perks, and prestige. Interest groups will pressure politicians and public servants for policies that benefit themselves, using a share of the accrued benefits to fund future political campaigns. In the logic of the public-choice model, the dovetailing self-interests of politicians, public servants, and interest groups require an ever-expanding public sector with a deep-rooted disinclination to effect substantive change of any kind (Borins, 1988, pp. 13–17). Jay became familiar with public-choice theory in the early 1970s and embraced its logic. With experience gained in his company, Video Arts, producing corporate training films that taught their lessons through the humor of managers making classic mistakes, Jay determined to turn his attention from private sector management to government. He enlisted a Video Arts collaborator as partner, the comedy writer, director, and actor Jonathan Lynn, and *Yes Minister* was born.

It is not hard to see why the two were attracted to the skepticism of the public-choice model, with its substitution of self-interest for public good as the engine of government. (In interviews, Lynn routinely attributes less specific influence to public choice, focusing instead on the universality of the series' critique of hypocrisy and self-seeking in high places. Its centrality for Jay remains.) Both men experienced early political epiphanies that left them deeply suspicious of politicians and bureaucrats alike. For Jay, it was the spectacle in 1964 of the newly elected home secretary in the Wilson government acting on the advice of his senior officials and rejecting a petition signed by millions of Britons, which he had himself organized when in opposition. (The petition concerned posthumously overturning the guilty conviction of a man executed for a murder he likely did not commit.) For Lynn, who has a law degree from Cambridge, it was insider knowledge of deception at the highest levels of government gained from his uncle, the former Israeli Foreign Minister Abba Eben:

> I remember learning the true story of the Suez Crisis in 1956 at the age of thirteen, the extraordinary conspiracy between Britain, France, and Israel, instigated solely by Anthony Eden to ensure the return of the canal. Eden subsequently double-crossed his Israeli and French allies in private and lied about it in public. This naturally had a significant effect on me—I knew the truth. And Harold Macmillan, later a respected and eminent figure, was both first in and first *out* of the Suez adventure—and emerged, incredibly, as Prime Minister. (J. Lynn, personal communication, August 19, 1987)

The distance between public utterance and private action is at the heart of *Yes Minister*'s comedy. And that distance exists because every agent within the system (politicians and civil servants alike) is motivated solely by his own personal ambitions and needs. This is the essence of the British political fable: public interest has nothing to do with it. Government ministries are, as one of Sir Humphrey's civil service colleagues notes, "a loose confederation of warring tribes" whose primary function is to prevent any other tribe from gaining an advantage. But there is another battle being fought, too, within each ministry itself, this conflict pitting career civil servants against their transitory (but elected) political masters. As Jay summarized the structural premise in a 2010 interview: "The people who have the permanence have the power but the ones with the elected office have the theoretical authority" (Rees, 2010). Few of *Yes Minister*'s heirs would retain the series' focus on the interactions of politicians and bureaucrats, focusing instead on the corruption, incompetence, compromises, and betrayals of the elected office holders (and would-be office holders). By *The Thick of It*, civil servants are peripheral to the story, a reflection, as we've noted, of changing perceptions regarding the locus of power within British government. But it is through the repeated confrontation of Hacker's "will" with Sir Humphrey's "won't" that Jay and Lynn establish their basic narrative premise. Each episode then becomes an extended illustration of the almost infinite ways self-interest trumps public good in government.

A closer look at two episodes from the first series of *Yes Prime Minister* (broadcast in 1986) demonstrates both how tightly structured the narrative is around that single conflict and how inventive Jay and Lynn were in devising plots that were both utterly credible—they had advice from an anonymous insider network of politicians, public servants, and political advisers—and increasingly farcical.[8] The first, "The Ministerial Broadcast," centers on newly elected Prime Minister Hacker's determination to use his first televised speech to the nation to announce the details of his "Grand Design": his plan to cancel the new £15 billion Trident nuclear weapon system and replace it with a less expensive package of spending on land forces and supportive technologies. This, of course, has strong echoes of the failed defense initiative of Snow's Roger Quaife, and it too quickly attracts the ire of "the Americans." But Hacker is not opposed to nuclear weapons on principle. Rather he is seeking a means of decreasing unemployment (increased land forces would require a reintroduction of mandatory military service for young people) and facilitating politically popular tax cuts.

Philosophically and temperamentally opposed to Hacker's proposed changes, Sir Humphrey swings into action. "It's tremendously refreshing to have a new mind on the old problem, challenging old ideas, questioning the whole basis of government thinking for the past thirty years," he remarks with acid affability to the Prime Minister when the subject of the speech is first brought up. The remainder of the episode sees the battle waged on two fronts. The Prime Minister's principal private secretary Bernard Woolley, a career civil servant answerable to Sir Humphrey, is deployed to prevent any specific mention of the new defense policy from being made in the broadcast. "Bernard, this doesn't say anything," an exasperated Hacker exclaims after reading the secretary's revisions to the speech. "Oh, thank you, Prime Minister," the gratified Bernard replies. Sir Humphrey, meanwhile, assured by the Prime Minister of his cabinet colleagues' full support for his initiative—"They all think it's a vote winner, I mean a major contribution to the defense of this country"—sets out to reverse the situation. Over tea with a group of like-minded permanent secretaries, he coolly arranges for their ministers to receive new briefings opposing the policy based on the perceived harm it will do to their ministerial interests, and the Prime Minister's cabinet support promptly evaporates. Sir Humphrey also commissions a public opinion poll with questions deliberately designed to elicit opposition to conscription, breathlessly presenting the results to Hacker immediately after the cabinet meeting. Hacker concedes (temporary) defeat and omits all reference to the Grand Design in his broadcast. On the advice of his press secretary, he accepts a host of media gimmicks—light-colored suit, high-tech furniture, bright backdrop, modern art on the walls—to create an illusion of energy and change and to mask the complete absence of substance in the address itself. Round one, Sir Humphrey.

"The Smokescreen" sees Prime Minister Hacker intent on securing his tax cut, over the objections of Sir Humphrey and the Treasury. When the Minister for State for Health, a physician and antismoking zealot, presents Hacker with a proposal for confiscatory taxation on tobacco products and a complete ban on tobacco advertising and sponsorships, thereby reducing government revenues by a projected £4 billion, the Prime Minister is at first dismayed. "Smoking should be stopped," Hacker sputters, "And we will stop it. In due course. At the appropriate juncture. In the fullness of time." The Health Minister understands the code: "You mean, forget it." But as he considers the implications of the proposal, Hacker sees an opportunity to leverage Treasury acquiescence in a tax-cut of £1.5 billion. He encourages the impassioned minister to promote the policy publicly and promises tacit support. When Sir Humphrey learns of the proposed £4 billion loss of government revenue, not to mention the ban on tobacco company sponsorship for favored upper-class institutions like cricket matches and the Royal Opera House, he is predictably incensed. In an inspired comic exchange, he demonstrates incontrovertibly why smoking remains the best option for Britain's citizens, concluding triumphantly, "So, financially speaking, it's unquestionably better that they continue to die at the present rate." Hacker is unconvinced and marshals answering statistics of his own. Sir Humphrey will have none of it. "I see," Hacker says, "So, your statistics are facts. And my facts are merely statistics." The Prime Minister eventually offers a quid pro quo: he will drop his feigned support for the anti-tobacco policy, if the Treasury will endorse the tax cut. Sir Humphrey immediately brokers the deal.

A final complication arises, however, which pushes the narrative into the dizzy realms of farce. The zealot Health Minister threatens to resign if his policy is abandoned and to go public with the reasons. A panicked Prime Minister turns to Sir Humphrey for help. With a succession of quick exits and entrances through multiple doors in the Prime Minister's office, the Health Minister, proving to be more ambitious than zealous, is bought off with a ministerial promotion to the Treasury, and the chain-smoking Minister for Sport (who had vigorously opposed any end to tobacco sponsorship) is promoted to Health Minister.[9] He accepts his good fortune with a cloud of cigarette smoke and a hacking cough. "What did he say?" the anxious Hacker asks. "I believe he said, 'Yes Prime Minister,'" Sir Humphrey smoothly replies.

There is a tendency among viewers of the *Yes Minister* series, both academic and lay, to assume that Sir Humphrey "would invariably have his way" (Adams, 1993, p. 70; Savoie, 2007, p. 75). In fact, Jay and Lynn were much too skillful to stack the cards entirely in the Cabinet Secretary's favor. Despite the acknowledged debt to age-old fables of clever servants like Figaro and Jeeves outwitting their masters, *Yes Minister* quite frequently allows Hacker to prevail, and often the two unite against a common foe (the Prime Minister and the Chancellor of the Exchequer in early episodes; recalcitrant cabinet ministers in the later).[10] From a purely technical point of view, this introduces an element of suspense into the series' tight narrative structure. What it might say about the relative powers of politicians and civil servants remains open to interpretation.

As much as Jay and Lynn's fable draws on the critical premises of public-choice theory for its depiction of the motivations of its characters and the outcomes of its plots, and for all the debt to Crossman's critique of "the Dame" and her colleagues, there are important continuities with Snow here too. With every face-saving deal, principle-shaving compromise, and back-channel maneuver, *Yes Minister* demonstrates in episode after episode the internal workings of closed politics. Sir Humphrey himself explains as much. In "The Ministerial Broadcast," Bernard tentatively suggests to the irate Cabinet Secretary that the Prime Minister might simply be trying to open a national debate on defense policy. Sir Humphrey snaps back with barely concealed exasperation: "Bernard, you do not open a national debate until the government has privately made up its mind." Like Snow, Jay and Lynn were concerned about the distortion of language for political and bureaucratic purposes, demonstrating it both through Sir Humphrey's arias of bureaucratic doublespeak as well as inversions of meaning ("courageous" as code for politically suicidal) and Freudian slips that reveal the self-interest that underlies expressions of concern about the public interest. Lynn and Jay, with the help of three indispensable lead actors, spun comic and satiric gold out of the spectacle of government privately making up its mind. The political narratives that follow *Yes Minister* have much more difficulty maintaining the balance between outrage and amusement.

FU Prime Minister: *House of Cards*

The remarkable popularity of *Yes Minister* ensured that other political series would follow. One of the most notable was *House of Cards*, a four-part miniseries based on the 1989 novel of the same name by Michael Dobbs, a journalist and former chief-of-staff of the British Conservative party. The series, which traces the machinations of the fictional Tory Chief Whip Francis Urquhart in the days following Margaret Thatcher's resignation, had the good fortune to air just two days before the actual parliamentary Conservative Party's choice of John Major as leader and Prime Minister in November of 1990.[11] Its over-the-top plotting—"skullduggery, treachery and thwarted ambition served up for breakfast" in Dobbs' words (http://michaeldobbs. com/uk/index.php?id=9,0,0,1,0,0)—its depiction of politicians as hapless, self-destructive, morally flawed, or all three, and in particular the delightfully malignant performance of Ian Richardson in the lead role earned the series a wide audience and a host of accolades.

Unlike *Yes Minister*, and perhaps in a deliberate attempt to distance itself from its illustrious predecessor, *House of Cards* pays no attention to the actual business of governing. Civil servants make no appearances, nor are the mechanics of policymaking or implementation ever addressed. Instead, the plot concerns itself solely with the internecine warfare of a party in decline, following Urquhart as he conspires, frames, blackmails, and eventually murders his way to the leadership. After handily disposing of the young journalist who has been both his lover and his pawn (he pushes her off a tower at Westminster), Urquhart is last seen driving off to Buckingham Palace to "kiss hands" and formally accept the office of Prime Minister.

Although Dobbs had killed off Urquhart in the original novel (it is he who takes the dive off the tower, not his lover), *House of Cards* proved so popular that two further series were made: *To Play the King* (broadcast in 1993) and *The Final Cut* (1995). The second installment focused on the new Prime Minister's adversarial relationship with a politically active (and

Labour-leaning) sovereign, the third on Urquhart's desperate attempts to cling to power as ghosts of past misdeeds begin to close in on him. Once again, the plots are laced with copious amounts of murder, blackmail, conspiracy, alcoholism, drug addiction, and adultery. Series three ends with Urquhart assassinated by his bodyguard on the orders of his equally ambitious wife to "preserve his reputation."

This brief summary should be enough to make plain that *House of Cards*, even in its first incarnation, was not seeking verisimilitude. (The plot of the television adaptation does differ in some significant respects from that of the novel, but it is mostly a question of degree. Screenwriter Andrew Davies notches up the melodrama still further and heightens both Urquhart's self-awareness and his villainy.) Unlike Lynn and Jay, who aimed for credibility in their satiric plots, Dobbs' acknowledged intentions were to create a Shakespearean villain in bespoke pin stripes, a Richard the Third for the age of Margaret Thatcher. "I'm sad to say that the entire concept derives from his initials, FU," Dobbs confessed on his Web site (http://michaeldobbs.com/uk/index.php?id=9,0,0,1,0,0). And the television production takes up the Shakespearean motif, granting Urquhart "soliloquies" in which he outlines his nefarious schemes while speaking directly to the camera.

Unsurprisingly, the character of Francis Urquhart walks away with the series, helped in large measure by the performance of noted Shakespearean actor Ian Richardson in the part. Richardson embraces the role of FU with evident relish, finding infinite shadings of malevolence and cunning in the raising of an eyebrow. His trademark phrase, "You might think that; I couldn't possibly comment" communicated fathomless depths of political mendacity and double-dealing in eight innocuous words. In an appealing instance of life imitating art, the mantra even made its way to the floor of the (real) House of Commons. So closely identified was Richardson with Urquhart that he would only consent to appear in the third installment of the series if the character would finally be killed off. And even then, his own obituary tribute in the British newspaper *The Independent* was headlined "Ian Richardson, the PM who couldn't possibly comment, dies aged 72" (Kirby, 2007).

House of Cards was an enormous hit with general audiences and, if the author is to be believed, political insiders as well. "John Major's entire campaign headquarters came to a standstill at 9 o'clock on a Sunday evening in order to find out what came next," Dobbs recalled in an obituary tribute to Richardson published on the BBC Web site in 2007 (Youngs, 2007). And it is not difficult to understand why a series portraying Tory politicians as scheming, adulterous, alcoholic, drug-taking, murderous, back-stabbing toffs with good tailoring might have had a broad audience appeal in the dying days of Thatcherism. But the narrative's satiric point has lost much of its edge in the years since. The scale of Urquhart's evil makes it difficult to consider *House of Cards* as offering a serious critique of politics or government, certainly much less serious than the insights provided by a single 30-minute episode of the sitcom *Yes Minister*. And the first series' director, Paul Seed, admits as much: "It was cheeky political television," he recalls in the same tribute cited above.

In its narrowing of focus from government (that is, the interactions of politicians and bureaucrats with policy as the disputed terrain) to politics, and its coarsening of tone from the corrective-satiric mode of Lynn and Jay to the more purely cynical, calculated outrageousness of Dobbs and screenwriter Andrew Davies, *House of Cards* marked a new stage in the development of the dominant British political fable, a movement from the astute, witty, well-polished satire of Lynn and Jay to something broader, blacker, and infinitely more frenetic. It is a trend that will reach its highpoint in the scabrous dialogue and bottom-feeding dramatis personae of *The Thick of It*.

"Kick, Bollock, and Scramble": New Labour and the Dominant Fable

The first episode of *The Thick of It*, broadcast on May 19, 2005, was as much of a landmark in its way as that of *Yes Minister* 25 years before. The series opens with an inspired comic savagery that makes it easy to see why British critics were reaching for their superlatives. Newly appointed Secretary of State for Social Affairs Hugh Abbott is gleefully preparing a major public announcement of a "snooper force" to reduce social benefit fraud. He has, he tells his somewhat dubious staff, the Prime Minister's enthusiastic support and is confident of a publicity coup: "He said that he's right behind us on this and it's very much what we should be doing" (Iannucci et al., 2007, p. 10). A media circus is accordingly rustled up, complete with a live news conference from a local school. En route, Abbott and his aides are sideswiped by a phone call from the Prime Minister's furious Director of Communications Malcolm Tucker, who is mopping up "a fucking hurricane of piss here" from the "neurotics in the Treasury" over the pending announcement (p. 16). Abbott is ordered to "kill" the policy. "'Should' does not mean 'yes'" Tucker acidly informs him. Abbott duly complies, live, in full view of the nation's media, disowning the policy as the invention of a "disgruntled civil servant" and denying any intention of announcing it, despite the carefully planted leaks to that effect just hours before. Returning humiliated to his ministry, he is greeted by Tucker with the news that the Prime Minister himself has already gone to bat publicly for the snooper force (despite the Treasury), and the Secretary of State must now contact the media yet again in order to reverse his reversal. He is to tell the press that he did, in fact, announce the policy earlier that afternoon, though he might have appeared to be assuring them that the policy had never actually existed.

At this point, even the new ministerial worm turns: "I'm not quite sure what level of reality I'm supposed to be operating on," he protests. "Look," Tucker barks back, "this is what they [the media] run with. I tell them that you said it, they believe that you said it. They don't *really* believe that you said it, they know you never said it... But it's in their interest to say that you said it, because if they don't say that you said it they're not going to get what you say tomorrow, or the next day, when I decide to tell them what it is you're saying" (Iannucci et al., 2007, p. 29). It is a brilliant comic moment and Peter Capaldi, the actor playing Tucker, makes the most of it, finding just the right note of baleful bravado to accompany the lunatic logic. It is also a perfect encapsulation of one of the series' main narrative preoccupations: the symbiotic relationship between politicians and press in the age of spin, an adversarial alliance based on mutual loathing and mutual need in which the biggest loser is always the public.

The series' other narrative premise, the substitution of a succession of poll-tested sound bites for substantive policy decisions, receives an equally inspired treatment. For much of the episode, Abbott and his advisors are left scrambling to find a replacement policy for the on-again off-again snooper force. It must be a policy that can be announced at a moment's notice, one that is "sexy and eye-catching and that is free and universally popular and instantly applicable, that no one can possibly object to" (Iannucci et al., 2007, p. 22). ("Return of capital punishment?" a disgusted young staffer suggests sweetly.) Improvising desperately in the car on their way to the press conference, the team hits on a perfect solution. The Big Announcement will be that there is no announcement. They will parade their determination to forego glitz and spin in favor of highlighting the "amazing work, bread and butter work, belt and braces work" their department has been doing every day. As Abbott and his advisors try the idea out, they grow increasingly excited at its media possibilities, and the platitudes come thick and fast. "Quiet bread and butter," the senior advisor muses. "On target, under budget," the Minister intones. "Coalface politics," the young aide interjects. They agree to take the unsung heroes line, with an austerity gloss: "Not wasting resources... Let's go for that... And we've probably got ten million we can throw at it" (p. 24).

This is *The Thick of It* at its best; intelligent, scathing, and unafraid of a good one-liner, scoring points through an inspired reworking of some of *Yes*

Minister's most effective verbal and structural devices: the contrast between public rhetoric and private motive, the note-perfect rendering of political boilerplate in all its impressive hollowness, the initially credible premise—a mistimed policy announcement, a mismanaged press conference—spiraling into bleak absurdity, a veneer of realism coexisting with wickedly funny caricature.

For creator and director Iannucci, the main goal of *The Thick of It* was always to create the feeling of an insider's view: "I wanted the viewer to feel like they were actually in a room watching politicians and civil servants do what they do" (Iannucci, 2005). The series employed as "accuracy consultant" a former BBC correspondent who had served as director of communications for various government departments in the early years of the Blair government. (A "swearing consultant" is also credited, though the director elsewhere attributes the "baroqueness of the swearing" to the native inventiveness of the show's co-writers.) And Iannucci makes use of many of the usual markers of "realism": roving, handheld cameras; overlapping, occasionally inaudible dialogue; absence of an opening credit sequence; no music of any kind. He also encouraged his lead actors to improvise, though Capaldi, in the interview quoted above, estimates that only about 20% of a given show consisted of unscripted material. The idea, as Chris Langham, the actor who plays Hugh Abbott, explained, was to use the actors' own "terror of improvisation" to replicate the frenzy of "day-to-day life in a ministry," which he characterizes in quintessentially English terms as "much more kick, bollock, and scramble than it is five-year plan" (Iannucci, 2005).

All of this succeeds remarkably well, the intelligence of actors, writers, and director creating a narrative that balances skillfully between a convincing semblance of government reality and impossibly profane outrageousness. Yet it is hard to watch more than a few episodes of *The Thick of It* without a sense of rapidly diminishing returns. Unlike *Yes Minister*, whose creators evinced a genuine interest in questions of policy and its implementation, the political and social issues *The Thick of It* invokes are largely interchangeable, meaningless counters in an ongoing game of political poker. Iannucci himself succinctly characterized the difference: "*Yes Minister* was about people trying to stop things from happening; nowadays, politics is about stopping things from being said" (Iannucci et al., 2007, p. 9). The third season does introduce a new minister, Nicola Murray, an inexperienced backbencher with a policy agenda she naïvely hopes to pursue.[12] But her "Fourth Sector Path Finders" initiative—an attempt to identify and enlist "ordinary extraordinary citizens" as community leaders—is greeted with universal derision by Murray's own aides and staff, and by something more pungent by Malcolm Tucker: "This fourth sector thing, right? It's fucking mad. She's fucking mad. But the great thing about it is, it's free, yeah?" Focusing so unrelentingly on the self-interest, venality, incompetence, and cynicism of its characters, reducing any questions of policy to empty public relations gestures, leaves the narrative with little else to do or say than to reiterate in more or less entertaining form the same essential premise, summed up by Tucker in his characteristic style: "It's a fucking war." Point taken.

Iannucci and his writing team went on to use the main characters of *The Thick of It* for a feature film in which Mr. Tucker goes to Washington with a looming Middle East war as backdrop and a (different) incompetent minister in tow. *In the Loop* was released in 2009 and was intended as hard-hitting satire of the Blair government's involvement in the second Iraq war, which was deeply unpopular in the UK. For some critics, this was indeed precisely what the film offered. A. O. Scott of the *New York Times* hailed it as both "a highly disciplined inquiry into a very serious subject" and "line by filthy line, scene by chaotic scene, by far the funniest big-screen satire in recent memory" (Scott, 2009). Such praise was far from universal, however. In the same week, Anthony Lane, film critic for *The New Yorker*, excoriated the film's reductive narrative premise—"everyone in politics is either a beast or a dithering dolt"—before going on to note the limitations this imposes on both character and action: "There is no basis for public service other than the foaming rage for power, and anyone who dares to dream otherwise—anyone who enjoys *The West Wing* for example—is the most credulous mug of all" (Lane, 2009). By the end of the film, Lane concludes, "you just want to get away from these people."

The comparison to *The West Wing* is instructive. If Iannucci and company are incapable of the sentimentality of their American counterparts, Aaron Sorkin, *The West Wing*'s creator, proved much more skillful at creating government actors who are neither beasts nor dolts, but rather highly intelligent, personally ambitious, frequently flawed and also, to use a word Malcolm Tucker would despise, genuinely public spirited: men and women who compromise, broker deals, manipulate, negotiate, lie occasionally, mislead quite regularly, and yet who are motivated by something other than a hunger for domination. There is no place for such characters in the political or narrative universes of *The Thick of It* and *In the Loop,* and that absence, in the end, limits the insight either can offer. Perhaps the most measured assessment of what is missing was provided by a rather unusual source: Alastair Campbell, director of communications to Prime Minister Tony Blair from 1997 to 2009 and widely acknowledged as the model for the ferocious and profane Malcolm Tucker. Reviewing *In the Loop* for the *Guardian* newspaper, Campbell commented, "Of course, politicians and advisers have their own ambitions. But they have more than that" (Campbell,

2009). And it is precisely that "more" that Iannucci's narratives leave out. Called to task by an interviewer who suggested that he disliked the film for the sharpness of its satire ("the portrayal was too close to home"), Campbell countered simply, "I didn't like it because it was so far removed from the motives of most of the people I know." For a satire that stakes its claims in realism, that is a damning objection: you got the mechanics right; you got the characters, and their substance, all wrong.

Open Politics and Closed Careers: *A Very British Coup* and *The Amazing Mrs. Pritchard*

It is difficult to imagine two fictional prime ministers further apart than Francis Urquhart and Harry Perkins, the heroic prime minister of *A Very British Coup*. Yet the narrative worlds these two contrasting figures inhabit— one a murderous upper-class schemer, the other a working-class idealist bent on socialist reform—ultimately differ very little. Far from questioning the assumptions of the fable that shapes both *House of Cards* and *The Thick of It*, *A Very British Coup* reaffirms its most basic premise: political life is both corrupt and corrupting, its sole animating principle being the attainment and retention of power. Anything else is window dressing for the press (which knows better, but colludes for its own purposes) and the public (who might still be fooled). The only real difference between the two versions (and it is this which qualifies *A Very British Coup* as a variant fable) is the possibility of the heroic exception. The occasional, inspired leader, a Harry Perkins say, can envision and pursue a different course, but he will not succeed. Indeed, he does so at the expense of his career.

The structure of *A Very British Coup*'s narrative is simplicity itself. The 1988 television miniseries, based on Labour backbencher Chris Mullin's (1982) novel, begins with the election of a left-wing Labour government headed by the politically skillful and charismatic Harry Perkins to replace Mrs. Thatcher's Conservatives. A series of crises confront Perkins as he attempts to fulfill his election promises and introduce a sweeping set of socialist reforms. This being television, the focus is not on the distinctly unglamorous issues of implementation and funding, but rather on the "establishment" conspiracy that seeks to block the popular new prime minister and his cabinet comrades. Enraged by Perkins' radical agenda, which includes renationalizing key industries, closing American air bases, and dismantling nuclear weapons (on national television), an unholy alliance of CIA agents, bribed union officials, shadowy figures from within Britain's security and defense establishments, and the requisite sinister press baron (the adjective is probably superfluous, benign press barons being in rather short supply in most political narratives) plots to bring Perkins down. The weapons of choice include covert surveillance, blackmail, smear campaigns in the popular press, personal intimidation, and murder.

If the structuring contest within the narrative of *Yes Minister* was between the elected politician and the appointed civil servant, and that of *In the Thick of It* between ministers and prime ministerial "spinmeisters," that of *A Very British Coup* pits the democratically elected (Labour) representatives of the people against what Perkins calls "that whole non-elected army that holds power in this country," a landed Tory oligarchy embodied by Perkins' Old Etonian nemesis, the director of cabinet security, Sir Percy Browne. Sir Percy resembles his fictional contemporary Francis Urquhart in the silky upper-class smoothness with which he pursues his undemocratic, and occasionally murderous, intentions. It is Sir Percy who organizes the plot against Perkins, culminating in a cabinet room showdown between the two men where Sir Percy reveals the forged bank statements that will be released to the (tame) press to implicate Perkins in financial wrongdoing, unless he agrees to resign for reasons of health. Perkins appears to concede defeat, commenting "In South America, they'd call this a coup d'etat." "But no firing squad," Sir Percy replies, "No torture. No retribution. No bloodshed. A very British coup, wouldn't you say?"

In fact, Perkins does not resign, proving the truth of the remark he'd made earlier to his loyal friend and press secretary, "I'm a good sport, but a very bad loser." Using the televised address which was to have been his resignation speech, he reveals the details of Sir Percy's plot, calls a general election, and appeals directly to the public: "You the people must decide whether you prefer to be ruled by an elected government or by people you've never heard of, people you've never voted for, people who remain quietly behind the scenes, generation after generation, yea even unto the middle ages." The enraged Sir Percy, watching Perkins on television, mutters ominously the words famously associated with the politically motivated murder of Sir Thomas Becket: "Who will free me from this turbulent priest?" The series ends as it begins, in the council flat of Perkins' elderly mother on election day, as he prepares to learn his fate. Perkins' mother predicts "another landslide," but the final frames suggest a much more uncertain outcome, perhaps a military intervention, possibly a genuine coup. (The last voice we hear is that of a news announcer declaring an end to "the recent political turbulence" and a "clarification of the constitutional situation." This is followed by a cacophony of static and the sound of hovering helicopters.)

The television series makes much use of shots of (now charmingly antiquated) high-tech surveillance equipment and of sinister dark-suited figures lurking in shadows, working hard to create an atmosphere of increasingly fevered menace. While the suggestion that the United States would have colluded with MI5 in a coup to remove an elected British prime minister from office might seem almost comically paranoid, author Chris Mullin recalled in an interview with me (C. Mullin, personal communication, January 29, 1990) and later in a newspaper article (2006) how very different things seemed in the 1980s. The Campaign for Nuclear Disarmament was then a major political force in Britain, attracting crowds of more than 200,000 to protest the arrival of cruise missiles at American air bases. U.S. diplomats were sounding out "authorized contacts" in London regarding Labour party defense policy, making no secret of their opposition to its antinuclear stance. And in 1987, a former MI5 officer published a book in which he claimed that he and other MI5 colleagues had plotted to undermine the Wilson government in the 1970s. "Suddenly," Mullin writes, "the possibility that the British establishment might conspire with its friends across the Atlantic to destabilize the elected government could no longer be dismissed as leftwing paranoia" (Mullin, 2006). For all Mullin's comments, the plotting of *A Very British Coup*, with its clandestine meetings, blackmail, forged documents, and officially sanctioned murder, remains its weakest feature, bringing its narrative world at times extremely close to the melodrama of *House of Cards*.

Unlike Ros Pritchard, the political novice who unexpectedly finds herself Prime Minister in *The Amazing Mrs. Pritchard*, Harry Perkins is portrayed as a skilled and experienced politician, a brilliant communicator, a shrewd strategist, an effective negotiator, and a born leader—every inch the "Labour statesman" Sir Percy acknowledges him to be. (It is the reason, Sir Percy says, he must be stopped.) The element of wish fulfillment in the character's creation seems indisputable. It must have been intensely comforting to the long-time Labour backbencher Chris Mullin to imagine such a hero into life, particularly in the early days of Margaret Thatcher's Tory ascendancy. Yet, as played by the marvelous Irish actor Ray McAnally, Perkins emerges as much more than an impossibly idealized old Labour saint, or working-class cliche. The intelligence and humor he brings to the role, as well as the hints of weariness and self-doubt, the passion with which he conveys Perkins' ideological commitments, the authority and the clear enjoyment of the political game that he suggests, create a much more complex character than perhaps Mullin, or screenwriter Alan Plater, actually devised. And McAnally is wonderfully adept at delivering Perkins' Northern-inflected one-liners. "I once tried middle of t'road," he comments to the compromising (and ultimately disloyal) Chancellor of the Exchequer who advocates a middle way, "I were knocked down by traffic in both directions." When he is welcomed to Downing Street by an impossibly supercilious civil servant with frigid pleasantries—"You've been to Number 10 before, of course?"—he answers with cheerful mockery: "Yes, but I were never allowed to handle t'silver."

Perhaps the most revolutionary aspect of Perkin's political program, certainly the one that disturbs Sir Percy the most, is his rejection of closed politics and the backroom back-channel maneuverings that are their hallmark. "This country hasn't kept a secret that mattered a damn in the last twenty-five years," he informs Sir Percy as he insists on being shown the surveillance equipment that is used to monitor government communications, "Open government. I'm answerable to the people. I'm not going to keep secrets from them." And Perkins extends the notion of openness to his new government's relationship with the press. He intends to do away with what his successors would know as "spin," the mutual manipulations of press and government. Briefing his new Press Secretary at a reception at Number Ten, Perkins instructs him: "No more lobby correspondents. No more whispering behind hands. No more unattributable leaks. We stand on our own two feet and we tell the truth. Original, don't you think?" The former journalist is skeptical: "What do I do in my spare time?" "Keep an eye on the bastards that work here," Perkins crisply replies.

By the end of the television adaptation of *A Very British Coup,* it is not clear that "the bastards" won't succeed in bringing Perkins down. (The novel is much less ambiguous in this regard. Perkins succumbs to Sir Percy's blackmail, agreeing to be hospitalized for exhaustion and to be replaced by his moderate Chancellor of the Exchequer, who repudiates his reform agenda.) "Are you going to win?" Perkins' mother asks him on the morning of the fateful election. "Well, all I can do is tell the truth. And let the people decide," he replies. "You're a bugger for lettin' the people decide," she comments in broad Yorkshire, "D'you think it'll ever catch on?"

Yet for all the narrative's despair at the ineradicable corruption of "the system" and the implacable elitism of "the establishment," there is an undercurrent of populist faith that prevents it from sharing the cynicism of *House of Cards* or *The Thick of It.* It is not merely that Perkins derails Sir Percy's plot by appealing directly to the country. The narrative also makes use of two highly symbolic "everyman" characters to epitomize the essential fair-mindedness and decency of the English electorate—the very people whose will Sir Percy and his co-conspirators are seeking to thwart and subvert at every turn. The first is Mr. Patel, the owner of the newsagent's shop in Perkins' Sheffield constituency. At a point when the beleaguered Perkins is surrounded by enemies, denounced in the tabloid press, and threatened on every side, he returns to his constituency and encounters Mr. Patel, who assures him that he and his family don't believe a word of the lies that are being spread. They have faith. Buoyed by his encounter, Perkins returns to London determined to fight on.

A still more significant role in the plot is assigned to the second representative figure, Inspector Page, the laconic police officer who serves as Perkins' body guard. An almost silent presence throughout most of the narrative, it is Page who intervenes to prevent Perkins' final television broadcast from being blacked out by the quisling Director General of the BBC, a chinless lackey of Sir Percy's. Page literally removes the man's hand from the control board, quelling him with a single look and a measured "Sit down, Mr. Alford." Mr. Alford sits and the broadcast continues. As the Inspector accompanies Perkins back from the television station, the soon-to-be-former Prime Minister thanks him for his actions. "With respect, sir," the inspector replies. "I don't actually vote for you, but I know what's right." In a sense, *A Very British Coup* seeks to have its ending both ways: "the establishment" might—or might not—defeat Perkins. But perhaps "the people," with their innate sense of rectitude and fair play, will still triumph in the end.

It is this strain of populist outrage, seasoned with large doses of old-school "sisters are doing it for themselves" feminism, that animates writer Sally Wainwright's 2006 miniseries *The Amazing Mrs. Pritchard.* Far less well received than any of the other political narratives we've been considering— one English critic (Cowley, 2006) went so far as to title his review "Politics for Morons"—the series lasted a single season. And it is, in many ways, the least sophisticated version of the British political fable that we will examine. Yet Ros Pritchard, working mother, manager of a supermarket in fictional northern Eatanswill, and accidental prime minister is worth a closer look.[13]

The premise of the series is a simple one. Disgusted by the antics of the two (male) candidates who come to blows while campaigning outside her supermarket, Ros Pritchard decides to stand for parliament as an independent. "I could do better than that lot," she comments indignantly. "They always say that, luv," the Labour candidate cheerfully replies. Through a series of highly improbable events over which the narrative leaps with understandable speed—unexpected financial support from the influential and very wealthy business woman who owns the supermarket chain that employs Ros, a number of high profile defections by female MPs and even cabinet ministers—Mrs. Pritchard finds herself at the head of a new women's party, the Purple Democratic Alliance, the winner of "the biggest ever landslide in modern British political history," and the newest inhabitant of 10 Downing Street. The first two episodes focus tightly on the campaign and its immediate aftermath, as an army of newly elected female MPs descends on Westminster, and the new Prime Minister's plain-speaking ways and radical ideas electrify the country. (These include a proposal to sell Whitehall and move parliament from London to Bradford—roughly analogous to relocating Congress from Washington to Madison, Wisconsin—in order to bring it back in touch with "the real people," and "carless Wednesdays" when all private motor traffic will be banned throughout the country.)

There is considerable entertainment to be found in these opening episodes as the new government, composed of refugees from the two main political parties, attempts to cohere around its tiny, indomitable new leader. ("Whingeing fucking liberals," is the disgusted comment of the former Conservative Catherine Walker after her first cabinet meeting. She, appropriately enough, is appointed Chancellor of the Exchequer.) And Jane Horrocks as Ros Pritchard is a warm, intelligent, engaging presence, transcending the cliché of the plain-speaking Northern lass and growing in stature as she begins to comprehend the magnitude of what she has taken on. Unfortunately, the series quickly embroils itself in a number of tiresome subplots. Ros' husband has financial irregularities in his past that might be brought to light. Her nubile teenage daughter "accidentally" poses nude for a racy men's magazine. The tough-as-nails new Chancellor is having an affair with a much younger aide and might be pregnant. Someone is leaking unfavorable insider information. Could it be the jealous Home Secretary?

It is easy to see why *The Amazing Mrs. Pritchard* annoyed so many English critics. The essentialist gender politics that animate the narrative—women are united by their gender regardless of political beliefs; "women don't muck about with the truth" as Ros emphatically announces early in episode one, unlike men who, apparently, invariably do; women naturally favor liberal social policies and reject military action—belong to a bygone era. The narrative's stance in relation to actual politics is no more sophisticated, its informing premise apparently being that the best qualification for holding public office is complete lack of any previous experience. "She knows nothing about government, absolutely nothing at all," a politician remarks in exasperation on election night as Mrs. Pritchard's victory takes shape. "But surely that's the point," his interviewer replies.

It is, in fact, a point that is made repeatedly throughout the narrative, perhaps most fancifully in the new prime minister's determination to create a policy agenda for her government through national debate, encouraging citizens to form local discussion groups and to forward their ideas. The result (in two weeks, no less) is a "sensible and balanced" program that the new government duly adopts. Compare this with the results of the consultation initiative undertaken by the Obama government in the early weeks of its transition, the Citizens' Briefing Books. The most popular ideas harvested, much to the new administration's chagrin, included decriminalizing marijuana use, legalizing online poker, and revoking the Church of Scientology's tax-exempt status (Borins, 2010).

It is this sort of narrative naïveté that led A. A. Gill, reviewing the series in *The Sunday Times*, to note with asperity, "The answer to bad politics isn't no politics, it's better politics" (Gill, 2006). Like Anthony Lane, Gill too cites *The West Wing* as the gold standard of intelligent, sophisticated political fiction, a standard *The Amazing Mrs. Pritchard* falls far short of. Yet if there is much about this narrative that makes it appear more feminist fairytale than political fable, there is at least one continuity with *A Very British Coup* that is worth pausing over. Like Harry Perkins, Ros Pritchard is a plain speaker, her northern English accent, like his, a badge of authenticity, and a mark of difference from the southern Establishment insiders. And Pritchard, like Perkins, links her open, direct speech to a larger principle: open government. "I love all this arcane crap we've got floating around Westminster. Like a secret code language for the posh, and the clever, and the initiated," she remarks to her (indisputably posh) cabinet secretary. But if Perkins' story was ultimately animated by a desire to return power to the democratically elected representatives of the people, the moral of Ros Pritchard's tale is somewhat different. She herself makes it explicit in her first televised speech as Prime Minister, delivered, symbolically, in the open air, outside the doors of Downing Street:

> The increased remoteness of the Westminster world has meant that ordinary people, the little people, people like you and me, have felt increasingly excluded from the forces that shape our lives. Increasingly disenfranchised, increasingly at odds with it all. Well that's going to change and it starts here. But remember this. You haven't just voted for me. You've voted for yourselves. You must no longer allow yourselves to feel locked out from the decision-making process. You must no longer allow yourselves to assume that other people know what's best for you, better than what you do yourselves... Okay, so it may only last for five minutes. But at least we'll have proved something.

What Wainwright appears to be suggesting is an end to closed politics through populist engagement, though what precise form that is to take beyond passionate discussion down at the pub and mail-in policy campaigns it is somewhat difficult to tell.[14]

Pritchard's election-day speech is the major set piece of the series, one of the only times, in fact, we will see Ros Pritchard acting publicly. Horrocks makes the most of the moment and so, too, does the director. As the camera pulls back from the slight, bird-like figure of Ros, it pans the faces of the initially skeptical civil servants and journalists in attendance. Gradually they are won over by Mrs. Pritchard's passion, conviction, and sincerity. By speech's end, they erupt in cheers.

Poor reviews and declining audiences meant that a projected second installment of *The Amazing Mrs. Pritchard* was never aired. Instead, the series ends with Ros Pritchard confronted by three moral crises: to cover up evidence of financial impropriety in her husband's past, to ignore the mounting evidence that her wealthy supporter (and former employer) had paid sitting MPs to leave their parties and join the emerging Purple Democratic Alliance, and to allow preferential review of contracts her benefactor is tendering to government ministries. Will the people's politician be corrupted by the system? Ros herself narrates her dilemma: "Everybody seems to think I should bite the bullet. Compromise my integrity and get used to it. Like a real politician. How can I do the one thing I promised the people I'd never do? Become one of them, self-serving, duplicitous tossers." In fact, Mrs. Pritchard does not betray her promise to "the people." She resigns from office, leaving her extremely capable chancellor to succeed her as prime minister and to win a second term for the Purple Democratic Alliance government she founded. The system has not corrupted her, but only because she has refused to participate. It is, still, the only way. To stay, as the dominant fable always assumes, would inevitably mean to become "one of them."

The Politics of Character: Peter Morgan's Tony Blair

Interviewed just prior to the launch of *The Thick of It* in 2005, the series' creator, Armando Iannucci, distinguished his project from the "dramas about politics" like *The Deal* that had preceded it. For Iannucci, these were "very acted pieces...fake dramas" focusing exclusively on what he called "the politics of personality." Without parsing the implications of "fake" within this context, it is not hard to understand why Iannucci reacted so critically to his perceived rival. Much of the immediate attention surrounding each of Morgan's films centered on the truly astonishing acts of imaginative identification achieved by the actors playing Blair, Brown, and most notably, the Queen. But Morgan also structures his narratives very deliberately around pairs of characters, each of whom represents constellations of ideas, choices, and principles. These are not, however, simple, schematic oppositions. Morgan is both too intelligent and too skillful for that. Nor do the outcomes of these stories produce clear-cut victories or defeats for either side. The drama resides, quite literally, in the conversations between the two principals and their principles—Blair and Brown, Blair and the Queen, Blair and Clinton—with all the shifting power dynamics, unspoken meanings, and implicit moral choices they enact.

Morgan's Blair is a deeply ambitious politician for the media age, a master of spin and the artfully staged display of genuine emotion; but he is also a man of vision and political conviction. Both the early films pit the modernizer Blair against representatives of an older, outmoded ethos, and it is clear that the narratives see history on his side. When Blair outmaneuvers Gordon Brown for the leadership of the Labour party in *The Deal,* or successfully exploits public grief over Princess Diana's death to consolidate his own fledgling government's popularity in *The Queen,* we are witnessing the operations of a man skilled at what a character (Labour politician Peter Mandelson) in *The Deal* calls "the ugly business" of modern politics. But we are clearly seeing, too, the limitations, blindness, and incapacity of those who oppose him. Brown might be the better (more authentic) man, but it is Blair who is the better (more effective) leader. The Queen's refusal to pander to public demands for emotional display might be admirable, but it alienates the country and ignores the realities of 21st-century public life.

Morgan's narrative mode is not satiric, though he too makes effective use of the by-now familiar "translation trope" to expose what lies beneath public political rhetoric. As Blair and an array of dispirited Labour party insiders listen disgustedly to a television interview in which one of their number heaps praise on Neil Kinnock, the leader responsible for their shattering 1992 election defeat to the Tory nonentity John Major—"He has united the party as a political force, modernized it as a campaigning organization, and quite apart from this legacy, his own natural charm and warmth of character will mark him down as one of the all time great leaders of this party"—Cherie Blair acidly remarks, "As long as Neil knows everyone wants him out by Monday."

If the dominant mode of *Yes Minister*'s fable is satiric, and that of *The Thick of It* cynical, the Blair fable tends to the ironic. All three of the narratives end with pyrrhic victories: Blair reneges on his implicit promise to his friend not to seek the leadership of the Labour Party—"We had an actual conversation," Brown protests. "But not an actual agreement," Blair counters—wins the post and goes on to a landslide electoral mandate. Blair will then, as the closing titles remind us, also renege on the deal Brown thinks he made to secure Brown's support; namely, that he will not serve more than a single term.[15] Two promises broken. A friendship betrayed. An ambitious reform agenda successfully launched. A party's fortunes reborn. The Queen abandons her privacy and silence, engages in the public performance of grief demanded of her, and the new Labour Prime Minister emerges as "Mister Saviour of the Monarchy Blair," as his wife, Cherie, mockingly remarks. The old values of stoicism, reserve, and self-control are drowned out by the noise of what the Queen Mother witheringly calls "a bunch of hysterics carrying candles." Watching the Queen's unprecedented televised tribute to Diana, delivered at Downing Street's suggestion "as a queen, and as a grandmother," Cherie Blair is disgusted by the insincerity: "She doesn't mean a word of this." "That's not the point," her husband responds, "What she's doing is extraordinary. That's how you survive."

What interests Morgan's narratives more than the satiric points to be scored, however, is what we might call the politics of character, and specifically, the character of Tony Blair. And this is where the interest lies for our analysis too. At first glance, Morgan's first Blair narrative, *The Deal*, might seem to conform quite closely to the dominant fable. Slick, ambitious Tony with his camera-ready demeanor and skill at simulating sincerity betrays both his friend and his own better nature to win "the big job" over the more principled but infinitely less media-friendly Gordon Brown. But the story *The Deal* tells is actually considerably more complex. Blair's personal ambition is clearly established (as indeed is Brown's) from the film's first frames, but so too is his genuine desire to rescue his party's fortunes and implement its progressive agenda. In other words, Morgan's narrative world can contain precisely what the real Alastair Campbell found lacking in Iannucci's, the mixture of motives, the imbrication of personal and public agendas, that characterizes those drawn to politics and government. As Gordon Brown explains to Blair in an early scene, they are all motivated by the same ambition, the desire for the ultimate power: "Isn't that what we came into politics for? We're happy to work as a team. It's all about a cause and public service, but deep down you won't change the world until you have the big job." It is a measure of the film's intelligence that it does not suggest that either the cause or the service is somehow negated by the ambition.

But if the Blair fable is about political survival, it is also about its costs. And history itself would add the final ironic coda. Less than a year after the release of *The Queen*, Blair would resign from office and parliament, deeply unpopular and widely suspected of having "misled" both parliament and the British public regarding Britain's participation in the second Iraq war. The fluency and persuasiveness that were the grounds of his success would prove his undoing. Those who live by the sound bite die by it too.

While *The Special Relationship* does not directly address the controversy surrounding the Blair government's handling of the Iraq War, it uses Blair's impassioned campaign for international intervention in Kosovo to foreshadow events to come. The climax of the movie—and the mark within the narrative of Blair's emergence as a world leader in his own right, out of the tutelage and the shadow of the larger-than-life Clinton—is his securing of an American commitment to broad-based NATO intervention in Kosovo. At this point, personal conviction and political ambition are entirely intertwined. The narrative makes clear Blair's genuinely anguished desire to prevent further genocidal attacks by Slobodan Milosevic's troops. "The lives of those people depend on the whim of an insane tyrant," he tells his wife, "And we have the power to change that. If Bill won't, or can't, then it's up to me." But at the same time, Blair is entirely clear about the political cost of failing to make good on his very public humanitarian commitments: "This could be the end of me. I'm completely out on a limb on this. If we don't win this thing, I'm the one who's going to have to answer for it." In the end, of course, Blair does "win this thing." Milosevic backs down, and the American press hails Blair as a model statesman and leader, in marked contrast to their own erring and prevaricating president. Blair benefits from his passionate espousal of the cause of intervention, the narrative makes no bones about that. But he is also allowed the full sincerity of his principled stand.

The final movement of the film deals with the election of George W. Bush, framing a moral choice for Blair: abandon his progressive, center-left principles and agenda, ally himself with Bush, and become "the senior partner" in a new special relationship, or distance himself from a controversial administration whose declared principles are antithetical to his own, and lose the influence and (reflected) power that might come with a close embrace. As the film's Clinton warns him, pictures of Bush and Cheney flashing on a television screen behind them, "Be careful. These guys. They play rough. Their administration has been born in controversy, national shame, and illegality. And it is my bet, that that's the way they'll go out. So the question you need to ask yourself is, what business does a progressive center-left politician from a tiny little island in Europe have making friends with folks like that?" The film ends with shots of the Clintons leaving Chequers, the Prime Minister's country residence, as Blair begins his congratulatory phone call to the newly declared American president. "Absolutely, George," we, like Clinton, overhear Blair remarking as he flashes his famous Cheshire cat grin. And the rest is (hotly debated) history.

Morgan's Blair narratives offer yet another variant on the dominant fable. This is not a counter-fable, for Morgan too retains the fundamental premise of the compromises, betrayals, and falsities of political life. It is rather a variation that allows principle and ambition, conviction and desire for power, ideals and spin, commitment and manipulation to coexist, not only within the same narrative universe but within the same character. Unlike the narratives of *A Very British Coup* and *The Amazing Mrs. Pritchard*, escape is not the only answer nor is utter moral defeat the only other alternative. For all Armando Iannucci's strictures on the "false" nature of Morgan's dramas, one can still argue for the greater realism of his narratives in this respect at least, that he peoples them with figures who are not monsters of ambition, nor comic incompetents, nor plain-speaking martyrs. There are neither indisputable heroes, nor villains, nor even antiheroes in Morgan's version of the fable. They are, rather, complex and contradictory human beings acting out private dramas of character on a very public stage.

The Lessons of Polyphony

From Snow and Crossman to Morgan, Iannucci, and Wainwright, the creators of the narratives we've been considering have shared a common urge to communicate what Iannucci called "a fixed unimpeachable truth about how we are governed." And that "truth" has varied surprisingly little over the decades, its essence encapsulated in Malcolm Tucker's four choice words: "It's a fucking war." That is the core fable of British narratives of government and politics, and its dominance, as we've seen, is almost total. Mainstream management literature typically favors success narratives over cautionary tales, stories of achievement featuring exemplary protagonists (whether individuals or institutions) as models for emulation. Our narrative set, clearly, offers little in that line, and this raises an interesting question: What, and how, do nonexemplary management narratives such as these teach us? Is it merely a question of negative example? When possible, do not betray your friends, your principles, or your electoral promises; it's bad for your character. Avoid launching wholesale attacks on entrenched special interests, especially if they have been used to running the country for the past seven centuries. Employing the F-word as verb, adjective, adverb, and noun in every one of your communications might terrorize your colleagues, but it won't win you much love when your power is on the wane. Murder is, on balance, not the most effective way to resolve leadership issues. If you campaign on a take-back-the-government platform, it helps to know what you're going to do with it once you've got it. Amusing as it is to generate such a list, and it could be extended considerably, there is another way to frame the question. What do these particular narratives, so closely allied in theme and mood, teach us about narrative engagement?

This is not to abandon questions of practice completely. If we accept the dominant fable's Hobbesian view of government and politics, there are at least three main rules of conduct to be extracted for Mr. Tucker's war. A particularly conspicuous plot element in virtually all of the narratives we've considered has been the manipulation of information, especially inside or secret information. It is one of the most useful weapons and most valuable counters, and the successful protagonists (successful in the satirical-cynical fable's terms of getting and/or keeping power) are those who are most adept at manipulating informal networks to obtain and barter it. In the two

Yes Prime Minister episodes we discussed, Sir Humphrey uses inside information and his informal network to thwart Jim Hacker's "grand design," just as Hacker uses his informational advantage to manipulate his seemingly idealistic health minister's antismoking policy to serve his own ends. Again, Malcolm Tucker speaks for all in a later episode of *The Thick of It* (series 3, episode 4) when he briefs ministry staff on the procedure for a visit from their opposite numbers in the shadow cabinet: "When the opposition are here, you tell them nothing, yeah? Except where the toilets are. But you lie about that."

A corollary to the law of manipulating information is derived from the premises of public-choice theory that inform *Yes Minister* and its successors. Every action, policy, or statement of a politician or public servant can be explained by the operation of self-interest. The trick is to penetrate the rationales that serve as camouflage: political ideology, party loyalty, public interest. Once the necessary inside information has been gained to reveal the personal stakes involved, it then becomes possible to calculate what would be required to satisfy that interest and win the support necessary to further one's own ends. In the narratives we've considered, this is often what is being enacted through the translation trope: the revelation of the hidden personal motive beneath the political or bureaucratic rhetoric.

This in turn leads to the third of Tucker's Laws: in the struggle for power, language, like information, is a weapon of choice. But this has little to do with the jargonistic obfuscation of a Sir Humphrey Appleby, the machiavellian dissimulation of a Francis Urquhart, or the verbal brutality of a Malcolm Tucker. The skillset involved is much more subtle and is dramatized most effectively in Peter Morgan's Tony Blair trilogy. In the modern media age, when the exposure of the machine (to use C. P. Snow's prescient phrase) has become a 24-hour fact of political life, success goes to those who can best use words to express, or at least simulate, authenticity of feeling. What is being modeled here is a highly skilled performance, a carefully calculated display of warmth, spontaneity, empathy, emotional connection, but above all genuineness.

This is not hypocrisy, or double-speak, still less is it deliberate deception. It is much closer to the doubleness that characterizes the best actors: the ability to be utterly "in the moment" and yet outside of it too; fully engaged yet always in control. And it is the quality that makes what a character in *The Special Relationship* calls "a bona fide, triple A, vote-winning political superstar." He is referring to President Clinton, but Tony Blair, in Morgan's narratives, is no less a master of the art. It is an aspect of the character that is dramatized repeatedly in all three films, the "people's princess" episode from *The Queen* being only one of many similar set pieces contrasting the public performance of deep feeling with the private political calculus that informed it.

Interestingly, the real Tony Blair addresses the issue explicitly in his 2010 autobiography, offering a (seemingly) frank assessment of the complex duality involved. He makes his comments in the chapter dealing with Princess Diana and her death, as he identifies in her public performances a similar skill; namely, a fully conscious exploitation of her apparent emotional spontaneity: "She knew its effect, of course, but the effect could never have been as powerful as it was if the feeling had not been genuine" (Blair, 2010, p. 140). Blair describes himself, and the princess, as "manipulative people, perceiving quickly the emotions of others and able instinctively to play with them."

The judgment of Morgan's narratives on this manipulation appears to shift over the course of the trilogy. In *The Deal*, it is undoubtedly the grounds of Blair's success over the emotionally tone-deaf, prickly Brown, a Scot for whom the adjective "dour" would appear to have been invented. Blair's media-friendly appeal, his skill with an emotional sound bite (even when he is cribbing his best lines from Brown), is framed by the narrative as a glibness that is inseparable from Blair's final betrayals. *The Queen* offers a more nuanced (and therefore challenging) depiction. However much the royals and their staff might mock the modernizing new Prime Minister, with his "Call me Tony" ways—and it is difficult to resist the sight of the actress Helen Mirren, in all her glory as Queen Elizabeth, putting "Call me Tony" in his place with an acid "This is a family funeral, Mr. Bair, not a fairground attraction"—it is Blair who wins out. As the queen herself acknowledges in the final frames of the movie, "I can see the world has changed. And one must—modernize." With *The Special Relationship*, as we've discussed at some length in our analysis of the film's handling of the Kosovo intervention, the narrative is unwilling to separate the political calculation, the public performance, the genuine emotion, the moral imperative, and the personal ambition. Rather the viewer is left to wonder whether Blair himself has any notion of where one ends and the other begins. And, in the final sentence of his memoirs, Blair (2010, p. 682) himself expressed that conundrum: "as you will gather from this memoir, it has never been entirely clear whether the journey I have taken is one of a triumph of a person over the politics or of the politics over the person."

This is a level of openness, even ambiguity, in its handling of the character that is largely absent from the other narratives we've been considering. In this sense, Morgan's films are polyphonic, multivoiced, in a way that the others are not. This might seem like a strange assertion, given the literal cacophony of characters in a narrative like *The Thick of It* (but all ultimately sounding very much alike), the strident conflict between Perkins and his foes in *A Very British Coup*, even the infinite variations rung on the trio of utterly distinctive voices in *Yes Minister*. Yet ultimately, these narratives framed their perspective from a single point of view: that of the cynical, disenchanted observer of "the ugly business" that is modern politics and government. Morgan's narratives, in contrast, seem increasingly willing to complicate that viewpoint, refusing to make ambition and conviction mutually exclusive. And it is this openness, I think, that ultimately makes Morgan's narratives more rewarding to engage with than, say, *The Thick of It*, brilliant, and scathing, and funny as it often is. Morgan's narratives are not constructed around a single "fixed unimpeachable truth." They are, at heart, more democratic in their structure than that. These are, indeed, as Armando Iannucci remarked, dramas of character, human character, with all that implies. Allowing the character of Blair a full measure of complexity, Morgan's narratives accord the business of government and politics their full complexity too. They undoubtedly see the ugliness, but they also see more. And through them, if we choose, so can we.

Endnotes

1. The so-called Barsetshire and Palliser novels are the best known of Trollope's work today. Both are a series of linked novels with recurring characters. The Barsetshire series (named for the imaginary county in which it is set) deals with various levels of the Anglican ecclesiastical hierarchy, from parish priests to wardens, deans, bishops and archbishops and includes the undisputed comic masterpiece *Barchester Towers*. The Palliser novels chronicle the fortunes of the aristocratic "Whig" statesman Plantagenet Palliser (later Duke of Omnium and Prime Minister) and his circle of grandees, cabinet ministers, political hostesses, MPs on the make, political agents, party hacks, ambitious young arrivistes, and assorted journalistic hangers-on. Trollope remains a touchstone in the history of British political narrative. His sustained exploration of political life—what Snow termed "his studies of the human political process" (1975, p. 109)—are still being invoked in discussions of *Yes Minister* posted on Jonathan Lynn's Web site.
2. The *Strangers and Brothers* novels all are narrated in the first person by Lewis Eliot, a character closely based on Snow himself (Snow, P., 1982; Ramanathan, 1978). Eliot is always a participant in the events depicted, but never a major player. Snow presents him as quintessentially tactful, hence a superb confidant. As author, Snow was attempting to modernize the 19th-century convention of the omniscient narrator writing in the third person. Eliot, as the universal confidant, communicated to the reader many other characters' thinking, thus performing the role of omniscient narrator in, to modern readers, a more natural manner.
3. Snow and Crossman were near-contemporaries and Wilson government colleagues: Snow served as parliamentary secretary to the Technology Minister

from October 1964 until 1966. Judging by slighting references made by Crossman in the *Diaries* and Snow in a book-length interview published in 1983, the two men cordially disliked each other. Literary rivalry might have contributed to the animus. In his *Diaries,* Crossman is dismissive of Snow's "novelistic talk" and routinely denigrates his political acumen (Crossman, 1975, p. 42). Snow returns the compliment, damning the *Diaries* with the faintest possible praise: "Well, they didn't teach me anything I didn't know already. I suppose to people who are not in that sort of world, they may have been a bit of a shock" and dismissing the man himself as "usually quite right, but he had no judgment, and he was a bully" (Halperin, 1983, p. 188). Yet each was, in his way, engaged in a similar enterprise: chronicling the inside workings of postwar political life, "lighting up the secret places of British politics" (Crossman, 1975, p. 12).

4. Crossman completed the first volume before his death, and the second and third volumes were edited by Dr. Janet Morgan.

5. As is so often the case in British politics, there is an element of class bias at work. Crossman came from a much more privileged background than Wilson: his father was a judge, Wilson's a "works" (industrial) chemist. I was surprised by Crossman's willingness to include in the published diaries snobbish comments concerning Wilson's "deeply petit bourgeois" lifestyle and remarkably left-handed compliments on the Prime Minister's ability *not* to cravenly "respect the upper classes for having superior cultural tastes which he would like to share." It is equally surprising to encounter, as another left-handed compliment, a sentence like "He [the Prime Minister] won't hold it against me that I live in a lovely manor house in the country and he doesn't" (Crossman, 1975, p. 230).

6. Spending weekends at his country house, every Saturday night Crossman sat down with the previous week's official documents, press clippings, and his engagements diary and reconstructed the most significant or noteworthy events of the week. On Sunday morning, he tape-recorded his ministerial diary, which later in the week was transcribed.

7. He wrote this at the same time he was giving his lectures at Harvard. I had the good fortune to attend them as an undergraduate, and recall that Crossman gave a superb performance, delivering them with a level of energy and enthusiasm that belied the ministerial fatigue he was privately writing about. Perhaps he was eagerly anticipating leaving politics, returning to his career as a journalist, and publishing the *Diaries.*

8. After each season, the broadcasts were published as Hacker's diaries. While not screenplays, they captured the plot and much of the dialogue and also, before the advent of high quality digitization, preserved the programs. For "The Ministerial Broadcast," see Lynn and Jay (1986, pp. 86–113) and for "The Smokescreen," Lynn and Jay (1986, pp. 187–211). The quotations in this book are from the broadcasts.

9. Anthony Downs, in his classic study *Inside Bureaucracy* (1967, pp. 79–111), one of the earliest and most influential public-choice texts, discusses a number of types of officials, one of which is the zealot, who is much more devoted to a particular cause than to the advancement of either his own career or the

organization. *Yes Minister* presents very few zealots, and even those who appear to be zealots reveal themselves to be what Downs refers to as "climbers"; namely, those who are most interested in their own advancement. One might even go so far as to interpret the health minister's vigorous advocacy of a war on smoking as a calculated attempt to attract Hacker's attention and thereby advance his career.

10. By my count, of the entire 38 episodes, Humphrey prevails in 39% of them, Hacker in 29%, and they cooperate successfully against a common antagonist in 24%.

11. The choice of chief whip, rather than some senior ministry, for Urquhart's position prior to becoming Prime Minister, is particularly well aligned with this cynical view of politics because the chief whip is, in essence, an enforcer who makes it his business to find out his parliamentary colleagues' weaknesses and use his knowledge of their weaknesses to ensure compliance with the prime minister. In this case, Urquhart used his knowledge to supplant the incumbent prime minister.

12. The plot development was in large measure forced on Iannucci and his creative team by the arrest, conviction, and jail term for possession of child pornography of the actor playing Hugh Abbott. With Abbott gone, the series broadened its purview to include members of the opposition shadow cabinet, and increasingly focused on Tucker's own fight to retain influence as the leadership of his party undergoes a transition similar to Tony Blair's mid-term resignation.

13. The name of Mrs. Pritchard's constituency is a direct borrowing from the election chapters in Charles Dickens' *Pickwick Papers,* published in 1837, a knowing wink to the long-standing tradition of English political satire.

14. The elements of "take back the government" and "politics is too important to be left to the politicians" in Ros Pritchard's fictional campaign invite comparisons to the anti-Washington-insider rhetoric of 2008 Republican vice presidential candidate Sarah Palin. There is a similarity, too, in the underlying logic that transforms lack of experience into a badge of honor. (Mrs. Pritchard, it should be noted, was much more willing to acknowledge the drawbacks of her limited knowledge than her real-life counterpart. Inviting a high-ranking Tory cabinet minister to join her government as Chancellor of the Exchequer, she remarks on the pressing need to find "someone who understands the fucking economy.")

15. While *The Deal* portrays Brown as believing he and Blair had reached an agreement about how long Blair would serve as prime minister, the actual Blair, (2010, p. 71), in his memoirs, denies it: "Though there was never a deal in the sense that his standing down [that is, not contesting the leadership of the Labour Party] was contingent on my agreeing to help him come after me, nonetheless there was an understanding of mutual interest. Had you asked me then what I would do and what might happen, I would have said I would do two terms and then hand over. . . . But, once again, looking back, I was too eager to persuade and too ready to placate. The truth is I couldn't guarantee it; and it was irresponsible to suggest or imply I could."

4

Churchill, Appeasement, Victory

The British Narrative of Leadership

Introduction

> You ask what is our policy? I can say: it is to wage war, by sea, land, and air, with all our might and with all the strength that God can give us; to wage war against a monstrous tyranny, never surpassed in the dark, lamentable catalogue of human crime. That is our policy. You ask, what is our aim? I can answer in one word: it is victory, victory at all costs, victory in spite of all terror, victory, however long and hard the road may be, for without victory, there is no survival.
>
> —Winston Churchill, May 13, 1940

The story of Winston Churchill's wartime leadership of Britain has acquired the status of a modern myth. Its power is indisputable. There is an almost biblical force to the narrative of the unheeded prophet, ridiculed, marginalized, exiled from power, returning to save his country in its darkest hour. It is a story of redemption, both national and personal, as Churchill fulfills his destiny and changes the course of history, silencing the defeatist voices of Appeasement with heroic defiance, galvanizing nations with his words.

Governing Fables: Learning from Public Sector Narratives, pages 103–134
Copyright © 2011 by Information Age Publishing
103

One measure of the myth's enduring power is the continued currency of the term "appeasement" as a political slur. The specter of Appeasement (and of his father's well-known support of it as official British policy during his tenure as Ambassador to Britain in the prewar years) would haunt President Kennedy throughout the Cuban Missile Crisis, as we will see. Analogies to Neville Chamberlain's futile conciliation of Hitler, and Churchill's heroic resistance, would be cited repeatedly during both the first and second Gulf wars on both sides of the Atlantic. The story of Churchill and the end of Appeasement is indisputably a historical dominant fable, inevitably shaping our understanding of Britain's experience in those cataclysmic years of war. Its influence continues to be felt, framing our perception of world events more than sixty years later. And Churchill himself remains a touchstone of heroic leadership, a statesman who has transcended not only politics, but even his moment in history, to become an enduring icon.

The contrast to the dominant satirical-cynical fable of the preceding chapter could hardly be stronger. Yet the two are products of the same geo-political and cultural shifts. As Britain slowly rebuilt after the devastation of the war years, only to find herself a former world power dependent upon the grace and favor of her American cousins, as politics and governance became increasingly synonymous in the public mind with media manipulation, bureaucratic obstructionism, and personal duplicity, the nostalgia for the heroic leadership and national sacrifice of the war years grew. Nostalgia, however, tends both to select and to simplify, reducing what is recalled to a generalized perfection that often bears little relationship to reality. From the vast literature on Churchill as war leader, this chapter focuses primarily on his role in the ending of Appeasement, exploring a necessarily select set of recent reconsiderations of both the man and the Appeasement story, narratives that, in very different ways, attempt to move beyond simple hero worship.[1] These include a notable biography, published in 2001 by the distinguished Labour politician and minister Roy Jenkins, as well as two more narrowly focused historical accounts. The first is John Lukacs' *Five Days in London: May 1940* (1999), a detailed study of the crucial days preceding the evacuation from Dunkirk, when Churchill united his deeply divided war cabinet to reject a proposal for a negotiated peace with Hitler, committing his government, and his nation, to all-out war. The second is Lynne Olson's *Troublesome Young Men* (2007), which focuses on the group of young Conservative Party dissidents who opposed Appeasement and helped drive Neville Chamberlain from office. We will also consider two films co-produced for television by HBO and the BBC depicting the same years and events: *The Gathering Storm* (2002), which chronicles the end of Appeasement and

Churchill's return to office as First Lord of the Admiralty, and *Into the Storm* (2009), a highly telescoped account of the key events of the war years.

These contrasting narrative enterprises make an illuminating set precisely because of the cross-currents between them. While Jenkins offers the closest to a canonical account of the end of Appeasement fable, his emphasis throughout falls largely on Churchill as a *political* rather than a military or international leader. Lukacs, in contrast, views those five critical days from the widest possible world-historical perspective, identifying them, literally, as the turning point that (narrowly) averted the defeat of Western civilization itself. Lukacs' Churchill, then, "inspired as he was by a kind of historical consciousness that entailed more than incantatory rhetoric," is very much the mythic hero of popular imagination (Lukacs, 1999, p. 217). Yet running parallel to the heroic leader narrative is another story, a submerged narrative of a skillful politician marshalling a range of managerial techniques and stratagems to secure a momentous decision from an inner cabinet of senior colleagues and rivals who often appear in the published minutes, in Jenkins' memorable description, as "five bewildered gentlemen firing off inconsequential remarks in a variety of haphazard directions" (Jenkins, 2001, p. 603).

It is in the light of this other, political narrative, that we will look briefly at a recent advice book for business leaders, Alan Axelrod's *Winston Churchill, CEO* (2009). Churchill has long been a popular figure in this literature: his speeches are quoted almost as invariably those of Shakespeare's Henry V. And Axelrod has many lessons to draw from his long and eventful public career. But in some ways, what is most interesting about *Winston Churchill, CEO* is what it doesn't do. Despite the promise of its title, it largely ignores the managerial narrative highlighted by Jenkins and embedded in Lukacs' work; namely, the story of Churchill's extraordinary skills as a political manager during a period of extreme crisis. Instead, Axelrod focuses predictably on the much more familiar story of Churchill's indomitable public persona, inspirational rhetoric, and military leadership, despite the often glaring incongruity of the analogies he then seeks to draw. It is a measure of the persistence and potency of the dominant Churchill fable. But it also points to the far greater narrative appeal of the hero-leader than the skilled and canny professional politician.[2]

Lynne Olson is not seeking the managerial narrative beneath the heroic fable. Rather, her interest is in uncovering the "behind-the-scenes story leading to Churchill's accession," a story that has been for the most part elided, or indeed eclipsed, by the "monumental figure, sweeping everyone else from center stage and claiming history's spotlight" (Olson, 2007, p. 6). For her, the story of the young Tory rebels is essential to the narrative of the end of Appeasement, the necessary cause that enabled Churchill to fulfill his destiny. This is not revisionism. Olson, no more than Jenkins or Lukacs, seeks to minimize Churchill's singularity or significance. What *Troublesome Young Men* speaks for is a more complex understanding of the other narratives in which Churchill's own epic story is enmeshed, an acknowledgement that the hero alone is rarely the whole story.

The two Churchill movies we will consider, both written by Hugh Whitemore, an award-winning British playwright and screenwriter, adopt a different perspective, seeking to humanize the icon, to uncover the personal story of the difficult, discontented man, the uncomprehending father, and self-centered spouse who finally became, for those crucial years, the national savior he always imagined he would be. It is, *Into the Storm* reminds us, a tale of redemption with an ironic twist. For Churchill was a hero who failed to retain his role as leader in the postwar world he made possible.

The chapter concludes with a structural inversion of the Appeasement fable: Kazuo Ishiguro's acclaimed 1989 novel *The Remains of the Day* and the 1993 Merchant-Ivory film adaptation. This might seem a tangential addition to a chapter centering on Churchill. And Ishiguro's interest is squarely on the fictional characters he places in the interstices of the historical events we've been considering. Yet Ishiguro seems to me essential to any examination of contemporary narratives of Appeasement, and not merely because the success of the film adaptation (it was nominated for eight Academy Awards) gave new currency to the subject. Arguably, his beautifully rendered narrative of the fictional Lord Darlington, as recalled most unreliably by his devoted butler Stevens, represents the most radical Appeasement counter-fable. Not only because it explores the events of those years from the perspective of those on the wrong side of history, nor even for the subtle political allegory it offers of aristocratic failure and blind working-class deference, but mostly for its searching consideration of Appeasement as a form of false consciousness, a psychic fracture that can neither be acknowledged nor healed. For both Ishiguro's characters, as we will see, though in different ways, there is no victory. Appeasement never ends and no peace is possible.

"The Greatest Human Being Ever to Occupy 10 Downing Street": Roy Jenkins' *Churchill* and the End of Appeasement

Roy Jenkins was a member of the House of Commons from 1948 to 1977 and a senior minister in both of Harold Wilson's Labour governments, serving as Chancellor of the Exchequer from 1967 to 1970. His long experience in parliament and government make him an astute and insightful biographer of Churchill, the more so as he too had the painful experience of "trying to remain within a party while disagreeing with its leadership on the central issue of the day" (Jenkins, 2001, p. 535).[3] His account of Churchill's opposition to Prime Minister Neville Chamberlain's Appeasement policy, and his return to office, accession to the Tory leadership, and first months as Prime Minister is particularly valuable for its shrewd insight into the political maneuvering, the "closed politics" in C. P. Snow's sense, which continued to play out even in this period of escalating national crisis. Jenkins neither displaces Churchill from the center of the narrative nor minimizes his extraordinary abilities. (Indeed, it is the closing phrase of the biography that provides this section's title.) Rather, he recognizes that the heroic leader was also, always, a working politician fully attuned to the necessity of building alliances, conciliating opponents, coopting critics, and outmaneuvering rivals—unheroic but essential skills often overshadowed by the public persona.

The historical frame of the Appeasement narrative can be quickly sketched. Following his election to the chancellorship of Germany in 1933 and subsequent coup d'etat, Hitler embarked on a program of rapid remilitarization to enable Germany to take control of contiguous regions with German-speaking populations, the first step in his planned domination of Europe. In addition, the Nazis began a systematic suppression of the rights of Jewish citizens and other targeted minorities. Britain's majority Conservative government, led by Stanley Baldwin from 1935 to 1937 and Neville Chamberlain from 1937 to 1940, adopted a policy of Appeasement: while Britain attempted to keep pace with Germany in rearming, they also hoped that territorial concessions, for example in Czechoslovakia, would satisfy Hitler's expansionist aims and avoid war. It was a policy that enjoyed the support of a majority of Conservative MPs (the party held a large majority in the House of Commons), but that was bitterly opposed by a growing group of Tory dissidents, young backbenchers for the most part (the troublesome young men of Olson's book), in addition to Churchill himself. The Labour party, while opposing Appeasement, generally features very little in accounts of its ending, the focus being, understandably, on the dramatic internal struggles of the Conservative party that ended with Churchill's accession to office as Prime Minister.

On September 30, 1938, Neville Chamberlain signed the infamous Munich Agreement, conceding annexation of the German-speaking *Sudetenland* along the Czechoslovakian border to Nazi Germany, an agreement which he claimed would bring "peace in our time" and even "peace with honor." Events quickly overtook Chamberlain's vain hope. Nazi pogroms against Jewish citizens intensified, culminating in the horrors of *Kristall-nacht.* A full-scale German invasion of Czechoslovakia on March 15, 1939, rendered the Munich agreement meaningless. A nonaggression treaty was signed between Germany and Soviet Russia on August 23. On September 1, Germany invaded Poland. On September 3, Britain declared war on Germany. After ten years in political exile, Churchill returned to the cabinet as First Lord of the Admiralty (minister for the Navy). He would become Prime Minister eight months later.

What is striking about the narrative Jenkins creates of these tumultuous weeks is the dual focus it provides, reflecting both Churchill the (soon-to-be) national leader and Churchill the working politician, facing challenges from a constituency mistrustful of his maverick behavior (Jenkins, 2001, pp. 531–534), a former senior minister eager for reentry to the inner circles of power, careful not to alienate those who might facilitate that return, and a shrewd public performer, calculating the timing of his parliamentary appearances to derive maximum press attention. Describing Churchill's famous speech during the debate on the Munich Agreement, a speech which ended in quintessentially Churchillian fashion: "This is only the beginning of the reckoning. The is only the first sip, the first foretaste of a bitter cup which will be proffered to us year by year unless, by a supreme recovery of moral health and martial vigour, we rise again and take our stand for freedom as in the olden times" (Churchill, 1938), Jenkins calls it "a powerful, even a noble speech." But he notes, too, the precise calculation with which Churchill waited until the third day of the debate to speak, to avoid being upstaged by the resignation of Duff Cooper, who left office as First Lord of the Admiralty in protest over the signing of the agreement. Jenkins dryly observes, "[Churchill] was always good at the timing of his speeches so as to get a full House and major press attention" (2001, p. 527).

This same balanced perspective characterizes Jenkins' treatment of Churchill's first months at the Admiralty and his eventual accession to the office of Prime Minister. Unlike the film *The Gathering Storm*, which treats Churchill's return to the Admiralty as a foreshadowing of triumphs to come and ends with a young sailor informing the new First Lord, "The message went out to the Fleet, sir. Winston's back," Jenkins astutely assesses the difficulties awaiting the national savior-to-be: "There was at once suspicion of him among most of his new ministerial colleagues and too much expectation of him among the press and public" (2001, p. 522). Nor does he present succeeding events as a simple, inevitable yielding to the force of the great man's vision. Jenkins pays particular attention to Churchill's skillful handling of relations with the man he was destined to replace: "Throughout the whole of these early war months, he was at pains to treat Chamberlain with respect and circumspection, which is generally a wise tactic for ministers in relation to the head of government, particularly when large sections of the press and public are elevating the subordinate minister over his nominal chief" (p. 555). He also notes that for all his deference, Churchill initiated a series of radio broadcasts about the progress of the war at sea, a move that effectively established him in the public's mind as the government's main spokesperson. And he began direct communication through diplomatic pouches with President Franklin Roosevelt at the latter's invitation. Fully aware that he was trenching on the Prime Minister's own privileges here, Churchill both entered heartily into the correspondence *and* made sure that Chamberlain was informed and amenable.

The extraordinary tact and discretion Churchill displayed in his relations with Chamberlain—not qualities typically associated with the Churchill myth—could not conceal the enormous differences between them on the question of basic war strategy. While Churchill advocated attacking the Germans in Europe, Chamberlain still hoped a negotiated settlement might be possible. Churchill's most ambitious proposal was for an invasion of Norway to disrupt the supply of iron ore to Germany. The cabinet delayed authorizing the Norway operation for several months, and by the time it was finally launched in April 1940, the Germans had already begun their own invasion of Norway. By early May, the British had been defeated and forced to withdraw. A parliamentary debate about the military failure in Norway led to a motion of confidence in Chamberlain's government. (While Churchill was very much a part of that government, and indeed spoke in its defense, the critics did not attribute the military failures to him. In Jenkins' words, "He retained the image of a bulldog who would first bark and then put things right" [2001, p. 576].) The decisive speech in the debate was given by Leo Amery, one of the dissident Conservative backbenchers, who in his powerful peroration looked directly at Chamberlain and quoted Oliver Cromwell's famous dismissal of the Long Parliament at the start of the English civil war: "You have sat too long here for any good you have been doing! Depart, I say, and let us have done with you! In the name of God, go!" (p. 579). Chamberlain won the vote with a majority so reduced that the victory was pyrrhic. He immediately decided to resign.

The parliamentary maneuvering that followed the resignation was intended to create a government of national unity. Again, Jenkins rejects the dramatic simplifications of myth to remind us that Churchill's triumph was not inevitable. There were in fact two choices for prime minister, the other being the Foreign Secretary, Lord Halifax. Chamberlain, most of the Conservative party, and the senior bureaucracy all preferred Halifax, who was both more pragmatic and less volatile than Churchill. Halifax, however, conceded the position to his rival. The reason he gave publicly was that as a member of the House of Lords, he would be disqualified from serving as prime minister. As a seat in the House of Commons could readily have been opened up for him, Jenkins surmises that more likely reasons were that he felt it would be impossible to control Churchill, that he himself would benefit politically and popularly from having declined the premiership, and that he expected that, if Churchill failed (a possibility he considered highly likely), he would be called upon to take over with nothing more to fear from his now-discredited rival. Halifax was not, Jenkins notes in an acerbic aside, called "Holy Fox" for nothing (Jenkins, 2001, pp. 583–585).

Far from arriving at Downing Street in a blaze of glory, Jenkins' narrative insists, Churchill assumed office with tepid political support: "He was not the choice of the King. He was not the choice of the Whitehall establishment, which reacted with varying degrees of dismay to the prospect of his alleged wildness. And he was not the choice of the majority party in the House of Commons" (Jenkins, 2001, p. 588). One consequence of his political vulnerability was the consideration he continued to show for Chamberlain, keeping him as one of the five members of the war cabinet, yet another instance of the coexistence of the two Churchills—the dauntless leader and the careful politician.

The military situation facing the new Prime Minister was grave, with the Germans invading the Netherlands, Belgium, and France, and French and British forces retreating toward the French coast. At this dire moment, Churchill's unique strengths came into their own: unwavering resolve, prodigious energy, an unshakable belief in his own destiny, and a unique ability to inspire a nation through his words to become the quiet heroes he told them they had always been. It was during Churchill's first speech to the House of Commons as Prime Minister, a speech now famous for its evocation of the "blood, toil, tears and sweat" that would be required, that he delivered the peroration quoted at the outset of this chapter, culminating in the ringing assertion: "without victory, there is no survival."

It was a resolve that was soon tested, first by the military collapse in France, then by divisions within his own war cabinet. Halifax as Foreign Secretary had been approached by the Italian ambassador (Italy having not yet declared war) offering to broker peace talks between Germany and Britain. Ever the pragmatist, he put the proposal forward, and the cabinet met nine times over five days to consider it. As will be discussed in greater detail below, Churchill was determined to reject peace talks, but understood that the political situation demanded that the rejection be unanimous. Ultimately, and with considerable difficulty, he achieved unanimity, bringing even a reluctant Halifax to agree. On June 4, 1940, following the rejection of the Italian proposal (a decision taken in secrecy) and the successful evacuation of the British Expeditionary Force from Dunkirk, Churchill made his second great policy speech to the House of Commons, famously concluding:

> We shall fight on the beaches, we shall fight in the landing grounds, we shall fight in the fields and in the streets, we shall fight in the hills, we shall never surrender, and even if, which I do not for a moment believe, this island or a large part of it were subjugated and starving, then our Empire beyond the seas, armed and guarded by the British Fleet, would carry on the struggle until, in God's good time, the new world, with all its power and might, steps forth to the liberation of the old. (Churchill, 1940b)

With this speech, the policy of Appeasement was finally ended, and Churchill claimed his place as the nation's indispensible wartime leader. It was the beginning of his entry into myth.

Churchill the Politician: *Five Days in London* and *Winston Churchill, CEO*

When Churchill came to write his own narrative of these events some eight years later, he would omit all mention of the struggle within cabinet, claiming that the question of a negotiated peace (effectively, a surrender) "never found a place upon the war cabinet agenda." It was, Jenkins asserts, "the most breathtakingly bland piece of misinformation" to appear in all six volumes of Churchill's wartime memoirs, combining in equal parts "charity (toward Halifax) and mendacity" (Jenkins, 2001, p. 610). It is interesting to speculate why he should have chosen to excise this crucial episode, omitting all reference to the nine cabinet meetings which, in the view of historian John Lukacs, changed the course of world history (Lukacs, 1999, p. 1). It might have been, as Jenkins assumes, an act of magnanimity toward Halifax, who went on to serve Churchill loyally as wartime ambassador to Washington. Or perhaps the pull of the narrative Churchill himself had worked so hard to impress upon the British public was simply too strong, the fable of the indomitable English fighting spirit awakened by his own call to arms.

It wasn't until the public release of the minutes of the 1940 war cabinet meetings in 1970 that Churchill's evasions were discovered. And it is these minutes that form the basis of Lukacs' study. It is an hour by hour, at times almost minute by minute account that recalls in some ways Robert Kennedy's narrative of the Cuban Missile Crisis *Thirteen Days* (to be discussed in Chapter 6). As a historian, Lukacs' interest is in illuminating as fully as possible those few days that he calls, borrowing the phrase from Churchill himself, "a hinge of fate," the days when "Adolf Hitler came closest to winning the Second World War" (Lukacs, 1999, p. 2). He does so through a counterpoint structure: parsing the cabinet records, while also drawing extensively on private correspondence, diaries, and memoirs to create a background chorus of contemporary voices. Lukacs makes particularly effective use of the transcribed observations and reports made by volunteer participants in the "Mass Observation" project (now lodged in the archives of the University of Sussex), a quasi-anthropological enterprise launched in 1937 as "a study of everyday life" in Britain (p. 34). If the meetings of the war cabinet represent closed politics at its most extreme—a handful of men engaged in secret discussions—Lukacs skillfully places those meetings within larger social, cultural, and military contexts. Yet it is Churchill who remains the cynosure; Churchill for whom Lukacs professes an unqualified, even partisan admiration: "His vision was such that he turned out to be the savior not only of England but of much else besides—essentially, all of Europe" (p. 213).[4] And the close scrutiny he brings to bear on his hero's conduct during those five days in London allows us to read another narrative within Lukacs' own. For whatever else those five days represented—a turning point, a hinge, a redemption, or a narrow escape—they also exemplify quintessential managerial leadership during crisis.

Reading for the managerial narrative that runs through the historical, we discover a set of skills and approaches that seem surprisingly modern. These include such core concepts as inclusion, the importance of "buy in," the persuasive force of a clearly articulated vision, the uses of cooptation and conciliation, and the strategic value of broad-based engagement in a decision-making process. This is not to turn Churchill into Axelrod's CEO. Nor is it to suggest any direct mapping onto current practice. This was leadership *in extremis*. Few private or even public sector managers will ever face the existential challenges or decisions Churchill and his colleagues confronted. My goal here, as with the exploration of the hero-teacher fable in Chapter 2, is to highlight the additional managerial narrative that tends to be discounted in favor of the heroic; an implementation narrative that depends less on charisma, dramatic gestures, and inspirational rhetoric and more on planning, strategy, tactics, alliances, and persuasion, on management, in fact, rather than magnetism.

Churchill's war cabinet met nine times between May 24 and 28, primarily to consider two matters: first, the rapidly deteriorating military situation in France and plans for an evacuation of Allied forces; second, the proposal by Halifax to approach the Italian dictator Mussolini to act as an intermediary for a negotiated peace with Hitler (Lukacs, 1999, pp. 91–94). The minutes of those meetings are detailed and frank, recording at length (though in the third person) what each participant said. There is much drama here, very little of the bland "sense of the discussion" that so irritated Crossman about the public service notetakers of the sixties. The momentousness of the deliberations must have been clear to Churchill's Cabinet Secretary Sir Edward Bridges. He took pains to preserve a complete record.

The composition of Churchill's inner or war cabinet itself speaks volumes about his approach to the deeply divided government he inherited, even before Halifax's contentious proposal. It included Churchill himself, Chamberlain, Halifax, and the Labour party leaders Clement Attlee and Arthur Greenwood. (Attlee would replace Churchill as Prime Minister in the 1945 postwar election.) While Churchill appointed some of his supporters in the anti-Appeasement faction of the Conservative Party (for example, Eden and Amery) to the full cabinet, he felt compelled to give the two leaders of the Appeasement majority—Halifax and Chamberlain—seats in the war cabinet. (His managerial strategy here illustrates a familiar adage, variously attributed to Sun Tzu, Niccolo Machiavelli, or the fictional godfather Vito Corleone: "Keep your friends close and your enemies closer.")

Churchill's strongest support within the war cabinet would come, in fact, from the Labour ministers. His strongest challenger would prove to be not the superseded Chamberlain, but Halifax, a rival who still privately saw himself as a better candidate for Prime Minister. The two men were, as numerous commentators have noted, temperamental opposites. Halifax's "inclination to seek compromises," his "profound dislike of anything overstated or overwrought," in Lukacs' words, made him particularly suspicious of the volatile, dramatic, and emphatic Prime Minister (Lukacs, 1999, p. 66). After Churchill's accession to office, the Foreign Secretary confided to his diary: "I have seldom met anybody with stranger gaps of knowledge, or whose mind works in greater jerks. Will it be possible to make it work in an orderly fashion? On this much depends. Certainly, we have not gained much in intellect" (quoted in Lukacs, 1999, p. 67). It is likely, the historian observes, that "Churchill understood Halifax better than Halifax understood Churchill." The beleaguered new Prime Minister's skillful handling of the "Holy Fox" during those crucial five days suggests just how true this was.

From the start, Churchill opposed Halifax's initiative to negotiate with the Germans. He was not, however, in a position to flatly veto it, especially if it would have led to Halifax's resignation from the war cabinet: "A real break between Churchill and the two eminent Conservatives would have been disastrous. Had Halifax or Chamberlain or both resigned, there would have been a national crisis, immediately reverberating in Parliament, and Churchill's position would have been gravely damaged, perhaps even untenable" (Lukacs, 1999, p. 71). The problem, of course, with having history on one's side, is that it only becomes apparent in retrospect. Churchill needed the war cabinet to be unanimous in its support if he was to have any chance of uniting the deeply divided Conservative Party behind his government. For that he needed to win over Halifax, or at least isolate him to the point of neutralizing his influence.

Halifax approached the issue of negotiation as a pragmatist, focusing his attention on what was likely to happen militarily in the immediate future, and on the effect of the anticipated disastrous military losses to the British Expeditionary Force in France on the UK's subsequent negotiating position (Lukacs, 1999, pp. 181–182). Churchill, in contrast, brought both a larger and a more visceral vision to the question, a vision conveyed in epic terms. He argued that, because the UK would be negotiating from a position of weakness, Germany would only settle for virtual destruction of the country's military capacity, loss of its colonies, and the establishment of a puppet government that would curtail civil liberties and treat so-called non-Aryan minorities with the same murderous criminality as in Germany. The only alternative was to defend democracy and liberty within the UK, preserving its military capacity and its Empire at all costs (pp. 127, 214).

Stark as the differences between them were, Churchill was careful at this point not to force Halifax's hand. Unsure of the extent of his own support, he made a carefully gauged concession, asking Halifax to outline his plan for using the Italians as intermediaries for negotiations and promising a full cabinet discussion (Lukacs, 1999, p. 117). At the same time, he stipulated that Archibald Sinclair, leader of the Liberal party, Secretary of State for the Air Force, and a firm supporter of Churchill, would be present for that subsequent discussion. It was a shrewd combination of cooptation and outflanking, conducted with a decorum that left Halifax no grounds for complaint.

The discussions of the following day, however, led to a more open split, with Halifax now attempting to force Churchill into an explicit (and potentially polarizing) statement of his policy, implying in veiled terms that he would resign if the answer were unsatisfactory: "His question was, simply and bluntly, Would Churchill consider *any* peace terms, at *any* time?"(Lukacs, 1999, p. 151). Churchill again refused to rise to the bait, working instead to defuse the situation, reining in his usual triumphalist rhetoric: "He would not join France in asking for terms; but if he were told what the terms offered were, he would be prepared to consider them" (p. 151). This was scarcely enough for Halifax, yet as much as Churchill felt he could concede.

It was at this fraught juncture that Halifax requested a recess and asked Churchill famously to "come out in the garden with him." It is a scene that should, by rights, play out as the climax of the narrative: the fate of nations hanging on the outcome of a single encounter. In fact, the crisis would not be resolved for another full day. Neither man left any account of the conversation in the garden, nor do the official minutes contain any record of what was said. Lukacs quotes Halifax's diary for the day in which he makes no mention of the garden walk, but does recount something of the discussion that preceded it: "I thought Winston talked about the most frightful rot, also Greenwood, and after bearing it for some time I said exactly what I thought of them, adding that, if that was really their view, and if it came to the point, our ways must be separate" (Lukacs, 1999, p. 155). With a historian's characteristic caution not to outrun his sources, Lukacs goes no further than to suggest an attempt by Churchill to impress on Halifax the need for cabinet unity and the disastrous consequences of a resignation at that time. It is, he writes, "very doubtful" that during that brief stroll Churchill was able to do more.[5]

Positioned between Churchill's heroic defiance and Halifax's grim and narrow pragmatism was the former Prime Minister Neville Chamberlain. And it was there that Churchill's earlier circumspection found its reward, for Chamberlain increasingly supported the new Prime Minister's position, and his continued influence within the Conservative party made that support all the more essential. (Churchill's tactful management of Chamberlain continued after his accession, inviting the former Prime Minister and his wife to remain at 10 Downing Street for several months after his resignation. Churchill himself lived at the Admiralty during that time.) While Chamberlain, more than any man present at the discussions, had reason to know the impossibility of making terms with Hitler, there is no doubt that Churchill's very public demonstrations of consideration and respect helped cement his allegiance at that critical time.[6]

On Tuesday, May 28, Churchill briefed the House of Commons on the progress of the war, specifically the status of the British Expeditionary Force at Dunkirk. He made no mention of the discussions within the war cabinet, speaking briefly (for him), and concluding with a declaration clearly addressed as much to the five men he would soon be meeting as to the uninformed House at large: "I have only to add that nothing which may happen in this battle [at Dunkirk] can in any way relieve us of our duty to defend the world cause to which we have vowed ourselves" (Lukacs, 1999, p. 179). Significantly, only two members chose to comment on the speech: one Labour, the other Liberal. No Conservative members were heard from.

Churchill went directly from the floor of the Commons to a nearby meeting room where he had asked his war cabinet to convene. The move was highly strategic. At 5 p.m., after another hour of fruitless debate, Churchill adjourned the meeting and went to his office. He had arranged to address the rest of the cabinet, a group in which his supporters in the anti-Appeasement faction were more abundantly represented, to enlist their support to sway or silence Halifax. He succeeded. Alluding in the most general terms to the possibility of opening negotiations, Churchill then outlined the stark choices facing Britain: capitulation and subjugation or continued all-out war, alone if necessary. The result was unanimous support for the resolve to fight on. As one participant recounted in his diary: "No one expressed even the faintest flicker of dissent" (Lukacs, 1999, p. 184).

At 7 p.m., armed with the knowledge of the full support of the rest of cabinet, Churchill returned to the war cabinet, reporting on the meeting he had just held, commenting, "He did not remember having ever before heard a gathering of persons occupying high places in political life express themselves so emphatically" (Lukacs, 1999, p. 185). This final piece of brilliantly stage-managed political theater was too much for Halifax. He offered no further opposition to the rejection of mediation by Italy, or any further discussion of a negotiated peace. Churchill had won, through an extraordinary combination of patience, vision, strategy, conciliation and—at the precise moment when it would do most good—carefully calibrated confrontation. What is extraordinary to remember is that all this was going on at precisely the same time that the evacuation from Dunkirk was being organized and carried out.

The narrative of the war cabinet crisis, Lukacs' five days in London, is undoubtedly a heroic one, but it is heroism of a kind largely ignored in the dominant Churchill fable that focuses almost exclusively on the inspirational public figure or the inspired military strategist. In fact, the first crisis of Churchill's wartime leadership came within the four walls of Downing Street, in five days of meetings with a small handful of men.[7] It was a crisis of political leadership, a crisis of political management. Had he not triumphed in that closed room, his story, and much else, would have been very different.

Given the richness of the historical record mined by Lukacs, Alan Axelrod's *Winston Churchill, CEO* (2009) reads increasingly like a wasted opportunity. The problem is encapsulated in the subtitle "25 Lessons for Bold Business Leaders." The book is constructed on a sustained analogy between the exceptional wartime leader who, undeterred by catastrophic military losses, "went about the business of saving his country" (Axelrod, 2009, p. 21) and corporate executives in the contemporary private sector.

The disjunction in scale is simply too great. (It is a dissonance highlighted by the bold-faced type on the dust jacket which proclaims, "We shall fight in the Boardrooms.") The book's premise is undoubtedly flattering to the egos of its intended readership, but the lessons offered often seem entirely unconnected to either Churchill or history. The application of Appeasement to the private sector ("Reject the Tyrant's Bargain"), to take the most relevant example, seems inappropriate to the point of incoherence. Axelrod counsels corporate leaders to "avoid extortionists or confront or defeat them" (p. 133). Is this to be read metaphorically and, if so, to whom does it refer? Who in this scenario plays the role of the genocidal Hitler? Or is this advice to be read literally as discouraging investment in countries where the rule of law is not well established? Is it a call to strengthen corporate security? Or to encourage businesses to report all attempts at extortion to the proper authorities?

I am not questioning the soundness of Axelrod's advice. That is beside the point. It is the insensitivity to context that amounts to a sort of narrative tone-deafness that I'm addressing. This is most evident in the book's last chapter, simply entitled "Win." Axelrod makes the rather obvious observation that the goal Churchill set for his nation was victory. He then recounts that on V-E Day (May 8, 1945), Churchill knew exactly what to say to the assembled crowds: "This is your victory." "No," the people shouted back, "It is yours." For Axelrod, this was "the perfect leadership moment, the moment at which leader and followers were revealed as one in purpose and values. It is the point of balance every great enterprise strives to attain" (Axelrod, 2009, p. 256). True enough. But what other enterprise could possibly be comparable to this one? Just what would "great" mean for the latter-day "bold business leaders"? Axelrod also praised Churchill for selling "the privilege of sacrifice" (p. 153), rather than selling an easier life, as most politicians would have done. He disingenuously omits, however, all mention of just how fleeting that perfect moment of unity proved to be for Churchill. The savior of the nation was defeated at the polls ten weeks later, rejected by those same ecstatic crowds who had now metamorphosed into an electorate looking for the promise of an easier life and convinced that Churchill was not the leader to provide it.

Focusing entirely on the most public, and dramatic, aspects of Churchill's wartime leadership, Axelrod pays little attention to the war cabinet crisis, despite its obvious relevance. While the chapter "Make Good Use of Adversity" refers to the crucial meetings in May 1940, it highlights only the triumphant full cabinet meeting on May 27 and the robust support Churchill received there, citing it as yet another instance of the great man's heroic defiance against all odds and his ability to redefine defeat (the British Expeditionary Force in France) as opportunity (Axelrod, 1999, pp. 160–168). Lost in the blaze of Churchillian rhetoric, which Axelrod quotes extensively, is the subtler narrative of political management we have been analyzing.

This is doubly disappointing as the chapter contains a very insightful analysis of the mechanics of Churchill's use of language, though couched in somewhat grandiose terms: "As armies of men crumbled beneath him, Churchill recruited an army of words" (Axelrod, 1999, p. 160). Axelrod's close reading here suggests that had he turned his attention to the differences in the public narratives Churchill and Chamberlain offered, for example, his observations would have been both shrewd and illuminating. (The importance of that comparison is a subject we will return to.) By limiting its purview to the Churchill of the dominant fable, *Winston Churchill, CEO* effectively focuses on the wrong narrative, choosing Churchill the heroic national leader over Churchill the skilled politician. In fact, as Jenkins and Lukacs in their different ways make plain, the two were inseparable. That was the genius of the man.

Churchill the Man: *The Gathering Storm* and *Into the Storm*

The opening frames of the 2009 docudrama *Into the Storm* show Churchill in his iconic hat and bow-tie exchanging glances with his famous ancestor, John Churchill, first Duke of Marlborough, on the battlefield of his most famous victory, Blenheim. It is, we learn later, a dream. The next shot cuts to a naked Churchill, filmed from behind, standing in his bathroom (urinating, in fact) and trying out fragments of oratory for a thundering parliamentary speech. The camera lingers almost lovingly on every detail of wrinkled sagging flesh (of which there is a considerable amount on display), clearly announcing the narrative's intention: to uncover the man behind the mythic figure, to show the hero laid bare. It is only the first of a number of such sequences both in this film and its companion *The Gathering Storm* (2002). And though two different actors play Churchill (Albert Finney in the earlier film, Brendan Gleeson in the later one), the emphasis on the distinctly unglamorous physical presence, all belly and sag, remains the same.

Again, the aim is not revisionism. Writer Hugh Whitemore and directors Richard Loncraine and Taddeus O'Sullivan are not seeking to counter the dominant Churchill fable. Instead, like Jenkins, though in a markedly different fashion, they attempt to maintain a double focus, interweaving in this case the public, heroic narrative with a private, much less triumphant story. When Churchill recounts his dream of Marlborough "riding off into history" to his wife, she remarks knowingly, "Stilton always gives you night-mares." It is both amusing and emblematic of the balance both *Into the Storm* and *The Gathering Storm* seek to maintain. The latter, which covers the period from the mid-1930s to Churchill's return to office at the Admiralty, spends considerable time exploring Churchill's financial difficulties (he is hover-ing near bankruptcy), his uncomprehending and unsuccessful attempts at parenting his generally disappointing offspring, and especially his volatile relationship with his long-suffering wife Clementine (played by Vanessa Redgrave). There is an extended scene of domestic tempest—Clementine throwing the lunch dishes; Churchill conciliating "Mrs. Pussycat" through a closed bedroom door—as well as several others that explore Churchill's fear of losing Clementine to another man. The Munich Agreement and Neville Chamberlain, in contrast, receive no screen time whatsoever. (The main political conflict depicted is between Churchill and Stanley Baldwin, Chamberlain's predecessor.) It is due largely to Finney's performance that the domestic drama enlarges rather than trivializes the figure of Churchill, suggesting the personal vulnerability, even insecurity that coexisted with the outsized ego and the unshakable belief in personal destiny.

Into the Storm (2009) employs a different doubled perspective, and here there is no question of downplaying the public narrative. On the contrary, so much incident is packed into the 98-minute film that it occasionally feels like a compendium of Churchill's "greatest hits," racing from one memo-rable public utterance (and extraordinary crisis) to another, slowing down only for an extended sequence showing a cross-section of English society, representative clusters of familiar English "types," listening to the broadcast of the famous "We shall fight on the beaches" speech. The double focus here is provided by the flashback time-frame employed. The movie begins with Winston and Clementine in France awaiting the results of the postwar election that would remove Churchill from office. (There was a consider-able delay between voting day and the announcement of the results, as large numbers of military votes from troops stationed overseas had to be count-ed.) His wartime triumph, then, is viewed, literally, from the perspective of the public rejection that followed and the "present day" Churchill (that is, the Churchill of the framing narrative) is shown to be restless, deeply irritable, inconsiderate, rude, irrationally obstinate, and increasingly out of touch—anything but heroic in fact.

These are narrative strategies that would appear to be designed, if not to resist the pull of the heroic myth, then at least to contextualize it: in the first instance through the emphasis on Churchill's personal struggles and failures, in the second through the structural reminder that Britain's indis-pensable wartime leader was very quickly dispensed with once the war had been won. *Into the Storm* is in no way unsympathetic to Churchill. In fact, its dramatizations of the wartime episodes explore in very familiar (mythologizing) terms his achievements and abilities. But the narrative also enacts his inability to shift from the pitch of crisis leadership to the less dramatic but no less crucial demands of postwar reconstruction. During the election campaign, Churchill gave a radio address replete with an exaggerated attack on the socialism of the Labour Party, implying that, if given power, it would enforce its policies through the creation of a British Gestapo. This deeply offended Labour Party voters who supported the wartime Government of National Unity. Labour leader Clement Attlee was entirely on the mark when he said that Churchill disillusioned his own followers. It is, the film implies, precisely the qualities that made him so successful as a war leader that disqualified him from an effective peace-time role. The 1945 election was the quintessential illustration that a rational electorate does not cast its vote as an expression of gratitude for an incumbent's past achievements, but rather as an attempt to chose the leader and policies most suited to future challenges.

While both films do succeed in restoring something of a human dimension to a figure who has long since become an icon, they too ultimately succumb to the power of the Churchillian myth. (*The Gathering Storm* ends, in fact, with a freeze-frame shot that fades to black and white, evoking not merely the famous wartime photos but Churchill's own reentry into history.) Perhaps it is simply that the events themselves are too dramatic to be contained by the personal narrative, or too momentous.

Churchill in Context: *The Gathering Storm* and *Troublesome Young Men*

Whatever its limitations as biography, *The Gathering Storm* does succeed in suggesting a more complex historical context for Churchill's struggle against Appeasement. Where the dominant fable tends to depict him as a solitary figure in the political wilderness, isolated by his prescience and unsupported by his party, screenwriter Hugh Whitemore interweaves Churchill's story with that of Ralph Wigram, a senior Foreign Office official who leaked secret documents concerning German rearmament for Churchill to use in his speeches against the Baldwin government. The movie makes clear the stakes involved for Wigram, who could have been convicted of a criminal offense for releasing the confidential documents. As suspicion mounts that it is he who is supplying the information that is enabling Churchill to attack the government with devastating detail and accuracy, Wigram is ostracized by colleagues and threatened by the Prime Minister's minions.

A self-confessed worrier about "almost everything"—"My wife. My son. The state of my finances. The state of the world. The state of my roof"—the slim, elegant, and sensitive Wigram is the polar opposite of the stocky and pugnacious Churchill. As his despair over his government's inaction mounts, he approaches breakdown, incapable of the resolution Churchill shows in driving off his own "melancholia." The poignancy of Wigram's story is compounded by the presence of Charlie, his profoundly disabled young son, who would have been murdered by the Nazis under their policy of "racial purity," a fact that clearly adds force to the father's principled opposition to continued Appeasement.

The historical Wigram died in 1936 of unexplained causes. *The Gathering Storm* depicts him as increasingly conflicted, frightened, and depressed, relying on Churchill's certainty and courage to sustain him. The narrative strongly suggests that his death was suicide (on Christmas morning, no less, to heighten the sacrificial symbolism) and includes a graveside scene where Churchill comforts Wigram's beautiful young wife with the assurance that his bravery and sacrifice will not have been wasted: "People often act heroically because they don't appreciate the dangers that lie ahead. Ralph saw those dangers and was afraid of them. But he did what he did in spite of his fear. No man can be braver than that." To which she can only reply (of course): "Thank you, Winston."

The narrative assumption is that by (indirectly) enabling Churchill to return to power, Wigram has made his contribution to history. The movie emphasizes Wigram's heroism because, unlike Churchill, he did not have the advantages of parliamentary immunity, independent income from his writing, and a national reputation. But here again we encounter the destabilizing effect on the narrative of the magnitude of the historical Churchill's achievement. However hard the movie works to place Wigram's heroism and tragedy at its center, his story is inevitably overshadowed, a footnote to the double redemption narrative of Churchill and England itself. The narrative appears to acknowledge as much when Wigram's grieving widow accepts Churchill's verdict on the meaning of her husband's story, gathers up her crying child and calmly departs the cemetery and the movie. (It's possible to imagine a much more unsettling coda to the Wigram story, focusing on the disabled son, but that would have overshadowed the subsequent scenes of Churchill's triumphant recall to office.)

Lynne Olson, the journalist author of *Troublesome Young Men: The Rebels Who Brought Churchill to Power and Helped Save England,* explicitly acknowledges the force field surrounding the story of Churchill in the 1940s, "one of the most compelling dramas in modern British history" (Olson, 2007, p. 7). The subtitle of her book makes plain that however heroic her subjects might have been in their struggles against Chamberlain's disastrous war policies, their ultimate significance lies in the assistance they provided to the man who would replace him. Her scrupulously researched and engagingly written study, then, proposes not an alternative fable, but a parallel one. Her focus is the group of young(ish) Tory backbenchers (her most frequent terms for them are "insurgents" and "dissidents," Chamberlain dismissively called them "glamour boys") who became the voice of opposition once Churchill had returned to office as First Lord of the Admiralty. Bound as he was by both the exigencies of cabinet solidarity and the need to prevent irreconcilable rifts between himself, Chamberlain, and Halifax (a key aspect of the political-managerial narrative we have discussed), Churchill himself could not publicly attack Chamberlain's half-hearted prosecution of the war in its early months. It fell to the rebels to do so, and to organize the parliamentary coup that led to the vote of confidence after the failure of the Norway invasion.

The story Olson tells is a compelling one: sons of privilege breaking with the gentlemanly traditions of their class, uniting to oppose their own party, bring down a government and save their country. The group included familiar names like Harold Macmillan and Anthony Eden, as well as less well-known figures Robert Boothby, Leo Amery, and Ronald Cartland. Olson is hampered somewhat by the fact that the heroic action she details largely took the form of political maneuvering, endless discussions of strategy, and the careful calibrations of influence and support that made possible the parliamentary insurrection of the Norway debate. She balances this with extensive details of the systematic harassment to which Chamberlain and the party establishment subjected the men they consider traitors (to the Tory party, if not the country itself): "They had been attacked as disloyal by the prime minister's many supporters in the press and government. Their phones had been tapped, their meetings spied on, their constituencies pressured to withdraw support from them at the next election" (Olson, 2007, p. 12). And she devotes considerable attention to the intertwined personal stories of the men (Macmillan's wife was conducting an affair with Boothby) and the "small, tight-knit, and insular" (p. 21) upper-class world they inhabited. The group portrait she paints is rich in detail. The evocation of the momentous months leading to Churchill's accession, the sense of a world hanging in the balance, is compelling. And the climax of the narrative, at the end of the Norway debate, with Amery's ringing denunciation "In the name of God, go" is deeply satisfying.

Much more than *The Gathering Storm*, which chose to focus solely on the bureaucratic supporters of Churchill, in particular the tragic Wigram, Olson's narrative makes clear that Churchill was not alone in opposing Chamberlain and that his return to power, far from being either inevitable or the result of his own unaided struggles, depended in great measure on the passionate conviction of other political figures; namely, the men who raised their voices and risked their careers. In the deeply moving words of the youngest of the troublesome young men, Ronald Cartland, who would die in battle on the road to Dunkirk, "No government can change men's souls. The souls of men change governments" (Olson, 2007, p. 7). The story of Cartland and his associates who changed a government when it was literally a question of life and death adds a necessary complexity to the dominant end-of-Appeasement fable, redressing the simplifications that have hardened into myth. (Re)placing Churchill within the full fabric of his historical and political milieu detracts nothing from his singularity. Without the Tory rebels, Churchill would not have become Prime Minister. Without Churchill, Halifax would undoubtedly have succeeded Chamberlain, followed by, we can speculate, a negotiated peace with Hitler. The single overriding factor remained Churchill himself.

"History Could Well Be Made Under this Roof": Ishiguro's Ironic Appeasement Fable

Speaking of *The Remains of the Day* in an interview published in the *New York Times* in 1989, Kazuo Ishiguro remarked: "I suppose I'm always trying to remind myself in my writing that while we may be very pleased with ourselves, we may look back with a different perspective, and see we may have acted out of cowardice and failure of vision. What I'm interested in is not the actual fact that my characters have done things they later regret, I'm interested in how they come to terms with it" (Graver, 1989). And one can read this first-person narrative of the butler Stevens recalling his life in service at Darlington Hall in the years leading to the Second World War as a masterful exploration of a belated coming to terms. Unfolding over the course of six days in the summer of 1956, the novel records Stevens' reflections as he journeys to a meeting with the woman he might have married some twenty years before. As his thoughts move backwards and forwards in time, the main threads of his personal narrative become increasingly intertwined: the story of Miss Kenton, the young woman who served as housekeeper at Darlington Hall whose love he failed to recognize or respond to in time, and that of Lord Darlington, the employer in the service of whom Stevens sublimated all hopes of personal emotional fulfillment.

This would be to read *The Remains of the Day* for its moving evocation of one man's belated journey to self-knowledge, culminating in an exquisite set-piece on a pier at twilight. For the astonishing artistic ventriloquism that creates Stevens' voice, a voice alternately comic and heartbreaking in its laborious formality, propriety, and self-repression.[8] For the skill with which Ishiguro deploys his self-deceived (or, in narratological terms, unreliable) narrator, generating bitter ironies from the distance between Stevens' own understanding and the other narrative he has so long suppressed, a narrative growing increasingly plain to the reader.

But this would be to ignore a dimension of the novel that broadens its thematic reach beyond the purely personal realm of moral consciousness Ishiguro invokes. For as Stevens journeys toward the knowledge of the life he might have had with Miss Kenton, he is also forced to recognize the truths he has refused to acknowledge for some twenty years: that his distinguished employer, Lord Darlington, that epitome of English gentlemanliness and aristocratic honor, was not merely a supporter of Appeasement, but a pawn in the hands of the Nazi regime who skirted dangerously close to treason; that all his lordship's desire for justice, and fair play, and decency did not prevent him from embracing a morally repugnant political and social creed; that the numerous "important international gatherings" (Ishiguro, 1989, p. 64) held at Darlington Hall in the 1920s and 1930s, events which represented, for Stevens, the pinnacle of his professional life, were simply cynical "propaganda tricks" (p. 224) devised by the Nazis to enlist aristocratic English voices against participation in the inevitable European war.

These fictional conferences of "powerful and influential gentlemen" (Ishiguro, 1989, p. 74) are, of course, another version of closed politics. And they structure Ishiguro's narrative, each memorable event of Stevens' recollected life coinciding with a gathering at Darlington Hall. In fact, Stevens makes explicit the larger meaning of these "off the record" events:

> The great decisions of the world are not, in fact, arrived at simply in the public chambers, or else during the handful of days given over to an international conference under the full gaze of the public and the press. Rather, debates are conducted, and crucial decisions arrived at, in the privacy and calm of the great houses of this country. What occurs under the public gaze with so much pomp and ceremony is often the conclusion, or mere ratification, of what has taken place over weeks or months within the walls of such houses. To us, then, the world was a wheel, revolving with these great houses at the hub, their mighty decisions emanating out to all else, rich and poor, who revolved around them. (p. 115)

C. P. Snow could not have put it better himself. If the closed politics of Churchill's war cabinet crisis represents the culmination of the end of Appeasement fable, the events at Darlington Hall are its fictional antithesis, an attempt by an unofficial opposition to force national policy (and history) in a different direction.

Ishiguro is drawing on elements of the historical Appeasement narrative here. Many English aristocrats in the interwar years were sympathetic to Hitler's Reich, a sympathy based on ties of friendship and even blood to the German aristocracy, but also on ideological affinities for the socially reactionary and anti-Semitic policies of the emerging Fascist regime. And it is known that Hitler's government sought to convert this sympathy to active support. (Darlington Hall and the meetings it hosted might have been inspired by accounts of the so-called Cliveden Set, a group of well-connected, upper-class German sympathizers associated with Viscountess Astor and named for her country house in Buckinghamshire.) There were secret talks between the German embassy and the highest levels of the British government about the situation in Czechoslovakia prior to Chamberlain's negotiation of the Munich Agreement in 1938 (Olson, 2007, p. 130). To imagine Darlington Hall as the scene of such meetings is not, therefore, stretching the historical record unduly. The climax of *The Remains of the Day* comes, in fact, on the evening when Lord Darlington hosts the German ambassador, von Ribbentrop, the Prime Minister Neville Chamberlain, and the Foreign Secretary Lord Halifax. The narrative remains with Stevens discreetly outside the door of the room where "the most powerful gentlemen of Europe were conferring over the fate of our continent" (Ishiguro, 1989, p. 227).

That Ishiguro also makes this evening the turning point in Stevens' relationship with Miss Kenton suggests the skill with which he intertwines the personal and the political narratives. As the young housekeeper makes one last effort to break through Stevens' self-suppression, telling him of her engagement to another man and all but inviting him to propose to her himself, he withdraws still further into the shell of his professional duty: "I do not mean to be rude, Miss Kenton, but I really must return upstairs without further delay. The fact is, events of a global significance are taking place in this house at this very moment" (Ishiguro, 1989, p. 218).[9]

It is a familiar "upstairs, downstairs" structure, the drama of the servants' hall mirroring and commenting upon events in the master's drawing room. What sets Ishiguro's use of it apart are the political and historical resonances Stevens' story carry. Between the lines of the butler's recollections can be read a fable of the death of the aristocratic political ideal and the final painful awakening of the English working class from centuries of political deference. For Stevens, the son of a butler (his father will in fact die in service at Darlington Hall), to be "in service" to an employer at the center of closed politics who embodies "all that I find noble and admirable"

(Ishiguro, 1989, p. 201), to serve him with utmost loyalty, subordinating all personal and emotional needs to his, is the most he can aspire to. "One is simply accepting an inescapable truth," he remarks near the end of his journey, "the likes of you and I will never be in a position to comprehend the great affairs of today's world, and our best course will always be to put our trust in an employer we judge to be wise and honourable, and to devote our energies to the task of serving him to the best of our ability" (p. 201).

The larger meaning of Stevens' literally self-effacing devotion to "service" is made plain in a scene of painful humiliation. Several of Lord Darlington's political guests have been having "rather too good a dinner," in Darlington's words, and the butler is summoned to be cross-questioned on the state of international affairs. To each increasingly more abstruse question—"Do you suppose the debt situation regarding America is a significant factor in the present low levels of trade?" "Would you say that the currency problem in Europe would be made better or worse if there was to be an arms agreement between the French and the Bolsheviks?" "What was M. Laval really intending, by his recent speech on the situation in North Africa?"—Stevens replies "I am sorry, sir, but I am unable to assist in this matter" (Ishiguro, 1989, p. 196). His tormentor then turns to the appreciative audience and remarks, "And yet, we still persist with the notion that this nation's decisions be left in the hands of our good man here and to the few million others like him."

As Stevens recalls the episode, he expresses no animus against either the "gentleman" who humiliates him, or Lord Darlington, who does nothing to intervene. Indeed, the conclusion he draws from it is precisely what his interlocutor could have hoped:

> The fact is, such great affairs will always be beyond the understanding of those such as you and I, and those of us who wish to make our mark must realize that we best do so by concentrating on what is within our realm; that is to say, by devoting our attention to providing the best possible service to those great gentlemen in whose hands the destiny of civilization truly lies. (Ishiguro, 1989, p. 199)

What is shocking is not the antidemocratic, quasi-Fascist views exchanged over the port and cigars by these various representatives of the upper classes. Ishiguro's pitch-perfect evocation of their voices has, as we've noted, ample historical support. It is Stevens' collusion in his own subordination, his insistence on the natural fitness of a political order that demeans and excludes him.

The narrative in the book clearly contrasts Stevens' self-abnegation and deference with an emblematic working-class figure, Harry Smith, whom he meets on his later journey. Smith is a local political organizer, scarcely a radical, but with a strong conviction of his responsibility to make sure *his* voice, and the voices of others like him, are heard "in high places" (Ishiguro, 1989, p. 189). And it is precisely his encounter with Smith that prompts Stevens to recall the earlier scene of his humiliation. The movie adaptation dispenses with Smith, but is equally careful to offer a working-class antithesis to Stevens, in the character of Miss Kenton's fiancé, Mr. Benn. Benn, too, is "in service," but he is determined to leave to start his own business, a humble smokeshop, expressing in clear terms both his desire for independence and his disgust at Lord Darlington's pro-Nazi sympathies, and the two are clearly linked. What's more, Benn (and Miss Kenton) reject Stevens's repressive disapproval of romantic relationships among the staff.

The handling of Darlington's political beliefs, what we can call the novel's Appeasement plot, marks one of the key differences between the film adaptation and the novel. Where Ishiguro allows Stevens to reveal only gradually the reasons why "a great deal of nonsense has been spoken and written in recent years concerning his lordship and the prominent role he came to play in great affairs" (Ishiguro, 1989, p. 61), Ruth Prawer Jhabvala's screenplay early establishes popular opinion of Darlington Hall as "a traitors' nest." Much of Darlington's backstory is also omitted. Where the novel details his gradual progression from sympathy for the plight of a German friend ruined in the hyperinflation after World War One (the friend commits suicide), to a conviction that the Treaty of Versailles, with its punitive war reparations, is an affront to the gentlemanly code by which such affairs ought to be managed—"'It is unbecoming to go on hating an enemy like this once a conflict is over. Once you've got a man on the canvas, that ought to be the end of it. You don't then proceed to kick him'" (p. 87)—to outright admiration for the Fascist regimes of Germany and Italy, which have "set their houses in order" (p. 198), the film version presents him as already fully embroiled in, and a dupe of, the pro-Nazi cause. The movie reemphasizes this point as Ambassador von Ribbentrop, arriving for his meeting with Chamberlain and Halifax, notices Darlington's magnificent art collection and in German asks an aide to make detailed notes about the paintings for future use.

The choice is part of the telescoping and compression necessary in adapting what is essentially an interior monologue covering two decades in a life for the screen. The series of international gatherings depicted in the novel is equally compressed for the film, which features only one such unofficial "conference" and pushes it significantly closer to the outbreak of war (from 1923 to 1936), thereby heightening the irresponsible (even treasonous) folly of Darlington's actions. This does not sacrifice, however, anything of the effect of Stevens' devastating realization of the truth of Lord Darlington's story. Not that this "classic English gentleman" is not "decent, honest, well-meaning" (Ishiguro, 1989, p. 102), but that he is all these things and also disastrously, almost catastrophically wrong in his sympathies and beliefs, obstinately clinging to an outmoded political and social ethos that has made him a pawn in the hands of a murderous regime.

The movie is aided immeasurably in this by the casting of James Fox in the role of Lord Darlington, whom Roger Ebert in his original review of the film rightly called "that most urbane and civilized actor" (1993), and by the trademark sumptuousness of the movie's period visual elements. The amber glow that typically bathes a Merchant-Ivory film, the impeccable costuming, and the lavishly detailed sets all work to imbue Darlington Hall with an elegance and an Englishness that are undeniably seductive. We feel, with Stevens, that there is something noble and fine in the life that is unfolded before us. The dissonance created by the growing awareness of what is really happening at Darlington is all the more disquieting for the beauty of the place and the charm and decency of its owner.[10]

The end of Lord Darlington's story is revealed by Stevens in his final meeting with Miss Kenton. As he reports his conversation with her, in which he learns that she had loved him and hoped to marry him, we learn that "throughout the war some truly terrible things had been said about his lordship," which he bore in silence "while the country remained in peril" (Ishiguro, 1989, p. 235). After the war, he sued for libel the newspaper that had been particularly loud in its denunciations. "His lordship sincerely believed he would get justice. Instead, of course, the newspaper simply increased its circulation. And his lordship's good name was destroyed for ever." He ends his days a recluse. Darlington can be seen as a paradigmatic illustration of the tragic outcomes in Erik Erikson's life cycle theory. Despite being handsome, wealthy, and titled, Darlington has no partner. His life's work turns out to have been, in Stevens's apt words, "a sad waste," and he passes his last years in despair and regret.

The end of Stevens' own narrative comes two days later as he reflects on the life he has failed to claim for himself and the tragic errors of the master he served so loyally, reserving his harshest judgment for himself. Sitting on a seaside pier at twilight, watching the passing crowds as the last daylight disappears, Stevens strikes up a conversation with a sympathetic stranger in the course of which he delivers an epitaph for himself, no less than Darlington:

> Lord Darlington wasn't a bad man. He wasn't a bad man at all. At least he had the privilege to say at the end of his life that he made his own mistakes. His lordship was a courageous man. He chose a certain path in life, it

proved a misguided one, but there, he chose it, he can say that at least. As for myself, I cannot even claim that. You see, I *trusted*. I trusted in his lordship's wisdom. All those years I served him, I trusted I was doing something worthwhile. I can't even say I made my own mistakes. Really—one has to ask oneself—what dignity is there in that? (Ishiguro, 1989, p. 243)

The film version transposes this revelation to a slightly earlier point in the narrative, muting its desolation somewhat as Stevens confesses, "You see, in my own small way, I did make my own mistake. But I still might have a chance to set mine right." The final movement of the film is thus reserved for Stevens's encounter with Miss Kenton, his understanding of her feelings, and his realization of everything he has lost forever. He then returns to Darlington Hall and to his life there, the final frames of the movie an increasingly distant view of his face framed (immured?) in a window.

It is hard to quarrel with the filmmakers' choice when it affords as fine an actor as Anthony Hopkins the chance to register by the subtlest play of expression in his eyes the repressed anguish of Stevens as he contemplates the prospect of the empty years ahead of him, and the wasted ones behind. It is hard, in fact, to imagine any actor playing repressed emotion more heartbreakingly than Hopkins does throughout the film. Yet placing the emphasis so fully on the emotional, rather than the political, narrative tends to diminish the force of a novel that so expertly interweaves the two.

It is this interweaving that makes *The Remains of the Day* so valuable as a counter-narrative within our analysis. Ishiguro commented in a radio interview broadcast on the BBC World Service in 2007 on his choice of Stevens as protagonist: "I thought a butler was a perfect metaphor for the relationship of ordinary people to political power."[11] It might also be a perfect metaphor for the relationship between public servants and politicians, whereby the former are constrained to obey and implement the decisions of the latter, even if they think them misguided. The other narratives we have been considering in this chapter focus on extraordinary leaders in extraordinary times, heroes (Churchill, Wigram, the Tory rebels) on the right side of history. Among the many remarkable things this extraordinarily moving novel does is to give voice to the other side of the heroic fable, not only to those who chose the wrong cause, but also to those ordinary individuals caught up in the cross-currents. Does reading (or watching) *The Remains of the Day* help us to analyze the managerial implications of the end of Appeasement fable? Perhaps not. Does Ishiguro's narrative enlarge our understanding of the moral implications of Appeasement and of the mindset of those who initially supported it and those who even years later were unable to renounce it? Does it question in a subtle and searching way our own relationship to the leaders we choose and the heroes we venerate and the stories we tell of them? Yes, I believe it does.

Conclusion: Leaders and Narratives

All the variants of the end of Appeasement fable we've been considering have been narratives of leadership. But we can also consider them as stories about leaders and narratives. And that is, in fact, what two leaders have done. For very different reasons, and from very different perspectives, both President John F. Kennedy and Prime Minister Tony Blair have considered the narrative of Appeasement and its lessons. For both, those lessons are inseparable from ideas about narrative. In his recently published memoir *A Journey* (2010), Blair recounts a day spent at Chequers (the Prime Minister's country residence) early in his tenure, planning strategy with his advisers. Despite all the external markers of success (the electoral victory, the strong public support), he is troubled by "an anxiety that something was missing, some dimension barely glimpsed, let alone understood, but important, crucial even" (Blair, 2010, p. 207). As he thinks about the history of the room in which he is sitting, his thoughts are drawn to Chamberlain, whose private diaries still sit on the shelves. He reflects on the odium that attaches to Chamberlain's name—"A comparison to Chamberlain is one of the worst British political insults"—and questions the justice of the place he is habitually assigned in the narrative of the early war years: "Yet what did he do? In a world still suffering from the trauma of the Great War, a war in which millions died including many of his close friends and family, he had grieved; and in his grief pledged to prevent another such war. Not a bad ambition; in fact, a noble one" (p. 207). Blair then recalls leafing through Chamberlain's diaries and discovering his account of the now infamous meeting with Hitler at the Berchtesgaden prior to the signing of the Munich Agreement. Chamberlain's fatal mistake, he concludes, was not in trusting that a madman (and Chamberlain fully recognized Hitler as such) could be contained by treaties. "The mistake was in not recognizing the fundamental question…Does fascism represent a force that is so strong and rooted that it has to be uprooted and destroyed?" (p. 208)

In other words, Chamberlain had misread the historical and political narrative and, having done so, had lost the means to respond appropriately: "By 1938, fascism was culminating in a force that was not going to act according to Chamberlain's canons of reason, but according to the emotions of [its] ideology" (Blair, 2010, p. 209). Moreover, driven by the urgency of his own personal story, and the scenes of public euphoria that greeted him on his return brandishing that infamous paper, Chamberlain allowed the signing of the Munich Agreement "to be a moment that seemed strategic not tactical" (p. 208). Instead of presenting the Agreement to the public as a necessary evil, a means to contain a madman until some measure of sanity could be restored in Germany, Chamberlain lost control of the public narrative too.

This failure is tragically apparent in the radio broadcast Chamberlain made announcing the declaration of war on September 3, 1939. (It can be heard in its entirety at http://www.youtube.com/watch?v=qtrOJnpmz6s.) He begins the speech from a purely personal rather than national perspective—"You can imagine what a bitter blow it is to me that all my long struggle to win peace has failed"—and devotes the bulk of his remarks to recounting the complicated diplomatic maneuvering by which war was supposed to have been averted. Only in the penultimate sentence does he even begin to engage what should have been the essence of the speech, the presentation of the new narrative that would now govern the nation's fate: "For it is evil things that we shall be fighting against: brute force, bad faith, injustice, oppression, and persecution." It was left to Churchill, speaking later that day in the House of Commons, to articulate the national, indeed global, narrative that had motivated him and his supporters for so many years, and that would quickly become England's story too: "This is not a question of fighting for Danzig or fighting for Poland. We are fighting to save the whole world from the pestilence of Nazi tyranny and in defence of all that is sacred to man. . . . It is a war to establish on impregnable rocks, the rights of the individual, and it is a war to establish and revive the stature of man" (Churchill, 1939).

In 1940, John F. Kennedy completed his senior honors thesis at Harvard on the subject of British military spending between the two world wars. Entitled *Why England Slept*, an allusion to Winston Churchill's *While England Slept*, an attack on the Munich Agreement published two years before, it was originally intended to be a purely private research paper. Kennedy's father persuaded him to publish it, and it went on to sell 80,000 copies in the UK and United States. Although it now mostly reads as the undergraduate thesis it originally was, *Why England Slept* contains one highly significant passage of analysis, in which the future president addresses the same fatal flaw Tony Blair had noted: the blindness that comes from misreading the political narrative. But there is more. For Kennedy, Chamberlain's ultimate failure was his inability to acknowledge, or respond to, the polyphony of the narrative confronting him. Kennedy writes:

> There is no doubt that Chamberlain made considerable efforts to build up England's armaments. At the same time, he had so much hope and confi-

dence in his appeasement policy that he could not conceive of a war being inevitable. The result is that his energies were split. Although, in one sense, his two aims were harmonious, in another sense, they pulled in opposite directions. A boxer cannot work himself into proper psychological and physical condition for a fight he believes will never come off. (Kennedy, 1940, p. 157)

As we will see in our discussion of the Cuban Missile Crisis, one of the extraordinary features of Kennedy's leadership was the combination of flexibility and resolve he consistently demonstrated. Kennedy refused to be limited ("locked in" in contemporary terms) by the escalating response scenarios his military advisers were advocating from the first hours of the crisis. His insistence on canvassing all possible options, of considering every way of averting a confrontation, even while preparing fully for that eventuality, were decisive. No less so was the careful control over, and communication of his government's narrative of the crisis. Kennedy and his family were present in England for Neville Chamberlain's radio broadcast. They were in the House of Commons for Churchill's speech. They were in London when the first German bombs began to fall. John Kennedy had read the narrative of Appeasement closely—firsthand. Clearly, he had learned its lessons well.

Endnotes

1. I capitalize Appeasement to refer to British policy regarding Nazi Germany up to declaration of war in 1939, distinguishing it from the inevitably pejorative term of reference for a policy of nonconfrontation and accommodation of an (unspecified) aggressor state, which is not capitalized.
2. Business book writers still show a decided preference for military figures as subjects and models. There are at work here both a self-aggrandizing impulse and a tendency to conceive of competition in the marketplace in terms of military analogies. It will be interesting to see if, as more women reach higher levels of corporate management, the bias toward heroic exemplars and battle metaphors and analogies begins to shift.
3. Jenkins' father was a coal miner and later Labour MP who rose to the rank of junior minister. Despite his life-long affiliation, Jenkins himself grew increasingly disenchanted with the "hard left" policies pursued by Labour in the 1970s. He was a member of the so-called Gang of Four, senior Labour figures who left the party to form the Social Democratic Party in 1981.
4. Lukacs' personal narrative is clearly relevant here. Born Janos Lukacs in Hungary in 1924 to a Christian father and a Jewish mother, he was forced to serve in a labor battalion during the early war years, barely escaping deportation to a death camp after the fall of Hungary in 1944. He fled to the United States in 1946, where he became, not surprisingly, a student and then a professor of European history, and a life-long admirer of Churchill.

5. Not all writers have been equally restrained. Michael Dobbs, the author of the *House of Cards* series, has also written four historical novels dealing with Churchill and the war years: *Winston's War, Never Surrender, Churchill's Hour,* and *Churchill's Triumph.* His motivation for doing so, he reveals on his Web site, was to use the resources of fiction "to fill in the gaps and gain a more complete understanding" of events and personalities than can be supplied by historians working from "fragmentary and incomplete" historical records (www.michaeldobbs.com/uk/index.php?id=9,0,0,1,0,0). One of the gaps he seeks to fill is precisely that famous walk in the garden. In his entirely fictional version, Churchill secures Halifax's support through self-described "deception and a bald lie": that if, after the evacuation from Dunkirk is complete, the cabinet decides to negotiate, he will step aside and "hold my silence" (Dobbs, 2003, p. 229). Halifax agrees to abandon the Italian option, and Churchill buys himself time with a few false promises. What might not be clear from this episode is that Dobbs is an ardent admirer of Churchill, even if he cannot help re-creating him in the image of Francis Urquhart, or embellishing already momentous historical events with fictional storylines replete with his trademark blackmail, betrayal, manipulation, and general "skullduggery." He notes cheerfully in the acknowledgments to *Never Surrender* that he has "taken all the dramatic liberties required to construct what I hope is an enjoyable read" (p. 341). Many of those liberties involve Churchill himself, creating a portrait of an indisputably heroic leader who yet appears to be operating within the political world of the cynical dominant fable of the postwar era and embracing its ethos wholeheartedly. One might call this an instance of internarrative polyphony. At times it appears closer to cacophony.

6. Chamberlain was discovered to have terminal colon cancer in July 1940 and died the following November. In the last months of Chamberlain's life, Churchill kept him in the war cabinet until he chose to resign and made sure he was sent cabinet papers until his death.

7. There was a final chapter in Churchill's relationship with Halifax. In December 1940, the British ambassador to the United States died, and Churchill appointed Halifax to replace him. His political standing enhanced by successful defense from air attacks in the Battle of Britain, Churchill no longer wanted or needed Halifax at the center of strategic decision making. He felt (correctly, subsequent events showed) that Halifax would faithfully represent the government to its most important ally (Lukacs, 1999, p. 204). Churchill also had his own direct lines of communication to President Roosevelt.

8. One could give many examples of Stevens' voice. Here is how he handles his choice to remain at his duties while his father was on his deathbed in the servants' quarters: "if you consider the pressures contingent on me that night, you may not think I delude myself unduly if I go so far as to suggest that I did perhaps display, in the face of everything, at least in some modest degree a 'dignity' worthy of . . . my father" (Ishiguro, 1989, p. 110).

9. Stevens's recollection of that evening included pride at his smooth handling of his professional responsibilities without being distracted by Ms. Kenton's emotional state. In addition to questioning the latter, both the novel and movie question even the former. That evening, Lord Darlington has a sur-

prise visit from his godson Reginald Cardinal, a journalist strongly opposed to Appeasement, who has received a tip about the meeting. Darlington banishes Cardinal to the basement. Cardinal accosts Stevens, saying "over in that room—and I don't need you to confirm it—there are gathered at this moment the British Prime Minister, the Foreign Secretary, and the German Ambassador...Do you know Stevens, what is going on here?" Stevens replies, "I'm afraid not sir" (Ishiguro, 1989, pp. 221–222). Of course, Cardinal was looking for confirmation and Stevens' answer, based on an acceptance of Cardinal's premise, provided it. Cardinal's article the next day would likely begin, "Unnamed sources at Darlington Hall confirmed that Prime Minister Chamberlain, Foreign Secretary Halifax, and German Ambassador von Ribbentrop met here last night."

10. Ishiguro (2005) also used this technique in his more recent novel *Never Let Me Go*, which initially appears to be about students at a boarding school in a pleasant countryside setting, but the reader slowly discovers a much more tragic story.

11. An audio version of the interview for the World Book Club can be accessed at www.bbc.co.uk/worldservice/specials/133_wbc_archive_new/page3.html. The interview also includes a brief but revealing discussion of Ishiguro's long-standing fascination with "what happens when social values in a country do a sort of topsy-turvy, leaving a whole generation stranded morally almost." Ishiguro was born in Nagasaki in 1954. His two novels preceding *The Remains of the Day* set personal narratives of failure and disillusion against the backdrop of recent Japanese history.

5

Cynicism, Idealism, Compromise

American Political Fables

Yes, Mr. President: American Political Fables in Context

The president (senator, congressman, mayor, candidate) is a cynical power seeker, loyal to no ideology larger than self-interest. A dabbler in dirty tricks who condones, if he does not practice, blackmail, press manipulation, intimidation, unauthorized surveillance, and occasionally murder. His marital unfaithfulness/sexual license is a marker of his moral failure. The political system he exploits is a by-now familiar witches brew of influence peddling, hypocrisy, special interest lobbying, self-seeking, and personal betrayal. A threat of violence—assassination or suicide—looms over his story.

The president (senator, congressman, mayor, candidate) is a pragmatist. A fundamentally decent man who might yet be motivated by principles of service to a larger ideal, but one who has occasionally bowed to the realities of "the system" as it exists. A flawed man who might have made one too many deals with the devil. A man who understands the necessity of compromise, of working within the "real world," but one who might have compromised himself too much in the process. The threat of violence has

---

Governing Fables: Learning from Public Sector Narratives, pages 135–175
Copyright © 2011 by Information Age Publishing
All rights of reproduction in any form reserved.

receded from his story, but still lingers. His fate, like his moral status, is often left unresolved.

The president (senator, congressman, mayor, candidate) is a grand old lion. He is Frederic March, facing down a conspiracy of his own generals in *Seven Days in May*, or Spencer Tracy, dying at inordinate length in *The Last Hurrah*, speaking out for the values of service, loyalty, decency, integrity, and community. He is the heroic (and aging) defender of patriotic/civic values increasingly under siege, the incarnation of all that is good in the American democratic tradition.

The president is Josiah "Jed" Bartlet of *The West Wing*, television's longest-serving Chief Executive. He is a man of wisdom, principle, and pragmatism. Loyal to his political ideals, yet skilled at the compromises and power games necessary to enact those ideals as policy. A man capable of compromise without sacrificing either his integrity or his vision for the nation. He is the presiding genius of a narrative that is sophisticated in its representation of the complex realities of contemporary American politics, yet idealistic enough to insist on the possibility of politicians like Bartlet being elected and even reelected.

What is striking about American postwar political fables is just how many of them there are. And how often a single narrative will incorporate more than one within its structure. The scenarios just outlined encapsulate narrative archetypes recurring across decades; fables that coexist and persist, creating a narrative field as diverse and multivoiced as the polity it takes for its subject. This chapter will consider representative examples of all these fables, concluding with an extended analysis of Aaron Sorkin's landmark television series *The West Wing*. This favored status deserves some explanation. It is not merely the sophistication of the dialogue, the intelligence with which complex political issues are dramatized, the appealing performances, or the heartening spectacle of seven seasons' worth of really smart (and generally attractive) people arguing passionately over issues of public policy and governance. What makes *The West Wing* so important for our purposes is the way it draws upon elements of all three of the operative fables—the cynical, the compromised, and the nostalgic/heroic—to create something genuinely new within the tradition of American political narrative.

For some scholars, it should be noted, such a tradition simply does not exist. Philip Gianos (1998), for example, contends that "nothing approaching a developed political film genre has ever taken root in the United States." Indeed, he believes "the United States has developed over the years a richer film vocabulary for gangsters, cowboys, and mummies raised from the dead than it has for citizens and presidents" (p. 7). Similarly, Christensen and

Haas (2005, p. 5) argue that political films lack the established and familiar conventions of plot and character found in other genres and claim that the audience for political films is so small that filmmakers, in pursuit of a larger market, are forced to incorporate elements of other genres, such as comedy, action-adventure, or romance if the movies are to be made at all.[1] To the extent that film scholars have identified a dominant fable for the political film genre, it is the cynical one with which I began (Chase, 2003, p. 529; Christensen & Haas, 2005, pp. 12, 278–279; Giglio, 2005, p. 250).

Clearly this chapter draws very different conclusions. Not only does it identify a diverse set of political narratives and the archetypal fables that inform them, but we begin by analyzing the unique features of the American political system and its culture that are reflected in the content of these otherwise very different narratives. The obvious comparators here are the British narratives on government that we examined in chapters 3 and 4. Where the British stories consistently focus on governing and the interactions of elected politicians and career public servants, the American narratives highlight politics, political appointments, and campaigning. Since many American political appointees must be confirmed by the Senate, and confirmation hearings give senators a mandate to examine an appointee's entire life, there is a tendency within the American political narrative to focus more on the personal life—the extramarital entanglements, mental and physical health issues, financial and family backgrounds—of protagonists, with converging private/public plotlines a common occurrence. Thus, a key policy issue coincides with a personal crisis; there is a dramatic private reason for the protagonist's public stance. The tight nexus between policy advocacy, political decisions, and campaign funding that characterizes American politics ensures that money (campaign financing) is always an important plot mechanism. The advice the informant "Deep Throat" gives to the *Washington Post* reporters Woodward and Bernstein in their investigation of the Watergate break-in—"Follow the money"—could be a tag line for many of the narratives we will be considering. Finally, campaign finance laws permitting interest groups and individuals to make large donations to political campaigns or to political action committees, coupled with frequent elections (particularly the two-year terms of members of the House of Representatives) ensures a fertile ground for plots centering on corruption, influence peddling, and, conversely, heroic resistance to pressure groups and lobbyists seeking to subvert the national interest.

These are structural features of the American political system, reflected in the plot structures and character relationships of the narratives that engage with it. But we noted at the outset another distinctive feature: the range of fables operating within this narrative set. Unlike the British narratives that tend to share public-choice assumptions positing a political world ruled by self-interest and personal ambition (even when individual protagonists prove exceptions, they are routinely defeated by the Francis Urquharts and Malcolm Tuckers), a significant subset of American political narratives consistently allow a greater range, and mix, of motivations and outcomes (what we are calling the narratives of compromise). In this respect, they are closer in outlook to Peter Morgan's Tony Blair trilogy than to *Yes Minister* or its successors.

This difference can be attributed in part to the tendency of the American narratives to focus much more on the personal development of their central protagonists, to frame the narrative in personal terms, whether as a *bildungsroman* or story of apprenticeship (the 1972 Robert Redford film *The Candidate*) or as a tale of midlife crisis and/or reinvention (Warren Beatty's *Bulworth,* 1998). If we recall the four-quadrant categorization outlined in Chapter 1 (Table 1.1), most of the British narratives of government we've considered group in the lower cells, with both protagonists and the political system within which they operate clearly in decline (moral if not material). As we examine the three sets of American narratives we have termed fables of cynicism, compromise, and heroism/nostalgia, we will find they disperse across all four quadrants of our schema, with *The West Wing* occupying a special position. While its protagonists—I include in this group not just the president but the key members of his staff—operate within a (fictional) political universe that shares many of the structural features of the cynical fable, they themselves retain their integrity, their idealism, and their commitment to service, emerging from the Bartlet administration with their principles and their personal lives intact. It is a happy ending for grown-ups who take politics seriously (and don't mind a little stars and stripes sentimentality along the way) and one inconceivable within the British narrative universe.

A brief word about selection. The narratives chosen for analysis in this chapter represent a very small sampling of a very large field. While I have tried to include examples from a range of eras, I have not attempted a chronological survey, and many titles have been excluded that could certainly have been discussed, but that would have made an already long chapter punitively so. What I present here is an alternative interpretive narrative, not an exhaustive one.

"This is Hardball": The Cynical Fable

Four of the five narratives we will be considering here were produced in the 1990s, a particularly fruitful period for political cynicism fostered by the policy shortcomings of the Clinton Administration—the Monica Lewinsky scandal, the impeachment vote, and the Kenneth Starr investigation—as well as the unprecedented rancorousness of political discourse and the virulent mutual animosity of the major political parties. We begin, however, with the grandfather of contemporary American narratives of political corruption, the 1949 film *All the King's Men*, directed by Robert Rossen and adapted for the screen from the Pulitzer Prize-winning 1946 novel of the same name by Robert Penn Warren. Inspired (if that is the right term) by the life and death of notorious Louisiana governor Huey Long, a radical populist nicknamed The Kingfish, *All the King's Men* is the story of Willie Stark, a self-made country lawyer, who enters politics in a primarily rural southern state as a populist and reformer. Campaigning on a platform of class resentment and economic grievance—"You wanna know what my platform is? Here it is. I'm gonna soak the fat boys and spread it out thin"—Stark wins the governorship on the strength of his powerful common-man rhetoric and despite the efforts of the Democratic party establishment's machine: "I'm the hick they were gonna use to split the hick vote. But I'm standing right here now on my hind legs! Even a dog can learn to do that. Are you standing on your hind legs? Have you learned to do that yet?"

While making good on the promises made to the increasingly wild mobs who elected him, delivering a college, museum, medical center, and four-lane highway to the unnamed "redneck" state he will control like a private kingdom, Stark becomes a dangerous demagogue, employing the state police as a private army to intimidate opponents, mobilizing crowds of impoverished supporters to march on the state capitol when charged with corruption, and driving at least one critic to suicide with the threat of public exposure of a long-forgotten misdeed. Stark's story ends, as Long's did, in assassination, gunned down by a scion of the patrician family he has brought to ruin.

The novel was narrated by a young journalist, Jack Burden, who is drawn increasingly into Stark's orbit. And it is his "old South" family that is destroyed by their contact with "the Boss." The film retains Burden as narrator, framing the action in retrospective voice-over. But the movie's heart is clearly Stark, played with uncouth and ferocious energy by the bull-like character actor Broderick Crawford. Contemporary critics like Bosley Crowther (1949), reviewing the film for the *New York Times*, focused on Stark the corrupt populist, singling out for praise the filmmakers' "frightening comprehension of the potential of demagoguery in this land." But Crowther also noted the care with which the movie traces Stark's evolution from a poor but honest defender of the little man against the "bosses" who exploit and manipulate him to a corrupt and brutal political boss himself, discovering, as Crowther memorably puts it, "the strange intoxication of his own unprincipled charm."

It is this aspect of the film that is central to our concerns. Stark embodies the essential premise of the American cynical fable: the political process is irredeemably corrupt and anyone who engages in it will succumb to its infection. The only difference between Stark and his "gentlemanly" opponents is the lack of pretense with which he bullies, browbeats, manipulates, lies, and plots. It would be too much to claim Stark as an antihero. The narrative is much too eager to dispose of him (on the steps of the statehouse no less). But there is a conspicuous absence of any narrative counterbalance to him, no other character who suggests a different possibility. It is all hypocrisy, lies, deception, greed, and the drive for power for its own sake. It is a story that will be retold, with minor variations, in all four of the successor narratives we will consider.

All the King's Men was remade in 2006 by writer/director Steven Zaillian, the Academy Award-winning screenwriter of *Schindler's List*. Zaillian, who claimed never to have seen the original film, transposed the action from the Depression to the 1950s. The novel clearly looks back to the populist political movements of the 1920s and 1930s (not just Huey Long, but still more sinister figures like Father Charles Coughlin, founder of the "Nation's Union for Social Justice" in 1934 with a membership that reached into the millions, and broadcaster of anti-Semitic radio diatribes railing against Jewish bankers and big business), as does the 1949 film adaptation, a thematic concern noted in contemporary reviews. Zaillian might have felt the historical resonances to be too remote for an early 21st-century audience, preferring to invoke the hysteria of the McCarthy era. (George Clooney's film about McCarthy and journalist Edward R. Murrow, *Good Night and Good Luck*, appeared the previous year.) In a lengthy interview with the Writers' Guild of America's online publication *Written By*, Zaillian claimed a timeless relevance for the fable. More than that, he offered a view of Stark that accords him a measure of heroic status as a truth teller and plain speaker (an interesting inversion of the plain-speaking heroes of our British political narratives):

> The book was written 60 years ago, but you could set it in any era...As I watched what was happening in the 2004 campaign, I particularly felt the absence of any politician brave enough to say something that mattered, and say it in plain English. To say things they believed in. I still feel that way. If somebody came along like Willie Stark today, he'd be president tomorrow. That's all it takes: Someone to just come out there, believe in it, and say it. Rather than just whatever will get you elected. (Feeney, 2006)

Zaillian returned to the novel as his source, interweaving passages of dialogue with excerpts from Long's own speeches into the screenplay. He also restored the character of Burden to equal narrative importance with Stark and retained much more of the novel's byzantine plot and backstory. Despite a high-profile cast, including Sean Penn as Stark, Jude Law as Burden, Kate Winslet, and Anthony Hopkins among others, and despite the titillating presence of James Carville, Bill Clinton's "Ragin' Cajun" campaign manager as executive producer, the movie was a resounding failure. While Penn was praised for the energy and intensity of his performance, the languorous pacing and murky plot elicited inevitable references to swampy bayous and overheated gumbo. (The spectacle of three estimable British actors defeated by their southern accents didn't help.) Peter Travers' (2006) dismissive review in *Rolling Stone* is a fair sample of the critical reception: "Overthought, overwrought and thuddingly underwhelming."

While Zaillian attempted to transform (or he would say, return) *All the King's Men* from a fable of inevitable political corruption to a drama of human character, ambition, and hubris, the other political films we will consider adhered much more closely to the vision animating the 1949 movie, what we are calling the cynical fable of American political narratives. We begin with a 1992 comedy directed by *Yes Minister*'s Jonathan Lynn, *The Distinguished Gentleman*. The movie itself is, in fact, entirely undistinguished, an increasingly lame vehicle for the fast-talking comic talents of its star Eddie Murphy. One can imagine Lynn's attraction to the project as an opportunity to apply the public-choice theory premises so influential in the UK to an American context. The film is unique, too, in choosing the House of Representatives as its setting (the White House and the Senate being much more usual choices). With its two-year election cycle, it is a setting in which interest group politics and campaign financing play crucial roles, and the movie duly finds venality, self-seeking, and greed everywhere it looks.

The plot can be quickly summarized: Murphy plays small-time con man Thomas Jefferson Johnson, who capitalizes on the death of incumbent congressman Jeff Johnson to run as an independent, basing his campaign entirely on (mistaken) name recognition. He is elected, meeting a like-minded group of freshman congressmen (a former television weather forecaster, a retired football player) who have done much the same. The con man soon realizes that he has joined the big time—"This job's not about helping people. It's about being here."—and he sets his sights on the Power and Industry Committee, chaired by the corrupt and ruthless Dick Dodge, as offering the richest pickings. Johnson's view begins to change, however, when he meets the inevitable beautiful lobbyist for a public interest group. And his conscience is further aroused when he is approached by a constituent who believes her young daughter's cancer has been caused by their home's proximity to power transmission lines. Dodge urges Johnson to pursue the issue no further than a photo op. An electricity industry lobbyist offers Johnson's political action committee $200,000 if he will drop his crusade. Johnson does not back down, and his conflict with Dodge escalates. Johnson secretly videotapes a meeting Dodge holds with electricity industry lobbyists while Dodge's staff digs up Johnson's extensive rap sheet. Each exposes the other publicly, and the film ends with both careers ruined and Johnson's attempt to advance the public interest thwarted.

As the presence of Eddie Murphy indicates, *The Distinguished Gentleman* is not a serious meditation on the systemic failings of the House of Representatives. Rather, it is a version of the cynical fable played for farce. What makes it an interesting precursor to the next film we will consider, a satire with significantly more bite, is the introduction of the politics of race into the narrative. Johnson's nemesis, Dodge, is White, and there is an amusing scene in which the con man, impersonating a member of the NAACP, harasses Dodge's office with questions about the composition of his influential committee, running down a list of the minority communities who have been excluded (African Americans, Latinos, Asians, Native Americans, homosexuals, the disabled), and concluding with a cheerfully ominous, "Well, you've been a great deal of help. Just forget I even called. Just tell him I said 'hi'."

Writer-director-star Warren Beatty's 1998 film *Bulworth* places its narrative in the Senate rather than the House of Representatives, following the wild last days of Jay Bulworth, a veteran Democratic senator from California running for reelection in 1996 who transforms himself from a disillusioned, centrist-platitude spouting Clintonian liberal into a rap-reciting political truth teller. The film's narrative premise draws audaciously on the assassination plot that runs through the cynical fable. Bored and disgusted by the political charade in which he has participated for so long, locked in a loveless marriage with a wife he rarely sees, Bulworth inveigles an insurance industry lobbyist to write, gratis, a $10 million life insurance policy with his daughter as sole beneficiary. Drawing on the services of an aide with underworld connections, he arranges a contract on his own life. Free to speak his mind, he intends to spend the last weekend of the campaign (and his life) becoming a plain-speaking truth teller, using rap lyrics as a vehicle. He has in effect, succumbed to Eriksonian despair, and his speeches of that weekend will be his suicide note to the public.[2]

Following a campaign stop at a Black church where his truth telling delights a posse of young women ("We all come down here. Get our pictures taken. Forget about it."), the Senator is taken by them to an after-hours club. There he encounters the beautiful Nina (played by Halle Berry). As Janet Maslin (1998) noted in her review of the movie in the *New York Times*, *Bulworth* supplies no other narrative justification for its white-bread, button-down lead character's sudden plunge into the world of Black culture, adopting homeboy clothing and delivering his home truths in deliberately amateurish rap style. A single close up of the indisputably gorgeous Ms. Berry is sufficient—for Jay Bulworth, and for the audience. (Roger Ebert (1998) is less tolerant, noting the narrative's reliance on that favorite movie assumption that "a man in a fight for his life can always find time in three days to fall in love with a woman half his age.")

Renewed by his romance with Nina, and exhilarated by his newfound freedom to speak openly to and about the special interests to which he previously was forced to pander (liberal Hollywood media types and the insurance industry draw fire as well as the Black community), Bulworth seeks unsuccessfully to cancel the contract on his life. His campaign now revitalized by his new identity, he is reelected with an increased majority. Dressed once again in the conservative business suit of the political establishment, he asks Nina to join him to face the media outside her parents' house. In the scrum that follows, the hit man finds his target. The movie closes with images of Bulworth wounded on the ground—a reference to the infamous photo of Robert Kennedy moments after he was shot—and of the horrified crowd pointing at a balcony where an insurance industry executive had been standing—a reference to the equally infamous photo of the immediate reaction to the assassination of Martin Luther King (Christensen & Haas, 2005, p. 30).

In view of both Warren Beatty's well-known liberal political leanings (he was an active "advisor" to the presidential campaigns of George McGovern and Gary Hart, and even considered seeking the Democratic presidential nomination for the 2000 election) and his tendency to make cinematic capital of them (his 1981 film biography of the American communist and journalist John Reed, *Reds*, won him a Best Director Oscar), there can be no doubt where *Bulworth*'s political sympathies lie. And the movie devotes an amount of narrative attention to the issue of national health insurance that appears prescient from our vantage point. But as Janet Maslin again points out, the film's real energy lies in its title character's free-wheeling attacks on the state of politics more generally: "One man, one vote; now is that really real? The name of our game is let's make a deal." It is, Maslin (1998) writes, "the all-purpose jaundiced eye" the film turns on the way "the game" is played that is most striking. Arguably, *Bulworth* ends in assassination because it can envision no other alternative for the visionary truth teller its protagonist has become. Certainly it suggests no hope of change in "the game." In this it is a true successor to the cynical tradition of *All the King's Men*.[3]

The 1997 film *Wag the Dog*, written by David Mamet and directed by Barry Levinson, takes the cynicism and the political stakes one step higher, moving from a senatorial campaign to a presidential election, and from a rap-spouting California Democrat, to a Hollywood-engineered war. It is ten days before the election and the incumbent's strategists have just learned that a teenage girl is accusing the president of molesting her during a tour of the Oval Office by her Girl Scout troop. Their only hope lies in the free-lance spin doctor Conrad Brean (played with panache and remarkable restraint by Robert De Niro) they hire for damage control. Brean's mantra is simple: "Change the story, change the lead." The story he proposes is war, specifically a made-in-Hollywood campaign against Albania. In a memorable exchange with the president's understandably startled chief aide—"Why *Albania?*"—he explains his rationale.

> "Why not?"
>
> "What have they done to us?"
>
> "What have they done *for* us? What do you know about them?"
>
> "Nothing."
>
> "See? They keep to themselves. Shifty. Untrustable."

As "Connie" hastens to assure his new employers, "We're not gonna have a war. We're gonna have the appearance of war," just long enough to secure the president's reelection and bury the Girl Scout scandal. To achieve the necessary verisimilitude, Brean brings in Stanley Motss, a blow-dried, fake-tanned, aviator-glasses-wearing Hollywood producer (played by Dustin Hoffman in loving homage to every self-described Hollywood mogul he surely ever encountered). This is the heart of the movie's satire, an extended sequence documenting the media manipulations, disinformation, and carefully staged spectacle that produce "the Albanian war," complete with soundstage-fabricated footage of a "refugee peasant girl" (dimwit starlet) fleeing the savage Albanian forces with her cat in her arms (cat to be blue-screened in later); self-important rock musicians recording an inspirational anthem in support of the war's innocent victims ("Albania's hard to rhyme" laments the drunken composer hired for the job); and the manufacture of a combat hero, the rescued POW Sergeant William Schumann (a recently released convict with a history of psychopathic violence—"He's fine as long as he gets his medications." "And if he doesn't get his medications?" "He's not fine.")

With the success of the Albanian campaign, the president is reelected and hostilities cease. "The President will be a hero," Motss notes, "He brought peace." "But there was never a war," Connie Brean objects. "All the greater accomplishment." Delighted with the production he has just staged, Motss unwisely decides to go public. Brean arranges for a Secret Service detail to return him to his palatial Hollywood home, where he is soon discovered dead (by his pool). The official cause of death: a massive heart attack. Although the movie loses much of its bite in its final half-hour, as improbabilities pile up and a subplot concerning the unstable "Schumann" takes over, its often hilarious rendering of the mechanics of modern-day "spin" adds a new element to the cynical fable. Where Willie Stark's power rested on his ability to give authentic voice to the grievances of the "hicks" and "rednecks" ignored by the political establishment, in the world of *Wag the Dog,* authenticity is manufactured to order on a Hollywood soundstage.

In the opening frames of Mike Nichols's 1998 film *Primary Colors* (adapted by Elaine May from the novel of the same name by journalist Joe Klein), we see southern governor and presidential candidate Jack Stanton speaking with heartfelt simplicity to participants in an adult literacy program about the shame his uncle, a military hero, experienced at being unable to read. We then watch Stanton as he employs much the same skills of sincerity, empathy, and eloquence to seduce the program's instructor before moving on to the next campaign stop, and the next willing victim. The movie, like the thinly veiled *roman à clef* on which it is based, follows the Clintonian Stanton through his New Hampshire primary campaign as he is forced to fend off allegations of sexual misconduct, including a long-term extramarital affair and the impregnation of a Black teenager, the daughter of an old friend and constituent. Focusing as much on Stanton's fiercely intelligent and no less ambitious wife Susan as on the governor himself, the narrative appears to promise a searching character study of two flawed but passionately committed political pros as they claw their way to the top of a no-less-flawed political system.

In fact, *Primary Colors* fails to deliver on that promise, despite impressive performances by John Travolta (in an uncanny channeling of Bill Clinton) and Emma Thompson (as a tightly wound yet highly sympathetic Hillary) in the leads, and a number of equally effective appearances by a roster of fine character actors (chiefly Kathy Bates as a long-time aide who commits suicide and Billy Bob Thornton as the volatile southern spin doctor given to lengthy and incomprehensible "folksy" anecdotes). It is a failure that illustrates both the structural limitations of the cynical fable (which we have considered before), and the particular burden this narrative labors under by being linked so closely to the Clintons' story.

Like *All the King's Men, Primary Colors* embeds an observer into its narrative structure—a *focalizer,* in narratological terms—whose perspective shapes the story as it unfolds (Prince, 2003, pp. 31–32). It is a measure of the distance separating the two narratives that the controversial southern politician with the down-home style and ability to speak directly to "the common man" is observed in the first instance by the heir of a decaying aristocratic clan, and in the second by the African American grandson of a celebrated civil rights activist. Henry Burton joins Stanton's campaign, seduced equally by the governor and his wife, by their intelligence, their ambition, and the promise of political renewal (change, commitment, hope) they project so skillfully. "That's how history is made," Susan Stanton promises him, "by the first-timers." The movie then charts Burton's progressive disenchantment as he watches the Stantons do whatever is necessary to quash the recurring sexual scandals, strong-arm potential rivals into dropping out of the race by threatening to disclose hidden histories of drug addiction and homosexual affairs, and emulate the worst behavior of the opponents whose "dirty" tactics they routinely condemn.

The climax of the film comes when Burton, repelled by the Stantons' hypocrisy, determines to leave the campaign. Summoning up all his reserves of righteous indignation and moral relativism, the governor delivers what amounts to his political credo:

> This is hardball. This is the price you pay to lead. You don't think that Abraham Lincoln was a whore before he was president? He had to tell his little stories and smile his shit-eating backcountry grin. And he did it just so that one day he would have the opportunity to stand in front of the nation and appeal to the better angels of our nature. That's where the bullshit stops. That's what it's all about. So we have the opportunity to make the most of it. To do it the right way. You know as well as I do that there are plenty of people playing this game who don't think this way. They are willing to sell their souls, crawl through sewers, lie to people, divide them, play on their worst fears—for nothing. Just for the prize.

The choice of Lincoln as exemplar is, of course, particularly loaded when made by a White southern governor to the Black American grandson of a civil rights leader. It is presumably the shock that prevents Burton from pointing out the obvious: whatever else Lincoln might have had to do to be elected, he did not use his office to seduce an endless parade of women, nor did he inveigle a staff member to assist in falsifying DNA tests to escape paternity charges. The movie ends shortly after Stanton's set piece, at the Inaugural Ball, as President Stanton and his First Lady waltz together, with Burton still there, looking on.

The problem with Stanton's speech, as Charles Taylor (1998) pointed out in a lengthy online review for Salon.com, is that nothing in the preceding narrative suggests that the Stantons are any different from those soulless power seekers who play the game for the prize alone. Bound by its source material to the focus on Stanton's sexual escapades, governed by the cynical fable's insistence on the inevitable corruption that is the price of a political career, the movie finds no means of convincingly registering, let alone exploring, any other dimensions of the Stantons' political lives. Indeed, the narrative effectively suggests that none exist. The few vague references to anything resembling policy are framed as empty gestures, meaningless phrases rolled out for the cameras. This is, of course, entirely consistent with the view of politics the movie proposes, but it removes the possibility of anything like a complex inner life for either of the two main characters. They remain as unknowable to the viewer as they are to Burton. Taylor summarizes all that he feels is wrong with both the novel and the film by noting their shared inability to allow "the political operator" and "the true believer" to coexist within the character of the erring governor. It is a problem shared by all the narratives we have been analyzing as exemplars of the cynical fable. Political operators are everywhere to be found. True believers exist only as observing presences waiting to be disillusioned and/ or destroyed. No other alternative seems possible.

The narrative offered by Chris Hegedus and D. A. Pennebaker's documentary account of the 1992 Clinton campaign, *The War Room*, accommodates precisely the complexities and contradictions *Primary Colors* does not make room for. In her introduction to the 2006 DVD version of the film, Hegedus (2006) made plain that their ambitions for the film were not to confirm the usual suspicions, however much subsequent events might have altered the meanings now attached to the story it presents: "I hope that when people watch the film they get a sense, not of the type of cynicism that people speak about today within political campaigns, but of the sort of idealism of a lot of the people in the Clinton campaign who really wanted to change things."

Hegedus and Pennebaker chose to focus on the campaign's communications operations (based in Little Rock) and the young made-for-Hollywood odd couple who ran it: the volatile, colorful chief strategist, James Carville, and the intense, boyish, intellectual director of communications, George Stephanopolous. Smart, quick, passionate, full of manic energy, and talking nonstop, the two were *West Wing* characters a decade before the fact. Watching them, and the youthful staffers they marshal, as the campaign gains momentum and moves toward victory is exhilarating and even inspirational. Yet the primary function of their operation is to counter what Carville and Stephanopolous call "the Republican attack machine." So we see the energy expended on the squalid task of discrediting Gennifer Flower's allegations of sexual impropriety. We see, too, a long episode of Carville developing an attack ad concerning the Bush campaign allegedly outsourcing the printing of its campaign advertising to Brazil—a "strategic" initiative that did not in fact come to fruition. While Carville and Stephanopolous argue, convincingly enough, that they are acting defensively, attempting to move the campaign away from personal attacks to a discussion of policy issues, there's no doubt they are getting their hands more than a little dirty (Levine, 2005). The energy invested in these episodes suggests something of the pleasure these adrenalin-fuelled young men found in hitting back twice as hard. On the last day of the campaign, an emotional Carville is seen telling the War Room staff that the most sacred things a person can give are "love and work." The film closes with a shot of a white board at the campaign headquarters with the words, "change versus more of the same, it's the economy, stupid, and don't forget health care." It is a perfect encapsulation of the narrative's ability to accommodate the coexistence of fierce ambition, a willingness to surrender the moral high ground and fight with whatever means necessary, and a genuine commitment to larger political ideals. Carville and Stephanopolous are massaging their message to the very end—"It's the economy, stupid"—but the last words remain: "Don't forget health care." That the Clinton administration would go on to disappoint most of the hopes of true believers like the War Room staff, not to mention legions of voters, does not invalidate the idealism the filmmakers had sought to capture. And it is a similar willingness to allow complexity of motive, conflicting impulses, and ambiguity of outcome that animates the narratives of compromise to which we now turn.

"What Do We Do Now?": The Fable of Compromise

We begin, again, with a film adaptation of a Pulitzer Prize-winning novel, Otto Preminger's 1962 film version of Allen Drury's 1959 novel *Advise and Consent*. (The title is taken, of course, from the Senate's constitutional power to confirm or reject presidential appointments.) The plot centers on confirmation hearings for an ailing Democratic president's nominee for Secretary of State, Robert Leffingwell. Leffingwell, the head of a federal agency, is a member of the left wing of the Democratic party, favoring nuclear arms negotiations with the Soviets. He is also, as he proudly proclaims in the unmistakable cadences of Henry Fonda, "an egghead" (that is, an intellectual), a status as suspect in American political discourse then as it is now: "I'm an egghead. I'm not only an egghead, I'm a premeditated egghead. I set out to become an egghead and at this moment I'm in full flower of eggheadedness, and I hope to spread the spores of egghead everywhere I go."

The Senate is split between those inclined to support the president's egghead nominee for reasons of ideology, fear of retribution, or hope of favor, and those opposed primarily on ideological (anti-Communist) grounds. Evidence is presented that Leffingwell was an active member of a Communist cell in the thirties. He denies it under oath. One of Leffingwell's key opponents, Senator Brigham Anderson of Utah, is threatened with public exposure of the homosexual affair he engaged in during the war. Anderson commits suicide. The senators turn against the president and the left-wing demagogue Senator van Ackerman who pressured Anderson. The confirmation vote is very close and the aging president succumbs to a heart attack while awaiting the outcome in the Oval Office. In fact, the final tally is tied. Learning of the death of the president while presiding over the vote, the vice president declines to break the tie. The nomination fails. The story ends with the new president informing the majority leader that he will propose his own nominee. And the process will begin all over again.

There are significant differences between the novel and the movie. Drury was explicitly and unrelentingly anti-Communist, and his narrative, with its insistent omniscient narrator, is almost ludicrously emphatic in its depiction of the cowardice, duplicity, and corruption of the president, the nominee, and his supporters. The antics of the repellent van Ackerman are particularly risible. At a rally of the lobby group COMFORT (Committee on Making Further Offers for a Russian Truce), he proclaims to the cheering crowd, "I would rather crawl to Moscow on my belly than perish under a bomb." The acronym COMFORT is a reference to the constitutional definition of treason: giving aid and comfort to the enemy. And Drury has performed an interesting authorial sleight-of-hand with van Ackerman, remaking Joseph McCarthy as a left-wing demagogue.

Preminger's film abandons Drury's ideological agenda almost entirely. (The casting of the arch-hero Henry Fonda in the role of Leffingwell clearly indicates the extent of the change in his narrative status.) Dispensing with the cynical fable's embedded observer and his privileged judgments, adopting a transparent visual style, with long continuous takes, Preminger allows the drama of the hearings to unfold in documentary-like fashion, effectively placing the viewer in the position of the listening senators themselves. It is a film that is, literally, polyphonic, much of its "action" consisting of testimony and cross-examination. The narrative interest here is not only in the relative merits of the conflicting ideologies being voiced, but also in the complex individuals who voice them: the mixture of motives animating the characters, the compromises they find themselves forced to make, and the means they use to make sense of their own actions. It is a film that is deeply interested in the workings of governance, in the ways in which the system operates. The film uses a set that is a replica of the Senate chamber, and many of the other scenes are shot in Washington. These two related narrative concerns will become markers of the fable of compromise: a serious engagement with the mechanics of governing, the daily business of doing the job, coupled with an interest in the tensions that inevitably arise between expedience and principle once one accepts the basic premise of electoral politics: you can't do any good if you haven't got any power.

When does expedience become corruption? Where is the line that should not be crossed? These are two of the questions the film version of *Advise and Consent* raises. They are also at the heart of the 1996 film *City Hall*. Marketed as a political thriller—its tag line was "Murder. Corruption. Cover up. Scandal."—the movie, which stars Al Pacino as popular New York mayor John Pappas and John Cusack as his trusted young aide Kevin Calhoun, has an almost anthropological fascination with the inner workings of a governing system. The plot centers on Calhoun's self-initiated investigation of a shooting that kills a plainclothes detective, a drug dealer with Mafia connections, and a six-year-old boy caught in the crossfire, an investigation that ultimately implicates the mayor himself. But the narrative's concern is less with the spreading web of corruption that encompasses a city councilor in thrall to organized crime, crooked cops, and a judge who bows to political pressure—familiar cinematic terrain—than with the ambivalent moral status of Pappas.

Pappas' connection to the initial triple murder is remote but still damning. His phone call to the presiding judge, made at the urging of the city councilor, secured parole for the drug dealer rather than jail time when he was charged with a previous offence. Pappas made the call, fully aware of the criminal's (and the councilor's) Mafia connections.[4] When Calhoun begins his investigation, Pappas tries only halfheartedly to distract him but, despite anticipating the likely outcome, does not obstruct him.

Calhoun is disillusioned by the discovery but hardly shocked. He is not a Henry Burton. The narrative makes clear that the young man, a Louisiana native who had served on the staff of a congressional committee, is no political naïf. He understands the networks of influence and mutual obligation within which Pappas must move. He knows why the mayor may truly grieve the death of a child and yet be grateful the fatal bullet came from the drug dealer's not the police detective's gun ("In my world," Pappas says, "that counts as good news."). He admires the skill with which this experienced politician can score media points by hijacking the murdered child's funeral with a brilliant, uninvited eulogy, while sharing the mayor's own distaste at the grandstanding. (The scene is a showcase for Pacino's virtuoso energy and theatricality.) And he, like the narrative itself, retains a deep sympathy with the charismatic and dedicated mayor, even as he rejects the political credo of "*menschkeit*" by which the older man lives.

This notion of menschkeit is central to the narrative's political vision. As the Greek-American mayor explains it to his "good Louisiana lapsed Catholic" aide, it is "Something about honor. And character. It's...untranslatable. That's why it's Yiddish." Pressed to clarify, he finally articulates it as "the space between a handshake." For Pappas, politics is all about the handshake, about the deals you make to do the good you intend, but, he adds, "Deep down, you know, there's a line you can't cross. And after a thousand trades and one deal too many, the line gets rubbed out."[5] What the movie leaves unsaid is the other side of the bargain: what benefit the councilor and Pappas received, or what harm they avoided, in exchange. Is there anything that could justify making deals with organized criminals? Pappas emerges, however, not as one of the political rogues or villains of the cynical fable, but as a tragic hero, a leader of many virtues who is undone by a fatal character flaw.

The movie's dramatic climax comes in a final confrontation between Pappas and Calhoun. Pappas is not evasive nor is Calhoun angry. Pappas quickly confesses what he knows Calhoun has already discovered and, while Calhoun is disillusioned, he has deep personal sympathy with Pappas. Calhoun's anger, however, is with Pappas's idea of menschkeit.

> Menschkeit is horseshit. It's 120 years of graft and sweetheart deals and featherbeds and inside information and golden parachutes.

Ironically, Calhoun's behavior illustrates the traditional idea of menschkeit—noble character, dignity, and ethical action—because, even as he forcefully points out Mayor Pappas's ethical and legal failings as a public servant, he treats John Pappas, the human being, with sympathy and respect.[6] The mayor's connection to the young boy's death will be made public. Calhoun suggests he resign before it does, perhaps use his connections to secure an ambassadorship. But his ultimate fate is not revealed. The young aide, far from withdrawing from "the system" whose corruption has now been revealed to him, resigns his position to run, unsuccessfully, for city council. The movie ends with his determination to try again.

As a movie, *City Hall* is as flawed as its protagonist. Dialogue and plotting often descend to the gritty city clichés familiar from every New York police drama. An entire subplot revolving around a suspiciously young and pretty lawyer representing the family of the fallen police officer seems to belong to a different story. Yet what makes the film so pertinent for our discussion is its paradoxical insistence on ambivalence. As in *Advise and Consent*, compromise here assumes a double meaning, connoting both the inevitable means by which political aims are realized and the moral implication those means entail. Is American city politics so structured that the participants are bound to descend the slippery slope from acceptable deals like public-private partnerships to illegal deals like arranging probation for a mafioso drug dealer? Is it possible to survive in politics without making deals with the devil? This is a quandary that former Secretary of Defense Robert McNamara will articulate most fully, as we will see in Chapter 6. Might we do evil, so that good may come of it? One of the questions *City Hall* raises, but does not answer, is where does that evil begin?

For Mike Nichols and Aaron Sorkin, director and screenwriter, respectively, of *Charlie Wilson's War* (2007), the intimate connection between political compromise and political heroism is the shaping premise of their narrative. The joint involvement of the two men on this project would almost be sufficient to justify its inclusion here. But the film merits attention for more than its production personnel. Based on journalist George Crile's bestselling 2003 book of the same name, it offers a fascinating variation on the fable of compromise we have been exploring, recounting, in the words of the book's prolix subtitle, "the extraordinary story of how the wildest man in Congress and a rogue CIA agent changed the history of our times."

The wild man in question was Charlie Wilson, the heavy-drinking, skirt-chasing, cocaine-using Democratic representative from Texas' second congressional district, who transformed himself into a clandestine hero, channeling millions of dollars of funds through disaffected CIA agent Gust Avrakatos to support the mujahedeen resisting the Soviet invasion of Afghanistan in the early 1980s. It was, to say the least, an improbable transformation. As Crile's nonfiction account, and Sorkin's screenplay, make clear, Wilson was in many ways a figure straight out of the cynical political fable: an adept political operator who quickly secured himself appointments to the House Appropriations Committee's Foreign Operations and Defense subcommittees. An aggressive pursuer of "pork" for his poverty-stricken congressional district, Wilson never, in Crile's words, "shied away from using his influence to get jobs for his constituents or contracts for local industry" (Crile, 2003, p. 77). Eager to gain a permanent appointment to the Board of the Kennedy Center (the better to impress an endless succession of interchangeable young women with access, at no cost to himself, to the most glamorous events in Washington), Wilson agreed to a quid pro quo that might have embarrassed even Eddie Murphy's Jeff Johnson. House Speaker and Democratic leader Tip O'Neill would secure his place on the Kennedy Center board in exchange for Wilson's services on the House Ethics Committee, with the understanding that those services would include derailing the committee's investigation of one of O'Neill's key lieutenants. Wilson, according to Crile, delivered completely (pp. 80–85).

To this point, Wilson and his narrative seem familiar enough: an amiably corrupt politician, gaming the system to benefit his constituents and himself, doing a little evil but also some good for the folks at home (and having a damn good time doing it). Wilson suffered little political damage from his corrupt behavior because he was handsome, charismatic, single, and completely upfront about it: it was who Charlie Wilson was, not evidence of his hypocrisy (Crile, 2003, p. 29). But that was not the full measure of the man. Wilson grew up during World War II, strongly influenced by the British resistance to Nazism and a great admirer of Churchill. He became profoundly anti-Communist, an ideology deepened by his youthful experience as a naval officer hunting Soviet submarines.

Good-time Charlie Wilson seems like an unusual choice of protagonist for a movie bankrolled by Participant Media, the socially conscious production company founded by Internet billionaire Jeffrey Skoll. Participant, whose previous projects included *North Country* and *Good Night and Good Luck*, tends to favor inspirational tales of heroic individuals speaking out against social evils, defending the values of civil society against predatory corporations (*North Country*) or political demagoguery (*Good Night and Good Luck*). It is, of course, Wilson's conversion experience that qualified him for inclusion in these ranks. One of the attending ironies is that it was precisely his skills at playing the system that qualified him for the heroic role he would undertake.

Characteristically, Wilson found his mission through the agency of a woman: the wealthy Houston socialite Joanne Herring (played in the film by Julia Roberts). Herring was both fiercely anti-Communist (a stance she shared with Wilson) and well-connected to the Pakistani government. (She served, rather surprisingly, as honorary consul.) She took Wilson to Pakistan to witness the plight of Afghan refugees and to meet President Zia ul Haq. Support for the fierce warriors defying the might of the Soviet military machine appealed to Wilson's bravura nature. His membership on the House's Defense Subcommittee enabled him to act upon that appeal.

But Wilson was not interested in merely increasing the CIA's budget to support mujahedeen operations. With the hands-on proclivities of a former naval officer who had hunted Soviet submarines, he sought to reach down into "the Company" to ensure the money would be spent effectively, something unprecedented for a member of Congress. His partner-in-crime would be the rogue agent of Crile's subtitle, Gust Avrakatos. Together they would form precisely the sort of odd couple team beloved of Hollywood—"You're no James Bond" Wilson informs Avrakatos at one point. "You're no Thomas Jefferson either, so let's call it even"—and it is no surprise that Sorkin's script makes their escapades the center of the narrative. Avrakatos, like Wilson, was a maverick; an aggressive, risk-taking, plain-speaking son of Greek immigrants, perennially at odds with the WASP elite that controlled the CIA's upper echelons. He first appears in the movie arguing with his Ivy League boss, his entrance line the truly memorable, "Excuse me, what the fuck?" As played by Philip Seymour Hoffman, Avrakatos walks away with the movie, leaving the rather miscast Tom Hanks as Wilson trailing in his wake.

The deal Wilson and Avrakatos eventually broker, in its complexity and cynicism, belongs in the realm of satire: to avoid giving any appearance that the United States is actually arming the mujahedeen, Israel will supply them with Russian-made weapons through Egyptian, Pakistani, and Saudi intermediaries. As their incredulous Israeli contact remarks, "Well, just one or two problems with that, just off the top of my head. Afghanistan and Pakistan don't recognize our right to exist. We just got done fighting a war against Egypt. And everyone who has ever tried to kill me or my family has been trained in Saudi Arabia." Not entirely true, Wilson points out, "Some of them were trained by us." Clearly, we are back in the moral universe of the cynical fable, where any deal is acceptable, so long as it is not made public. Yet neither Crile's account, nor Nichols and Sorkin's film suggest that Wilson did not believe in the justice of the cause he was advancing. However skeptical Avrakatos might be of Joanne Herring—"You know, I've found, in my business, that when rich people with time on their hands get involved in politics, I start forgetting who I'm supposed to be shooting at"—he too believes in the strategic, indeed global importance of their self-appointed mission. *Charlie Wilson's War* confronts us with the spectacle of a deeply compromised protagonist marshaling all the skills of manipulation, deal brokering, deception, and finagling acquired in a long and energetically misspent political career to change the course of history. And it is precisely his compromised status that enables him to do so entirely unsuspected. In the words of Avrakatos, "As long as the press sees sex and drugs behind the left hand, you can park a battle carrier behind the right hand and no one's gonna fucking notice."

In standard Participant Media fashion, the movie begins and ends triumphantly (accompanied by the obligatory inspirational score) with a 1993 ceremony at which Wilson is given the first ever Honored Colleague Award by the Clandestine Service, the CIA's core group of agents responsible for directing and participating in covert operations. And there is no doubt that Wilson and Avrakatos have triumphed. The Soviets do leave Afghanistan. The cost of the invasion to the government, both in material terms and in loss of prestige, contributes directly to the defeat of Communism. But the armed mujahedeen freedom fighters of the eighties would mutate into the oppressive Taliban government of the nineties, a tragic irony both narratives explicitly highlight. Toward the end of the movie, Charlie and Gust are at a party celebrating the Soviet retreat from Afghanistan. Gust takes Charlie out on the balcony and informs him that the latest intelligence assessment is that "the crazies are streaming into Kandahar" and then tells him a story about a zen master who responds to a variety of conflicting developments in a boy's life with the same ambiguous comment: "We'll see." Charlie then meets with his congressional subcommittee and fails to convince his previously supportive colleagues to provide funding for postwar reconstruction. As one puts it, "No one gives a shit about schools in Afghanistan," to which Charlie cryptically responds, "The ball keeps on bouncing."

The three narratives of compromise we have considered so far have all also been narratives of governance. The last we will look at is a classic campaign tale, hailed by Vincent Canby in his *New York Times* review as "one of the few good, truly funny American political comedies ever made" (Canby, 1972). It is also the movie which has the dubious distinction of having inspired Dan Quayle to enter politics. *The Candidate* (1972), directed by Michael Ritchie from a screenplay by Jeremy Larner, stars Robert Redford as Jim McKay, a young, liberal California lawyer who runs a rural legal aid clinic. The son of a former long-serving governor, McKay is precisely the fresh face veteran Democratic party organizer Marvin Lucas is seeking to run against the popular third-term Republican incumbent. (It doesn't hurt, of course, that the face is also preternaturally handsome.) Convinced that he will lose no matter what, McKay agrees on two conditions: he will say and do what he wants, and go where he wants throughout the campaign.

The narrative setup is familiar enough. The idealistic young candidate will be disillusioned and corrupted by "the system." But the script is more subtle and more rewarding than that. As Larner made plain in a 2001 interview recounting the genesis of the movie, his interest was not in a predictable moral melodrama of external corruption, but in the much more insidious process by which a candidate loses himself. "They [Redford and Ritchie] wanted a liberal Senate candidate who sold out. I said I don't think they sell out. They get carried away. They get lost" (Larner, 2001).

A novelist and political activist, Larner was also a speechwriter for Senator Eugene McCarthy during the 1968 presidential campaign, and he clearly understands intimately the alternative reality of modern campaigning. McKay does no backroom deals. He doesn't mortgage his soul to special interests or dirty money. (When introduced by his father to a teamsters' union leader who asserts they have much in common, McKay retorts, "We don't have shit in common." The union leader supports him nonetheless.) McKay merely succumbs to the twin pulls of popularity and ambition, alternately fascinated and repelled by the power he acquires over the crowds who embrace him in spite of himself. It is what Larner called in a 1988 reconsideration of the film, "the problem of political success." Whatever the motivations, beliefs, commitments, and aspirations a candidate brings with him into a campaign, Larner wrote, "forces larger than any candidate will eventually dictate his behavior—forces such as his looks, marketability, and what others see in him" (Larner, 1988).

The narrative is also a remarkably detailed illustration of the median voter hypothesis that asserts that candidates holding strong positions on issues, on either the right or the left, will modify their positions to appeal to the majority of the electorate in the center. McKay begins his campaign as a plain speaker of the left: favoring a generous welfare program, strong environmental initiatives, school busing, and abortion rights. As the McKay effect gathers momentum, the man who ran to lose begins to be packaged as a candidate who can win. The previously hippie-ish McKay cuts his hair and shaves his sideburns. His position on busing is neutered to anodyne and ambiguous sound bites: "You can't let a bus carry all the responsibility for educational improvement" and "I want to preserve neighborhood schools," and his stand on abortion dwindles to "I'll think about it." His commercials emphasize his good looks and youthful energy (in contrast to his aging opponent), with a slogan that means anything, or nothing: "McKay: The better way." Though he mocks his own empty stump speech in the privacy of his limo—"Can't any longer play off Black against old, young against poor. This country cannot house its houseless, feed its foodless"— McKay ends the campaign mouthing the same platitudes as his opponent. In Larner's words, "his star outshines his soul and events sweep him, blind and lost, to victory" (Larner, 1988).

McKay's relationship with his wife deteriorates during the campaign, mirroring his political loss of self. Early on, we see a close and passionate relationship. Midway through the campaign, McKay returns home to find her, as an accomplished equestrian, being interviewed, in her full riding gear, by a tabloid. McKay immediately realizes that this photo-op will undercut his image and throws the interviewers out. Her attempt at getting attention thwarted, she and McKay argue. As he campaigns, McKay is surrounded by groupies, one showing off his campaign button pinned to her panties, another flashing her bra and asking him to sign it. While McKay avoids the groupies, he does have an affair, and we occasionally see the woman signaling to him in a crowd or the two emerging separately from a hotel room.

The movie concludes with McKay winning an unexpected but decisive victory. McKay's father, beaming, congratulates him with the words, "Son, you're a politician," and the son looks distinctly uncomfortable. In the movie's famous final words, set during the victory party, the nervous and distressed McKay takes his campaign manager aside and asks, "Marvin, what do we do now?"

It is a testament to the subtlety of Larner's screenplay that this can be viewed as an open question. Some commentators, in particular former Vice President Dan Quayle, a man considered by many the avatar of political vacuity, saw McKay's story as a political *bildungsroman*, a tale of education, a primer for would-be politicians. Larner's devastating rejoinder, "Sorry, Senator Quayle, you thought we were telling you how-to, when we were trying to say: watch out. You missed the irony. Unless, in a way we could never have foreseen, you are the irony" (Larner 1988), makes one hesitate to suggest an alternative reading. Perhaps it is the intelligence and attractiveness of Redford's performance (in the view of many critics, the best he's ever given) that suggests McKay might yet survive the campaign to become something more than a hack politician. No longer a freewheeling iconoclast, perhaps, no longer nearly as innocent, aware of his own ambitions and the lengths to which they will lead him, but still a man with convictions who will find some of his soul again. In this interpretation, McKay's self-mocking during the campaign is what can be expected when an intelligent person is forced to endlessly repeat the same message. And McKay's final question of his campaign manager represents merely the nervousness if not fear any politician (as recounted recently by Tony Blair [2010, pp. 8–9] in his memoirs) would feel on the verge of assuming a major office. McKay, once he takes his seat in the Senate, might begin to compile a record that will soon be considerably different than his Republican opponent's. Larner's retrospective interpretation of the movie suggests that, after a decade in the Senate, McKay will experience the same sort of disillusionment as Bulworth, while the alternative interpretation suggests that he might feel the same sense of achievement as, say, Teddy Kennedy.

The Candidate is a movie that, thirty years after it was made, is still visually rewarding. Atypically for its time, it was shot with a jerky handheld camera in a documentary style. The producers ran a pseudocampaign capitalizing on the 1972 presidential campaign, staging mock-rallies, photo-ops, and interviews. The crowds drawn to the project and to Redford's pseudo-candidacy provided vitality and spontaneity, but also demonstrated Larner's larger point that it is possible to generate political excitement that is devoid of political substance.[7]

Grand Old Men: The Nostalgic-Heroic Fable

Turning back from the world of *The Candidate* to that of *Seven Days in May* and *The Last Hurrah* is to enter an entirely different cinematic, narrative, cultural, and political universe. Although only eight years separate the John Frankenheimer thriller (*Seven Days in May*) from the Redford film, the generational divide could not be more apparent, while *The Last Hurrah*, produced in 1958, belongs to another era entirely. The difference is encapsulated in the lead actors: Redford is the embodiment of counterculture youth and a crown prince of a new era of filmmaking (*Butch Cassidy and the Sundance Kid* was released in 1969); the two older movies feature grandstanding performances by legends of Hollywood's golden age, Fredric March (born in 1897) and Spencer Tracy (born in 1900). Both bring with them the extranarrative authority, and star power of images honed over decades of leading-man status. It is no surprise to find them inhabiting political figures of impeccable rectitude, characters who function within the narrative as representatives of an ethos seen as threatened in one instance, displaced in the other.

Seven Days in May was adapted from a popular political thriller by Rod Serling (better known as the creator of the cult television series *The Twilight Zone*). Its director, John Frankenheimer, had recently made the paranoid political melodrama *The Manchurian Candidate,* and the film shares something of the earlier movie's obsession with betrayal and covert manipulation, the "trust nobody" atmosphere, without the heavy Freudian overlay. The plot centers on a military coup masterminded by the Chair of the Joint Chiefs of Staff, General James Scott (played with dignified restraint by Burt Lancaster). The president, Jordan Lyman (Fredric March), is deeply unpopular, having recently signed a comprehensive nuclear disarmament treaty with the Soviets, a treaty Congress has yet to ratify. General Scott is outraged by what he sees as the president's capitulation to the Soviets, giving a rousing speech to a senate committee on the perfidy of the Russians and the weakness of negotiation: "Now we're asked to believe that a piece of paper will take the place of missile sites and Polaris submarines, and that an enemy who hasn't honored one solemn treaty in the history of its existence will now, for our convenience, do precisely that." To preserve the country, Scott and his fellow chiefs plan to remove the president from office before the treaty can be ratified. A senior Air Force officer, Colonel Martin Casey (Kirk Douglas) learns of the intended coup and, despite his own philosophical opposition to the treaty, informs the White House. Lyman springs forcefully into action and the remainder of the film explores the maneuvers of both sides as they battle for control. With the assistance of Casey, and drawing on his own reserves of authority, principle, courage, and dedication to the Constitution, as well as impressive counterplotting skills (he obtains incriminating letters written by Scott, sufficient to convict him of treason, secures statements from officers who refused to join the plot, and extracts incriminating information from Scott's former mistress), Lyman confronts the rogue general, secures his resignation and those of the other joint chiefs, and overpowers him with the force of his reasoned rhetoric. (Interestingly, despite his burst of biblical eloquence at movie's end, the narrative presents Lyman as a plain speaker, in contrast to the technical jargon and frequent euphemisms of the military men who surround him. When Casey refers to "possibilities...what we call, uh, capabilities in military intelligence," meaning the intended coup, Lyman asks "You got something against the English language, Colonel?")

The film shares the thematic terrain of *Advise and Consent* (nuclear policy and relations with the Soviet Union), and Frankenheimer too avoids demonizing either ideological position. Scott might be treasonous in his inclinations, but he has none of the caricatured belligerence of *Dr. Strangelove*'s military madmen (whom we will discuss in Chapter 6). It is his methods, not his rationale, that mark him for failure. Still, there is little doubt of the heroic status of the president, who faces him down, and March brings to bear all the authority of his decades of movie stardom in the climactic confrontation in the Oval Office. He is the plain-speaking voice of reason, of democracy itself—the voice of America's better (older) nature. Scott begins by accusing the president of betraying the country:

> And if you want to talk about your oath of office, I'm here to tell you face to face, President Lyman, that you violated that oath when you stripped this country of its muscles—when you deliberately played upon the fear and fatigue of the people and told them they could remove that fear by the stroke of a pen. And then when this nation rejected you, lost faith in you, and began militantly to oppose you, you violated that oath by not resigning from office and turning the country over to someone who could represent the people of the United States.

Lyman immediately understands Scott to mean himself and comments sardonically on his ambition. The general denies any interest in personal advancement, claiming only a wish to serve his country. Lyman silences him with a final, unanswerable peroration: "Then, by God, run for office. You have such a fervent, passionate, evangelical faith in this country—why in the name of God don't you have any faith in the system of government you're so hell-bent to protect?"

Even in victory, however, Lyman remains a man of honor. He returns the incriminating letters to Scott, says nothing publicly about the generals' actions, and concludes the film with a press conference in which he speaks, in biblical cadences, of America's ultimate triumph:

> There's been abroad in this land in recent months a whisper that we have somehow lost our greatness, that we do not have the strength to win without war the struggles for liberty throughout the world. This is slander, because our country is strong, strong enough to be a peacemaker. It is proud, proud enough to be patient. The whisperers and the detractors, the violent men are wrong. We will remain strong and proud, peaceful and patient, and we will see a day when on this earth all men will walk out of the long tunnels of tyranny into the bright sunshine of freedom.

It takes an actor of March's authority and experience to carry off a speech like this. What makes the role and the performance even more interesting is their inversion of recent history, when America's youngest elected president stood down "the violent men" on both sides of the Cuban Missile Crisis.

President Jordan Lyman's cinematic faultlessness might well be an implicit tribute to the recently murdered Kennedy, and we will look in much more detail at the figure of Kennedy as president-hero in the next chapter. As a narrative device, however, Lyman's selfless dedication to the constitution, his willingness to sacrifice popularity for principle with no apparent regret, his seeming lack of all personal ambition or even enjoyment of power, drains the character of both ambivalence and complexity, making him in the end much more a symbol than a man.

It is not clouds of perfection that hang over *The Last Hurrah*'s depiction of the final days of Frank Skeffington, the Irish-American mayor campaigning for his fifth term in an unnamed New England city (assumed to be Boston). It is something more like hagiography. Adapted from Edwin O'Connor's 1956 novel and directed by the Irish-American John Ford, the movie is an extended celebration of a politics of ethnic solidarity and working-class consciousness, a highly sentimentalized and sanitized evocation of big-city political-machine politics as a benign agency delivering benefits to common citizens (Coyne, 2008, p. 103).

Skeffington's opponent (also Irish-American) is a young lawyer and war veteran who uses the then-cutting-edge technology of television advertising, is endorsed by the major newspapers, and financed by the very banks Skeffington has defied in his working-class constituents' interests. He is callow, politically inept, and unconnected to the working-class electorate, but he is young and forward looking, a product of the advertising age. The mayor, in contrast, does little campaigning, and what he does, takes the form of traditional speeches and public meetings: the man of the people speaking directly to them. The narrative, of course, is setting Skeffington up for defeat. After the votes are in, Skeffington has a heart attack, and the movie concludes with what *New York Times* film critic Bosley Crowther (1958) called "an unconscionably long-drawn and liturgical death-bed scene" involving farewells to both supporters and opponents. While this scene was trying to depict the sense of integrity Erikson associated with a life well lived, it failed because it was devoid of any dramatic tension.

Lacking the slickness and suspense of *Seven Days in May*, *The Last Hurrah* rests primarily on the authoritative performance of Spencer Tracy, looking much older than his years, but projecting the warmth, humanity, decency, and frailty of the dying politician. And this is the problem. Where O'Connor's novel had not sought to whitewash the less savory aspects of Skeffington's machine politics, the movie bathes every action in an altruistic, even beatific light. Nothing Skeffington does is for personal gain. Any remotely dubious tactic, any deal done, is intended to benefit "the little people." In effect, Ford has transformed a compromised hero into a secular saint. In its resistance to any shade of gray, the narrative world of *The Last Hurrah* shows a similarity to the absolute moral universe of the cynical fable. Both *Seven Days in May* and *The Last Hurrah* offer vivid illustrations of the difficulty of creating compelling portraits of effective political leaders who might fairly be termed heroic. It would take more than thirty years, and several revolutions in America's political culture, for a fictional chief executive to arrive in the Oval Office who could lay claim to the title.

The United States of Sorkin: *The West Wing* and a New Presidential Ideal

The prospects on September 22, 1999, for a debuting weekly hour-long television series about politics and government that would deal seriously with issues of policy, agenda setting, and implementation did not look good. (Its competition among new series included *Family Guy*, *The Sopranos*, and *Law and Order: Special Victims Unit*.) Improbably, *The West Wing* (*TWW*) was a spectacular success. The series ran for seven seasons, airing 154 episodes. In its first three years, *TWW*'s audiences in the United States averaged 20 million, peaking at the beginning of its second season at 25 million. It won numerous awards, including 27 Emmy awards, nine of which were for its first season alone. Even as its audiences waned during the series' later seasons, it remained popular among a coveted television demographic of high-income viewers, rarely dipping below 16 million.

Much like *Yes Minister*, the series also assumed an important place in contemporary political discourse. The program attracted the attention of Washington insiders, some of whom provided anonymous tips for plot lines, others who served as consultants. During the program's third season, its creators aired a companion documentary that featured interviews with former presidents Clinton, Carter, and Ford and a variety of former White House advisers (most notably Henry Kissinger and David Gergen) comparing their own experiences with scenes from *TWW. The West Wing* also responded to the 9/11 terrorist attacks by beginning its third season with a special episode ("Isaac and Ishmael"), introduced by cast members, though not speaking in character and making plain the episode is not a part of the series' ongoing story line. In the episode, a group of visiting schoolchildren are caught in a White House "lock down" after a security threat is discovered. They spend their time discussing issues raised by the likely response to 9/11 (ethnic profiling, enhanced surveillance, the geopolitical causes of terrorism) with various members of the West Wing staff. The inclusion of this special episode offers clear evidence of *TWW*'s creators' belief in the necessity of responding directly to this cataclysmic change in the country's political climate.

TWW has been the subject of extensive analysis by intellectuals and academics (collected in Rollins and O'Connor, 2003) and of two book-length academic studies (Crawley, 2006; Parry-Giles & Parry-Giles, 2006). As is often the case when popular culture is put under the microscope, the series functions for these writers as something of a Rorschach text, with authors analyzing it for a range of tendencies and reasons: evidence of the elision of gender and race from the national political narrative (Parry-Giles & Parry-Giles, 2006); misrepresentation of the mechanisms of policy formation and implementation, particularly the role of the bureaucracy (Levine, 2003); and inevitably, given its Democratic incumbent, demonstrations of "liberal bias" and the promotion of a "left wing" political agenda (Podhoretz, 2003). (It should be noted that much of this analysis has focused on the first four seasons of the series, before the departure of its creator. Sorkin left the series in 2004, having written or co-written 85 of the first 88 episodes.)

Clearly, my analysis of *The West Wing* has its own agenda. Placing the series within the context of what we have called the operative fables of the American tradition of political narrative, sampling 32 episodes over the entire life span of the series (with a preference for those focusing on political issues rather than the private lives of the protagonists), I seek to trace the ways in which the series fuses elements of all three of the fables we have examined, creating as a result something genuinely new: a realistic fable of heroic political leadership—or, perhaps, a heroic fable of political realism.

At the core of this fable is a seeming contradiction, or at least tension, between elements that have generally been seen by our narratives as irreconcilable; namely, political realism and political heroism. What makes Sorkin's narrative universe unique in our analysis is its realistic depiction of the compromises, the deal making, the negotiating, and trading off the daily business of government entail, a depiction that coexists with an enduring belief in the continuing decency, rectitude, and devotion to public service of the individuals who engage in it. Josiah Bartlet and his staff are clearly believers in the possibility of serving the national good through the political system as it exists. They are not innocents waiting to be disillusioned, nor are they on a slippery road to moral ruin, betrayed by their own ambitions or corrupted by the evil around them. They will not even, or very rarely, cross that invisible line that separates legitimate compromise from illegal deals. They simply devote their considerable intelligence, energy, passion, and conviction to the daily practice of politics and government. In a lengthy interview in 2000 (fittingly broadcast on PBS' august NewsHour with Jim Lehrer) Sorkin himself explicitly addressed the significance of this:

> Our leaders, government people are [usually] portrayed as dolts or as Machiavellian somehow. The characters in this show are neither. They are flawed, to be sure, because you need characters in drama to have flaws. But they, all of them, have set aside probably more lucrative careers for public service. They are dedicated not just to this president, but to doing good, rather than doing well. The show is kind of a valentine to public service. It celebrates our institutions. (Sorkin, 2000)

An important part of this valentine is the stress Sorkin placed on the intelligence of his protagonists, noting in a subsequent interview that one of the pleasures of the series for him as a writer was the opportunity to create dialogue for people who were much smarter about politics than he. That trademark Sorkinese, delivered at breakneck speed and generally while in motion, those dazzling riffs of insider political shorthand, he described in a wonderful phrase as "a phonetic re-creation of the sound of political sophistication" (Sorkin, 2002). It is no surprise that he identifies the playwright David Mamet, with his unique cadences, idioms, and rhythms, as a major influence.

Intellect is, indeed, the defining trait of President Josiah (Jed) Bartlet, played with authority, wit, and conviction by Martin Sheen. Bartlet is a former professor, a Nobel laureate in economics, and a former New Hampshire Congressman and Governor. (This intellectual background alone, in the era of George W. Bush's presidency, was enough to earn the series one of its nicknames, "The Left Wing." It was not intended as a compliment.) But what implications does his status have for the narrative's characterization of his leadership? *The West Wing* presents Bartlet as erudite: he makes frequent use of Latin, has a wide command of factual information, and an easy grasp of cutting-edge research. He is also an articulate and effective public speaker. But the essence of Bartlet's intellectualism is in his approach to decision making. He does not rush to decide, but takes the time to consult his staff, Congress, the bureaucracy, and sometimes still more widely; he also expands the set of alternatives and thinks carefully about their implications. Thoughtfulness, however, does not imply indecision, and ultimately—sometimes with the prodding of his staff to meet inexorable deadlines—Bartlet decides.

Surprisingly, for a character whose chief marker is intellect, Bartlet is also religious, a practicing Catholic who converted from Protestantism in his youth, and who uses Catholic theology to inform the moral code he brings with him to the White House. The series makes effective use of the conflicts Bartlet experiences between his religious beliefs and his political allegiances. "Take this Sabbath Day," episode 14 of the first season, centered on capital punishment. Bartlet, faced with the weighty decision of whether to commute the death sentence of a drug dealer convicted under federal law, consults both Catholic theology and other religious traditions. In the end, he determines not to commute, allowing his personal and religiously influenced opposition to be overridden by a legal mandate, clear evidence in the case, and strong public support for the death penalty. American screen treatments of intellectuals have tended to emphasize their generic elevation of reason above emotion. Bartlet's religious beliefs function as a counterbalance to his intellectualism, imbuing his character with compassion and a moral compass that redeems him from the sin of "eggheadedness." The scholars Trevor Parry-Giles and Shawn Parry-Giles (2006, p. 50) rightly emphasize the narrative importance of Bartlet's constant struggle to do "what is right, just, and moral"—a struggle the narrative often, but not always, allows him to win.

Bartlet is married to a physician who has a set of policy concerns of her own, and who, by advocating about these issues, functions as one of his advisers. The relationship is often argumentative, as the two often disagree about politics and policy, but the marriage is close, with no hint of any extramarital interest by either spouse.

One of the strengths of *The West Wing* as television drama was the quality of the large ensemble cast that peopled it. But this has a structural and thematic importance too. If, as Melissa Crawley contends in her 2006 study *Mr. Sorkin Goes to Washington*, Sorkin conceives of politics as "workplace drama," then the president does indeed become "the ideal employer" (Crawley, 2006, p. 80). Bartlet's core West Wing staff all joined him during his first campaign for the presidency and virtually all remain with him to the last days of his administration. The West Wing staff are all exceedingly hard working and all single, the demands of work in the West Wing making it difficult to initiate or maintain romantic relationships. The staff ultimately took on the characteristics of a family, with the president treating the senior staff as brothers and the younger staff as his children.

He consults with the staff extensively (the structural premise for all that crackling dialogue) and is sufficiently open-minded that they are not afraid to disagree with him, sometimes heatedly. Sorkin's West Wing is a dramatic democracy in the sense that the protagonist is surrounded by a group of equally strong and well-developed characters, all of whom receive large amounts of narrative attention. It is a polyphonic narrative with a vengeance, peopled with memorable and distinctive voices that never stop talking: Chief of Staff Leo McGarry (experienced, politically savvy, a street fighter with a conscience); Deputy Chief of Staff Josh Lyman (a pragmatic idealist, explosive, manic); C. J. Cregg, Press Secretary and later Chief of Staff (the smartest woman in the room, sardonic, principled, a feminist) and Communications Director Toby Ziegler (outspoken, driven, a liberal intellectual who doesn't particularly like liberals). That the president can inspire the loyalty of this impressive inner group and has the confidence, and the wisdom, to listen to their advice even when it runs counter to his own wishes, is clearly presented as an essential component of his leadership and a measure of the intellectual and moral stature of the man.

Politically, Bartlet is a liberal Democrat facing a Republican-controlled Congress. Choosing this political dynamic, of course, ensured that the series would not run out of conflict or adversaries. The driving plot mechanism is thus the struggle between Bartlet doing what his conscience and political beliefs dictate and attempting to convince Congress to go along, on the one hand and, on the other, doing what is politically popular, as revealed by public opinion polling, or politically feasible, in that it will readily receive enough Republican votes to be enacted. Sometimes Bartlet's decisions reflect his preferences. At other times he does what is popular or politically expedient. The outcome is often of much less narrative importance than the process by which the decision is made.

In *The West Wing*'s early years, conservative critics took vocal exception to the program's liberal inclinations, interpreting it as an ad hominem attack on the principles and policies of the Bush administration (Podhoretz, 2003). This is ground that has been covered extensively elsewhere. It is impossible to watch the series and not interpret its characterizations as at least an implicit critique, in particular of recent residents of the White House. I would simply add that if you are a screenwriter contemplating the creation of a parallel political universe, it makes imaginative sense to elect a president from the party that is not currently in power. *Yes Minister* avoided the issue by refusing to identify the party of its Prime Minister. It would hardly have mattered. Since the essence of that series' vision was the irrelevance of political principles or ideology to governance, its satire was emphatically nonpartisan.

Is Josiah Bartlet a perfect president, a Jordan Lyman for the 21st century? The narrative is too smart to push his virtues that far. Bartlet is often gripped by anxiety and self-doubt. His crises of confidence during his initial campaign for the presidency are shown in flashback throughout the third season, establishing him as human enough to fear the magnitude of the job he undoubtedly covets. He can be irritable with staff, infuriated by the irrationality of opponents, intellectually arrogant, and quite frequently makes mistakes, which, however, he acknowledges openly and redeems. The character is further humanized by a major plot development introduced midway through the first season: the president suffers from multiple sclerosis (it was in remission during the campaign), a fact he has chosen to keep secret. This becomes a continuing feature of the plot, as news of his illness becomes public, and a special prosecutor is appointed by Congress to investigate allegations that this failure to disclose constituted electoral fraud. Bartlet ultimately accepts responsibility for his deception and is censured by resolution of Congress.[8] Throughout his second term, Bartlet is shown increasingly weakened by his illness. This careful shading of the character— though we might note that as recent presidential deceptions go, Bartlet's concealment of his medical status is of little consequence or, in Catholic terminology, venial—works well to establish a credible contemporary leader, a humanly heroic figure who "faces physical infirmity, professional anxiety, self-doubt and personal turmoil as he leads the nation" (Parry-Giles & Parry-Giles, 2006, p. 153).

The West Wing is no more perfect as political narrative than Bartlet is as president. Like the West Wing staffers who serve him so loyally, however, viewers are happy to put up with the occasional flaws. The series has a strong vein of sentimentality running through it. (It can be quite shameless in its deployment of the symbols of Bartlet's office, for example, and its occasional paeans to the spirit of democracy and the essential decency of "ordinary" Americans would make Frank Capra blush.) It is also more than happy to exploit melodramatic conventions. Season 1 ends with an assassination attempt. We don't find out who is actually hit until season 2. The personal lives of the staffers (and the president's family) are mined for myriad romantic entanglements and personal drama. And there is a noticeable tendency to send off young, attractive, secondary characters into the line of fire (assassination, terrorist bombings in unnamed middle-eastern countries, violence at home).

More serious limitations include the highly idealized relations among the West Wing staff and their unswerving devotion to the president. Real-world advisers are more likely to constitute rival factions. They are less likely to speak their truth to power as forcefully as the staff on *TWW* and much more likely to compete with one another for the president's favor, leading in some cases to pulling punches, in other instances to simple sycophancy. They are also, given the demands of the job, much more prone to burnout, which would result in shorter tours of duty at the center than on *TWW* (Baker, 2010b). Finally, actual advisers are less likely to make a career of continued service to a constituency of one, even the president, and thus are more likely to move on to other careers, for example in elective politics or in the media (Levine, 2003).

While Sorkin's view of politics in the Oval Office and public service in the West Wing is, if not exactly idealized, then air-brushed, this does not extend to the entire public sector. Indeed, the inexorable demands of series television requires ongoing conflict, and Bartlet enjoys a steady stream of political adversaries. His main antagonists are found in Congress, among both parties. *The West Wing*'s Republicans pursue an agenda of budget cutting, and in the fifth season they and Bartlet come to a budgetary impasse that leads to a shutdown of the federal government (episode 8, "Shutdown"). Democratic legislators are depicted as largely unconcerned about the national interest as Bartlet attempts to define it, primarily seeking largesse for their constituencies to ensure their own reelection. In season 5, episode 5, "A Constituency of One," a Democratic senator from Idaho blocks military promotions to induce the president to reinstate funding for the construction of a missile launcher that was being built in his state. When the White House refuses and publicizes the senator's maneuver, he retaliates by switching to the Republican side. It is precisely through ancillary plot lines like these, and the ongoing necessity for compromise, conciliation, and the occasional strong-arm maneuver (that frequently backfires) that the Bartlet administration's political circumstances entail, that *TWW* establishes the nature of the daily business of governance. It's not all clever policy disputes at 90 miles an hour in the hallways of the West Wing. Nor is it graft and corruption. It's simply politics in a flawed system with a frequent election cycle, 24-hour media saturation, and loose campaign finance laws.

There is one serious omission from *The West Wing*'s narrative world, however. The executive branch of government is for the most part conspicuous by its absence. Few departmental secretaries have significant roles in the series. When we do see secretaries or the occasional career public servant, their concerns tend to be predictably parochial, defending their traditional mandates or their budgets. In season 4, episode 14, "Inauguration, Part 1," President Bartlet seeks to mobilize the government to prevent ethnic cleansing in a country in equatorial Africa. Both the State and Defense Departments work to derail his initiative; State because it is worried that Bartlet will elevate humanitarian concerns to a foreign policy priority and Defense because it feels overcommitted and does not want to send troops to Africa. Clearly, the public-choice view of politics and policy is not banished from *TWW*, but it functions largely as an internal counternarrative, the negative contrast to the dedication of Bartlet and his West Wing advisers to decision making on the basis of the public interest.

This might suggest that Bartlet is presented as a unique specimen, an exception to the general rule exemplified by the members of Congress on both sides of the party divide. In fact, while self-seeking, or simply inept, politicians exist within the narrative, so do a number of other Bartlet-like figures. Bartlet's second-term Republican opponent, Robert Richie, the governor of Florida, is not one of them. Richie, widely believed to have been based on George W. Bush, is inarticulate, faux-folksy, and defiantly anti-intellectual, described by Bartlet as "a .22 caliber mind in a .357 Magnum world." (Richie's verdict on the president is: "superior sumbitch.") Informed of the recent murder of a Secret Service Agent, Richie ponders, then pronounces, "Crime. Boy. I don't know." To which Bartlet replies, "In the future, if you're wondering, 'Crime. Boy. I don't know' is the point when I decided to kick your ass" (season 3, episode 21, "Posse Comitatus"). Bartlet's two vice presidents are also less than ideal; the first, forced to resign after leaking confidential information to the woman with whom he is having an extramarital affair (season 4, episode 21, "Life on Mars"). His successor is a lightweight representative known derisively by West Wing staffers as "the Congressman from the Western Colorado Mining Company."

Later seasons of the series, however, develop two worthy successors to Bartlet in the competing Democratic and Republican presidential candidates. If any single character on *The West Wing* constitutes a liberal electoral fantasy come to life it is surely Democratic Congressman Matthew (Matt) Santos, a Hispanic American former Marine fighter pilot who saw service in the Gulf War, who is also a two-time mayor of Houston. The son of a barber and a domestic worker, Santos is the first member of his family to graduate from college. He is passionate, articulate, highly intelligent, a savvy politician, a skillful strategist, young, and good looking to boot. He is played with enormous charm, and saving humor, by Jimmy Smits. His opponent, Arnold Vinick, is that rarest of birds, the moderate, intellectual Republican. As embodied by veteran actor Alan Alda (the much-loved star of the popular 1970s television series *M*A*S*H*), he is every centrist's dream of a candidate: cultured, experienced, knowledgeable about international affairs, devoted to public service, a man of honor who will not make use of illicitly obtained private information about his opponent. When the two men meet in a debate broadcast live on November 6, 2007 (season 7, episode 7, "The Debate"), viewers could be forgiven for feeling that they had entered political nirvana. The seriousness of the issues being canvassed; the measured, thoughtful, and substantive responses from the candidates; the general civility and fluency of the exchanges made the outcome of the election entirely understandable. The country could barely choose, with the last state to be decided, Nevada, providing the slimmest margin of victory for Santos. If it is not Josiah Bartlet all over again, the continuity is clearly there. The nation is in good hands. (One of Santos' first actions is to invite Vinick to join his administration as Secretary of State.)

Shortly after Aaron Sorkin announced his departure from *The West Wing* at the end of the series' fourth season, Richard Just, writing in *The American Prospect Online*, summarized the show's signal achievement: its insistence that "intelligence and moral purpose are the two most important attributes we ought to expect from our political leaders." It is, he concludes, in somewhat valedictory style "a smart show whose central message was about the virtue of intellectual passion" (Just, 2003). Subsequent writers echoed Just, putting even more emphasis on the thematic implications of the role of dialogue/debate within the narrative. Political scientist Samuel Chambers cites the series' weekly policy debates as an example of "agonistic discourse," genuine political debate among people who, while strongly disagreeing with each other, maintain mutual admiration and respect (Chambers, 2003, p. 96). Parry-Giles and Parry-Giles, referring specifically to the special "Isaac and Ishmael" episode (season 3), invoke the classical concept of *methexis*, dialogue intended as a means of promoting cultural understanding, healing, and community (Parry-Giles & Parry-Giles, 2006, p. 160).

In their own ways, these writers too are addressing the issues of characterization and polyphony, primarily at a thematic level, with an emphasis on their prescriptive function. But we can also consider the thematic importance of *The West Wing*'s multiplot structure and characteristic visual style. A television series about government raises the inevitable question of what the protagonists actually do in the course of a (very long) work day. In some instances, the president makes a decision himself, for example to appoint a certain person to the Supreme Court or to order military action. In others, there are collective decisions to which the president is a party, for example when Congress passes, modifies, or rejects his legislative proposals. And in other instances, the action is communications through the media to the public; for example, C. J. Cregg's daily press briefing. But, as a backdrop to all these actions, there is the process of deliberation. Some reviewers (Pompper, 2003) have argued—correctly, in my view—that *TWW*'s distinctiveness rests in its taking its audience behind the scenes to depict C. P. Snow's "closed politics"—the deliberation, debate, and negotiations that precede government decisions.

The West Wing's originality lay in the means it chose to depict the process of making decisions simultaneously about a variety of issues. *TWW* adopted the standard convention of television drama that incorporates an ensemble of actors who are involved in multiple story lines that are linked from episode to episode. The agenda for a typical episode could include the White House attempting to gather congressional support for gun control legislation, an offshore oil spill, allegations in the media that the White House has softened an EPA report about an environmental hazard, ethnic violence in an equatorial African country, and a hostage-taking of American embassy staff in Latin America. Some of these issues were resolved in a given episode, and others persisted from one episode to another and were never resolved or ended in an ambiguous outcome. This convention of television drama neatly fits the context of the central agency of any major government, particularly that of the United States. There are numerous political priorities to be pursued, crises breaking out either domestically or overseas, and communications issues to be managed. Staffers are inevitably overstretched and stressed, as they attempt to control the agenda and to communicate the president or prime minister's message.[9]

Sorkin's scripts have his characters, particularly the White House staff, discussing policy issues, usually taking different sides (for example, C. J. Cregg arguing from a feminist point of view against weapon sales to a fundamentalist Islamic state that oppresses women, even if it is a strategically significant ally, and Leo McGarry making a realpolitik argument in support of weapons sales (season 3, episode 8, "The Women of Qumar"). The issues are discussed passionately, but as the West Wing staffers have many issues to consider (as well as personal relationships with one another), their discussions shift rapidly from topic to topic, interpolating serious affairs of state with personal banter. In addition, the conversations often include unexplained acronyms and references to past events at either a personal or professional level. In the real world, these discussions might be pursued in e-mail messages on BlackBerries, phone calls, and face-to-face meetings. E-mail messages and phone calls, however, do not make for very exciting television. Sorkin and his producers chose to concentrate on face-to-face communications in what have become known as "walk and talks." *TWW*'s set was constructed to include long corridors, and these conversations unfolded as the actors walked, often in haste, up and down them. The conversations generally involved pairs of actors and often switched from one pair to another, sometimes moving in different directions and shifting focus as the two pairs passed. The scenes were shot in close-up with a handheld Steadicam, which as the name suggests, preserved a steady picture that avoided the jerkiness of the cameras used to achieve the *cinema verite* atmosphere of *The Candidate* and *The War Room* (Smith, 2003; Vest, 2003).[10]

The use of the Steadicam has the effect of bringing the audience into the corridor with the actors. The rapid pace and deliberately oblique nature of Sorkin's dialogue heighten the engagement, challenging viewers to follow the policy debate and determine which position they support, as well as follow the story, filling in gaps such as the meaning of acronyms or the significance of references to previous personal or political events. Enjoying *TWW* demanded a high level of engagement, and its success indicated that a large audience (generally of higher income and education) was willing to provide it (Crawley, 2006, p, 68–69). Equally importantly, Sorkin and his co-writers ensured that the content of the ongoing policy debates matched the complexity of their dramatic presentation. Issues are analyzed from a variety of perspectives, with characters moving unpredictably between positions. Nor is any particular ideological viewpoint allowed to triumph consistently. The cumulative effect is to create a convincing representation of the magnitude and complexity of the business of making policy, as well as the dizzying speed at which events can unfold and the range of issues that must be canvassed in the course of a single day of a government's life.

While multiple plot lines over seven seasons are difficult to track, the series paid increasing attention to international stories, in particular terrorism against the United States and American interests abroad. This is likely a reflection of the changed political agenda in the United States following the terrorist attacks of 9/11. But it might also have been dramatically motivated: domestic politics involved continual negotiation with a Republican-controlled Congress and self-interested Democrats. To make progress, Bartlet must make deals and engage in the same sort of political calculus as the legislators. Bartlet's power as commander-in-chief is less constrained by Congress. He can sit in the high-tech Situation Room, watching military and political developments overseas, and then, after consulting the military and his advisers in the National Security Council, make his decision, which can immediately be implemented either by diplomatic initiative or military action. This allows the series to contrast the president as constrained player in domestic politics with the decisive Commander-in-Chief. It also provides occasions for nail-biting crises watches, late-breaking reprieves or disasters, and the occasional tune-in-next-week cliffhangers.

Any analysis of *The West Wing*, like discussion of *Yes Minister*, will inevitably be beset by the temptation to assess its influence on public perceptions of politicians and politics. The marked similarities between Barack Obama and Matt Santos—acknowledged in an interview with *The Guardian* by the series' writer and producer Elie Attie, who was responsible for most of the Santos episodes, as deliberate borrowings—only increases the urge (Freedland, 2008). Sorkin himself, in the interviews cited earlier, made plain his desire to offer corrective representations of politicians and the staffers who work for them. I have neither the desire nor the confidence to make assertions concerning the effect of this highly intelligent and beautifully acted series on the wider culture. My concern throughout has been to focus on the significant addition it makes to a distinctive tradition of American political narrative. What Sorkin and his colleagues achieved through seven seasons of *The West Wing* was to create a convincing dramatic representation of the full complexity of politics and governance in contemporary America and to people it with a cast of passionate, intelligent, dedicated characters seeking to do the right thing for their country and its citizens and, quite frequently, actually doing so. The narrative's consistent ability to demonstrate political sophistication without cynicism, depict compromise without moral degradation and offer positive characterization without idealization (or without too much), sets it apart within the tradition we have been considering. The last episode of *TWW* ("Tomorrow") was broadcast on May 14, 2006, and dealt with the inauguration of President Matthew Santos, the United States' first non-White Chief Executive. Much has happened in the real world of American politics since then. Could another *West Wing* be created now? And if it were, could it find the same dedicated audience? It would be nice to think so.

The Political Narratives We Deserve

Movies and television have long been considered the great democratic art forms. It seems fitting that a chapter analyzing American political narratives should focus so extensively on film. (And no less fitting to discover how eagerly Hollywood seizes on political source material: *All the King's Men, Advise and Consent, Seven Days in May, The Last Hurrah, Primary Colors, Charlie Wilson's War* all began life as printed texts that were very quickly adapted for the screen.) And *The West Wing* was written for the other screen. The British television critic A. A. Gill (2006), in an irascible review of the soft-centered political satire *The Amazing Mrs. Pritchard,* cited it as "another example of British drama's inability to treat politics as anything other than a joke." Professing an extreme case of *TWW* envy, Gill went on: "Perhaps one of the reasons we get the politics and politicians we do is that, like sniggering kids, we refuse to take them seriously." The political narratives we have been considering range over a period of almost sixty years. They encompass a spectrum of genres including melodrama (*All the King's Men*), thriller (*Seven Days in May*), satire (*Wag the Dog*), character study (*The Candidate*), documentary (*The War Room*), and simple farce (*The Distinguished Gentleman*), at times combining elements of all these, and more, within their narrative frame. Within this artistic democracy, we have traced three operative fables, noting at the outset how they coexist, persist, and overlap, and locating in *The West Wing* a uniquely persuasive convergence of all three. Perhaps the most important point to make in conclusion is to note the variety and vitality of this narrative field, to highlight the imaginative pull the political narrative has exerted over decades of cultural change. Unlike their British counterparts, American creators of political narrative have always found politics to be something more than a joke, a means to give shape to their vision of and for their country. The challenges facing their nation today are no laughing matter. Will the narratives and fables that emerge find room for both cynicism and idealism, sophistication and the occasional hero worship? Or will the expansiveness of the tradition prove to be a uniquely 20th-century phenomenon? Within the last five years, new hybrid genres have begun to appear: military-political narratives of the Iraq war and financial-political narratives of the recent global economic crisis. New operative fables are taking shape. The only certainty perhaps is that the story never ends.

Whatever the fable, the American narratives share a common concern about political leadership. Unlike the dominant British fable that, drawing on public-choice theory, dismisses the possibility of exemplary political leadership, the American fables seek to define it, either by its presence or its absence. What are the common features that define this ideal? They include a politician's agenda; namely, the set of policies or programs he wishes to maintain or introduce; the sort of conceptual and emotional intelligence she brings to the decisions she must make in response to unanticipated events and crises; and the way he conducts those aspects of his life usually deemed personal but which at any moment could be become public. As most of the narratives discussed in this chapter are fictional, I prefer not to develop notions of exemplary political leadership on that basis alone. Instead, drawing upon not only the fictional narratives of this chapter, but also the historical narratives of other chapters, I will in the final chapter discuss an ideal of responsible political leadership.

Endnotes

1. I have deliberately excluded such mixed-genre films from this chapter, including Aaron Sorkin's 1995 precursor to *The West Wing*, *The American President*, which featured Michael Douglas as a liberal, widowed president in an election year, who falls in love with a beautiful environmental lobbyist (Annette

Bening) and has to defend her from the slanders of his rabid Republican opponent (played with evident relish by Richard Dreyfus). It's an amusing film and co-stars Martin Sheen (soon to be elevated to the Oval Office himself as President Bartlet) as an acerbic but still idealistic Chief of Staff, as well as Michael J. Fox and Anna Deavere Smith as hyperverbal staffers. Any resemblance to serious political narrative, however, is purely accidental. Similarly, I don't consider action and/or thriller narratives that feature high-ranking government officials like *Independence Day* (1996) and *Air Force One* (1997), or the immensely popular television series *24*, a subgenre I have privately dubbed President-in-Peril flicks.

2. Another 1990s political film that also makes satirical use of the assassination plot, Tim Robbins's *Bob Roberts* (1992), is not discussed in this chapter. This mock-documentary of the career of folk singer/conservative politician Bob Roberts who survives an assassination attempt (possibly staged) to campaign successfully for the senate from his wheelchair, strongly suggests that the sinister Roberts has faked his own injuries while inciting his increasingly rabid young supporters to attack (and murder) the journalist seeking to expose him. While the movie makes clever use of the conventions of contemporary political documentary, its increasingly preposterous (and paranoid) plot line undermines its effectiveness as satire. It is silly in a way that *Bulworth*, for all its improbabilities, never is and shares nothing of the later movie's sophisticated understanding of the mechanics of the political "game."

3. Some viewers have interpreted the film's ending as at least holding out the possibility that Bulworth will survive his wounds. I disagree. The tenor of the narrative seems to me to leave its protagonist with no other possibilities. A sacrificial death (of his own conniving) at the moment of his electoral rebirth seems more in keeping with the bleak political vision that animates both Bulworth and *Bulworth*.

4. The two other men who complete this triangle, the councilor, Frank Anselmo (a searing performance by Danny Aiello) and the judge, Walter Stern (a dignified but underused Martin Landau) are structural counterparts to Pappas. All three are middle-aged men of ethnic backgrounds, passionate and effective in their public roles, who cross the invisible line that separates pragmatic compromise from moral transgression. Anselmo commits suicide, urged by his Mafia patron to "make it easy" for his family, and Stern resigns.

5. A legitimate deal the movie presents involves the city councilor representing a group of real-estate developers willing to build a financial center in Brooklyn if Pappas can provide transport access. Pappas was able to find money in the city's budget for an expressway off-ramp and willing to go to the state government for funding for a new subway stop, in effect creating a public-private partnership.

6. The principal screenwriter for *City Hall* was Ken Lipper, a New York businessman and author, who also served as a deputy mayor for finance and economic development from 1983 to 1985. One of Lipper's earlier screenplays was for Oliver Stone's movie *Wall Street*. The theme of a flawed mentor is also apparent in *Wall Street*, though in that case, the mentor, corporate raider Gordon

Gekko, was contemptuously exploitive of his protégé, and the protégé's revenge more vindictive, delivered with cold fury rather than deep regret.

7. *The Candidate* had a direct successor in the early HBO production *Tanner 88*, a "mockumentary" directed by Robert Altman from a script by Gary Trudeau (best known as the creator of the Pulitzer Prize-winning satirical cartoon strip *Doonesbury*). The miniseries follows the fortunes of fictional Michigan congressman Jack Tanner in his bid for the Democratic presidential nomination. Like *The Candidate*, *Tanner 88* is filmed in *cinema verite* style. Where the earlier film had run a pseudocampaign during filming, *Tanner 88* introduced its star, Michael Murphy, and supporting cast into the 1988 Democratic primary season, featuring footage of (real) candidates stumping and staging encounters with them. (Cameo appearances included Bruce Babbit, Kitty Dukakis, Bob Dole, Gary Hart, Jesse Jackson, and Pat Robertson.) The series had difficulty finding an audience, its unusual (for the time) mix of fiction and reality confusing some viewers. HBO did not extend the series beyond its initial 11 episodes. Its prestige has increased over time, however, and its satire of the escalating, media-fed insanity of a presidential campaign remains remarkably relevant. The series was rebroadcast in 2004 on the Sundance Channel (a Robert Redford connection) with framing commentary from the main actors (in character). The channel subsequently produced a four-part sequel, *Tanner on Tanner*.

8. The illness is first introduced in season 1, episode 12 "He Shall from Time to Time"; it is a major focus in season 2, episodes 18, 19, and 20 "17 People," "Bad Moon Rising," and "The Fall's Gonna Kill You," respectively. The Special Prosecutor's investigation comes to the fore in season 3 episodes 3, 4, 5, and 10.

9. In contrast to *TWW*'s television drama, *Yes Minister* is a situation comedy. Its episodes deal with one issue or at most two, and are neatly resolved in 30 minutes, usually with a deal between Jim Hacker and Sir Humphrey Appleby. Its episodes stand alone, while *TWW*'s are part of a long-running saga designed to invite ongoing engagement.

10. In contrast, *Yes Minister* was set in a traditional three-walled studio, with the viewer observing from the front through the lens of a mounted camera. Episodes were rehearsed and then recorded live before a studio audience. *TWW* used a mobile Steadicam, closely following the actors as they walk and talk.

6

Kennedy, Cuba, History

Lessons of a Crisis Management Narrative

Introduction

It is a scene familiar from every summer's Hollywood blockbuster: the Chief Executive confronting the unthinkable amid the grandeur of the Oval Office. Grim-faced men in uniforms or dark suits arranged in a phalanx before him. The solemn announcement: "Mr. President, we have a situation." He meets their gaze, resolute, undaunted. "How serious is it?" Then the aliens land, or the virus is unleashed, or the secret weapon is triggered, and the future of the free world is once again at stake for two hours in the multiplex. The scene is so familiar we might forget (the multiplex audience likely never knew) the historical events that are its progenitor: those thirteen days in October 1962 when, as Defense Secretary Robert McNamara, speaking in Errol Morris's 2003 documentary *The Fog of War,* recalled, "we literally looked down the gun barrel of nuclear war." It is ironic that those unparalleled days of crisis whose outcome might have "altered the course of world history in ways we can only dimly imagine" (Allison & Zelikow, 1999) should have spawned so many pop culture iterations. Yet in some ways the events themselves were always already a narrative. As the authors of a landmark study of the Cuban Missile Crisis observe, the events of those thirteen days, the possibilities of global thermonuclear war they raised, "appear conjured from some fantastic story or movie" (p. 77) and the early sixties did indeed see a rash of novels and films on that very theme. The story of the crisis, moreover, has become "among the most studied episodes in modern history" (p. 1), generating innumerable new narratives in its turn.

This chapter will consider a necessarily selective set of Cuban Missile Crisis narratives and the lessons those narratives offer, identifying a dominant fable that echoes the idealizing presidential fable of the previous chapter. Here, too, cynicism regarding corruption is abandoned as an exceptional leader prevails over less reasoned minds and spirits to pull the world back from the brink of nuclear insanity. Clearly there is an enormous difference between the fictional narratives of the presidency we analyzed previously and world-shaking historical events that have been exhaustively reconstructed by several generations of scholars. But, while the details of the historical record are by now well established, the meanings we attach to the narrative remain fluid. One of the paradoxes of the Cuban Missile Crisis literature is the extent to which every retelling (historical or fictionalized) insists on the unprecedented and unique nature of the events, while also invariably seeking to extract their (presumably transferable) lessons. We insist on reading for the moral, though the moral sought will vary. Is it about leadership? Governance? International relations? Defense policy? Nuclear deterrence? Decision making? Or the inevitable limitations of human rationality? And this need to wrest a larger meaning raises still larger questions. What does it mean to learn from history? What do we expect the past to teach us, and how far does that alter our perceptions of it? How much of even the recent past remains essentially unknowable? Is a narrative produced in hindsight more or less true?

These are some of the questions haunting Errol Morris's *The Fog of War*, an Academy Award-winning documentary portrait of Robert McNamara, Secretary of Defense during the Missile Crisis and a principal architect of U.S. policy during the escalation of the Vietnam conflict. Morris's film is subtitled *Eleven Lessons from the Life of Robert S. McNamara* and its subject, directly addressing the camera and speaking almost nonstop for most of the film's running time, offers more managerial maxims than even the subtitle promised. But the lessons Morris's film suggests are far less easily summarized, open-ended inquiries into history, truth, knowledge, and narrative, and the complex relationships among them, an exploration of the innumerable ways that, as Morris says, "narrative trumps evidence" (Morris, 2008b). Morris and McNamara's often competing narratives (and it is precisely the fact that they do compete that makes the film so compelling) stand as this chapter's defining counter-fable, an unsettling, and timeless, tutorial in the limits of human reason.

The Cuban Missile Crisis: October 16, 1962 to October 28, 1962

We begin with a brief review of the central facts of the Cuban Missile Crisis, drawn from its two most recent retellings: Munton and Welch's *The Cuban Missile Crisis: A Concise History* (2007) and Michael Dobbs' *One Minute to Midnight; Kennedy, Khrushchev, and Castro on the Brink of Nuclear War* (2008). Munton and Welch based their work on a careful review of the voluminous literature. Michael Dobbs (a journalist, not to be confused with the author of the novels discussed in chapters 3 and 4), in addition to drawing on the secondary literature, conducted his own original research, visiting government archives and interviewing many participants in the crisis, particularly Americans, Cubans, and Russians who were on the front lines.

The crisis was set in motion in the summer of 1962 when the Soviets began to send a variety of nuclear weapons, military aircraft, and defensive weapons such as surface-to-air missiles covertly to Cuba. Troops were also sent, amounting to a presence of 50,000. The main motivations for this action—a matter of desperate speculation during the crisis and fiercely debated by historians since—would now appear to have been closing the missile gap between the United States and the USSR and deterring a feared American invasion of Cuba.

The American government received intimations of the Soviet weapons buildup from a variety of sources, but the definitive confirmation came from films taken by a high level reconnaissance flight of an American U-2 spyplane on Sunday, October 14, 1962. President Kennedy was informed two days later. Rather than act immediately out of anger, shock, or alarm, the president established a secret high-level advisory committee, the Excom (Executive Committee of the National Security Council) to explore options. The Excom spent six days in increasingly agonized and polarized secret debate. Two main options quickly emerged: air strikes on the missiles followed by an invasion of Cuba versus a naval blockade. While these discussions were going on, Soviet Foreign Affairs Minister Andrei Gromyko made a previously scheduled visit to President Kennedy and, to Kennedy's astonishment and disdain, categorically denied that the Soviet Union had sent offensive weapons to Cuba.

Ultimately, President Kennedy decided on the naval blockade of ships carrying armaments and announced the naval "quarantine" to the world on Monday, October 22. His speech carefully left open the possibility of the use of increased force to remove the Soviets' offensive weapons from Cuba. The consequences of the decision became apparent during the course of the week. The United States put the quarantine into effect, intensified its military preparations to attack Cuba, and began regular low-level over-flights to continue photographing the Soviet military installations. (Previous surveillance flights had been carried out at a much higher level. These planes were literally operating under the radar, exposing the pilots to much greater risk of anti-aircraft fire from the ground.) The Soviet leadership, while ordering its weapons-transporting ships to reverse course, nonetheless ordered its forces in Cuba to make the missiles operational as soon as possible. On Friday, October 26, Soviet Premier Nikita Khrushchev sent Kennedy two telegrams. The first, more conciliatory in tone, offered to remove the weapons if the United States agreed not to invade Cuba. The second added a demand that the United States remove its own nuclear missiles based in Turkey.

On Saturday, October 27, while Kennedy and his advisers were struggling to determine a U.S. response, the military situation grew increasingly tense. The Soviets shot down an American U-2 flying over Cuba, killing the pilot, Major Rudolph Anderson. The Cubans opened anti-aircraft fire at the American low-level reconnaissance planes. The U.S. Navy tracked down a Soviet nuclear submarine in the Atlantic and forced it to the surface. An American U-2 flight monitoring atmospheric radiation over the Arctic strayed several hundred miles over Siberia before returning to base. (The President's response to this last incident, according to Dobbs, was "a short, bitter laugh and a truism from his Navy days: 'There's always some sonofabitch who doesn't get the word'" [Dobbs, 2008, p. 270].) Against this backdrop of accumulating military errors, provocations, and hair-trigger encounters, President Kennedy agreed to accept the proposals Khrushchev put forward in his first telegram. Attorney General Robert Kennedy met secretly with Soviet Ambassador Dobrynin, confirming (but not for public disclosure or attribution) that the American missiles would be removed from Turkey in several months. He also gave the Soviets a one-day deadline for a diplomatic resolution of the problem, with the threat of American military action beginning the next day should the Soviets refuse. Khrushchev's acceptance of Kennedy's final offer, delivered on Sunday, October 28, ended the crisis.

The narratives considered in this chapter will encompass a range of forms and genres spanning some 40 years. These include insider memoir, historical analysis, fictional (and fictionalized) feature films, and documentary. We begin with the best known early account of the crisis, Robert Kennedy's posthumously published *Thirteen Days: A Memoir of the Cuban Missile*

Crisis (1969), edited by JFK speechwriter Theodore Sorensen, with an introduction by Robert McNamara. We conclude with a portrait of McNamara himself, *The Fog of War* (2003), whose DVD tagline promises "A Whole New Story." In between we consider journalist Michael Dobbs' *One Minute to Midnight* (2008), a skillful and conscientious work of popular history, as well as the enormously influential *Essence of Decision*, political scientist Graham Allison's landmark reconceptualization of the crisis, first published in 1971, and revised with Philip Zelikow in 1999. Different as the two works are in every respect, they will be considered along with Kennedy's memoir as variations of a dominant crisis fable. Positioned against them are an equally heterogeneous group of films: the 2001 Hollywood recounting *Thirteen Days*; Stanley Kubrick's groundbreaking nuclear comedy *Dr. Strangelove* (1964); and Errol Morris's *The Fog of War*, a work memorably described by one critic as "a moral travelogue" (Angell, 2004). The chapter's central thesis is reflected in this structure. If Kennedy's account provides the clearest delineation of the dominant crisis fable, McNamara's "new" stories (the plural is used advisedly) constitute its most devastating revision.

Reason Triumphant: Robert Kennedy's *Thirteen Days* and the Heroic President

"On Tuesday morning, October 16, 1962, shortly after 9:00 o'clock, President Kennedy called and asked me to come to the White House. He said only that we were facing great trouble" (Kennedy, 1969). With these two simple sentences, Robert Kennedy begins his account of his participation in one of the most extraordinary events of modern history. As his title makes plain, he focuses entirely on the thirteen days of the crisis itself, from the American discovery of the Soviet missiles in Cuba to the eleventh-hour agreement that resulted in their removal. Kennedy concentrates on his own participation in the Excom, as well as the informal meetings and conversations (particularly with the president) in which he participated, and his responsibilities for implementing various decisions. The tone remains coolly analytical throughout, seemingly uninflected with emotion or partisanship, the narrative viewpoint determinedly limited in its chronological scope. Although he employs flashbacks as needed, as *in medias res* narratives have traditionally done—"I thought back to my meeting with Soviet Ambassador Anatoly Dobrynin in my office some weeks before"—there is no assumption of (retrospective) omniscience (p. 24). Nor is Kennedy himself the main protagonist. At the center of the narrative is the president. His character and conduct provide the resolution, and the moral, of Kennedy's fable. For Kennedy, the crisis is ultimately a story of the triumph of reason as embodied by his brother. It is a story of the world brought back from the brink of nuclear madness (madness not limited to the Soviet enemy) by the heroic restraint, intellectual clarity, compassion, and courage of a new breed of international leader, a statesman for the nuclear age. This image of the president, and this framing of the crisis' core conflict, would prove remarkably enduring. We will encounter versions of both in Dobbs, Allison, and the film *Thirteen Days*, while *Dr. Strangelove* will testify to its influence by the extent of its inversion. Only *The Fog of War* reframes the narrative entirely, exposing the terrifyingly precarious foundations of its hero's achievement.

Before looking in detail at the portrait of presidential leadership Kennedy paints, it is worth considering the ambiguities of his own position as narrator. Kennedy wrote a draft of *Thirteen Days* during the summer and fall of 1967, only four years after JFK's assassination and just preceding his own declaration as a candidate for the 1968 Democratic presidential nomination. (The memoir was edited and published posthumously in 1969.) Positioned at the time of publication as the ultimate insider's story, "a second-by-second account" of the crisis viewed from "the center of power," according to the first paperback edition's cover, Kennedy's project can clearly also be considered a literary memorial to his murdered brother, a consciously designed contribution to JFK's historical legacy, and perhaps the most prestigious campaign ad in the history of American presidential elections. None of this is to cast doubt on the veracity of the account. Rather it is to underline the multiple stories Kennedy the narrator was seeking to tell. How conscious Kennedy the author was of his narrator's multiple motivations is impossible to say. That they are present, and that they necessarily influence both what Kennedy recalls and how he does so, seems undeniable. The virtual absence of then-Vice President Lyndon Johnson from Kennedy's pages is a relatively minor example of this. At the time of writing, Johnson was, of course, the presumptive presidential nominee for 1968, a rival whose accomplishments Kennedy had no interest in publicizing. More significantly, the studied neutrality of tone Kennedy maintains throughout the memoir, the cool, statesmanlike restraint he brings to bear, even when writing of advice and opinions utterly inimical to his own, his judicious framing of events, all function as a textual enactment of the intellectual and temperamental qualities he celebrates in the president, and thus a narrative demonstration of his own fitness for the office. Does this necessarily make Kennedy an "unreliable" narrator? The issue is hardly so simple. Memory is always selective. The greater the pressure of conscious (and unconscious) narrative needs upon that memory, the more it is likely to be so. Does that invalidate the story, or more accurately stories, that are being reconstructed? Or does it make them still more revelatory? The reader alone must determine.

From its understated opening, Kennedy's narrative moves quickly to the president's first decisive action, an action which Kennedy clearly views as determinative of all that was to follow: the formation of the Excom.

> This was the group that met, talked, argued and fought together during that crucial period of time. From this group came the recommendations from which President Kennedy was ultimately to select his course of action. They were men of the highest intelligence, industrious, courageous, and dedicated to their country's well-being. It is no reflection on them that none was consistent in his opinion from the very beginning to the very end. That kind of open, unfettered mind was essential. For some there were only small changes, perhaps varieties of a single idea. For others there were continuous changes of opinion each day; some, because of the pressure of events, even appeared to lose their judgment and stability. (Kennedy 1969, 31)

The significance of the Excom, both to the historical record and to the other narratives Kennedy creates, cannot be overemphasized. It was the forum through which the president solicited the broad range of expertise and opinions upon which to exercise his own analytic powers. It was the talking, arguing, fighting proof of his determination to explore every possible option. The Excom's membership encompassed a variety of advisers, including not only those leading organizations with a formal mandate for involvement (the Secretaries of State and Defense, Director of the CIA, Chair of the Joint Chiefs of Staff) but other senior officials whose wisdom Kennedy valued (Attorney General Robert Kennedy and Treasury Secretary Dillon), as well as a variety of deputy secretaries and undersecretaries in State and Defense, and knowledgeable outsiders (former Secretary of State Dean Acheson). Questions of rank and of proper channels were disregarded. As Kennedy notes, "We all spoke as equals . . . the conversations were completely uninhibited and unrestricted" (p. 46). This too was the mark of a flexible and creative presiding intelligence willing to bypass traditional lines of authority, unafraid (as a later generation would say) to think outside the box, demanding that his advisors do the same.

It is equally clear from Kennedy's account that the president's management of the Excom was highly conscious and deliberate. Fully aware of the potentially inhibiting, or at least distorting, effect of his presence, he chose not to attend all its meetings. Kennedy's editorial comment is succinct: "This was wise." Yet for all the free-flow of debate, the president remained firmly in control, committed to action—"It would be difficult; the stakes were high—of the highest and most substantial kind—but he knew he would have to act"—raising "probing questions," insisting on better answers, clearer options, sending the wise men back to their deliberations when those answers weren't forthcoming (Kennedy, 1969, pp. 33, 43).

The outlines of the portrait are beginning to emerge. Unlike some of the "open and unfettered minds" in the Excom, the president never loses his bearings amid the pressure of events. Interrogating his advisers on every aspect of their recommendations, repeatedly demonstrating his grasp of implication and detail, he is yet capable of taking the long view, referring in private conversation to historian Barbara Tuchman's account of the origins of the first World War and drawing further analogies to Germany in 1939: "They somehow seemed to tumble into war, he said, through stupidity, individual idiosyncrasies, misunderstandings, and personal complexes of inferiority and grandeur" (Kennedy, 1969, p. 62). It is a history the president is determined not to repeat. Throughout the tense days of standoff and negotiation, the young president repeatedly demonstrates the "grace under fire" that others of the Excom circle—as Kennedy notes, discreetly naming no names—were unable to muster: "That kind of pressure does strange things to a human being, even to brilliant, self-confident, mature, experienced men" (p. 46). His calmness and confidence, maintained throughout, even allow an occasional flash of humor, strategically deployed. A tense exchange with Air Force chief of staff General Curtis LeMay, in which LeMay makes an astoundingly impolitic reference to appeasement, culminates with the general's impertinent (and inaccurate) comment: "You're in a pretty bad fix at the present time." The president's rejoinder is immediate: "Well, you're in there with me. Personally." (Kennedy, 1969, pp. 35–37; Dobbs, 2008, pp. 21–22). When the philosopher and pacifist Bertrand Russell sent a message praising Khrushchev's conciliatory stance and condemning American belligerence, the president replied personally: "I think your attention might well be directed to the burglar rather than to those who caught him" (Kennedy, 1969, p. 74).

If Kennedy's narrative highlights the president's extraordinary qualities of mind and spirit, it pays equal attention to his administrative role as Commander in Chief, in particular to the balance of restraint and resolution he maintains. Skeptical in the face of the Joint Chiefs of Staff's unanimous recommendations of immediate military action (Kennedy, 1969, p. 36), refusing to be goaded into precipitate shows of force, he maintained strict control over the military once the naval quarantine went into effect, carefully supervising frontline operations to ensure there would be no mistaken initiation of hostilities. (This was not done through direct personal contact, but by his frequent presence in the White House situation room and through Defense Secretary Robert McNamara.) On a number of occasions, the president himself intervened to restrain military operations, letting an East German passenger ship through the quarantine to Cuba (pp. 77–78) and refusing to permit a retaliatory strike on the Cuban SAM (surface-to-air missile) launch site that destroyed the American U-2 plane piloted by Major Anderson. Prepared to fight, clearly every inch the war leader, the president stands alone in his ability to see beyond the immediate provocation, resisting the atavistic urge to strike back harder when struck:

> At first, there was almost unanimous agreement that we had to attack early the next morning with bombers and fighters and destroy the SAM sites. But again, the President pulled everyone back. "It isn't the first step that concerns me," he said, "but both sides escalating to the fourth and fifth step—and we don't go to the sixth because there is no one around to do so." (p. 98)

The image could not be stronger: one man alone preventing a rush into the abyss, once again, one heroic figure pulling everyone back.

Kennedy's profile of the president-hero is now all but complete. Only one attribute remains to be addressed, but it is, for the author, of the utmost importance: the human factor, the powers of empathy and compassion which the president repeatedly displayed even at the height of the crisis. It was not merely his constant awareness of the generations of children whose fates rested in his hands. It was, equally, a capacity to extend his insight into the mind of his adversary, to empathize, to see with a largeness of vision that transcended the more limited capacities of even his closest advisors, coupled with the moral courage to insist on the validity of that vision: "Against the advice of many of his advisers and of the military, he decided to give Khrushchev more time. 'We don't want to push him to a precipitous action—give him time to consider. I don't want to put him in a corner from which he cannot escape'" (Kennedy, 1969, pp. 76–77). This aspect of the president's response is so important for Kennedy, he returns to it again at a later point in his narrative. What is fascinating about his analysis here is the way in which the subject himself frames the issue as a question of narrative, the story that will be told of the events he is then enacting:

> "I am not going to follow a course which will allow anyone to write a comparable book about this time [comparable to Tuchman's *The Guns of August*], *The Missiles of October*," he said to me that Saturday night, October 26. "If anyone is around to write, after this, they are going to understand that we made every effort to find peace and every effort to give our adversary room to move. I am not going to push the Russians an inch beyond what is necessary." (p. 127)

This is the actor on the stage of history, conscious of the judgment of future generations. It is the leader called forth by an extraordinary crisis who rises to it triumphantly, a larger-than-life figure who has joined the ranks of the titans. But the image with which Kennedy closes his account is in a more minor key, though no less significant. After word is received that Khrushchev has accepted the president's proposed resolution, Robert Kennedy leaves his brother alone in his office, writing a letter of condolence to the widow of Major Anderson, the individual life remembered even while history is being made.

"I often thought afterward of some the things we learned from this confrontation" (Kennedy, 1969, p. 111). Like most of the chroniclers and historians of the crisis who would follow him, Kennedy's narrative concludes with the lessons he feels compelled to draw, lessons offered as a means to replicate the president's successful resolution of the crisis. Interestingly, Kennedy's rationale for offering them is not the extraordinary singularity of the events that produced them, but just the opposite: "We could have other missile crises in the future—different kinds, no doubt, and under different circumstances" (p. 123). The implication is clear: It could happen again, and if it does, this is what you do. The lengthy discussion that follows (some eighteen pages in the paperback edition), frequently expressed in the imperative, focuses on five main points:

- Build strong multilateral support.
- Cultivate empathy for the adversary and express that empathy through careful management of communications and their timing.
- Explore all possible options as part of the decision-making process encouraging as much free-ranging debate as time permits.
- Elicit a full range of opinions without consideration of rank or deference to a presumed preferred course of action.
- Bring as many departmental viewpoints to the table as possible, regardless of "turf" or traditional bureaucratic demarcations.

All five are unexceptionable managerial formulations gleaned from firsthand experience, and they remain valid today. They are also, though Kennedy nowhere explicitly says so, entirely dependent upon precisely the sort of extraordinary moral and intellectual leadership that President Kennedy so singularly displayed throughout the crisis. In effect, they are a further restatement—in administrative and institutional terms—of the Cuban Missile Crisis' dominant narrative: reason triumphs; rational debate, the free play of ideas, and compassionate courage will produce the necessary creative thinking that routs irrationality and the engrained recourse to force. But only if that heroic reason, rationality, and compassion are embodied in the person of an outstanding leader, a president-hero. The lessons, then, can be reduced to a single, perhaps impossible, injunction: make sure you have a John F. Kennedy on hand.

Commander in Chief, Analyzer in Chief: Two Historical Narratives

Michael Dobbs' *One Minute to Midnight* (2008) is a carefully researched and engagingly written account of the Cuban Missile Crisis, informed by the scholarly literature and incorporating the results of Dobbs' own interviews with participants. It is, in the words of the author's preface, "a minute-by-minute account of the drama" (p. xiii), but it is also offered as something of a corrective to previous omissions, a representation of the experience of the lesser figures who participated in that world-altering drama, the "accidental figures whose role in history is often overlooked: pilots and submariners, spies and missileers, bureaucrats and propagandists, radar operators and saboteurs" (p. 23). In effect, Dobbs is seeking to restore the polyphonic range other versions of the crisis narrative have silenced, literally giving voice to the "minor characters" who are generally not granted speaking parts. Unlike the Hollywood film *Thirteen Days*, which attempts (unsuccessfully) to displace the figure of the heroic president from the center of the crisis narrative, Dobbs' history offers numerous supplementary story lines radiating from, and returning to, the undisputed center: the figure of greatness whose "sane and level-headed" management of the crisis brought the madness under control, the uncommon man whose compassionate humanity was "his—and our—saving grace" (pp. 352–353).

Dobbs writes as a journalist (he was a reporter for the *Washington Post*) not a historian, with a journalist's eye for the telling incident. His book's target reader would appear to be the proverbial (and often elusive) interested layperson. As the title, with its cinematic evocation of the ticking clock, indicates, this is a narrative constructed around principles of chronology, driven by the premise of time running out and of simultaneous events unfolding while the clock hands inch ever closer. Dobbs himself functions as a fully omniscient narrator, secure in his knowledge of the complete story and rendering judgment throughout on the motives and characters of the players he marshals. Although he comments frequently on President Kennedy's sense of history, which he encapsulates early in this narrative as "a chaotic process that can occasionally be given a shove in a desired direction, but can never be completely controlled" (Dobbs, 2008, p. 23), Dobbs himself has little interest in abstracting any larger conceptualizations from the drama.

Dobbs, like Lukacs (1999), writes in the hinge-of-history genre. While Lukacs focuses on debates in Churchill's five-man War Cabinet over a five-day period, Dobbs devotes over half his pages to a minute-by-minute reconstruction of the events of "black Saturday," October 27, 1962, the critical day when, amid escalating military tensions, President Kennedy and the Excom advisers decided on and communicated the American response to Khrushchev's two inconsistent offers of the previous day. While Lukacs touches on aspects of the multifaceted story of the evacuation of Dunkirk as the human and military context for his narrative, Dobbs engages in great detail with the handful of instances of military engagement (or near-engagement) that threatened to trigger nuclear war. While most other accounts of the crisis have focused on the Excom deliberations, which have long been available in transcript, Dobbs emphasizes the military episodes, intercutting in a highly cinematic way between the talking heads and their policies and the frontline military actors. Interestingly, it is precisely the approach taken by director Roger Donaldson in his film *Thirteen Days,* a narrative that is much preoccupied with gleaming *Top Gun*-style visuals of soaring jets, battleships in pounding seas, sinister hazmat-suited technicians wrangling mysterious looking hardware, gunners aiming their sites, and the like. Donaldson's narrative choices seem designed largely as eye candy, a visual relief for moviegoers bored with the spectacle of white-shirted policy wonks arguing amid clouds of cigarette smoke over the wording of a diplomatic communiqué. Dobbs has more serious narrative purposes. Not only does he present interviews with surviving participants in the events, many of whose stories had not been recorded before, but he marshals the survivors' evidence in support of his larger thesis: the difficulty experienced by the political leadership on both sides of the crisis in controlling their own military machines, and the natural tendency of those machines to pull inexorably toward their natural end—war.

Dobbs draws several lessons from his intercut narratives of policy and action. Unlike Robert Kennedy, his injunctions are historical rather than managerial, preoccupied with the irony of national hubris and anticipating decades of debacles to come. For Dobbs, a main lesson of the Cuban Missile Crisis is that the participants themselves drew the wrong lessons. The Soviets determined that they must gain nuclear parity with the United States to avoid future humiliations. The result was the vast program of ICBMs, which did indeed achieve parity. The enormous cost in resources, however, contributed materially to the fall of Communism itself. The strategists of the Kennedy and Johnson administrations, triumphant in having forced the Soviets to back down in Cuba, concluded, in Dobbs' words, "that the United States could force the rest of the world to do its bidding through a finely calibrated combination of 'toughness and restraint'"

(Dobbs, 2008, p. 346). The disastrous consequences of this approach when adopted against an adversary impervious to American "logic" and unfamiliar "with game theory as taught at Harvard and promoted by the RAND Corporation" (p. 347) would soon manifest themselves in the unrelenting escalation of the Vietnam conflict.

Ultimately, the most important lesson for Dobbs is also the simplest, a restatement of Robert Kennedy's contention for a post-Iraq War generation: "Character counts." Like Kennedy, Dobbs insists on the "pivotal role of personality in politics" (Dobbs, 2008, p. 351), and he makes an explicit comparison (it is a running theme throughout) to the "essential difference" between JFK and George W. Bush. Singling out President Kennedy's "great virtue...that he had an instinctive appreciation for the chaotic forces of history," Dobbs (p. 350) insists on the uniqueness of the president's experience, intellect, character and imagination. In his singularity, and his greatness, JFK was the indispensable determining factor that prevented the rush into destruction. If Dobbs' narrative project begins as an attempt to return the overlooked and underappreciated "little men" to the stage of history, it ends with a more familiar image: a towering hero alone in the spotlight.

Graham Allison's *Essence of Decision: Explaining the Cuban Missile Crisis* was first published in 1971 and revised, with Philip Zelikow, in 1999. The two editions have a cumulative Google Scholar count of over 5,600, and the book has become (as the authors note bemusedly in the preface to the revised edition) a fixture on the curriculum of "graduate schools of government and public policy, business and other professional training programs" (Allison & Zelikow 1999, p. viii). Its influence in the academic world is indisputable; in many ways it has set the terms of the debate over how institutions and their managers come to act as they do. For Allison himself, the book's subject was, and remains, something different: "How should citizens try to understand the actions of their governments?" with the emphasis resting as much on the trying as the understanding (pp. vii–viii). In this respect, the book's epigraph stands as both caution and summation: "The essence of ultimate decision remains impenetrable to the observer—often, indeed, to the decider himself." (The words come from President Kennedy's preface to Theodore Sorensen's *Decision-Making in the White House* [1963].)

Essence of Decision is an analysis of ways in which government actions can be "read"; that is, framed, interpreted, and learned from. It is a narrative about narratives. More specifically, it is a narrative about polyphony and the multiple narratives a single fable may yield. It is also, itself, a polyphonic text constructed around three explanatory master narratives Allison labels simply Models I, II, and III. The book's method is straightforward: detailed analysis of each model as methodology and theoretical construct, followed by application of the model to some of "the central puzzles of the Cuban Missile Crisis." The goal is a double illumination: a deeper understanding of "the defining event of the nuclear age" *and* an exploration of "the influence of unrecognized assumptions upon our thinking about events like the missile crisis" (Allison & Zelikow, 1999, pp. ix–x) and on the stories we tell about them.

Unlike Dobbs, Allison is not seeking to expand the historical record. His focus is the necessarily subjective relationship of the observer/analyst to that record. Exploring three "alternative conceptual lenses," Allison demonstrates the ways in which each leads us "to see, emphasize and worry about quite different aspects of events" (Allison & Zelikow, 1999, pp. ix–x). This is not to suggest that there are not better (more sophisticated, more sufficient) explanatory narratives and worse. In fact, the core of the book's argument is precisely the limitations of Model I, the "classical model," with its largely unexamined assumption that the behavior of a government collectively, and of its key players individually, should always be understood as "action"; that is, as "purposive, goal-directed activity" (p. 17). In the interpretive paradigm that results, nations are always rational actors whose leaders choose from a menu of clearly formulated alternatives, with every action undertaken by every one of a nation's agents down to its frontline soldiers, consciously designed to advance the objectives chosen by those leaders. Against the simplifications of Model I, *Essence of Decision* posits two alternatives: analyzing governmental action as organized output, the product of institutional inertia as embodied in frontline personnel following standard operating procedures (Model II), or as political resultant; namely, the outcome of complicated bargaining games and power struggles among organizational leaders (Model III).[1] At the time of first writing, Allison's Model I dominated the discourse of academic foreign policy analysis. It is a measure of the book's influence that, by the time the revised edition was published, Model I had been largely displaced.

Allison's stated narrative aim is to demonstrate the different effects the three conceptual lenses he identifies will have on the observer's vision of events. His application of Models II and III to the Missile Crisis, however, also generates a further narrative about those particular events. It is a narrative of intellectual heroism centered on an "Analyst in Chief" (Allison & Zelikow, 1999, p. 347), a president whose personal experience and attributes grant him unique insight into the forces and processes Allison's Models II and III define, as well as the unique ability either to channel or to offset them sufficiently to resolve the crisis. Behind Allison's intellectually and methodologically sophisticated analysis lies another story, whose outlines are surprisingly familiar: the story of a flexible and penetrating intelligence transcending the institutional and political forces that would trammel a lesser mind (and soul). The nature of the protagonist's role has been re-defined, the arena of his action shifted into the realm of the intellect; his heroic and exceptional stature, however, remains undiminished.

Both biography and historiography are relevant here. Allison's academic mentor was the renowned historian of the American presidency Richard Neustadt. In his 1960 study *Presidential Power* (revised 1980), Neustadt argued for a very particular understanding of the president's role and scope for action. Given the separation of powers among governing institutions, Neustadt posited, the power of the president is often limited to persuasion. Government action results only from institutional cooperation. To achieve a desired outcome, the president must be able to persuade other governmental players that their interests lie in cooperation with him. Neustadt's view represents an inversion of Model I's assumption, which Allison characterizes as "government behavior as the choices of a unitary decision maker" (Allison & Zelikow, 1999, p. 255). And it is Neustadt's view that Allison builds upon in Models II and III, each of which represents a further departure from, and complication of, the classical model's assumptions about the forces that produce governmental action.

Allison's chapter title for his explication of Model II ("Organizational Behavior") suggests a general focus, viewing government through an all-purpose organizational lens. The examples cited within the chapter, however, reveal a primary interest in large government bureaucracies (as opposed to entrepreneurial start-ups, say, or small nonprofits). And the premise of the subsequent analysis is clear: nations, and governments, do today what they did (in slightly altered form) yesterday and what they will go on to do again (with minor variations) tomorrow. Barring extraordinary intervention from above or outside, the machinery that produces government action is preprogrammed and largely self-sustaining. And this has clear implications for interpreters of government action. To attempt to read agency into any particular example of "standard operating procedure" is to misread inertia as intent: "If an analyst observes behavior by members of an organization that is consistent with the organization's established routines, that behavior provides zero evidence about any specific intentions of state leaders in the particular case" (Allison & Zelikow, 1999, p. 173).

A crisis is, by definition, a nonstandard event disrupting an organization's (or nation's) established routines, but the further implication of Model II is precisely the continued influence of such routines on the approach to, and implementation of, crisis management. For Allison, the point is indisputable: "Existing organizational capabilities influence government choice," however unusual or indeed potentially earth-shattering the events necessitating those choices may be. While Allison prefers the neutral term "influence," the tenor of his analysis equates that "influence" with constraint.

What happens, however, when standard operating procedures prove insufficient, when the game is changed, when, for example, Soviet missiles appear in Cuba? Model III explores the web of personal and political transactions out of which nonstandard governmental action emerges. Again, Allison's premise is clear: "If a nation performed an action, that action was the resultant of bargaining among individuals and groups within the government" (Allison & Zelikow, 1999, p. 304). Decision making is always a political process, "the intranational game," involving players motivated by an unpredictable amalgam of "national, organizational, and personal goals" (p. 255). Allison's Model III insists on the many other narratives in which key players are enmeshed and that continue to operate even (especially?) during times of crisis. Polyphony, again. As Allison notes, with considerable understatement: "The nature of foreign policy problems permits fundamental disagreement among reasonable people about how to solve them" (p. 256).

It is a strength of Allison's Model III that it is rooted in a recognition of the messy nature of the business of government as it is carried out daily by fallible human beings. "For those who participate in government," he notes in a rebuke to academic critics whose analysis ignored such mundane considerations, "the terms of daily employment cannot be ignored" (Allison & Zelikow, 1999, p. 257). Many of the propositions he then goes on to formulate retain this awareness of the human factor: "Where you stand, depends on where you sit" (p. 307); "Resultants emerge from games among players who perceive quite different faces of an issue and who differ markedly in the actions they prefer" (p. 306); "Because they must compete with others, reasonable players are forced to argue much more confidently than if they were detached judges" (p. 309). And Allison notes, too, the typical plot lines of the policymaking narrative Model III suggests: misexpectation (expectations of other players that are ultimately disappointed), miscommunication, and misleading reticence ("hesitant silence and only partially intended soft-spokenness") all play their part in the process (p. 310).[2]

Allison's application of his Models II and III to the Cuban Missile Crisis narrative sheds valuable new light on key aspects of the story, including long-standing puzzles regarding the Soviets' process for actually installing the missiles and the American delay in ordering U-2 overflights to confirm their existence. In the first instance, the application of Model II reveals Soviet Rocket Forces following standard procedures; in the second, Model III focuses attention on rifts within the interdepartmental Committee on Overhead Reconnaissance (between CIA Director John McCone, who advocated the flights and Secretary of State Dean Rusk, who feared jeopardizing diplomatic initiatives in other areas). In both instances, the interpretations offered are precisely what we would expect these particular conceptual lenses to produce.

When Allison turns his attention, and his Model III, to the work of the Excom, however, a subtle shift in the tenor and tendency of the analysis begins to be felt; a shadow narrative emerging to challenge in some ways the premises of the Model itself. Initially, the president of this narrative appears both more stymied and more angered than in other accounts, frustrated by the difficulty he encounters asserting his will over his own government. While other accounts also emphasize the president's clashes with the military (a theme we'll return to in our discussion of *Dr. Strangelove*), Allison and Zelikow also detail a serious conflict with the State Department. When the naval blockade was imposed, the president asked Secretary of State Dean Rusk to contact the Turkish government immediately, paving the way for the removal of American missiles from Turkey, a concession the president knew would have to be part of any settlement. Instead, the State Department used the president's request as an opportunity to begin promoting its own long-term agenda of replacing nuclear deterrence in Europe with multilateral force. No one contacted the Turkish government. The president's frustration over what he perceived as a deliberate misinterpretation of orders was repeatedly expressed both during and after the crisis: "Have we had any conversations in Turkey? With the Turks?" he demands in exasperation at one point (Allison & Zelikow, 1999, pp. 241–242).

But as Allison's narrative focuses on the undoubted turning point of the crisis-fable—Black Saturday and the desperate Excom deliberations—Neustadt's constrained and exasperated Negotiator in Chief is displaced by a much more proactive and forceful figure: "President Kennedy becomes the driver of the debate . . . On each issue, he presses his colleagues to probe deeper implications of each option; to explore ways of circumventing seemingly insurmountable obstacles; to face squarely unpalatable tradeoffs; and to stretch their imagination" (Allison & Zelikow, 1999, p. 357). The narrative becomes one of mastery rather than constraint, of leadership that sets the terms of the debate. It is, as Allison and Zelikow (p. 346) phrase it, "a story of the most subtle and intricate probing, pulling, and hauling, leading, guiding, and spurring." In the final hours of the crisis, the president clearly demonstrates his understanding of, and control over, the "closed politics" that ultimately generate policy. He adjourns the full Excom and continues with a smaller, selected group to put the finishing touches on the reply to Khrushchev's telegrams and to brief Robert Kennedy for his face-to-face meeting with Dobrynin. Like Churchill in his handling of the conflict with Halifax over whether to negotiate with the Germans, the president chooses the players to produce the desired outcome. Churchill expanded his circle of advisers to encompass the full Cabinet to resolve in his favor a struggle previously confined to the War Cabinet. President Kennedy reversed the process, narrowing the circle to achieve a similar result. In both instances, the stratagem could not have succeeded without the particular leadership qualities—the force of intellect, character and personality—unique to each statesman.

In the end, Allison and Zelikow's narrative remains truly polyphonic, speaking with several voices, telling at least three different stories. One is the methodological narrative that defines and applies Models I, II, and III to the facts of the Cuban Missile Crisis, offering rich theoretical material that continues to influence public sector studies of the interaction between politicians and large bureaucracies on the one hand and individuals, groups, and committees in leadership roles on the other. Another story is the meta-analysis that reflects on the influence of conceptual frameworks (like the very models it employs) on the facts to which they are applied and the interpretations that result. The third is a reframing of the dominant Cuban Missile Crisis fable in intellectual and political terms, revealing how indispensable the figure of the president-hero continues to be to our imagining of that story.

"Rationality Will Not Save Us": Counter-Factuals and Counter-Fables

"If seeing is believing, then we better be damn careful about what we show people, including ourselves" (Morris, 2008a). The remark was made by documentary filmmaker Errol Morris in an online essay defending his use of visual reenactments. All three of the counter-fables we will consider are visual narratives: movies. It is worth pausing for a moment to consider the implications of this. As discussed in Chapter 1, movies can reach a far wider audience than printed materials. Visual narratives can also augment their persuasive powers with an array of immersive strategies unavailable to the creators of print narratives. It's reasonable to assume that movies might influence popular ideas about the subjects they dramatize, more so than even the most groundbreaking scholarly treatment or conscientiously researched popular history. The issue becomes more complicated, however, when we attempt to track the extent, nature, or significance of that influence. What are the appropriate metrics? Audience numbers, critical reception, media coverage, rankings on the Internet Movie Database (IMDb) all provide only partial information. That is why this book also focuses on the relationship of narratives *to each other*—the core concepts of internarrative polyphony and of dominant and counter-fables—rather than attempting to "prove" their influence upon the wider culture. But this is not to deny that influence. Clearly, narratives do matter. The stories we see, or read, or hear establish conventions and expectations (conscious or unconscious) that in turn determine how we imagine and perceive similar stories in the future, even how we "read" our own personal experience.

Arguably, no single narrative of the Cold War has had a greater influence on subsequent retellings than Stanley Kubrick's *Dr. Strangelove or: How I Learned to Stop Worrying and Love the Bomb* (1964), to give the movie its full title. It is almost impossible to imagine or represent the geopolitical and cultural history of the United States in the 1960s without reference (acknowledged or otherwise) to this counter-factual parable of nuclear catastrophe. Tracing its influence here, I will be focusing specifically on *Strangelove*'s depiction of the military as the embodiment of the forces of unreason, those same forces vanquished in the dominant fable by the president-hero. Noting the importance of the figure of Air Force Chief of Staff General Curtis LeMay (in fictional, fictionalized, and recollected form) to all three of our counter-fables, we will discover in *The Fog of War* both an answer to and an affirmation of Kubrick's ur-narrative of military madness. It is one of the most surprising, and unsettling, examples of internarrative dialogue we will encounter.

Acceptable Losses: *Dr. Strangelove* and the Generals

The year 2004 marked the fortieth anniversary of the release of *Dr. Strangelove*. The occasion prompted the usual two-disc special edition DVD with accompanying bonus features and a wave of critical essays and reflections. Long acknowledged as both a satiric masterpiece and the progenitor of a new genre of war movie, the anniversary reconsiderations were hardly needed to affirm the movie's canonic status. (It had already been selected for inclusion in the U.S. Library of Congress' National Film Registry in 1989, a distinction reserved for movies deemed to be "culturally significant.") One writer, however, did introduce a new note to the chorus. Writing in the *New York Times* in October 2004, Fred Kaplan, online columnist for *Slate* and author of a study of American nuclear strategists (*The Wizards of Armageddon*), heralded Kubrick's black comedy as "a remarkably fact-based and specific guide to some of the most secretive chapters of the Cold War," noting its "weird accuracy" and "eerie" resemblances to "the policies, debates and military leaders of the day" (Kaplan, 2004). Kaplan devotes much of his essay to considering the "real-life counterpart" to the character of Dr. Strangelove, whom he identifies confidently as Herman Kahn, nuclear strategist at the RAND Corporation and author of the 1960 work *On Thermonuclear War,* a book Kubrick is known to have read repeatedly while researching his film. (Other contenders for the honor of being the original of Strangelove have included, over the years, Edward Teller, Henry Kissinger, and Werner Von Braun.)

My focus, however, is neither Strangelove nor Kahn, but another historical figure whose presence looms large in the film and in the crisis narratives we've been considering: General Curtis LeMay, the "cigar-chomping, gruff-talking general" (the phrase is Kaplan's), who had been among those military advisors advocating most strongly for an immediate military response to the Soviet missiles in Cuba and who had clashed directly with President Kennedy over actions the general equated with appeasement. Kaplan emphatically identifies LeMay as the inspiration for Kubrick's deranged General Jack D. Ripper, commander of Burpelson Air Force Base. It is Ripper whose psychotic paranoia concerning Communist plots to "sap and impurify all our precious bodily fluids" causes him to order an unprovoked and unstoppable nuclear strike against the USSR. This in turn triggers the Soviet's fictional "Doomsday Machine," an equally unstoppable nuclear response mechanism, and the rest is mushroom clouds. This, essentially, is the plot of Kubrick's film, its 96-minute running time divided among intercut scenes of the Air Force base where the suicidal Ripper is besieged, the War Room where President Merkin Muffley fruitlessly attempts to avert the impending nuclear catastrophe, and the cockpit of the unreachable B-52 bomber unleashed by Ripper, heading to Soviet territory to drop its payload and usher in annihilation.

But Ripper is not the only mad general in *Dr. Strangelove.* Running increasingly amok in the War Room is Air Force Chief of Staff General Buck Turgidson (played with manic glee and the occasional pratfall by George C. Scott). It is Turgidson who proposes an immediate full-scale attack on the USSR to disable its nuclear capacity, memorably defending his plan with an estimate of the "acceptable" losses that would result: "Mr. President, I'm not saying we wouldn't get our hair mussed. But I do say, no more than 10 to 20 million killed, tops. Depending on the breaks." Behind Turgidson, too, stands LeMay, who had played a pivotal role in the American fire bombings of Japan during World War II, in which more than 100,000 Japanese civilians were killed in a single night. However broad, even cartoonish the characters appear in outline (Ripper, it should be noted, is played absolutely "straight" by Sterling Hayden, who invests him with a sweaty, psychotic earnestness that leaves no room for farce), these unhinged generals are the heart of Kubrick's counter-fable: they are the embodiment of unreason triumphant, of military "logic" (specifically the logic of nuclear deterrence) pushed to its inevitable conclusion: total mutual destruction. What Kubrick does in *Dr. Strangelove* is to invert the dominant crisis narrative, proposing an alternative reality where the presidential voice of reason is drowned out by increasingly delusional military ranting, and the machinery of war (including its highest ranking officers) proves to be a Frankenstein's monster that turns on its creators. It is a reimagining of the missiles of October without John Kennedy (or his Soviet counterpart Nikita Khrushchev) to prevent the rush into the abyss.

By reimagining the crisis narrative in this way, Kubrick effectively reaffirms the centrality of the president-hero. (It is entirely fitting that the first preview screening of *Dr. Strangelove* was scheduled for November 22, 1963. It was postponed.) In its own absurdist way, Kubrick's film is as much a tribute to the uniquely heroic status of the president as any of the dominant crisis narratives we have looked at. But the movie also did more. It established a pop culture archetype whose influence would extend well beyond the movies: the general whose belligerence borders on insanity, the high-ranking officer so in love with war and its destructive power that he is treasonously willing to subvert or ignore civilian oversight. "War is too important to be left to politicians," Kubrick's General Ripper intones, "They have neither [sic] the time, the training, nor the inclination for strategic thought." If the inspiration came from Kennedy's own Air Force Chief of Staff—according to Kaplan, "General LeMay's distrust of civilian authorities, including presidents, was well known among insiders, several of whom Mr. Kubrick interviewed" (Kaplan, 2004)—the figure would break free of its biographical origins to appear and reappear in the antiwar movies, novels, plays and nonfiction writing that were soon to become a recognizable genre in their own right. The ubiquity of the type would then feed back into our imaginings of the Cuban Missile Crisis itself, so that history is viewed through the lens of cinema, courtesy of a genre-bending movie that had itself taken recent (now historic) events as its inspiration. The recursion is complete when we (re)encounter LeMay in Roger Donaldson's 2001 retelling of the crisis narrative, *Thirteen Days*. The bellicose, insubordinate, and vaguely seditious generals of Donaldson's movie have clearly come straight from the War Room of *Dr. Strangelove*. "These goddamn Kennedys are going to ruin this country," Donaldson's LeMay barks to his brother officers at one point, "if we don't do something about this." It might well be Turgidson himself speaking.

A Few Bad Men: *Thirteen Days* and the Generals

Approximately ten minutes before the end of the movie, *Thirteen Days* dramatizes the crucial closed-door encounter between Attorney General Robert Kennedy and Soviet Ambassador Anatoly Dobrynin that would prove the crisis' turning point. As the two men bring their conversation to a close, the sad-eyed middle-aged diplomat turns to his young American interlocutor and remarks, with all the melancholy with which Hollywood typically invests screen Russians: "You're a good man. Your brother is a good man. I assure you there are other good men. Let us hope the will of good men is enough to counter the terrible strength of this thing that was put in motion." It is the movie's emblematic moment, a distillation of its narrative. For *Thirteen Days*, the Cuban Missile Crisis is the story of an epic confrontation not between two global superpowers but within the government of the United States; a war of nerves between the young, idealistic president and his civilian advisors, on the one hand, and the war-hungry, hardened, old (or at least middle-aged) Joint Chiefs of Staff and their supporters on the other. The Soviets, in this retelling, are for the most part incidental. The real enemy is the Pentagon and its scheming, highly decorated denizens:

> This. This is a set up. The Chiefs want to go in. They need to redeem themselves for the Bay of Pigs. They gotta go in this time. They gotta do it right. They're boxing us in with these rules of engagement. If you agree to 'em, and one of our planes gets knocked down, or one of their ships won't stop for inspection, the Chiefs will have us by the balls and will force us to start shooting. They want a war, Jack, and they're arranging things to get one.

The speaker is Kenneth O'Donnell, special assistant and political advisor to the president and an old friend and schoolmate of the Kennedy brothers. He is played by Kevin Costner with a brush cut and an improbable accent, and he is inescapable: bolstering JFK's resolve in resisting his angry generals ("You didn't freeze. You did exactly what you should have done. You stayed out of the corner."), coaching the beleaguered leader before his television address on October 22 ("You're the President of the United States. They can wait for you."), rousing UN Ambassador Adlai Stevenson for a key international debate ("You gotta be tough, Adlai. You need to find it."), reassuring an anxious Robert Kennedy before his all-important meeting with Dobrynin ("There's no one else I'd rather have going in there"). But O'Donnell is more than a cinematic version of the *ficelle* or string character whose function is to reflect upon and highlight the significance of narrative events (Prince, 2003, p. 30). Within the movie's highly schematic structure, the street-smart, wisecracking political operative with his fierce loyalty and his blunt wisdom is positioned as the Everyman hero of the narrative. It is O'Donnell who is the true antagonist to the recklessly belligerent LeMay, countering the military madness of the generals with the sanity and decency of the ordinary American husband, father, and friend.

While the historical O'Donnell was occasionally present at Excom meetings, the taped records record his voice very infrequently (Allison & Zelikow, 1999, p. 326; May, 2001). For the cinematic O'Donnell, *Thirteen Days* imagines a full roster of activities that might have occurred in the interstices of the historical record, beyond the confines of the Excom. While none of the encounters noted above are impossible, the cumulative strain on the narrative of attempting to maintain O'Donnell as its center is palpable. The movie labors to keep Costner/O'Donnell as its focus, only to be upstaged by every glimpse of the relatively unknown (Canadian) actor Bruce Greenwood as a restrained, thoughtful, and authoritative JFK. At a crucial point, the narrative effectively admits defeat, inventing an intervention for O'Donnell that had no basis in fact. Determined to stop the "plot" being engineered by the Joint Chiefs (and LeMay in particular) to secure a pretext for a full-scale attack on Cuba, O'Donnell trumps the Chiefs by telephoning Navy Commander William Ecker, the lead pilot on a low-level reconnaissance flight, and appealing to him to report that he is not fired upon, whatever actually happens. The scene unfolds in O'Donnell's characteristic idiom—plain-spoken, sincere, authentic—while the camera offers close views of his troubled eyes and the deep concern playing across his face: "If the President has to protect you, Commander, he may have to do it with the bomb. Now, I've known the man for fifteen years. The problem is, he will protect you. So I'm asking you, don't make him protect you. Don't get shot at." The scene shifts to Ecker's flight, when he is indeed fired upon, and then follows him as he reports to the Joint Chiefs in Washington later that day. This affords another opportunity to frame an emblematic encounter between the overblown, war-hungry LeMay and a sane, decent voice of reason (in this case the square-jawed blue-eyed Ecker standing in for O'Donnell). "Son," LeMay blusters, "I want to know just one thing: those bastards so much as shoot a BB gun at you?" Ecker's eyes flicker a moment, sizing up the preposterous general, before he calmly replies: "It was a cakewalk, sir."

Does this rather flagrant cinematic license matter? It's possible to argue that this invented episode represents nothing more than a conflation of documented facts in the service of effective storytelling, a narrative strategy common to fact-based dramas. Navy Commander Ecker did fly a low-level reconnaissance mission on Tuesday, October 23 and did report to the Joint Chiefs in Washington on his return, although he was not fired upon. Reconnaissance pilots were fired upon on Black Saturday, but there was no attempt by the pilots to deny the fact. There is no evidence that the Joint Chiefs sought to use this as a pretext for launching military action without the president's explicit authorization, however much some may have felt that a preemptive strike was the only viable military option. In fact, this radical departure from the historical record represents an extreme instance of a narrative bad faith that dogs *Thirteen Days* throughout. Seeking to recast the dominant crisis fable as an Everyman's story, attempting (unsuccessfully) to sideline the heroic president in favor of his man-of-the-people advisor, framing the conflict as a struggle between civilians who monopolize all feelings of compassion, restraint and decency and high-ranking officers recklessly bent on global conflagration results in significant distortion of the historical record and a radical misrepresentation of the role of the U.S. military in the crisis, a point noted by historians when the movie was first released (May 2001). It also makes for a narrative defeated by its own premise. For it is simply impossible to accord O'Donnell, or the actor who plays him, the status or significance the movie seeks for both.

Thirteen Days is, in fact, a very good example of a polyphonic narrative whose multiple voices end up in sharp conflict. As one delves further into the movie's backstory, it becomes clear that a number of other imperatives beside historical accuracy are at work. One might well be filial obligation. Kenneth O'Donnell's son, Kevin, an Internet tycoon, purchased Beacon Films, the company that produced *Thirteen Days,* before the film was made. Although he claimed not to have influenced the movie's content, he is also on record as insisting (contrary to the views of other Excom members and White House insiders) that his father's role was not exaggerated (Ringle, 2001). That the senior O'Donnell's story after his White House years was a chronicle of failure, alcoholism, and untimely demise suggests a strong (if unacknowledged) motive for revisionism. It's worth noting too that Kevin Costner, the movie's only recognizable star, was also one of its producers. Given his demonstrable inability to play the president, it seems likely that his role was enlarged in accordance with his Hollywood standing. This might also explain much of the movie's framing, which puts O'Donnell squarely in the foreground, relegating the Kennedy brothers to the edges of many key shots, or cutting repeatedly to O'Donnell's reactions and to the significant glances he continually exchanges with the two principals.

In the end, however, none of this succeeds in displacing the focus from the undeniable center of the story: the young president in his finest hour. The fact that Greenwood's performance transcends impersonation to present a credible portrait of a searching intelligence fiercely at work gives his understated scenes an authority and importance the movie's narrative cannot downplay, however much it might try. And this is a president Graham Allison would have no difficulty recognizing, an Analyzer in Chief indeed. David Self's screenplay repeatedly calls on Greenwood to do the two hardest things an actor can onscreen: think and listen. But it also explicitly positions him as the interpreter, the one who makes sense of it all. The scenes in which the president listens intently and then summarizes the options, or outlines the possibilities, or construes the implications of what he (and we) have just heard are too numerous to count. And each recurrence places him more securely at the movie's center. Late in the story, O'Donnell reassures his wife that nuclear war will not happen: "Honey, we're not going to let it come to that. I promise. Jack and Bobby they're . . . they're smart guys." "You're smart too," she interjects fiercely. "Not like them," O'Donnell replies. It is impossible for the viewer not to agree. Despite the best efforts of screenwriter, director, producers and star, the dominant fable reasserts itself. *Thirteen Days* remains the story of an extraordinary leader (and a quietly authoritative actor), not his Everyman aide, nor even the Hollywood star who plays him.

"There is No Veritas Lens": Robert McNamara, Curtis LeMay, and *The Fog of War*

It is a measure of Errol Morris's accomplishment in *The Fog of War: Eleven Lessons from the Life of Robert McNamara* that it is extremely difficult to extract a single topic or theme from the movie for separate discussion as I attempt in the analysis that follows. This is partly a reflection of the movie's recursive structure, the thematic and chronologic doubling back in which it constantly engages, and which itself bears a thematic weight. (In the concluding moments of the movie, McNamara quotes T.S. Eliot: "'We shall not cease from exploring. And, at the end of our exploration, we will return to where we started and know the place for the first time.' And that's in a sense where I'm beginning to be.") It is equally a function of the subtlety with which Morris transforms the self-told narrative of the life of Robert Strange McNamara, Secretary of Defense under Presidents Kennedy and Johnson, into a metaphysical inquiry into the morality of war.

The movie's formal features can be briefly summarized. Using his patented "Interratron" video system, linked cameras in which subject and interviewer face each other's images in a camera lens and speak directly to it, Morris was able to intercut footage of the aged McNamara speaking full-face to the camera with an extraordinary range of archival imagery and visual effects, some directly illustrative of events and people being described, others much more allusively related. These are sometimes accompanied by McNamara's narrative in voice-over, or by archival audio recordings (of President Johnson and McNamara discussing Vietnam, of JFK, of Roosevelt), at other times by Philip Glass' unsettlingly beautiful score. At intervals throughout, we hear (though never see) Morris himself posing questions. The movie is punctuated visually with titles enumerating the number and substance of the accumulating "lessons"—"1. Empathize with your enemy." "2. Rationality will not save us." "7. Belief and seeing are both often wrong."—and occasional key dates, always appearing as white letters or numbers on a black screen. What this brief summary cannot convey is the cumulative effect of the interactions of voice, image, and score. Nor can it suggest the power of the moments when Morris's supremely fluent and articulate subject falls silent, and the camera lingers on the face of an old man who remains—maddeningly for some critics of the movie, inevitably for others—an enigma.

Yet choosing to focus this discussion of *The Fog of War* on the Cuban Missile Crisis and Air Force Chief of Staff General Curtis LeMay does not violate the spirit of the movie. The two recur like leitmotifs throughout the narratives McNamara and Morris are creating. And with each appearance, the familiar stories and interpretations that have accreted around them shift and realign. Here, the Cuban Missile Crisis figures both as a mirror image of the Vietnam debacle to come and the retrospective turning point of McNamara's narrative journey, while LeMay emerges, not as the almost ludicrously belligerent hawk, familiar from so many other crisis narratives, but as an increasingly troubling embodiment of the intolerable moral calculus war entails. It is these two thematic strains, working together, that make *The Fog of War* the most radical crisis counter-fable we will encounter.

McNamara's account of the crisis, which effectively begins the movie, initially follows a familiar form, foregrounding the leadership of the president, in particular his insistence on seeking any means possible to gain insight into the minds and motivations of the Soviets, the empathy that McNamara will later describe as "put[ting] ourselves inside their skin," something he and his colleagues would fail utterly to do in the case of North Vietnam. In this first account, LeMay features prominently, also in a familiar role: "General Curtis LeMay was saying 'Let's go in. Let's totally destroy Cuba.'" This would appear to be yet another version of the dominant fable, with Allison's Analyzer in Chief augmented by an Empathizer in Chief, whose insight counters and ultimately defeats LeMay's blind belligerence. Very quickly, however, McNamara offers a corrective, and the crisis narrative takes a radically different turn: "I want to say—and this is very important—at the end we lucked out. It was luck that prevented nuclear war. We came that close [gestures with thumb and forefinger] to nuclear war in the end. Rational individuals. Kennedy was rational. Khrushchev was rational. Castro was rational. Rational individuals came that close to total destruction of their societies."

In a sense, Morris and McNamara's narratives (they coincide here, but by no means always do so; a point we will return to) will reenact the journey of discovery McNamara himself is describing, from celebration of the United States' victory over the Soviets, apparently achieved through a combination of leadership, empathy, restraint, and resolve, to a shocked recognition of how little all of this counted for in the end. It is a moment of pure *anagnorisis*, the Aristotelian term for the critical recognition of a truth that triggers the climactic reversal of tragedy. It comes when McNamara describes an encounter with Fidel Castro thirty years after the crisis, at a meeting of high-level participants convened to discuss those far-off events. It was then, in 1992, that he learned for the first time that during the most volatile days of the crisis, when an American invasion of Cuba seemed almost inevitable, there were already 162 operational nuclear warheads on the island, some 70 of which were capable of reaching targets within the United States itself. And if McNamara did not know this during the crisis, JFK also would not have known it. Thus, if JFK had ordered the threatened attack on Cuba, it would have been met with nuclear retaliation, putting the world on a fast-track to nuclear war. McNamara's retelling of the scene is intensely dramatic. What makes it unforgettable, however, is the final frame of the sequence, a lingering shot of McNamara's face staring into the camera in a silence which Morris sustains for what feels, by Hollywood movie standards, like an eternity. The sequence deserves quoting at length:

> I couldn't believe what I was hearing. And Castro got very angry with me because I said, "Mr. President, let's stop this meeting. I ... I ... This is totally new to me and I'm not sure I got the translation right. Mr. President, I have three questions to you. [He raises a finger for each.] Number one: Did you know the nuclear warheads were there? Number two: If you did, would you have recommended to Khrushchev, in the face of a U.S. attack, that he use them? Number three: If he had used them, what would've happened to Cuba?" [Quick cut to black.] He said, "Number one: I knew they were there. Number two: I would *not* have recommended to Khrushchev that he use them, I *did* recommend to Khrushchev that they be used. Number three: What would have happened to Cuba? It would've been totally destroyed." [Pause. McNamara stares.] That's how close we were. [He gestures with thumb and forefinger, eyes tearing.]
>
> [Morris's voice] And he was willing to accept that?
>
> Yes. Oh, and he went on to say, "Mr. McNamara, if you and President Kennedy had been in a similar situation, that's what you would have done." I

said, Mr. President, I hope to God we would not have done it. Pulled the temple down on our heads. My God. [Long silence.][3]

In a single sentence, McNamara demolishes the dominant crisis fable. "I hope to God we would not have done it." The mood is conditional. He has no certainty that he and the other men of reason, intelligence, and empathy, the conventional heroes of the fable, would have behaved any more rationally than to choose national suicide, as Castro by his own admission *had in fact done*. It is not in the end the military machine, or even its leaders, that are to be feared. It is human nature itself. Rationality will not save us, because it cannot be counted on to defeat the atavistic urge to destruction. All that is left is hope. And luck.

After the long silence, McNamara offers a qualified ending to his account of the crisis: "In a sense, we'd won. We'd got the missiles out without war." It is an ending he immediately proceeds to put in question through the figure of LeMay: "LeMay said, 'Won. Hell. We lost. We should go in and wipe 'em out. Today.' [McNamara laughs. His eyes tear.] LeMay believed that ultimately we were going to confront these people in a conflict with nuclear weapons and by God we better do it when we have greater superiority than we will have in the future." The return to LeMay here is key, significantly shifting his role both in the crisis narrative McNamara narrates and in the existential drama Morris unfolds. Within the counter-fable McNamara has framed, the "extraordinarily belligerent" general, as McNamara will go on to describe him, ceases to be the almost parodic voice of military madness. Rather, he begins to embody an inexorable truth. It is a process of revision (in the literal sense of seeing again) that will dominate the next three lessons of the film as Morris circles back to McNamara's early years, most significantly his wartime experiences with the man he calls "the finest combat commander of any service I came across." (McNamara was serving with the Air Force's Office of Statistical Control and his primary responsibility was analyzing and improving bombing efficiency.)

In March of 1945, McNamara recounts, LeMay, as commander of the B-29 bomber group stationed in Guam, made the decision to bring his planes, embodying the latest technology and capable of flying at an altitude of 25,000 feet, down to 5,000 feet and to employ incendiary bombs. The combination of increased target accuracy and firebombs proved devastating: "In that single night we burned to death 100,000 Japanese civilians in Tokyo. Men, women, and children." Questioned by Morris whether he was aware this was going to happen, McNamara's discomfort is palpable. "Well, I was, I was part of the mechanism that, that in a sense recommended it," he acknowledges, his hesitations and repetitions a notable contrast to his usual fluency. "I don't want to suggest that it was I who put into LeMay's mind that his operations were inefficient and had to be drastically changed," he quickly continues. "But anyhow that's what he did."

What is striking here is the absence of any condemnation of LeMay. And the reason for this refusal soon reveals itself as McNamara recounts the debriefing he witnessed after that night of destruction. Flying the bombers at much lower altitude had exposed the crews to much greater risk. A pilot who had lost his wingman in the raid confronted LeMay over the changed orders. Again, McNamara's narrative of the encounter must be quoted at length as he assumes the voice of LeMay himself:

> LeMay spoke in monosyllables. I never heard him say more than two words in sequence. It was basically, "Yes," "No," "Yup." That's all. Or "To hell with it." That's all he said. And LeMay was totally intolerant of criticism. He never engaged in discussion with anybody. He stood up. "Why are we here?" [Mc-Namara's eyes tear.] "Why are we here? You lost your wingman. It hurts me as much as it does you. I sent him there. And I've been there. I know what it is. But you lost one wingman and we destroyed Tokyo."

If the monosyllabic commander who will brook no criticism recalls the caricatured figures of *Dr. Strangelove* and *Thirteen Days*, the man who can utter the impossible equation of the passage's conclusion—"you lost one wingman and we destroyed Tokyo"—is something else entirely. He has become the symbol of the moral impasse of war.

McNamara himself makes this transformation explicit. Responding to Morris's question "The choice of incendiary bombs: where did that come from?" McNamara replies, "I think the issue is not so much incendiary bombs. I think the issue is: In order to win a war, should you kill a hundred thousand people in one night?" LeMay's answer, McNamara adds, would be clearly yes. Then, in an extraordinary act of ventriloquism, he assumes the persona of LeMay and argues the case. For a split second, the viewer wonders if she is watching the final fracturing of a deeply conflicted man:

> "McNamara, do you mean to say that instead of killing 100,000, burning to death 100,000 Japanese civilians in that one night, we should have burned to death a lesser number, or none? And then had our soldiers cross the beaches in Tokyo and been slaughtered in the tens of thousands? Is that what you're proposing? Is that moral? Is that wise?" [Quick cut to black.] Why was it necessary to drop the nuclear bomb if LeMay was burning up Japan? And he went on from Tokyo to firebomb other cities.

The "lesson" from which this scene is taken is titled "Proportionality should be a guideline in war." As McNamara's unanswerable questions accumulate (posed in his own voice as well as LeMay's), the inadequacy of the formulation becomes more and more evident. There is no proportionality in war. There are no longer moral absolutes when the destructive power of the forces engaged can obliterate 100,000 civilians in a single night and burn up entire cities. (McNamara returns to the number with obsessive repetition.) And again, it is LeMay who figures in McNamara's narrative as the bearer of this unwelcome truth. By this point, his status has been utterly changed. The easy judgments invited by earlier versions of the crisis fable, the cartoonish depictions that reduce him to a malign, bomb-crazy blusterer, have proved inadequate. And McNamara, again quoting LeMay himself, concludes with yet another question: "LeMay said if we'd lost the war, we'd all have been prosecuted as war criminals. And I think he's right. He, and I'd say I, were behaving as war criminals. [Shift to voice-over, camera holds on McNamara's silent face.] LeMay recognized that what he was doing would be thought immoral if his side had lost. But what makes it immoral if you lose and not immoral if you win?"

In the silence that follows, we see a spiraling line of dominoes toppling on a map, followed by a white date on a black screen: 1964. We have arrived at Vietnam.

This is, for many critics, the heart of *The Fog of War*, the defining chapter of McNamara's story and the core of the indictment they believe the movie offers. (For some, the case against McNamara is not made nearly explicit or damning enough. Fred Kaplan [2003], writing in *Slate*, faults Morris for the "free ride" he gives his subject in his frequent displays of "mendacity.") [4] This entire last movement of the film, with its haunting combat footage; its staggering use of audio tapes of Johnson and McNamara discussing policy; its montage of newspaper stories, still photos, television news footage and caricatures of an increasingly demonized McNamara, is extraordinary. It deserves extensive analysis for its formal qualities no less than the content of the narrative McNamara supplies. Yet it does not stand alone. McNamara himself frames the story of Vietnam by turning back to the Missile Crisis— "Let me go back one moment"—while his reflections on moral responsibility return, inevitably it now seems, to the figure of LeMay.

It is notable that the literal polyphony of the movie—the interplay of two different voices, Morris questioning or commenting, McNamara answering—becomes much more insistent here. For it is here that the distance between the explanatory personal and historical narrative McNamara is creating and the story Morris is telling becomes most obvious. Writing shortly after McNamara's death in 2009, and replying to the critics of his movie who had accused him, often very bitterly, of enabling McNamara to continue to deny his culpability (even criminality), Morris defined explicitly the story he had sought to tell. McNamara's admissions of error, he wrote, might have seemed woefully inadequate or entirely self-serving to many. But McNamara offered more than self-justification. "What he did give us was his struggle to understand the meaning of what he had done. We got to see him wrestle with history" (Morris, 2009). And through Morris's artistry, we got to see more: an implicit narrative of the emotional and psychic costs of that struggle for one extraordinary individual living what one reviewer called "an extraordinarily pertinent public life" (Angell, 2004).

McNamara returns to the Missile Crisis as he begins his explanation of the Vietnam catastrophe because, for him, they feature as mirror images:

> "Let me go back one moment. [Still photo of Robert and John F. Kennedy and the Excom.] In the Cuban Missile Crisis, in the end, I think we did put ourselves in the skin of the Soviets. In the case of Vietnam, we didn't know them well enough to empathize, and there was total misunderstanding as a result. They believed that we had simply replaced the French as a colonial power and we were seeking to subject north and south Vietnam to our colonial interests. Which was absolutely absurd. And we, we saw Vietnam as an element of the Cold War, not what they saw it as: a civil war."

While McNamara explicitly puts the emphasis on the failure of empathy, the implicit point seems clear: the ease with which highly intelligent, rational men could be so disastrously mistaken and could persist so tenaciously and so tragically in their error. It is the counter-fable again: the role of luck (good or bad), the insufficiency of reason. Even imagining an alternative history, if the heroic president of the crisis story had lived, McNamara can again only summon a conditional hope, an inclination to believe rather than belief itself: "I do—I am inclined to believe that if Kennedy would have lived, he would have made a difference. I don't think we would have had 500,000 men there."

As he moves from causes to implications, McNamara himself raises questions of criminality and moral choice. "How much evil must we do in order to do good?" he asks the camera. "We have certain ideals, certain responsibilities. Recognize that at times you will have to engage in evil. But minimize it." And it is here that he returns, for the last time, to LeMay in a complex invocation in which he appears both to identify with the general and distance himself from him: "That's the way LeMay felt. He was trying to save the country. He was trying to save our nation. And in the process he was prepared to do whatever killing was necessary." Ultimately, the lesson McNamara offers here is a deeply unsettling one: nations that fight wars must necessarily engage in evil, must necessarily rely on the generals who are willing to do whatever killing is necessary (and who face the prospect of being charged with war crimes should they lose). The fable here is not that the LeMays can be defeated by the men of empathy and reason, but rather that the men of empathy and reason can be just as morally culpable, and just as wrong.

Errol Morris begins *The Fog of War* with an excerpt from an archival "CBS Reports" feature on McNamara. Over footage of the young Secretary in his office juggling statistics and graphs on a presentation chart, we hear a period "Voice-of-God" announcer intoning, "This is the Secretary of Defense, Robert McNamara...Walter Lippman calls him not only the best Secretary of Defense, but also the only one who ever asserted civilian control over the military. His critics call him a con man, an IBM machine on legs, an arrogant dictator." From its first frames, then, McNamara is positioned as an enigma, and he remains stubbornly unknowable to the end.[5] Morris's technique invites us, as viewers, to read McNamara's presence like a narrative, seeking meaning in his gestures, glances, silences, hesitations, and reversals as much as in his words. We can never be certain, however, that we have read the story correctly. And it is Morris's willingness to leave us in this uncertainty that might explain the critical responses of those who were seeking simple exposure, condemnation, or demonization. Morris's movie asks more of us as viewers. It asks for recognition of the impossible choices McNamara faced. It asks for acknowledgment of the complexity of the issues he confronted. It asks for acceptance of the truths McNamara discloses. It asks for attention to an implicit narrative its own subject cannot openly acknowledge. In the end, I believe, it also asks for compassion. "It's the endless juggling of personal morality, loyalty, political possibility and the caprice of history," Morris wrote in the obituary essay quoted earlier. "If he failed, it is because he tried to bring his idea of rationality to problems that were bigger and more deeply irrational than he or anyone else could rationally understand."

Lessons, Questions, Narratives

Early in the *Fog of War*, Robert McNamara remarks, "My rule has been to try to learn. Try to understand what happened. Develop the lessons and pass them on." In very different ways, all of the narratives we've looked at (with the possible exception of *Thirteen Days*) have been concerned with the lessons to be derived from the Cuban Missile Crisis, or from the narratives generated by and about it, from Robert Kennedy's list of five injunctions to Allison's three models, to McNamara's and Morris's 11 aphorisms. Even *Dr. Strangelove*'s satire, for all its exaggerations and excesses, has a clearly corrective purpose. While we can, and will, enumerate specific lessons for managerial practice drawn from the crisis narratives we've examined, we will also consider some questions these very different texts raise, questions about lessons and about narratives. It is worth noting that here again McNamara uses a conditional formulation: "*try* to learn, *try* to understand." And this might be the most important lesson his story teaches: the difficulty of actually doing either.

If we list our narratives' managerial lessons in order of emphasis, the first must surely be the importance of empathy. Specifically, the importance of borrowing the perspectives of those on the other side—whether of a conflict, a negotiation, or simply a transaction—in order to understand the motivations and needs, both personal and organizational, informing their choices and actions. It is a cultivated awareness of the other stories that are in play beyond one's own, an effort of imagination and an act of interpretation. Failure to recognize the often very different narratives that inspire behavior, projection of one's own narrative onto another, as McNamara points out explicitly in the case of Vietnam, will lead to impasse.

But how to ensure that such recognition is at least attempted? Here, another lesson comes into play: organizational leaders have considerable latitude to structure their ad hoc advisory processes for crisis decision making. The choices they make matter importantly for the quality of advice they will receive. Consider President Kennedy's establishment and direction of the Excom, a subject canvassed extensively by Robert Kennedy as well as Allison and Zelikow. The president had to make numerous determinative choices about how to structure the process. Any leader creating an ad hoc advisory process would need to consider similar issues. Who will the advisers be? Will the group be limited to organizational heads with a strong interest in the issue, or will it include middle-managers with special knowledge as well as informed and experienced outsiders? How will the question or issue be defined and what is the objective to be achieved? How much of the deliberations will the leader attend, or will others be delegated responsibility for leading the process? Will the process involve brainstorming, rigorous analysis of alternatives, or other approaches? Will the leader choose an "inner" group to have the last word before taking a decision?

Clearly, decision making cannot rest upon empathy or opinion alone. Evidence and data must play their part. Yet it is also clear from McNamara's narrative that the injunction "Get the data" (lesson six) must be balanced against lessons seven and eight: "Belief and seeing are both often wrong," and "Be prepared to reexamine your reasoning." The point could be generalized under the rubric "Remember the human factor." No data is immune to bias in the gathering process. No analysis is free from the impress of unconscious wishes or beliefs—of those generating and those receiving it.

And there is a corollary, as Allison and Zelikow's Model II demonstrates. Large organizations are blunt instruments that function on the basis of standard operating procedures and rules of thumb. A clear understanding of those procedures and rules can keep the analyst from drawing the mistaken assumption that all of the actions by another organization's staff or agents are expressions of the intentions of its leaders. Armed with this understanding, a leader will also know to limit his expectations about the ability of his own organization to provide creative responses to unprecedented situations and will move to the ad hoc expedients described above.

A further insight, addressed most fully by Allison and Zelikow's Model III, can be summarized in the words of *Yes Minister*, namely, the tendency of government to behave as "a loose confederation of warring tribes" even or indeed especially in times of crisis. The warfare expresses itself in the inevitable advocacy, tugging, hauling, turf fights, and internecine competitions of organizational politics. Remembering this enables the analyst to understand why it takes so long for both his own government and others to arrive at decisions, and why, when decisions are finally taken, they reflect the logic of consensus and compromise.

Many of the lessons we've been considering emphasize either the collaborative aspects of decision making or the importance of the human factor. But our narratives have also repeatedly demonstrated another truth: character counts. More specifically, they have made plain the ultimate importance of a strong leader assuming clear control of the authority to make decisions involving organizational (or, in this case, national or even human) survival. Delegation to either field commanders or automata do not provide the negotiating advantage hypothesized by game theory, but rather lead to the nightmare scenarios of *Dr. Strangelove*'s rogue generals and doomsday machines.

Concluding with lessons in this way is entirely consonant with the dominant fable we have been exploring; a testament to the power of reason to benefit from experience. Yet there is a counter-fable, too. If the lesson of Michael Dobbs's narrative was precisely that the *wrong* lessons were learned by the best and brightest minds of their time, McNamara and Morris's narratives dramatize how such failures can occur. Their explanation, and they are in agreement here, is the persuasive power of the explanatory narratives we create for ourselves. Discussing the infamous Gulf of Tonkin incident, in which false reports of a North Vietnamese torpedo attack on a U.S. warship led to a major escalation of the conflict, McNamara remarks, "We see incorrectly. Or we see only half the story at times." Morris's voice then adds "We see what we want to believe." McNamara replies, "You're absolutely right. Belief and seeing, they're both often wrong." Arguably, McNamara's statement could stand as a summary of the thematic concerns of all Errol Morris's films. His interest, as he himself has written, is in "how we fail to see how our mental narratives prevent us from seeing evidence" (2008b). The issue, as Morris goes on to explain, is rarely deliberate deception, of oneself or others. It is rather the unconscious pressures that lead us to author the narratives we desire and then invest them with the authority of revealed truth. "Lie detectors and writers about lie detection often neglect this point," Morris observes. "We can lie and not know we're lying." Some critics have read *The Fog of War* as an extended meditation on this theme, a remarkably subtle exposure of a brilliant mind blinded by its own exculpatory narratives. We do not have to agree with them to read in it a cautionary tale of the difficulty of seeing the true narrative amid the competing false ones we are driven to create, and the further difficulty, once we find it, of learning from it.

Endnotes

1. While Allison made no reference to them, it is interesting to note that at the same time he was writing, French deconstructionist scholars in literature, psychology, linguistics, and philosophy (for example, Lacan, Foucault, Saussure, Derrida, Cixous, and Althusser) were all making the case for subjective interpretation, indeterminacy, and ambiguity in their own fields.

2. Allison's terms offer an extraordinarily apt summary of the "closed politics" that is at the heart of C. P. Snow's (1984) novel *Corridors of Power*, which we discussed in Chapter 3. "Misexpectation, miscommunication, and misleading reticence" captures precisely the scenes of quasi-official, and deadly serious, verbal maneuvering that quash reports, perpetuate policy, shift ministers, and end careers.

3. McNamara's biblical allusion (to the blind Sampson in the temple of the Philistines) is interesting in light of the frequency with which commentators have read McNamara's story in prophetic and/or tragic terms. Roger Angell, writing in the *New Yorker*, memorably invokes "old Robert McNamara—who at times appears to stand in our path with the bony finger and crazy agenda of a street saint" (Angell, 2004). James Carroll, writing in the *Boston Globe* after McNamara's death, employs an extraordinary extended metaphor in which McNamara features as Captain Ahab, Herman Melville's mad visionary in the classic 19th-century tale of misadventure and obsession, *Moby Dick*: "But what if Melville had ended his novel differently? What if, in defeat, Ahab had been cursed to survive for decades more . . . an embodiment of impotence and hubris? Then the story would have been not Ahab's, but Robert S. McNamara's" (Carroll, 2009). And there is something of the seer in Morris's McNamara. Despite his striped shirt and his blue suit, he appears before the viewer like a 21st-century prophet of the apocalypse, staring urgently into the camera, compelled to share the dark visions he has been vouchsafed.

4. Morris himself has addressed the issue of subjects who (consciously or unconsciously) lie and the status of their narratives within his films, commenting, "There is no mode of expression, no technique of production that will instantly produce truth or falsehood. There is no *veritas lens*" (Morris, 2008a). His point, I think, is to remind us as viewers/readers that the onus is on us to question the narratives we see and hear. His purpose and his technique, as he describes them in the same essay, consist of providing the means to assemble new and perhaps more truthful narratives out of the materials his subjects present. It is to invite revision. "I take the pieces of the false narrative, rearrange them, emphasize new details, and construct a new narrative."

5. In teaching *The Fog of War,* I ask students to debate the issue of whether Robert McNamara committed crimes against humanity, and the question always elicits heated argument on both sides.

7

Matters of Life and Death

Two American Jury Narratives

"Collective Decision Making in a Complicated Situation": Juries, Narratives, Management

Many of the narratives we have considered in the course of this book have featured high-profile, at times larger-than-life, public figures acting on the most prominent of political stages. We began, however, with more modest protagonists, teachers in inner-city American schools. It seems fitting to conclude with another "frontline" fable that is itself deeply concerned with narratives: two stories of decision making by ordinary citizens randomly chosen to perform an essential civic duty, jury service.

The law has long been a popular subject for narrative, from the great 19th-century novelists to contemporary bestseller lists (Posner, 2009). Yet jury proceedings, for all their inherent drama, have featured much less prominently than the trials that precede them. Graham Burnett, whose narrative of his own jury duty we will discuss in this chapter, calls the jury room "a most remarkable—and largely inaccessible—space in our society...We expect much of this room, and we think about it less often than we probably

---

Governing Fables: Learning from Public Sector Narratives, pages 213–238
Copyright © 2011 by Information Age Publishing
213

should" (Burnett, 2001, p. 13). It is inaccessible in a double sense. Potential jurors face widespread challenges by attorneys and are allowed numerous reasons for being excused. Only a small percentage of citizens actually serve on juries. And those who do generally seem to feel constrained by the confidentiality of their deliberations not to write about them subsequently (Weisselberg, 2007). Confidentiality of proceedings means, of course, that no other observers can be present, and there are stringent restrictions on the observation and reporting of jury composition, interactions, and behavior during court proceedings within the American legal system. There are, however, two significant American narratives about jury decision making, both based on their authors' lived experience, though separated by almost 50 years in time.

Reginald Rose, a television writer who was known for his "slice of life" dramas for CBS's influential anthology series *Studio One*, served on the jury for a manslaughter case in 1954. "We got into this terrific, furious, eight-hour argument in the jury room," Rose subsequently recalled. "I was writing one-hour dramas for 'Studio One' then and I thought, 'Wow, what a setting for a drama'" (at http://www.imdb.com/name/nm0741627/bio#quotes). The experience became the basis of the television drama, movie, and stage play *Twelve Angry Men*. D. Graham Burnett, a professor of the history of science now at Princeton, was impanelled as a member of the jury of a murder trial in 2000 while on a research fellowship. By his own account, a highly self-conscious aspiring academic with a "pseudo-monkish devotion to the world of the past and its books" nurturing "a mostly private contempt for people I deemed unserious" (Burnett, 2007, pp. 553, 552), Burnett seized on his jury service as an opportunity for self-transformation, "a rare opportunity to participate in something important, weighty, real, something very different from my academic life" (Burnett, 2001, p. 29). Subsequently (one might say, inevitably), he described his experience in a book, *A Trial by Jury* (2001). However much one might agree with Burnett's strategic self-deprecation in describing the "miasma of metaphysics and megalomania" (Burnett, 2007, p. 552) that accompanied him into the jury room, he produced a fascinating and thought-provoking account that both inverts and reenacts Rose's landmark drama.

Both these narratives have a dual claim on our attention. At the heart of each is a fable about the interpretation of competing narratives. And each concerns itself, in a particularly intimate and compelling way, with what Burnett calls with considerable understatement "collective decision-making in a complicated situation," (Burnett, 2007, p. 554); that is, with questions of leadership and decision making that have been recurring themes throughout this book. If Kennedy's Excom represented small-group decision making at its most exalted, Rose and Burnett's sequestered citizens struggling to resolve the perennial tension between law and justice afford a very different perspective.

Juries are a unique form of decision-making body, dissimilar in many ways from public sector bodies (cabinets), corporate bodies (boards of directors), or the ad hoc task forces widely used in both sectors. Juries are initially chosen at random and are intended to reflect the diversity of the population from which they are chosen. The prescribed size of twelve, besides providing for diversity, is intended to be large enough to counteract the tendency to "group think." Juries are by definition ad hoc, brought together for the purpose of making a single decision and then dispersed. But this decision making is notably constrained. The judge's interpretation of the law limits the set of alternatives juries can consider, and they are of course permitted to consider only admissible evidence presented during the trial. Strict rules of evidence limit what is admissible; for example, excluding hearsay as well as a defendant's previous convictions not directly relevant to the case. Jury members can interpret the evidence in the light of their experience but are not allowed to gather their own. Burnett commented on the difficulty of the jurors' constraints: "How could one even begin to investigate a problem without being able to engage with it directly?" (Burnett, 2001, p. 37). Similarly, he bridled at the restriction on evidence about previous convictions: "I was being asked to decide if a crime occurred—in other words, if *someone* did *something* to *someone else*. How could the nature of either "someone" stand off-limits?" (p. 71, emphasis in original).

In addition to these constraints on the admissibility of evidence, the actual decision-making process is also dramatically constrained. A jury's verdict must be unanimous. If unanimity cannot be achieved, the resulting hung jury requires the case to be reheard by another. Juries have no hierarchy other than the foreman selected by the judge, and the foreman's powers are limited to acting as chair. Juries are sequestered, meeting in secret, and are kept virtually incommunicado when not meeting, so as to prevent jury members from being influenced by other individuals, by the media, or by online commentary. Burnett wryly evokes the continuous attendance by armed guards "who extended their affable surveillance into all lavatories" (Burnett, 2001, p. 12).

The contrast between a jury and a parliamentary cabinet or a president and his advisers is considerable. Ministers have an ongoing relationship, making many decisions together. There are considerable status differences among the first minister, ministers holding senior portfolios, and junior ministers. Rules of evidence are loose, and there are no constraints upon ministers finding out whatever they can about issues under consideration and bringing their own evidence, in addition to their own experience, to bear upon the deliberations. The available options are not strictly limited, and sometimes the head of government, as President Kennedy did during the Cuban Missile Crisis, will urge his colleagues to be creative and develop new options. Decisions are usually made by consensus, with the first minister defining the consensus. It is well known that occasionally a first minister will define as the consensus an option that she alone prefers and that is opposed by the rest of the cabinet.

Yet we can identify some ways in which juries and cabinets are analogous. Both operate in secrecy. The practice of cabinet solidarity means that all members, regardless of what they said or how they voted (if the cabinet took a vote), must publicly support the decision that was taken or resign from cabinet. This gives the minority some measure of influence in shaping decisions. As we saw in the discussion of Churchill's leadership of the War Cabinet in May 1940, some decisions are so critical that unanimity is a practical necessity. While there is an evident hierarchy in cabinet, and juries are formally egalitarian, we can expect some sort of informal hierarchy to emerge within a jury in terms of the intellectual ability, skill at argument, and force of personality of the jurors. Most significantly, in the last analysis, both cabinets and juries are composed of groups of people, and there are some group dynamics in terms of the nature of the process or the roles played by individuals that inevitably assert themselves.

Unlike previous chapters, our analysis here will deal with only two narratives, and this narrowing of focus deserves some explanation. While juries do feature quite regularly in popular legal fiction (John Grisham's 1996 novel *The Runaway Jury* is an obvious example) and at least occasionally in more recent movies (the Grisham novel was made into a film in 2003), narratives whose primary concern is the internal dynamics of jury decision making are rare (Papke, 2007, pp. 742–748). While it would certainly be possible to survey the field of jury stories, tracing *Twelve Angry Men*'s continuing influence, I have chosen a different approach. What this offers, I hope, is the opportunity to reconsider themes of leadership and management from the perspective of citizens rather than public servants or politicians. For the jury narratives we will explore here are, above all, citizens' stories.

"This Gentleman Has Been Standing Alone Against Us": Anatomy of a Classic

If there is a dominant jury fable, *Twelve Angry Men* surely is it. As Graham Burnett himself notes in the introduction he wrote to a symposium published by the *Chicago-Kent Law Review* (Marder, 2007a) celebrating the 50th anniversary of the film, even those who have never seen the movie know—or think they do—that bare institutional room, the ticking clock on the wall, those twelve men in their white shirt-sleeves and narrow ties, the speeches, explosions, confrontations, and reversals (Burnett, 2007, p. 553). Most of all, they know that single figure, Juror 8, Henry Fonda, the epitome of impassioned decency, making his plea for reflection: "It's not easy for me to raise my hand and send a boy off to die without talking about it first . . . I just think we owe him a few words" (Rose, 2006, p. 12). It is not only scholars and critics (Ebert, 2002; Posner, 2009, p. 54) who accord the film classic status. The hundreds of management students to whom I have taught the movie over two decades respond to it with equal enthusiasm and engagement. And, at the time of writing, it has received 134,000 votes on www.imdb.com, with an average vote of 8.9 out of 10, the seventh-highest of any film.[1]

Twelve Angry Men begins with the judge's final instructions to the jury as he sends them to their deliberations. The choice clearly indicates that neither the crime itself nor the trial that followed it is the core of the drama. In fact, the killing (as it is evoked in the jurors' discussions) is a deliberately unsensational episode of domestic violence. A father and his teenage son have an argument in their apartment after dinner. The father slaps the boy several times. The son leaves the apartment at 8:00, goes to a neighborhood store and buys a switchblade. He then meets three friends at a diner, shows them the knife, and they talk until 9:45. He returns home at 10. According to the prosecution, he then has another fight with his father around midnight, stabs him in the chest, and flees at 12:10 a.m. Two witnesses are produced for the prosecution. An old man in the apartment below was awakened by the commotion, claimed to hear the teenager shout "I'm going to kill you," and to hear a body fall to the floor. He also claimed to see the teenager run out of the apartment. A middle-aged woman in an apartment across the street was also awakened by the struggle and, looking through the windows of a passing elevated train, claimed to see the teenager murdering his father by raising the knife and stabbing him (Rose, 2006, pp. 34–35). The teenager returned to the apartment around 3:15 a.m., was questioned by the police, who had been called by the elderly witness, and was arrested. During the trial, the accused teenager claimed that he left the house at 11:30 p.m. to go to a late-night movie, and lost the knife while he was out.

I have summarized the prosecution's account of the crime in detail because the essence of the film's "action" is precisely the gradual deconstruction of this explanatory account. What we witness, in effect, is a collective if adversarial interpretive process in which a group of "readers" (the jury) are led to contest the prosecution's narrative, casting sufficient doubt for it to fail to reach the required standard of "beyond a reasonable doubt," formulating alternative narratives, which are to them at least equally plausible. The legal scholar and appellate judge Richard Posner has observed that the unraveling of the prosecution's case "injects a strong whodunit element rare in jury deliberations" (Posner, 2009, p. 54). He goes on to say, "This is not a flaw in the film but an aspect of its art." Francois Truffaut, the noted director and critic agreed. The film's audience, he wrote, "experiences intensely the feeling, not of something done, but of something being done" (Landsman, 2007, pp. 756–757). Posner notes that it is the absence of a compelling counternarrative from the defense that involves the jurors in this unusual detective work (2009, p. 426). And Rose does indeed build into Juror 8's explanation of his doubts the seeming indifference and/or inexperience of the court-appointed defense lawyer.

> It could mean he didn't want the case. It could mean he resented being appointed. It's the kind of case that brings him nothing. No money. No glory. Not even much chance of winning. It's not a very promising situation for a young lawyer. He'd really have to believe in his client to make a good fight. As [another juror] pointed out a moment ago, he obviously didn't. (Rose, 2006, p. 38)

But is it not merely the "whodunit" mechanisms of the film that account for its power. The narrowness of Rose's focus—these twelve men, this one room—was the choice of a seasoned dramatist who understood the impact the gradually accumulating tension would produce. While many other legal narratives incorporate juries or individual jurors—the wait for the return of the verdict is a courtroom drama staple—no other has presented as detailed a portrait of all the jurors involved nor delved as deeply into their interactions (Papke, 2007). Director Sidney Lumet structured his visual narrative to heighten wherever possible the effects of claustrophobia, fatigue, and mounting pressure activated by Rose's structural choice, restricting the film's action to the jury room or the adjacent washroom (with the exception of brief framing scenes at the beginning and end). He also shot the film with progressively longer lenses, moving his camera from a position above the actors to one below them. This had the effect of making the room seem smaller, providing a visual correlative for what he called "the sense of entrapment the men must have felt in the room" (Lumet, 1995, p. 8). In the same memoir in which he described these technical choices, he also provided a one-word summation of what he felt *Twelve Angry Men* was about. His word was "Listen" (pp. 13–14).

And indeed the power of the voices that speak continuously throughout the film cannot be discounted. One of the reasons Rose's play is so frequently revived is the opportunity it provides to assemble what is inevitably referred to as "a powerhouse ensemble." The movie undoubtedly had its own. In addition to Henry Fonda, in one of the touchstone performances of his career, the cast included Lee J.Cobb (Juror 3), E. G. Marshall (Juror 4), Martin Balsam (Juror 1), and Jack Klugman (Juror 7). Equally important is the initial dramatic setup, which ranges Fonda's dissenting voice against the rest. The spectacle of Fonda facing down the eleven other jurors, armed only with his own integrity and an innate sense of fairness ("We owe him a few words"), then gradually winning the skeptics to his side, has an archetypal resonance acknowledged within the narrative itself. As Juror 9 explains, "This gentleman has been standing alone against us. Now, he doesn't say that the boy is not guilty, he just isn't sure. Well it's not easy to stand alone against the ridicule of others, so he gambled for support and I gave it to him. I respect his motives. The boy is probably guilty, but, uh, I want to hear more. Right now the vote is ten to two" (Rose, 2006, pp. 27–28).

Among management instructors, Juror 8 is a hero equivalent to Shakespeare's Henry V, an equally favored source of what Marjorie Garber calls "exemplarity" (Garber, 2008, pp. 178–200). And it is easy to understand why. For it is not just the force of his integrity and conviction (and no one played those qualities better than Henry Fonda) that moves his fellow jurors. It is also the powerful techniques of persuasion he employs and the quiet assertion of leadership. Watching these unfold, witnessing their effect on the other men in the room, feeling the balance tipping first one way then another, generates a psychological suspense that survives even repeated viewings. (It also makes *Twelve Angry Men* a classic management text, and we will consider Juror 8 as leader/manager in much more detail shortly.)

For original viewers of *Twelve Angry Men*, the narrative would have had an immediate social resonance, linked to, but not identical with, its timeless concern with issues of justice, law, and standards of proof. The defendant in the case, never named and most frequently referred to as "the kid," is clearly a member of an ethnic minority. (He is assumed by most commentators to be Puerto Rican.) Government provision for impoverished and disadvantaged defendants in capital cases were much less generous then than they are now, and the narrative engages indirectly but powerfully with issues of racial prejudice and the justice system through the diatribes of Juror 10, whose racist slanders discredit him at a crucial point in the plot.[2]

Viewed from a more distant perspective in time, the film seems equally engaged with issues raised by the anti-Communist frenzy of the McCarthy hearings, in particular the heroic individualism of those who dared to stand against the prevailing hysteria. (As a successful screenwriter whose professional career began in 1950, Rose would have been well aware of the Hollywood blacklist associated with the House Committee on Un-American

Activities, of those who succumbed to the pressure and those who resisted.) Juror 11, a European immigrant, indirectly invokes this very recent past when he responds to the abuse of those determined to convict by saying, "I have always thought that in this country a man was entitled to have unpopular opinions" (Rose, 2006, p. 27).

It is a measure of the power of *Twelve Angry Men*'s central thematic concerns—justice versus legality, the elusiveness of truth, the power of the individual conscience—that viewers can engage with the film completely without any knowledge of these historical contexts. The *Chicago-Kent Law Review* symposium demonstrates conclusively the range of that engagement. With nineteen different contributions, and running an impressive 350 pages in length, it covered topics as diverse as research on decision making by juries (for example, the frequency of juries reversing themselves during the course of their deliberations and the frequency and dynamics of hung juries); responses to and dramas inspired by *Twelve Angry Men* in Spain, Germany, and Russia; and discussions of religious imagery (Hay, 2007) and the theme of fatherhood (Sarat, 2007) in the movie. Most of the contributors shared the premise assumed here; namely, the heroic status of Juror 8, whose leadership inspires the other jurors to examine the evidence the prosecution presented at the trial with a skeptical eye and thus ensure that justice is done (Babcock & Sassoubre, 2007; Burns, 2007; Hay, 2007; Landsman, 2007; Marder, 2007b; Papke, 2007; Sarat, 2007). Surprisingly, none of these articles addresses the rhetorical and persuasive techniques Juror 8 used, the subject we will turn to in a moment.

The symposium, however, did include three counter-narratives. Both Vidmar, Beale, Chemerinsky, and Coleman (2007) and Asimow (2007) argued that there was very strong circumstantial evidence (for example, the absence of any physical evidence of a break-in at the apartment) inculpating the accused, and that the accused should in fact have been convicted. Weisselberg (2007) argued that the jury exceeded its mandate in several ways, most notably Juror 8's self-authorized gathering and production of evidence, and that, had a judge discovered this, (s)he would have discharged the jury and ordered another trial. The fact of this controversy is a further testament to Reginald Rose's skill. While the jurors in *Twelve Angry Men* do indeed reach a verdict, the film itself offers no "solution" to the crime. What we have witnessed is a triumph of persuasion. The film undoubtedly stacks the deck heavily in Juror 8's favor, beginning with the casting of Fonda in the role, but however persuasive his alternative explanations, they remain no more than that. In the end, we have arrived only at reasonable doubt.

"Listen": Juror 8 as Heroic Manager

What did the director Sydney Lumet mean when he attempted to encapsulate *Twelve Angry Men* in the injunction "Listen?" I choose to interpret his remark within the context of the management concept of "active listening" first popularized by the American psychologist Thomas Gordon in the 1960s and 1970s as an instrument of conflict resolution. Its first application was in Gordon's practice consulting to business in the 1950s. It became more widely known as part of his Parent Effectiveness Training model, which he developed in California in the following decade (Gordon, 2000). Active listening connotes close attention to the message(s) conveyed by the speaker's tone, facial expression, and body language, but it also implies listening for the unspoken information, the implicit perspectives and biases, the unacknowledged (even unconscious) needs that inform the speaker's words. It is, in a sense, a practice based on the recognition of the essentially polyphonic nature of all human communication. Throughout *Twelve Angry Men*, both Juror 8 and the camera function as active listeners, discovering in the other jurors' words much more than they actually say.

But "Listen" can also be the storyteller's injunction to his audience, and while Juror 8 was clearly an active listener, he also displayed a number of other narrative-related skills—argumentation, dramatization, empathy, and empowerment—skills that have made him an exemplary figure for management audiences. In many ways, Juror 8's biggest challenge comes at the beginning of the deliberations. The strongest advocates of a guilty verdict quickly made clear where they stood and, as will be discussed below, in some instances revealed their personal agendas. The foreman immediately showed himself to be unassertive, starting the meeting by saying, "Now you gentlemen can handle this any way you want. I mean, I'm not going to have any rules" (Rose, 2006, p. 10). Some jurors then called for a preliminary vote, and it was 11–1 for conviction, with juror number 8 voting for acquittal.

The cinema verite style employed by Lumet throughout the film (Babcock & Sassoubre, 2007; Burns, 2007), with its tight focus on the actors and avoidance of obvious visual effects, reinforces Juror 8's strategy in the deliberations. He reveals little about himself, his initial assessment of the evidence, or his intentions in the deliberations to his fellow jurors, leaving the audience as uncertain of his motivations as the men in the room. Does he actually think the accused is not guilty? Or does he only have doubts as to the prosecution's case? Whatever his own assessment of the evidence, his challenge is to begin a discussion that many of the other jurors believe unnecessary. He achieves this in a number of ways. Rather than challenge the almost unanimous verdict of the others, thereby alienating the men he hopes to sway, he asks only for a chance to talk first, reassuring them he has no other designs: "I'm not trying to change your mind. It's just that we're talking about somebody's life here" (Rose, 2006, p. 12). He then reminds them of the accused's youth and the difficult circumstances of his life, clearly seeking to redefine him in the others' minds: "Look, this boy's been kicked around all his life. You know, living in a slum, his mother dead since he was nine. He spent a year-and-a-half in an orphanage while his father served a jail term for forgery. That's not a very good head start. He's had a pretty terrible sixteen years" (p. 13). As discussed above, Juror 8 also casts doubt on the effectiveness of the accused's lawyer, implicitly legitimizing his own assumption of the advocate's role. These arguments and strategies do not deal directly with the prosecution's evidence. They do begin a conversation. More importantly, they succeed in subtly shifting the onus to the other jurors to convince the one holdout among them. Juror 12 suggests they each present their own arguments for their guilty votes. Effectively, Juror 8 has reframed the conflict, clearly defined his own role, and engaged his adversaries in a collective enterprise.

Juror 8's first attempt to dispute the prosecution's evidence concerned their argument that the murder weapon was unique and that it was the same knife that the accused had shown his friends. His tactic is a dramatic narrative disruption. The night before the deliberations, Juror 8 went walking in the neighborhood where the crime was committed and purchased an identical knife.[3] Early in the deliberations, he asks to have the murder weapon shown to the jury and then pulls the second knife from his pocket, thrusting it into the table beside the murder weapon. It is, as one of the other jurors immediately notes, "a trick," but it is enough to put this element of the prosecution's narrative in doubt. Juror 8 then takes a calculated risk, agreeing that if all the others now vote, anonymously, for conviction, he will accept their decision. One other juror now votes to acquit, not necessarily because he believes the accused is not guilty, but because he wants to continue the discussion (Rose, 2006, pp. 27–28). This marks a turning point (though hardly a tipping point) in the deliberations. Having broken the opposing jurors' unanimity, Juror 8 assumes a more active role, becoming increasingly forceful and self-confident. Taking control of the discussion, he no longer appears to be playing devil's advocate—if he ever was.

Once this turning point has been reached, Juror 8 begins to propose alternative narratives to the prosecution's, using information supplied by the defendant's lawyer about the murder victim (his father):

> He was in prison once. He was known to be a compulsive gambler and a pretty consistent loser. He spent a lot of time in neighborhood bars and

he'd get into fistfights sometimes after a couple of drinks. Usually over a woman. He was a tough, cruel, primitive kind of man who never held a job for more than six months in his life. So here are a few possibilities. He could have been murdered by one of many men he served time with in prison. By a bookmaker. By a man he had beaten up. By a woman he'd picked up. By any one of the people he was known to hang out with. (Rose, 2006, p. 33)

His aim, as he himself makes plain, is not to prove anything, but simply to multiply interpretations, to insist on the existence of other explanatory narratives that could also be sufficient.

He employs narrative disruption in other ways as well, linking the two witnesses' testimony to discredit one, forcing his listeners to acknowledge discrepancies between them. (If a subway train was passing by at the time of the murder, as the woman testified, then it would have been unlikely for the old man to have heard the accused shout "I'm going to kill you.") Varying his tactics, he further tests (and discredits) the old man's claims that after he heard a body fall he had dragged himself from his bed to the window and then saw the accused leaving the apartment. The old man, who walked with a limp, said that it took him fifteen seconds to get from his bed to the window. Juror number 8 marks out the distance in the jury room and, forcing himself to limp, demonstrates that it took him forty-two seconds to cover it. (The implication being that the witness could not then have seen the accused leaving the apartment as he claimed.) Having secured agreement on the time discrepancy, Juror 8 then uses this to advance yet another alternative.

Clearly, Juror 8 had a flair for dramatic self-presentation that buttressed his arguments. As mentioned, he brandished his own knife and acted out the old man's movements. Early in the deliberations, two jurors, one of whom was one of the leading proponents of a guilty verdict, were playing tic-tac-toe. Juror number 8 didn't simply ask them to stop, which the unassertive foreman failed to do, but he leapt to his feet, snatched the paper, crumpled it up, and threw it out, saying, "This isn't a game" (Rose, 2006, p. 35). Thus, he forcefully established his own moral seriousness and explicitly challenged the others to meet the standard he had set. And Juror 8 continued to use his physical presence to reinforce his refusal to be intimidated by ridicule or abuse. When the most belligerent and uncontrolled of the men (Juror 3) determines to reenact the actual stabbing (to settle questions of the angle of the wound), he challenges the others to play the victim. No one moves, until Juror 8 steps up and unflinchingly allows the man, who had already lashed out at him physically, to bring the knife within an inch of his chest (p. 60). It is a completely silent moment, and yet one in which an important story of aggression, attempted intimidation, and forceful resistance has been communicated.

While Juror 8 shows himself to be skillful in managing confrontation, he works carefully to avoid it where possible. His strategy is first to build bridges to those he senses are uncommitted, empowering them to contribute their ideas and experience to the discussion. He remains cordial toward those who are the strongest proponents of a guilty verdict, waiting to secure more support before attempting to convince or discredit them.

In one instance, however, Juror 8 deliberately departs from his calm demeanor and launches an ad hominem attack on one of the jurors who most strenuously argued for a conviction. Juror number 3, who revealed early on that he had a deeply conflicted relationship with his own teenage son, was unwilling to consider the evidence and kept repeating that the accused was a kid who committed murder and had to pay for it. He exclaimed to the other jurors, "What's the matter with you people? Every one of you knows this kid is guilty. He's got to burn. We're letting him slip through our fingers." Juror 8 seizes on his words: "Slip through our fingers? Are you his executioner?" He goads the irate man further, asking if he'd "like to pull the switch" and accusing him of behaving like "a self-appointed public avenger." A final accusation of sadism leads Juror 3 to lose control completely, lunging at his tormentor and threatening to kill him. This confrontation, for which Juror 3 later apologizes, destroys his credibility. It also effectively establishes the material interpretive point Juror 8 had been making; namely that "I'll kill you" is a common threat that is rarely meant literally (Rose, 2006, pp. 47–48). This confrontation ended the first act of the play on a suitably explosive note. Both play and film conclude with Juror 3, the last holdout, finally admitting that his judgment has been warped by his own feelings of anger, shame, and regret toward his son. Standing against the others, he now occupies the structural position of Juror 8 at the film's opening. Emotionally shattered, he changes his vote.

Juror 3: That whole thing about hearing the boy yell? The phrase was "I'm gonna kill you." That's what he said. To his own father. I don't care what kind of a man that was. It was his father. That goddamn rotten kid. I know him. What they're like. What they do to you. How they kill you every day. My God, don't you see? How come I'm the only one who sees? Jeez, I can feel that knife goin' in.

Juror 8: It's not your boy. He's somebody else.

Juror 4: Let him live.

[There is a long pause.]

Juror 3: All right. "Not guilty."

After all the other jurors leave, Juror 8, in a gesture of sympathy and reconciliation, helps the distraught man put his jacket back on.

Juror number 8, in keeping with his focus on the decision, revealed less about himself in informal discussions with the other jurors than many of them did, only that he was an architect and had two children. But his skill at persuasion and interpersonal relations strongly suggests that he would have been a leader among professionals; for example, the managing partner of a large firm. (This also suggests, ironically, that because of his organizational responsibilities, he would likely have been excused from jury duty.) Juror number 8 also displayed the intellectual flexibility and empathy with his adversaries that Robert Kennedy and Robert McNamara identified as President Kennedy's character traits that were so decisive to the peaceful outcome of the Cuban Missile Crisis.

Some of the other jurors whom juror number 8 encouraged deserve mention, particularly for their listening skills. Juror 9—an old man who was the first to change his vote and had been encouraged by Juror 8—proved to be an experienced and acute observer of people. For example, he noticed that the middle-aged woman who claimed to have witnessed the murder had grooves at the sides of the bridge of her nose from wearing glasses, but did not wear glasses in court. He hypothesized that she was not wearing her glasses when she was awakened by the sounds of the midnight struggle and thus saw only a blur through the subway train, rather than a clear image of a murder (Rose, 2006, p. 69). Juror 5, who shared the same ethnic background as the accused, showed from his own experience with knife fights that someone accustomed to using a switchblade would have thrust up, rather than stabbed down, thus adding to the jury's doubts about whether the boy was the murderer (p. 62). Juror 11, an immigrant watchmaker, analyzed the evidence closely, in particular asking why the boy, if he committed the murder, would have so quickly returned to the scene of the crime (pp. 38–40). The jurors demonstrated that the eyewitnesses might have been physically incapable of seeing what they thought they saw (for example, the middle aged woman without her glasses) or led by bias or prejudice to "see" what they wanted to see or "hear" what they wanted to hear.

In contrast to these three jurors, Juror 12, a writer at an advertising agency, came to epitomize the lack of seriousness Juror 8 deplored. He was one of the tic-tac-toe players, and he often used ad industry witticisms in the deliberations: "Um, if no one else has an idea, I may have a cutie here. I mean, I haven't put much thought into it. Anyway, lemme throw it out on the stoop and see if the cat licks it up [laughs]" (Rose, 2006, p. 50). Unsurprisingly, none of the other jurors was interested. Juror 12, by his clothes and profession, was one of the higher status jurors who should thus have had considerable influence, but his frivolous demeanor ultimately dissuaded his fellow jurors from taking him seriously.

The four jurors who believed most strongly that the accused was guilty present some interesting contrasts. Juror 4, a stockbroker, initially harbored a bias against the accused on the basis of his background, saying "slums are breeding grounds for criminals... Children from slums are potential menaces to society" (Rose, 2006, p. 18). But he didn't permit his bias to distract him from the evidence. He was as focused and as serious about his task as Juror 8. A glasses wearer himself, the key argument that changed his mind was the doubt about whether the female witness to the crime was wearing her glasses at the time.

Jurors 3, 7, and 10 all made it clear in the "meeting before the meeting"—the unstructured discussion before the foreman called the jury to order—that they strongly favored a conviction. They also, however, quickly communicated their personal agendas. Juror 7 had seats for the baseball game and wanted the deliberations to end quickly. Juror 8 challenged him on this, and as the deliberations wore on, Juror 7 lost interest and focus. When the jury was split 6–6, he proposed that they report a hung jury. When the jurors continued to debate, Juror 7 attempted, but failed, to assume control: "Listen, I'll tell you something. I'm a little bit sick of this whole thing already. All this yakkin's getting us nowhere, so I'm going to break it up here. I'm changing my vote to not guilty...I've had enough" (Rose, 2006, p. 62).

Juror 10 made clear right at the outset his prejudice against Puerto Ricans: "Listen, I've lived among 'em all my life. You can't believe a word they say. I mean, they're born liars" (p. 11). As the trial progressed, he refused to discuss the evidence and simply grew increasingly angry at the other jurors because they were changing their minds. Toward the end of the deliberations, he made a long speech laying out the rationale for his prejudice: "They don't care. Family don't mean anything to them. They breed like animals...They're against us, they hate us, they want to destroy us....They're gonna breed us out of existence" (pp. 64–65). As he spoke, the other jurors physically separated themselves from him, and ultimately Juror 4, even before changing his vote, told him, "We've heard enough. Sit down. And don't open your filthy mouth again" (p. 66). In the final vote, Juror 10, while still proclaiming that the defendant was guilty, recognized that he had been discredited and changed his vote. Juror 3 made clear early on his troubled relationship with his son: "When he was nine he ran away from a fight....So I told him 'I'm gonna make a man out of you or I'm gonna bust you in half trying.' Well, I made a man out of him all right. When he was sixteen we had a battle. He hit me in the face. He's big, y'know. I haven't seen him in two years. Rotten kid. You work your heart out..." (p. 18). As discussed above, it became increasingly clear to his fellow jurors that this bitter experience, rather than any logical analysis of the evidence, drove his judgment.

Jurors 3, 7, and 10, as a group, were singularly ineffective advocates. Incapable of suppressing the personal narratives that motivated them, they made clear early on that their votes were being driven by personal agendas. As the deliberations went on, it became increasingly obvious to their colleagues that they were unwilling to assess the evidence objectively and that their personal agendas, ranging from the trivial (tickets to a baseball game) to the profoundly disturbing (blatant prejudice, a failed father-son relationship), were unacceptable. As other jurors changed their minds, these three attempted to claim a bond of loyalty, a bond Juror 11 refused to accept: "I don't believe I have to be loyal to one side or the other. I am simply asking questions" (Rose, 2006, p. 39). More than any others, Jurors 3, 7, and 10 were the angry men referred to in the title. More than any others, their anger outweighed their ability to assess the evidence. And their anger made it impossible for them to do the thing Lumet summarized as the narrative's key point, to listen.

"Henry Fonda I Was Not": Graham Burnett's *A Trial by Jury*

The jury deliberations in which Graham Burnett participated, like those in *Twelve Angry Men*, involved a murder trial in New York City in which the defendant was a member of a visible minority, in this case an African-American. The differences, however, were significant. The deliberations lasted four days, and the jurors experienced the disruption of sequestration at suburban hotels for three nights. (Burnett explains that almost two full days were spent attempting to understand the judge's highly technical instructions concerning the possible charges on which the defendant could be found guilty, a task made much more difficult by his refusal to supply a written transcript (Burnett, 2001, p. 83). Only four of the jurors were men. While Burnett came to doubt the intellectual capacity of a few of the jurors, there was only one who displayed an unacceptable personal agenda comparable to those of Jurors 3, 7, and 10 in *Twelve Angry Men*. Most importantly, the defendant had capable legal representation, so that the jury's work was much closer to Posner's ideal of choosing between conflicting narratives than *Twelve Angry Men*'s collaborative authorship of an alternative or counter-narrative.

The murder itself was no garden-variety domestic homicide either. According to his statement to the police, Monte Virginia Milcray, a young black man, contacted "Veronique" (Randolph "Antigua" Cuffee) on a date line phone service and arranged to meet Cuffee at her apartment. There Cuffee revealed himself to be a transvestite and then attempted to sodomize Milcray. Milcray, who was carrying a knife, was positioned under Cuffee. He resisted, stabbing Cuffee in the chest, touching his aorta—a fatal wound that led to his death within a few minutes. Before Cuffee died, Milcray, still positioned underneath, stabbed him approximately twenty more times on the right side of his head, neck, and spine. There was no doubt that Milcray killed Cuffee, but the question the jury had to decide was whether this was murder or legitimate self-defense. More precisely, the judge gave the jury three alternatives. It could find Milcray guilty of second degree murder if he acted with intent to kill or with "depraved indifference to human life." It could find him guilty of manslaughter if, by acting recklessly, he caused Cuffee's death. Finally, under New York State law, the jury could find Milcray not guilty if he was deemed to be protecting himself from what he reasonably believed was imminent sexual assault (Burnett, 2001, pp. 81–83).

Burnett's narrative form, too, could hardly be more different from that of *Twelve Angry Men*. First and foremost, Burnett was providing a first person account of his experience as juror. At the outset, he made it clear that he was not attempting to retry the case by interviewing the participants or performing additional investigation or research. He was writing his own story and, as befits a good post-modernist intellectual, was well aware that each of his fellow-jurors would have their own narratives of events that would differ markedly from his own:

> I have no idea what those who shared the experience with me would make of this document should they pick it up. Or let me speak more frankly: I am sure each would contest my story in different ways . . . If one learns anything from a criminal trial under the adversary system, it is that sincere folk can differ vehemently about events, and that there is seldom any easy way to figure out what actually went on. (Burnett 2001, p. 14)

As this excerpt makes clear, Burnett uses the first person throughout, apparently revealing his thoughts and intentions as he describes his words and actions during those life-altering four days. Of course, this transparent, revelatory account of what "I" did, thought, and felt is as much a construction as any other narrative mode, and at least as unreliable, but its emphasis on the interior view does differentiate it from the narrative perspective of *Twelve Angry Men* which remains resolutely on the outside, looking in.

In his foreword to the Chicago Kent symposium on *Twelve Angry Men*, Burnett explicitly presents his narrative as the antithesis of the falsities of the famous movie, with its "trick endings" and "false discoveries." He takes particular exception to what he calls "the dramatic cleanliness of the progress toward a verdict" and offers his story as an antidote to the "collective fantasy about participatory judicial rationality" the movie engenders (Burnett, 2007, pp. 552–553). For all his protests, it is interesting to see how closely his own behavior through the proceedings comes to mirror that of the fictional character, Juror 8, though with a level of self-consciousness utterly foreign to that earlier era.

Burnett begins his narrative with Milcray's killing of Cuffee—as described by Milcray—questioning if events could indeed have happened that way. While this was clearly done to capitalize on the sensational aspect of the case, plunging the reader directly into the exotic world of New York's gay transvestite community, Burnett then eliminates any suspense by announcing the outcome of the trial. The jury acquits Milcray of both second-degree murder and manslaughter. Burnett then returns to the beginning of the story and presents, chronologically, the selection of the jury, the trial and finally, the primary focus of the book, how the jury deliberations led to the outcome. The trial featured both the forensic evidence of police investigators and the testimony of some of Cuffee's drag queen friends who were to meet him on the night of the murder. Milcray took the stand at the end of the trial. Burnett found the prosecution's case flawed because they had not been able to establish a motive other than self-defense. Equally importantly, he admits, he had conceived an intense dislike to the melodramatic and aggressive prosecutor who had attempted to intimidate Milcray under cross-examination into admitting he had stabed Cuffee from behind, a point Milcray steadfastly disputed. In a scene reminiscent of the reenactments of *Twelve Angry Men*, the prosecutor "furiously dramatized" every one of the twenty stabs with the murder weapon.

> So egregious did I find the whole performance that, as Milcray returned to his seat—slightly hunched, as if afraid of bumping his head on something—I felt a deep desire to see the prosecutor lose the case. How did that whisper of a thought affect what followed? It is difficult to say. (Burnett, 2001, p. 72)

Difficult, undoubtedly, but surely material? It is typical of the narrative strategy Burnett adopts that he raises the issue without pursuing its implications. This is part of what can make Burnett so deeply annoying as a narrator, the ostentatious willingness to confess coupled with an immediate self-granted immunity from prosecution.

The jury's first vote revealed that a majority, initially eight of the twelve jurors, concluded that the prosecution had not proved beyond the shadow of a doubt that Milcray did not act in self-defense. Getting from a majority to unanimity, however, was difficult. A possible compromise on a charge of manslaughter was considered, but rejected by the proponents of a not guilty verdict because they saw their task as strictly applying the law, and a finding of self-defense precluded a conviction of manslaughter. The third day proved to be the most dramatic. There was considerable sentiment in the room that, even if Milcray acted in self-defense, and even if the prosecution had failed to disprove beyond a reasonable doubt that he had done so, he still deserved some measure of punishment; the jury came to express this dilemma as a conflict between respecting the letter of the law or moving beyond it to see justice done. The implications of the conflict were eloquently articulated, not by Burnett himself, but by his closest counterpart (and rival for the position of resident intellectual) within the group, an academic he calls Adelle who, as quoted by Burnett, was strongly advocating for a guilty verdict:

> [W]hat I keep wanting here is for us to figure out some way to do justice, but I am starting to realize that the law itself may be a different thing. What is my real responsibility? The law? Or the just thing? I'm not sure what the answer is. We've been told that we have to uphold the law. But I don't understand what allegiance I should have to the law itself. Doesn't the whole authority of the law rest on its claim to be our system of justice? So, if the law isn't just, how can it have any force? (Burnett, 2001, p. 129)

Another juror, Leah, responded with a long, increasingly emotional plea to respect the letter of the law, citing the utter disregard for legal rights of dictatorships in Central America and police brutality in Turkey. The supporters of a guilty verdict took this as a personal attack, and bottled-up anger and resentment among the jurors results in furious confrontations recalling the angry interactions of *Twelve Angry Men*. Burnett played his part in calming the furor, with a long narrative contrasting various historical systems of justice intended to contextualize the struggle they were experiencing. But it is still another juror who truly broke the impasse. Speaking directly from his own experience, with none of Burnett's academic sophistication and references to "the punitive systems of democratic Athens" (Burnett, 2001, p. 136), Dean concluded:

> I've been listening to these things people are saying, and I have tried to pray about all this. Now I've decided what I have to do. I believe Monte Milcray did something very, very wrong in that room. But I also believe that nobody

has asked me to play God. I've been asked to apply the law. Justice belongs to God; men only have the law. Justice is perfect, but the law can only be careful. (Burnett, 2001, p. 138)

The jury began its fourth day of deliberations (a Saturday) with another vote and, with Burnett using his role as chair to push for acquittal, reached a unanimous verdict of not guilty. The narrative had something of a twist in its ending. In the hubbub after the trial, one of the jurors spoke with Milcray's lawyer, who told her that previously a young man had complained to the police about Cuffee for allegedly posing as a woman and soliciting sex to entice him into "her" apartment. As the victim did not press charges, the judge did not admit this story into evidence (Burnett, 2001, pp. 175–176). Further buttressing the legitimacy of the jury's finding of self-defense, this was the antithesis of the Hollywood reversal Burnett would later denounce. Had the jury been able to include this fact in their deliberations, they might well have reached their verdict much sooner.

This account of Burnett's narrative omits his own role in the proceedings almost entirely. But it is clear from his account that his role as foreman was almost as significant as that of Juror 8, and that the techniques he used to manage the process and to drive it to a desired outcome, whether consciously deployed or not, merit analysis. Of course, this is a self-reported presentation of managerial behavior, which should induce caution. Was Burnett the proverbial "legend in his own mind?" Burnett, to protect the privacy of the other jurors, used pseudonyms, so I could not contact any of them. I did e-mail Burnett to ask if his book elicited any published or oral reaction from the other jurors. The juror whose reaction most interested me was "Adelle." In an e-mail to me, Burnett (personal communication, March 29, 2009) confirmed that Adelle told him he had captured much of the crucible-like feeling of the room and did not criticize his work. He added that a number of the other jurors contacted him and seemed to be genuinely enthusiastic about the book. I take Burnett's e-mail (and the absence of anything published by the other jurors, particularly Adelle, to contradict his narrative) to be as much confirmation as I can possibly gather for using Burnett's narrative to discuss his managerial behavior.

As the trial began, Burnett displayed an affect that he described as "a species of aloofness." He dressed down ("parachute pants, hiking boots, and a fleece"), and when the court was not in session sat alone, either working on the proofs of a book or reading, which contrasted with what he called the "basic sociability" most of the jurors showed to one another. The foreman of the jury mysteriously disappeared several days into the trial, and the judge selected Burnett to replace him. Burnett responded by changing to jacket and tie and, especially when deliberations started, began to social-ize with the other jurors.

At the outset of deliberations, Burnett first suggested that the jurors collect their thoughts during several moments of silence and then offered to cede his place to whomever the jury would choose by show of hands. When there were no other volunteers, he had established his authority by common consent. He then set out ground rules, including beginning all sessions with several moments of quiet reflection (in a secular group, the equivalent of a prayer) and speaking in turn, for which he as foreman would keep track of requests. The moments of silence were intended to emphasize the seriousness of the jury's work and the setting out of ground rules to establish authority. (As the deliberations continued, Burnett found it increasingly difficult to maintain the rule of speaking in turn. By day three it was all but abandoned.)

One of Burnett's challenges was dealing with Felipe Rodriguez, a par-ticularly unfocused juror, whom Burnett described as "not clearly able to distinguish daytime television from daily life" and who, in the jury's initial discussion of the case "launched vigorously into an incoherent yarn about pig killing in his native Mexico" (Burnett, 2001, pp. 16, 88). Unable to fol-low the discussion, Felipe became anxious and expressed the desire simply to have the jury reach a conclusion. When this happened on the second day, Burnett reports that he raised his voice and said that "those kinds of remarks didn't belong in the discussion, that we were doing something too serious, and that I was going to lose my temper" (p. 108). On the third day, Felipe said "that he would vote for anything that would get us out of the room—he didn't care." When Felipe then criticized Adelle for supposedly letting her emotions get the better of her, several other jurors turned on him. Recogniz-ing that the rest of the jury was exasperated with Felipe, Burnett summed up the jury's consensus that "[Felipe] could keep his opinions on the whole case to himself . . . given that he had now expressed a willingness to side with whatever position prevailed. The best thing he could do would be for him to keep quiet for the rest of the deliberations" (pp. 140–141). Felipe is remi-niscent of Jurors 7 (the salesman with baseball tickets) and 10 (the bigot) in *Twelve Angry Men,* and Burnett, speaking for the other jurors, dealt with him in a similar way: silencing him.[4]

The most difficult moment in the deliberations was the explosion on the third day provoked by the juror's analogy to South American dictator-ships. Burnett's initial reaction, to call for several minutes of silence for people to collect themselves, was appropriate. In a voice little louder than a whisper, he reminded the jurors of "the importance of civility" and "the difficulty of the task" and the need for "passionate seriousness." He next resorted to narrative; he asked the jurors if he could "tell them a story, a brief history that [he] hoped would make peace in the room." His story was about a friend who completed a dissertation on the justice system of the Athenian city-state. In Athenian justice, jurors were charged not only with establishing guilt or innocence but also with determining the punishment the accused deserved. This contrasts with Anglo-Saxon jurisprudence, where the jury's role is "to find a verdict within the narrow strictures of the law, as described by the judge" and "to put aside any consideration of punishment." Put differently, in the Anglo-Saxon system, "the law was a thing apart from people—an abstract system laid over the messy reality of individuals and their specific situations," while in the Athenian system, "the law emerges from the texture and character of people and the details of their cases." Burnett's point was that both were reasonable systems of justice, but our society had chosen the former. Burnett's expressed intention was "to give a patina to our conflicts, to dignify the opposing positions so that we could make peace, see intelligence in the opposing views, and rise to the occasion of such a worthy disagreement." Burnett reports that his intervention did lead to making peace. Burnett's intervention was much more effectively put as a story about an actual person writing an actual dissertation than as an abstract point about differences in legal systems. Much more importantly, it created the opportunity for Dean to rephrase Burnett's lecture in a deeply personal way. As Burnett himself remarks "This statement centered the room . . . a repudiation of sophistication that suddenly seemed overwhelmingly sage " (Burnett, 2001, p. 138). Would Dean have achieved his insight without Burnett's story? It seems unlikely.

We now turn to Burnett's role in the jury's endgame. Burnett reported that, for quite a while his first choice had been a hung jury. The typical reason jurors might prefer that outcome is that it absolves them of the difficult, time-consuming, and potentially ego-bruising interpersonal work of bringing a refractory group to unanimity. But Burnett's rationale for a hung jury was atypical, and markedly narratological. As a humanist academic, he felt that the objective of thinking and talking was more thinking and more talking. In this view, one never "solved" a text, but one read it and reread it for the multiple interpretations it could afford. His intellectual task was to keep the questions open. For Burnett, a hung jury was a way of not resolving the question, of keeping the question open. Narratologically, he would be preserving polyphony. "By handing the question back to the court—by saying, in essence, 'Thank you, very interesting, now go ahead and do all of this again with another class—I would feel our deliberations had remained an exercise in thought, a splendid instance of thinking for the purpose of thinking." (Burnett, 2001, pp. 157–158).

After the third day of deliberation, Burnett came to reject his attraction to a hung jury. He speculates why, and gives a variety of explanations, without privileging any one. The judge instructed the jury to remain open to persuasion, and the foreman specifically to work toward unanimity if there were only one or two holdouts. Dean's persuasive formulation of the conclusion reached after the third day's interpersonal explosion; namely, that true justice was God's affair, left open the question of what Milcray ultimately deserved, even if the jury, by applying the law to the facts, decided to acquit him. Burnett also speculates, egotistically, that he might have been proving his own leadership skills by wrangling the jury to unanimity. Perhaps Burnett applied his notion of passionate seriousness to himself and concluded that the responsible thing was to work to achieve a verdict, not a hung jury. In any event, he emerged from his reflections between the third and fourth days with a commitment to work toward an acquittal.

Once he turned his mind to working toward acquittal, Burnett developed some specific tactics. He would call for a vote right at the outset of the fourth day of deliberations, a Saturday. Recognizing that at least one juror, Adelle, still remained committed to a guilty verdict, he prepared a statement to the judge that, despite its not-guilty verdict, the jury did not feel it had delivered "a truly just verdict"—a small concession, at least, to Adelle's position. He would sum up the case, arguing that, as the jurors had themselves witnessed the power of the state to, in effect, imprison them, they should fear the state's power to deprive Milcray of his liberty, also arguing that the prosecution had not proved beyond reasonable doubt that Milcray's account was a lie and finally, arguing that, unlike a work of fiction, "there are no trick endings here, no surprise discovery that will suddenly swing down and change everything." Finally, rather than vote on scraps of paper, Burnett was able to obtain from the clerk a set of index cards that would impress upon the jurors the importance of the choice they were about to register. Clearly, Burnett was visualizing an acquittal and, just as important, strategizing the means to achieve it.

The Saturday morning deliberations went essentially as Burnett visualized. Prior to calling for a vote, he made a long and carefully crafted "spontaneous" speech framing the rationale for acquittal in clear and emotionally appealing terms. Burnett remarks: "I cannot say how this peroration sounded. I meant what I was saying, but I had certainly crossed into the terrain of oratory—pausing, rounding my sentences, deployed the tropes. Did this matter? I do not know." (Burnett, 2001, p. 165). The vote was taken. When voting, Adelle, still conflicted, was the last one to mark her ballot, and Burnett conspicuously put it on the bottom of the pile so that "the full dismay of the room [would] land on her if she had voted for a conviction."

Adelle indeed voted to acquit, making it unanimous. Burnett called for the bailiff. But, just as the bailiff came for Burnett's written message that the jury had reached a verdict, Adelle had second thoughts. Thereupon, Burnett reconvened a near-frantic jury and read his prepared concession that "we the jury wish it to be known to the open court that we feel most strongly that the strict application of the law to the facts established by the evidence does not lead to a truly just verdict. We have, however, reached a verdict in accordance with our charge." This was sufficient to keep Adelle on board and confirm the verdict (Burnett, 2001, pp. 158–168).

Burnett was not in any way trained as a manager. Nevertheless, at least by his own report and not publicly contradicted by any of the other jurors, he displayed many effective managerial techniques. He established his authority as foreman right at the outset by calling for a ratification vote and then setting out ground rules for the discussion. He established a tone of seriousness both in his own dress and by his use of moments of silence to begin each day's deliberations. He recognized the group's consensus to silence a juror who proved incapable, and acted on it. He drew upon both narrative and philosophy to reconcile a conflict within the group. As the consensus in the deliberations moved to an acquittal, he overcame his own intellectual predisposition to a hung jury, visualized an acquittal, and worked out tactics to achieve it. He increased the formality of the vote and the pressure on the strongest dissident, while developing a compromise that would allow the dissidents to accept the verdict.

As with much else in this often annoying yet intensely moving narrative, Burnett seeks to have it both ways. For while he ultimately yields to the necessity of the verdict, he has successfully used the trial to construct the polyphonic narrative he sought for so long:

> The act of writing has been, all along (without my knowing), the doing of the thing I wanted so badly from the start, the writing has done the thing I wanted so badly from the start—it has made the trial into words, a thing to read, to interpret, to circle back through. A text. Like art. Meaning something different to each person. Keeping the large questions open. But the trial was not that. (Burnett, 2001, p. 183)

It Takes a Narrative

As argued at the outset, juries are a unique decision-making context. But the content of their decisions is closer to that of other public sector tribunals than private sector bodies, because public sector tribunals deal with decisions involving peoples' liberty, their health, and occasionally their very lives. Private sector decision makers, in contrast, deal with peoples' wealth and, at most, their material well-being. As such, the tone of jury decision making should be closer to the tone of other public sector tribunals than to private sector bodies. What lessons can we draw about jury, and possibly more broadly, public sector decision making and narrative skill from the two narratives discussed in this chapter? I begin with the lessons that seem most directly relevant to the jury context.

First, in both narrative about, and decision making by, juries, a tight focus is essential. One of the reasons *Twelve Angry Men* came to be regarded as a classic is that the narrative is completely and intensively focused on the jury deliberations. The jurors who were most effective—Jurors 8, 4, and 9 in *Twelve Angry Men* and Burnett in *A Trial by Jury*—were able to concentrate their sustained attention on evaluating the evidence and applying the law. Conversely, the jurors who failed to find an appropriate focus—Felipe, who couldn't regulate his attention or comprehension, or jurors 3, 7, and 10, who couldn't abstract from their own concerns—were least effective.

Second, because of the severity of the consequences, jury decision making demands what Burnett called "passionate seriousness." This particular organizational culture was something the effective jurors recognized. Juror 12 is the most compelling case of someone lacking seriousness of purpose. His light-hearted brainstorming approach was entirely appropriate in his chosen occupation of advertising copywriting, but it was entirely out of place in jury deliberations. Essentially, his light-hearted approach lacked the necessary gravitas.

Third, as discussed at the outset, jury decision making is more constrained regarding both the set of alternatives that can be considered and the evidence that can be used than other forms of public sector decision making. These constraints make it difficult for juries to achieve the required unanimity. In *A Trial by Jury*, convicting Milcray on a lesser charge than second-degree murder was not available as a compromise option. Nonetheless, Burnett was able to come up with a face-saving compromise that brought the juror most strenuously arguing for a conviction to accept acquittal; namely, a statement in open court about the verdict not being "truly just." The constraints of jury decision making mean that jurors must exert extra effort to develop compromises they can all support.

In addition to these lessons for decision making in juries, there are other lessons applicable more broadly in the public sector. The two narratives raise the question for participants in group deliberation of how much of themselves to reveal. Because he was challenging the jury's initial consensus, Juror 8 chose to reveal very little, so that the group would not be able to reject what he was saying on the basis of who was saying it. At the outset, he left unclear whether he was playing devil's advocate or expressing his actual assessment of the evidence. Jurors 3, 7, and 10, by revealing their hidden agendas, were revealing too much; what they revealed about themselves ultimately discredited whatever arguments they made. Burnett's first-person-narrative approach brings into sharp relief the difference between what a decision maker might be thinking and how he expresses his views. Burnett kept his counsel about several matters, such as his evaluations of the other jurors he had to work with or the deepest motivations driving his decision to push for an acquittal.

Because they are chosen at random from the general population, many jurors may lack the subtlety to keep their own counsel. In contrast, Allison (1971), in his description of collective decision making by experienced and shrewd public sector players (Model III), observes that they often display so much reticence about the considerations they are weighing that their deliberations are characterized by miscommunication and misexpectation. In a way, meetings become prisoner's dilemmas, with all participants agreeing that more openness on everyone's part would lead to a better outcome, but each fearing that if he is open and the others are not, the others will take advantage of him.

These narratives demonstrate various types of self-dramatization as management technique. Juror 8 was extremely effective at symbolic physical gestures and actions: stabbing his knife into the table, snatching the paper on which two jurors were playing tic-tac-toe, and reenacting the movements of the elderly witness and the victim. His dramatic and animated self-presentation thus attracted the attention of the other jurors and ultimately established his position of leadership within the group. Burnett was not as dramatic as Juror 8, but he was cognizant of his self-presentation in dressing up when he was appointed foreman, whispering to hold the jury's attention after the blowup on the third day of deliberations, and using index cards, rather than scraps of paper to emphasize the seriousness of what he hoped would be the jury's final vote.

Burnett also demonstrated the importance of visualization as a management technique, developing a mental picture of an event he wanted to occur (in this case an acquittal) and then working out the steps necessary to achieve that event.

Finally, both narratives illustrate the use of narrative as a management technique. In Burnett's case, presenting the story of a friend's dissertation research on jury practice in the Athenian city-state calmed the jury after its blowup and put his deeper philosophical point about the differences among legal philosophies within a context that all the other jurors, even Felipe, could understand.

One of the important issues regarding narrative in any context is whether it is sufficient to call into question a narrative one opposes or whether it is necessary to create an alternative narrative. Even though criminal trials situate the burden of proof in such a way that the defense need only raise reasonable doubts about the prosecution's narrative, it appears that, in fact, it is necessary for the defense to present an alternative narrative. In *Twelve Angry Men*, Juror 8 developed two short narratives: first, why the defendant's lawyer did a poor job preparing the case and second, how someone other than the accused could have been motivated to kill his father. These narratives certainly supported the jurors' efforts at disrupting the prosecution's narrative. In effect, it requires a narrative to defeat a narrative.

Endnotes

1. Rose adapted the film's screenplay from his original CBS teleplay. He also created a stage version that is revived regularly. Harold Pinter directed a production at the Bristol Old Vic in 1996; a 2004 Roundabout Theater Company production ran on Broadway for 328 performances. Plot references and dialogue are taken from the Penguin Classic 2006 edition of the play, which was used for the 2004 Broadway revival and is virtually identical to the 1957 screenplay.

2. Juror 8's function as the voice of White, liberal, middle-class values, intervening literally to save the life of the unnamed ethnic youth, and the heroic status the narrative unproblematically assigns him, clearly marks the movie as a product of an earlier era. While this is not the focus of our analysis here, it is worth noting how important issues of race and class will be in Burnett's jury narrative and how much more problematic they will prove, for this reader at least. Where Rose's narrative silences the voice of racism (Juror 10), Burnett's silences the voice of the ethnic "other" in the name of intellectual privilege.

3. This is one of the most implausible elements in the narrative, in that jurors are not permitted to gather additional evidence nor present it during the deliberations. If they are not permitted to gather additional evidence and are so instructed by the judge, even though jury deliberations are confidential, it is unlikely a jury member would so flagrantly ignore the prohibition (Weisselberg, 2007).

4. There could, of course, be a counter-narrative here, reflecting on the dynamics of class and race that Burnett ignores. His comfortable assurance that he speaks for the rest of the jurors in silencing Felipe scarcely compensates for the ugliness of the moment or the enormous disdain that Burnett the narrator makes no effort to conceal.

8

Conclusion

A Story that is Just Beginning

Endings, as any storyteller knows, are hard to get right. Rush them, and we feel cheated. Draw them out too long, and all sense of urgency is gone. A neat resolution with every loose end tied is often, paradoxically, deeply unsatisfying. Yet some sense of a conclusion, of a destination reached, is essential. The number and variety of the narratives we've been considering, the wide range of forms, subjects, approaches, even dates of creation offer a particular challenge in conclusion. How to summarize without simplifying? How to generalize without misrepresenting? My own preference (it has probably made itself clear) is always for narratives that resist definitive readings, narratives that invite multiple interpretations. How to honor that in my own practice while still leaving the reader with a sense of journey's end? As so often, my answer is to look for the structuring patterns.

Throughout this book, we've moved back and forth between considerations of the managerial content of the narratives we've analyzed and formal, narratological issues, always keeping in view the relationship be-

Governing Fables: Learning from Public Sector Narratives, pages 239–264
Copyright © 2011 by Information Age Publishing
239

tween the two. This final chapter will maintain that doubled focus, first summarizing recurring content-related themes in our narrative sets (using the analytic matrix introduced in Chapter 2), then looking at the particular formal challenges public sector narratives pose and the recurring narrative strategies adopted to address them. From the thematic analysis, we will formulate a cumulative model of what we can call responsible political leadership, a dominant fable for this book. From the discussion of narrative form, we will consider implications for storytelling within the public sector. The book concludes, in what I hope is a sufficiently open-ended manner, with suggestions for where the story of narrative and public management might go next. But I cannot quite resist the indulgence of a final word: a highly subjective "Top Ten" list drawn from the narratives we've been engaging. (Authorship does have its privileges, in the end.)

Classifying the Fables

Chapter 2 outlined a clear structure for the transformational teacher fable (summarized in Table 2.1). The dominant fable involves a charismatic and dedicated teacher who dramatically enhances the life prospects of the students (s)he teaches and strengthens the school (s)he teaches in by putting in place an innovative program to deliver academic improvements on a regular basis. This also brings new resources, such as foundation grants, into the school. The teacher's efforts are recognized at the national level and (s)he leaves the classroom to become an educational leader encouraging the diffusion of his/her innovations. There is a clear counter-fable of teachers who attempt to be transformational but fail, either because of personal demons (*Half Nelson*), an inability to navigate the school's organizational politics (*Dead Poets Society*), or failure to connect in an empathetic way with the students (*Entre les murs*). In these cases, no transformation occurs: the students do not make educational gains, the school is not improved, and the teacher's career either falters or, at best, remains on its current course. We did encounter two movies that are ambiguous in their outcomes: *Cheaters* and *The History Boys*. In these, teachers work intensively with a small group of students to achieve a prized goal: victory in the Academic Decathlon and admission to Oxbridge, respectively. The students in *The History Boys* benefit by succeeding on the admissions exams and the students in *Cheaters* are at least unharmed by the Steinmetz cheating scandal, but in both cases, the teacher's career falters, and the school is not transformed.

The British political fable set out in Chapters 3 and 4 differs markedly from that of the transformational teacher, though it too is very clear in its core structure (see Table 8.1). It is a fable of political decline. As discussed

TABLE 8.1 The British Political Fable

	Personal Growth of Protagonist	Personal Decline of Protagonist
Organizational Renewal	End of Appeasement (Churchill, Eden, Macmillan, George VI) Morgan's Tony Blair narratives	End of Appeasement (Chamberlain, Halifax) *The Remains of the Day* (Darlington, Stevens) *The Amazing Mrs. Pritchard*
Organizational Decline	*Yes Minister* (Hacker, Sir Humphrey) *House of Cards* (Urquhart) Morgan's Tony Blair narratives	*Corridors of Power* (Quaife) Crossman Diaries (Crossman, Wilson) *A Very British Coup* (Perkins) *The Thick of It* *In the Loop*

in Chapter 3, this is consistent with the UK's postwar political and economic experience of slow recovery from the devastation of the war, the loss of the Empire together with the growing hegemony of the United States within the NATO alliance, and class struggle as manifested by labor-management conflict. This fable shares the political pessimism, even cynicism, of public-choice analysis: namely, an assumption of increasing economic stagnation as self-interested politicians, public servants, and interest groups collaborate to use the power of the state to shift resources from the private to the public sector through taxation and to constrain the assumed dynamism of the market through regulation and cartelization.

Whether the narratives are framed as satire or tragedy, the fortunes of their protagonists usually decline. In *Corridors of Power*, Conservative Defense Minister Roger Quaife, opposed by the U.S. State Department as well as hardline elements within his party, the civil service, and the scientific community, fails to win sufficient support for a policy of nuclear disarmament. He resigns his office and leaves politics. Toward the end of his diaries, cabinet minister Richard Crossman ruminates about the aimless drift of the Wilson government as well as his own deteriorating health and expresses regret that the magnum opus on which he had labored so long would likely be seen as "the dull detailed history of the last days of the British *ancien regime*." While *A Very British Coup* advocates a radical socialist program for British society, the narrative assumes that such a program would so threaten the Establishment it would be suppressed by a military takeover. The socialist Prime Minister Harry Perkins is a clever strategist and charismatic leader, but is ultimately undermined. The more recent satires, *The Thick of It* and

In the Loop, do not focus on single central protagonists, but rather portray a cadre of political players jostling one another in a Hobbesian battle for survival. In *The Thick of It,* the government cynically puts in place policy gimmicks designed to capture public attention, with no expectation that they will make any difference in confronting real social and economic problems. *In the Loop* deals yet again with the strategic hegemony of the United States, and concludes by marking the UK's irrelevance to the American policymakers' military calculus.

Yes Minister and *House of Cards* are also set within the context of political and economic decline. In *Yes Minister* and *Yes Prime Minister,* few political initiatives survive bureaucratic opposition or foot dragging, and British society suffers from public sector waste and inefficiency. But, ironically, both protagonists advance. Sir Humphrey is elevated from Permanent Secretary to Cabinet Secretary and Jim Hacker from minister to Prime Minister, and both thrive politically, evidence primarily of their finely honed Whitehall and Westminster survival skills. In *House of Cards,* Francis Urquhart, blackmailing and murdering his way from party whip to Prime Minister, literally embodies the utter corruption of the political system.

There is only one narrative, albeit an extremely significant one, of unambiguous renewal; namely, the ending of Appeasement and the national commitment to securing the decisive defeat of Nazi Germany. As the political leadership of the Conservative Party was split between the opponents and supporters of Appeasement, the personal consequences for both groups were dramatically different. Not only did Churchill become Britain's wartime leader, but the "troublesome young men" who supported him went on to major roles in the postwar leadership, most notably Prime Ministers Anthony Eden (1955–1957) and Harold Macmillan (1957–1963). Their narratives clearly occupy the upper left quadrant of Table 8.1. (The 2010 movie *The King's Speech* offers another variant on the ending of Appeasement narrative. Though a constitutional monarch is not a political decision maker, he is a spokesman for the government. George VI's overcoming his stammer represented a process of personal growth that enhanced his effectiveness in his political role, thereby contributing to national renewal. It was the skillful and engaging presentation of this heroic fable that won it so much acclaim.)

The appeasers, particularly Chamberlain and Halifax, suffered political defeat, increasing isolation and, in the case of Chamberlain at least, the harshest of posthumous judgments. The compliant young men who supported Chamberlain and Halifax on Appeasement, most notably R. A. Butler, failed to realize their highest aspirations in postwar politics. *The Remains of the Day* explores Appeasement as a psychological state, through two linked characters, Lord Darlington and the butler Stevens, figures for whom appeasement, at the political and personal levels respectively, never ended. It thus presents a narrative of personal decline within the context of national renewal. It constitutes a counter-fable to the triumphant narratives of Churchill and the "troublesome young men." *The Amazing Mrs. Pritchard* occupies the upper right quadrant because it hypothesizes that the feminist-populist Purple Democratic Alliance enacts popular reforms, but Mrs. Pritchard herself, unwilling to compromise her integrity or expose her family, renounces her ambition and resigns.

The Tony Blair narratives, as presented by Peter Morgan (or interpreted by political commentators or historians) ambiguously occupy either the upper left or lower left quadrants. Politics for Blair was a personal triumph, with three electoral victories and a postpolitical career as author and international statesman. The impact of his premiership on the nation is hotly contested, however, with his supporters lauding the Northern Ireland peace accord and intervention in Kosovo; his critics denouncing Britain's involvement in Iraq and Afghanistan, and both debating whether public services such as health, education, and policing had improved or deteriorated on his watch.

The narratives from which we can derive an American political fable present much more diversity than the British case, as shown in Table 8.2. Reviewing Chapters 5, 6, and 7, we find a considerable number of narratives from which a heroic fable can be inferred (the upper left quadrant). Congressman Charlie Wilson and CIA agent Gust Avrakotos collaborate to give the Afghan mujahedeen the weapons they need to defeat the Soviets. Candidate Jim McKay unseats a conservative Republican senator in California, bringing a liberal voice to the Senate. In *The War Room*, political strategists James Carville and George Stephanopoulos neutralize the Republican attack machine to help Bill Clinton capture the White House. *The Last Hurrah* presents a retrospective, rather than forward-looking view of politics, but in it, a populist mayor looks back with an Eriksonian sense of personal integrity on his achievements on behalf of his lower-class ethnic constituents. *Seven Days in May* imagines a strategic president who, with the help of one senior officer loyal to the constitution, peacefully and quietly thwarts a military coup, and exhorts the nation to be both "strong and proud" and "peaceful and patient"—two contrasting sets of virtues. *The West Wing*, in seven seasons of series television, presents a portrait of a thoughtful president, served by a loyal staff, all devoted to defining and advancing the public interest and often, but not always, succeeding. The various narratives about the Cuban Missile Crisis—Robert Kennedy's memoir, Graham Allison's history, and despite itself, the movie *Thirteen Days*—all develop a consistent

TABLE 8.2 The American Political Fable

	Personal Growth of Protagonist	Personal Decline of Protagonist
Organizational Renewal	*Charlie Wilson's War* *The Candidate* (my interpretation) *The War Room* (Carville, Stephanopolous) *The Last Hurrah* (Skeffington) *7 Days in May* *The West Wing* *Thirteen Days* (RFK) *Essence of Decision* (Allison) *Thirteen Days* (film) *12 Angry Men* (Juror 8) *A Trial by Jury* (Burnett)	*Advise and Consent* (President, Sen. Anderson, Sen. Van Ackerman, Leffingwell) *12 Angry Men* (Jurors 3, 7, 10)
Organizational Decline	*Primary Colors* (the Stantons) *Charlie Wilson's War* (Taliban takes control) *City Hall* (Calhoun) *The Candidate* (Larner interpretation)	*The Distinguished Gentleman* (Johnson, Dodge) *Bulworth* *Wag the Dog* *All the King's Men* *City Hall* (Mayor Pappas) *Dr. Strangelove* *The Fog of War* (McNamara re. Vietnam)

picture of President Kennedy acting with firmness, thoughtfulness, caution, and empathy to resolve a confrontation that could easily have led to nuclear war. Turning finally to narratives about jury deliberations, an instance of public sector decision making writ small, we find two examples of jurors forcefully leading their colleagues to what they believe are just verdicts.

Clearly, there is in American public sector narratives a strong heroic fable. This conclusion is at odds with the work of film scholars such as Chase (2003), Gianos (1999), Giglio (2005), and Christensen and Hass (2005), all of whom describe the American political film genre as being predominantly pessimistic. It is no less surprising in view of the strong belief in market economics and the accompanying aversion to big government that are so frequently voiced in American political discourse. The story these narratives tell is that many Americans do still believe in a well-intentioned, activist, and effective government, or at least would like to. Unlike the UK's dominant fable of individual failure within a context of national decline, these are stories of individual public sector achievement in a country that has generally seen its future optimistically. Deep recession, irresolvable military conflicts abroad, and a looming public debt crisis have clearly already qualified the national optimism. The deep divisions and sharp polarizations within current political discourse might well shape future narratives, pulling the dominant American fable of governance much closer to the pessimism, even cynicism of the British.

We should also note the great diversity of protagonists in these American stories. Many of course feature a president hero (*Seven Days in May, The West Wing, Thirteen Days*) or chief executive (*The Last Hurrah*), but in others it is an individual legislator (*The Candidate, Charlie Wilson's War*), political staff (*The War Room, The West Wing*), or individuals who are not office holders (*Twelve Angry Men, A Trial by Jury*). Political heroism is not solely a leader's prerogative. Despite their differences in position and power, all these political actors are characterized by a desire to serve the best interest of their polity or collectivity, quiet determination, persistence, and an ability to persuade and enlist their fellow citizens to support their cause. They are, to use Mark Moore's (1995) now well-known phrase, creating public value. The heroic protagonists in these narratives may often prove creative in their use of power against their political opponents, but they always stay within the limits of the law.

In contrast to the heroic fable, there is also an American fable of organizational decline accompanied by the decline or defeat of the protagonist, as inferred from the narratives assigned to the lower right quadrant of Table 8.2. I have not chosen to designate either the heroic fable of the upper left quadrant or cynical fable of the lower right quadrant as dominant because there seems to be a balance between the two. There are a considerable number of significant narratives that give rise to a cynical fable. *All the King's Men* traces the career of a populist despot who corrupts the political process and is eventually assassinated. *The Distinguished Gentleman* applies public choice theory to the House of Representatives, painting a picture of an institution captured by special interests; the two congressmen whom the story revolves around enter into a confrontation that destroys both careers. In *Bulworth*, a disillusioned and despairing liberal senator is gunned down when he attempts to speak frankly about the capture of the legislative branch by interest groups. In *Wag the Dog*, a cynical president successfully uses marketing savvy to win reelection, but the marketer who assists him is killed at the initiative of a key presidential adviser for the "crime" of wanting to go public. In *City Hall*, a crime family is discovered to have used their influence on a popular and effective mayor to keep one of their members from jail, and this discovery likely will cost the mayor his job. The classic satire *Dr. Strangelove* shows how, within a Cold War context, interacting Russian and American approaches to providing second-strike capability lead to a global nuclear holocaust. Finally, in *The Fog of War*, documentary filmmaker Errol Morris' meditation on the meaning of the life and career of Robert McNamara, we witness a bitter reckoning and a burden of knowledge almost too great to be borne.

What are the common features that define a cynical fable of American politics and government? Protagonists, consistent with public-choice theory, treat politics as an opportunity to pursue their self-interest, seeking power for its own sake or power as a means to personal gratification. There is frequent corruption, encompassing both the protagonists' ends and the means used to pursue those ends. The corrupt protagonists are situated in a variety of political roles, such as president, governor, mayor, legislator, or advisor. Violence, including assassinations and suicides, is a frequent aspect of these narratives. When the electorate enters into the fable, it is easily tricked by political marketers or spin doctors.

While the American political narrative has its fable of heroic political leadership and its opposing fable of decline of both protagonist and polity, there are a considerable number of narratives that are off the diagonal, in either the upper right or lower left quadrants in Table 8.2. Those in the upper right include instances of retribution, where a character who opposes a process of organizational or political renewal is ultimately defeated, to the detriment of his career, and also instances of sacrifice, where a character's negative personal outcome contributes to the success of a process of organizational or political renewal. Thus, in the novel *Advise and Consent*, the desirable outcome from author Allen Drury's inferred point of view—the refusal of the Senate to confirm a pacifist as Secretary of State—is achieved, but the narrative focuses much of its attention on the characters who suffer in the process. The president, who was unscrupulous in his use of influence, dies of a heart attack and the nominee, who lied to the senate, is not confirmed. Both fates can be considered instances of retribution. There is sacrifice too: a senator opposing the nomination commits suicide under the threat of blackmail. Finally, *Twelve Angry Men*, while focusing on the heroic Juror 8, highlights the much less heroic, analytical, and creative jurors who opposed him. In other words, these narratives of political struggle or conflict do not simply heroicize the protagonist and demonize the antagonist, rather they seek to represent the opposing forces on both sides, taking seriously the motivations and significance of characters who are ultimately defeated.

A second off-diagonal approach involves the irony that derives from success for the protagonist in a setting of organizational decline (the lower left hand quadrant in Table 8.2). In *Primary Colors*, a satirical treatment of

Bill Clinton's first campaign for the presidency, charismatic southern governor Jack Stanton achieves his goal of being elected president, but only after engaging in a variety of dirty tricks that covered up, or distracted attention from, his own serious moral lapses. The narrative concludes with the suggestion that Stanton's sense of invincibility—his hubris—will eventually lead to the weakening of his presidency. *Charlie Wilson's War* can be read antiheroically, with history adding the ironic coda that Wilson's success at strengthening the mujahedeen contributed to the Taliban's eventual takeover of Afghanistan. *The Candidate* can also be read antiheroically, with Jim McKay securing election as senator by selling out his original supporters and compromising his policy positions. *City Hall*'s idealistic assistant to the mayor emerges from the scandal that will likely bring down his boss with his own reformist fervor intact, but there is no suggestion that the influence of the mafia on city politics will be ended.

It is fitting that American political narratives should display such diversity, encompassing not just a highly democratic array of heroic protagonists and happy endings, but a full range of ironic and even tragic outcomes, featuring complexly imagined antagonists experiencing both retribution and sacrifice. In addition, there are a number of narratives that are sufficiently ambiguous that they resist definitive readings. Does Jim McKay lose his soul in his attempt to gain power, or will he be able to redefine himself as the liberal Democratic senator he set out to be? Is Charlie Wilson's contribution to the defeat of the Russians in the Cold War of greater significance than his unintended support for the Taliban? Do we remember Robert McNamara as the man who, by tightly controlling the military, succeeded in keeping the Cold War from becoming a hot war or even a nuclear war for most of a decade, or do we remember him as the architect of the war in Vietnam? (Morris' narrative, of course, refuses to take sides.)

One of the benefits (I hope) of constructing the analytic matrices for the fables we've been considering is the cross-chapter structural comparisons they invite. Looking at Tables 2.1, 8.1, and 8.2 together, an obvious question arises: Do the transformational teacher fable and the American political fable have more in common because of a shared national context than the American and British fables of governance have in common despite their shared theme? Put differently, what seems to unite both sets of American fables is a continuing belief in the possibility of individual heroic action (at least) within the public sector, however dysfunctional the larger institutional context might be. It is a belief completely absent from the contemporary British fable of governance. Churchill is the obvious historical exception, whose looming presence makes the postwar cynicism, pettiness, incompetence, self-seeking, and dishonesty all the more glaring. It is tempting to read into this a fundamental, temperamental difference between the old world and the new. It is probably more accurate to see in it the reflection of the very different postwar histories of the two countries. The fascinating (if potentially painful) development to chart will be the directions the American fable of governance and politics will take next. The financial and military crises of the first decade of the 21st century have already begun to produce narratives that look increasingly similar to the dominant British fable. Are these a sign of fables to come?

A Final Fable: Managing Narratives

As promised at the outset, each chapter of this book has sought to develop context-specific lessons for public managers from both the dominant and counter-fables and the individual narratives they presented. Chapter 2 laid out lessons for how would-be transformational teachers could work both inside and outside the classroom to improve student performance and to influence the educational system to provide support and additional resources. The dominant British fable of government presented in Chapter 3 yields lessons for individual survival in a Hobbesian political world, while implicitly raising questions of the price to be paid (by the survivor and by the public). The discussion of the ending of Appeasement (Chapter 4) yields insights from Churchill's ability to define a clear vision and his mastery of the closed politics of bringing his rivals on board to support it. The fictional American political narratives in Chapter 5, despite their diversity, suggest traits that would characterize ideal political leaders. The Cuban Missile Crisis, as discussed in Chapter 6, provides insights into decision making in crisis situations, in particular the importance of a thorough analysis of options from a variety of perspectives, however orthogonal to established policy or precedent, as well as the strategic importance of empathy. (This last point is an acknowledgment of the human factor as it operates on both sides of a crisis.) Robert McNamara's narrative asks searching questions about the unreliability of human perception and the limits of our rationality. Chapter 7 dramatizes the dynamics of small-group decision making in a jury setting, exploring the strategies by which individuals reconcile the tensions between consensus and informal leadership to influence the outcome of the deliberations. In each instance, I have tried to show how often the narratives themselves complicate any attempt to elucidate simple principles, embedding counter-narratives within their own structures, or at least (inadvertently at times) suggesting how much more of the story is being left out.

It is still possible, however, to generate a cumulative model of responsible public sector leadership from our analysis, in effect, a dominant fable for this book. It is a fable structured by the management of three narratives: the *public* narrative of goal or agenda setting; the *internal* narrative of decision making and implementation; and the *personal* narrative of professional conduct, personal commitment, and moral or ethical choice. As both politics and governance come increasingly to be enacted in the continuous glare of what C. P. Snow presciently called "the exposure of the machine," control of these narratives and particularly of their public presentation becomes both more essential and more difficult. This has nothing to do with "spin," or "image control," or "sound bite politics," or any of the other expedients that drive the narratives of political and personal decline we've looked at. The model I am defining takes its inspiration from the fables of heroic political leadership and educational transformation, predicting better societal, organizational, and personal outcomes through conscious individual action.

The public narrative: agenda setting. The first priority for public servants is to create public value, to use Mark Moore's words. The adjective carries two connotations. First, the value created is public because it is defined for a collectivity rather than for the public servant him/herself. (Clearly, a difference with the hypothesis of public-choice economics that public servants are motivated solely by the desire to create private value for themselves). Second, value is public in the sense that it comes through the creation of public goods that are widely available for use within the polity and not constrained through pricing mechanisms that make them equivalent to private goods.

In any organization, the creation of value for those who use its services depends on the articulation of a polyphonic institutional narrative; that is, a narrative that is descriptive (How do the services provided benefit users? Who are they?), evaluative (Are we reaching present goals? How can the organization improve in delivering benefits?), and aspirational/predictive (What more or what else could the organization do? What might change in the future?). For reasonably simple organizations, such as a classroom or a school, defining the institutional narrative should be relatively easy—the desired goals (endings) are evident; the beneficiaries equally so. Measuring progress in its implementation is also straightforward.

Formulating the goal-setting narrative in the political arena is more difficult because of the inevitable diversity of any polity, especially at the national level. There will always be groups that will never agree to the goals set or policies proposed by a particular candidate. As opinion polling has come to play an increasingly important role in formulating electoral agendas, we have become accustomed to political narratives that suffer from an excess of polyphony, seeking to speak in many voices to many different ears, with parties calculating that a sufficiently fragmented platform will attract enough assorted interest groups to enable them to take power. Courting the "winning coalition" has become so much the norm that it is worth reminding ourselves what the alternative might be: a political agenda derived from a coherent narrative based on a set of philosophical premises. These might come from either the left (inspired by the application of Rawls's (1971) difference principle, focusing on improving the social safety net), or from the right (focusing on unfettered markets, minimal government, and low taxation), or from alternative ways of thinking about politics and policy; for example, those that promote a third way combining components of both. Tony Blair's (2010, pp. 66–107) discussion of the origins of the philosophy of New Labour as an attempt to modernize Labour Party doctrine to be relevant to a society with a large middle class provides a relevant example. To state the obvious again: the value of approaching politics with a coherent agenda is that it does more than appeal to the self-interest of a collection of narrow constituencies. Rather, such an agenda attempts to define the broader interests of the polity, to create a national narrative. Thus, a politician could make a decision not just because it is in the immediate interest of a constituency that supports him or her, but because it is consistent with his or her broader vision of how the polity should evolve. Indeed, a politician might also use that broader vision as a rationale for opposing the immediate interests of his or her constituents.

The internal narrative: decision making and implementing. Many of the narratives we've encountered focus on politicians acting as decision makers in either legislative or executive capacities. These are decisions of the utmost importance that cannot be delegated—existential decisions affecting the very survival of the organization. The emphasis here is on the explanatory narratives that frame the alternatives, the first rule being to gather as much information as possible in the time available to make the decision. In gathering information, be concerned about authorship and viewpoint (bias). Remember that quantitative data and the technical experts who interpret it are not neutral. Even (especially) seemingly relevant personal experience has been interpreted and re-presented by unconscious needs and expectations. For making major decisions, it might be desirable to establish an ad hoc advisory group that includes a diversity of perspectives and backgrounds (the classic example being the Excom that JFK established in the Cuban Missile Crisis). In such a group, permit open discussion of alternatives, including those you instinctually disagree with. Listen actively and skeptically to alternatives being discussed, and ask questions about them. (Indeed, the quality of the questions asked is a measure of the decision maker's analytical talent.) Don't rely to any great degree on instinct: Malcolm Gladwell's (2006) notion of "thinking without thinking" is a poor approach to difficult decisions. If the decision flows from a relationship with another party, especially an adversary, understand as much as you can about that party, and empathetically put yourself in their situation. Recognize that communication with adversaries might be difficult, so make sure that they understand you. As you approach the moment you take a decision, debate and discussion should stop (a necessity occasionally lost on advisers who want to make one last pitch for their preferred option). As your choice becomes clear to you, you will recognize that some of those you have consulted will agree with and others will disagree with your likely course of action. At that point, you might want to either expand (as Churchill did when deciding to reject negotiation with Germany) or contract (as Kennedy did when deciding what to communicate to the Soviets on Black Saturday) your advisory group to provide support and affirmation.

While some decisions might call for the establishment of an ad hoc advisory group, in many other instances a public sector executive would turn to regular advisors. Ideally, they should be comfortable speaking truth to power. Whether or not this happens depends on your willingness to hear advice you might find uncomfortable or disagree with. It also depends on the courage of the adviser. Some advisers might feel that if their advice makes you uncomfortable, they will soon be ostracized. The best advisers are those who, paradoxically, are willing to give up their role as adviser rather than pull their punches or say what they don't believe in order to retain favor. *The West Wing* imagined a president who was consistently willing to listen to frank and sometimes uncomfortable advice, advisers who were willing give it, and relationships between the president and his advisers that were strong enough to withstand such openness. It was, of course, fiction.

While a vote in a legislature is an act complete in itself, an executive decision is not. The decision must be implemented by one or more public sector organizations. When a decision has been taken, a complementary narrative is necessary, one that visualizes the outcome that will ultimately embody the decision. Organizations are blunt instruments and often have difficulty implementing an action that differs from their current repertoire and, if cooperation among organizations is required, the difficulties are compounded, perhaps exponentially. In addition to their intended consequences, decisions also have unintended consequences, so put in place a way of broadly tracking the results of a decision, especially the unintended consequences.

The personal narrative: conduct, commitment, choices. Throughout this book, we have analyzed a diverse set of political narratives (the distance between, say, *Advise and Consent* and *The Amazing Mrs. Pritchard* in every respect could hardly be greater). Yet one constant has been the importance of scandal as both a major engine of the plot and a moral litmus test for its protagonist(s). We could in fact generate a separate political fable matrix, positioning narratives and characters solely by their relationship to impropriety (financial, sexual, ethical). There is a simple explanation, of course. Scandal (as the British novelist Michael Dobbs is clearly aware) makes a better story. To draw lessons from this aspect of our fables might seem like an extended statement of the painfully obvious: public legitimacy for politicians and public servants depends on respect for the law. Law breaking will result in forfeiture of office: even Francis Urquhart cannot escape in the end. As more recent narratives remind us, information technology (for example, searchable data bases and cell phone cameras) and the greater transparency enabled by access to information laws have increased the level of scrutiny brought to bear, while the Internet has made worldwide dissemination of its results the work of a few hours at most. And this scrutiny extends from manifestly illegal behavior to actions considered by the media and public to be inappropriate, ill-judged, or simply inconsistent with the public narrative claimed by the agent/agency involved. In the United States today, and increasingly in the UK, every aspect of the life of political candidates and senior public servants, including their medical and tax histories, their domestic arrangements, personal recreational habits, and of course, past and present romantic/sexual stories are considered public information (Tony Blair itemizes this in his memoir [2010, pp. 129–130].) Medical and tax records, e-mails and text messages, and records from social networking sites are all readily recoverable.

All of this is, of course, well known by every politician and public servant. And yet, as the headlines constantly remind us, even the most intelligent, accomplished, and experienced still ignore these facts of public life and pay with their careers. Why? The answer former New York governor Eliot Spitzer gives in the recent documentary *Client 9* is almost as old as the Western narrative tradition itself: hubris. Tony Blair's explanation (2010, pp. 583–584) differs slightly. Success in politics, he notes, demands rigid self-control in every public aspect of one's life, so illicit behavior represents a concession to "your free-bird instincts [that] want to spring you from that prison of self-control." Another way to view it is as the result of a mistaken belief in authorial control, where the protagonist assumes that he is the sole author of his public narrative. That assumption tends to generate its own story: exposure, resignation, and sometimes prosecution.

The political and transformational teacher fables also address a less extreme aspect of the personal narrative; namely, the balance (or more often imbalance) between professional commitment and a meaningful private life. The stock figure of the devoted aide who lives only for the success of her candidate/minister appears in virtually every iteration of the political fable, as indispensable to the narrative as he or she is to the protagonist. When Mayor John Pappas in *City Hall* encourages Kevin Calhoun to "get a life," Calhoun speaks for all the aides when he replies "I've got your [life]. It's quite enough." But these fables also raise questions of the personal price paid for the dedication that makes transformation (in the case of the teachers) or heroic leadership (in the case of the politicians/public servants) possible. As is so often the case, Robert McNamara's narrative raises the most searching questions and provides the fewest definitive answers. It is not merely that his controversial role as Secretary of Defense during the Vietnam War, and the public vilification this entailed, exacted a huge toll on his family. (Both his wife and son opposed the government's war policy and both suffered health problems due to the tension within the family. McNamara himself recounts that he responded by "bottling up his emotions" and refusing to discuss the situation, a failure he recalls as "a grave weakness" [McNamara & VanDeMark, 1995, pp. 217, 297].) It is also that, at the end of his life, as Errol Morris' film reveals, he found himself in the position of the fictional butler Stevens of *The Remains of the Day*, confronting the knowledge that the narrative of his professional life has been tragically different from the one he believed himself to have been creating.

Questions of Form: Narratives of Democracy

We have been considering recurring themes (and associated character types and plot elements) among our narrative sets, generating from them a cumulative model of public leadership. Given our insistence throughout the book on the interrelationship of content and form, this raises some inevitable questions: Do the narratives share formal features as well? What meanings might we attach to them? We have, of course, included a wide variety of genres and media within our narrative sets (visual narratives whether feature films, documentaries, or television series, novels, dramas, historical accounts, biographies, memoirs), and each form brings its distinctive conventions and resources to its narrative task. Yet, there is one striking commonality. Most of the narratives we've engaged with have been multivoiced; that is, they have been characterized by an unusual degree of polyphony. (We recall that this can involve both the *intranarrative* proliferation of narrating voices and points of view and the *internarrative* interplay of retellings of a particular fable.)

This should not, in fact, surprise us, for the narrative enterprise in which these texts are engaged is the representation of public action within a democratic polity. Most of the narratives include at least one emblematic scene of passionate debate between opposing positions. Jaime Escalante and his students must decide whether to retake the Advanced Placement exam after being accused of cheating in *Stand and Deliver*, a choice ironically inverted in *Cheaters* (to cheat in the Academic Decathlon or not?). *Yes Prime Minister* is structured as an ongoing debate that is never conclusively resolved between politicians (Jim Hacker) and public servants (Sir Humphrey) over which group's view of management and policy will prevail. A number of the British narratives (*Corridors of Power, A Very British Coup, In the Loop*) debate military policy, with the United States always attempting to keep Britain in line as a supportive player in the NATO alliance and some British protagonists advocating a more independent stance. In the U.S. narratives (for example, *Advise and Consent, Seven Days in May*, and those concerning the Cuban Missile Crisis), the military issues inevitably concern how hard a line to take toward the Soviet Union. Debates between the left and right on domestic policy issues were a feature of both *The Candidate* and *The West Wing*. And the two jury narratives center on the impassioned debates of the proponents of guilt and innocence.

These are all instances of explicit polyphony, but many of our narratives also involve various forms of implicit polyphony, whether embedded counter-narratives (as in Errol Morris' masterful use of visual imagery, archival footage, and an unsettling Philip Glass score as counterpoint to McNamara's recollections), open or indeterminate endings (the relative places of expedience and principle in *The Candidate*'s Jim McKay's future career; the ultimate value of Charlie Wilson's victory in aiding the mujahedeen; the nature of Tony Blair's triumphs in *The Deal, The Queen*, and *The Special Relationship*), or the structural choice to present other stories within, and other contexts to, familiar fables (Roy Jenkins' attention to Churchill as political manager, Graham Allison's modeling of three different interpretive perspectives on the Cuban Missile Crisis).

But does this formal feature matter? Does it bear a larger meaning? For me, its recurring presence registers the challenge of representing the democratic narrative, the range of voices, positions, stories, interpretations, and experiences that are always at play; the often contradictory demands, expectations, and assumptions that must be accommodated; the elusiveness of definitive endings and the messiness of the provisional solutions that can be found. It is a reflection of the always ongoing story of a democratic society that is continually engaged in the process of remaking itself.

Narrative Competence, Again

In the introduction to this book, I proposed the idea of "narrative competence" as encompassing both the engagement with, and creation of, narratives. And I have striven throughout to model something of that competence in the story I sought to tell. There are increasing numbers of practitioner-oriented guides available on the subject of storytelling and its use within managerial contexts (Armstrong, 1992; Denning, 2005, 2007; Ganz, 2008; Simmons, 2001, 2007). Are there specific lessons that can be drawn from our analysis here that might inform such practical applications?

The narratives discussed in this book provide a few instances, either historical or fictional, of characters telling stories. Winston Churchill's famous "We shall fight on the beaches" speech was an oral narrative about the progress of the war in spring 1940, in particular the evacuation at Dunkirk. The jury deliberations discussed in Chapter 7 involved considerable narrative construction. The jurors arguing for a conviction in *Twelve Angry Men* started by telling the story of the crime as they understood it, and Juror 8, while ultimately destroying that story, initially proposed several stories of why and how someone other than the accused could have committed the crime. Graham Burnett used storytelling (the anecdote about a friend's doctoral dissertation) to calm his jury after a heated argument and to make the philosophical point that juries' functions and philosophy depend on the larger judicial system. One aspect of the Excom deliberations briefly touched upon in the Cuban Missile Crisis narratives is that its members were in part attempting to develop convincing stories about why and how the Soviets decided to place missiles in Cuba, and such stories would have significance in determining how President Kennedy would react.

The narratives that practitioners tell might thus be elaborate, like Churchill's 45-minute recounting of the war to that point; or very brief, like Juror 8's two-sentence hypothetical stories of how the murder occurred. They might be told for a variety of purposes, such as inspiring, rationalizing, or exculpating. They might be delivered in a speech or in a conversation. They might take advantage of new technology, for example, embodied in a Powerpoint display or a YouTube video that includes text, speech, and images. This section does not aim to provide a thorough handbook for practitioner storytelling, but it makes suggestions in six areas based on the narratives analyzed in this book.

Use the Fables: I hope that readers, upon seeing the categorization of the various types of fables and counter-fables, will conclude that this systematizes and makes explicit their own intuitive readings. If these fables indeed strike a chord with practitioners, then practitioners can use their structure and conventions in constructing their own stories. Their audiences will also recognize and appreciate the stories because they are part of their own experience. The use of narrative in election campaigns provides an illustration. Incumbents campaigning for reelection construct a narrative to fit the upper left quadrant of our analytic matrix (Table 1.1), along the lines of "our country has done well over the last four years, while I have grown in stature as a leader, and this will continue in the next four years." Indicators of a leader's growth in stature include becoming more comfortable in the job, becoming less partisan and more statesmanlike, or being recognized as a leader on the world stage. Another narrative strategy for an incumbent seeking reelection would be to present a sacrificial upper right quadrant narrative along the lines of "our country has risen to an enormous challenge over the past four years, but rather than retiring I will accept the burden of office to complete my work in the next four years"—FDR's narrative in 1944. An opposition party will present a lower right quadrant narrative of both national weakness and the leader's loss of energy, hope, or optimism—Ronald Reagan's campaign against Jimmy Carter in 1980. One could also develop campaign narratives for both incumbents and challengers that would be associated with each of the other quadrants.

How Narrowly to Focus? A crucial structural decision in framing a narrative is, as we've seen, how narrowly to focus. Many of the transformational teacher narratives focus almost exclusively on the relationship between teacher and students, while *Yes Prime Minister* rarely addressed anything other than the dyadic relationship between politics and bureaucracy, as represented by two key characters and an intermediary. The virtue of focusing so narrowly is that it cuts to the heart of the matter, allows the author to explore the key relationship, and is a natural response to the perpetual constraint of time or space available to tell the story. The cost of focusing so narrowly, particularly for a historical narrative, is that the story might be oversimplified and important aspects excluded. Thus, I argued that the transformational teacher stories, by rigorously focusing on the classroom, ignored another important factor accounting for the success of transformational teachers; namely, their ability to establish productive relationships with important decision makers and institutions in the external environment. So a choice the storyteller must make is how complex the story should be. Einstein's dictum that theories should be made as simple as possible, *but not simpler,* seems to me to be equally relevant to narratives.

Begin at the Beginning? One of the narrative conventions in modern communications, for example, newspaper and television, particularly when space or time is constrained, is the inverted pyramid model, which communicates the end of the story (its outcome) at the outset, and then fills in the details to the extent that time or space allow. It has the obvious advantage of communicating quickly in a world where audience attention is limited. The success of Twitter indicates the willingness of many people, even eminent novelists, to develop narratives that can be communicated within 140 characters. The great disadvantage of this type of storytelling is that it lacks the suspense of the traditional chronological approach. But the rationale for that approach is not only a matter of aesthetics. A story may be more effective at leading the audience to agree to an action if it takes them through the reasons for it. Churchill's "We shall fight on the beaches" speech, by keeping that exhortation to the very end, is a clear example. Churchill ultimately made a huge demand of his audience, to endure attacks on civilians at home and commit themselves to total war. Would he have been nearly as effective or convincing by asking that at the outset? The historical narrative, in fact, preceded the demand by recounting the course of the campaign in which the Germans drove the British and French to Dunkirk, praising the British forces for their resistance in the field and their ingenuity in the evacuation and finally, anticipating the looming Battle of Britain, recalling the stories of the Spanish Armada and Napoleon's planned invasion. Having established his rationale and context, Churchill then made his demand to an audience primed to respond.

There are, then, situations where a chronological narrative structure might be most effective. And there are obviously other means of controlling time frame and sequence beside those we've discussed. Two common devices include foreshadowing, leaping forward to hint at what is to come, and flashbacks, interrupting a chronological presentation to refer to something that happened in the past that will have consequences for the future. The point I am making here is simply to reiterate the importance of careful attention to these issues in the framing of a narrative structure.

Whose Story? The choice of narrator is a key issue in narratives developed by practitioners, whether stories of political, policy, or organizational advocacy. Consider the following: Contemporary political advocacy often involves using representative cases to make a broader point. The debate in the United States about national health insurance has involved stories about the consequences of a serious illness for someone who is uninsured, told by the advocates of national health insurance, and stories about someone in a system with national health insurance suffering unconscionable delay due to rationing, told by the opponents. Should such cases be presented in the first person by the individual in question or in the third person by a documentary-style narrator? The advantage of first-person presentation is the immediacy of someone talking directly to the audience about her experience. The disadvantage is that, once the story has been told, the media will attempt to contact the individual involved and might discover discordant or conflicting components to it; very quickly the story is no longer under the control of the advocates who introduced it. In contrast, a documentary-style story provides less heart-stopping immediacy, but more authorial control.

How much Polyphony? As is evident from the discussion in the previous section, my taste in public management narratives tends toward those with considerable polyphony, incorporating contending stories, opposing points of view, policy agendas presented by political rivals, or ambiguous outcomes open to a variety of interpretations. I find them thought-provoking and evocative of the multitude of conflicting voices and the complexity of policy-making in a democratic society. But is such polyphony effective in the narratives that political, policy, or organizational advocates produce? For many, advocacy involves knowingly distorting complicated situations and ambiguous evidence to arrive at simplistic and partisan policy prescriptions. Many audiences prefer the clarity of a world painted in black and white, and there are many advocates who are more than willing to provide it. More sophisticated audiences, however, tend to discount simplistic and partisan narratives. They would be more likely to prefer narratives that acknowledge ambiguity and polyphony, that address the legitimate counterarguments they face, concede validity where it exists, and offer a reasoned alternative. Using greater narrative polyphony is an approach worth exploring, at least for some audiences.

A Visual Narrative? Practitioners producing narratives now have the means easily and inexpensively to incorporate visual elements into their stories. This is a result of both the multitude of still and moving images that are available on the Web and in the public domain, ready to be copied or mashed up, and the ability of anyone with a videocamera or cell phone to record or create their own images. YouTube is readily available for disseminating political narratives, even those that involve primarily text and still images. Visuals, either still or moving, can be incorporated into Powerpoint presentations accompanying speeches. This has opened entirely new dimensions in practitioner storytelling, but it has created new pitfalls too. The ease of access to visual effects can result in overload. Not every story belongs on YouTube. The most important questions still remain: What story am I telling? Who is speaking? To whom? Why?

Directions for Future Research

In this book, I have tried to break new ground by introducing narratological concepts and approaches to public management and applying them to a selected group of narratives. I have tried to go beyond the "management lessons from film and literature" literature by outlining the structure of fables and counter-fables and using that structure as a basis to deduce lessons that will enhance a number of management skills, including skill at the creation and analysis of narratives. What research projects or areas of research could follow from the approach suggested here?

The most readily available option for extending this research is to look at the most recent narratives in the areas discussed in the book. While I have tried to include novels and movies produced in the last few years, as long as these genres are of significance and of interest to audiences, more such narratives will be produced. The economic turmoil, intractable military engagements, and technological advances of the last few years are providing much that will provoke creators of narratives. Three films receiving Academy Awards for 2010—*The King's Speech, The Social Network,* and *Inside Job*—all fit within the management narrative genre. Analyzing these and subsequent works will provide an explicit test of whether the structure of fables and counter-fables presented in this book remains a relevant conceptual framework.

The topics discussed do not in any way exhaust the universe of public management narrative. I have deliberately stayed away from war stories, even though war is an activity traditionally monopolized by the public sector. That genre contains a multitude of narratives, but many of them are "action adventures," narrowly focused on the battlefield. Only a minority deal with what is important to public management scholars; namely, military leadership and organization. The wars of the last decade, in particular the War on Terror and the wars in Iraq and Afghanistan have led to the production of a wide variety of contemporary military narratives. One example of a film that would be considered in such a discussion is Errol Morris's *Standard Operating Procedure*, about abuse and torture in the American prison at Abu Graib. My expectation is that a serious discussion of contemporary military narratives of leadership, organization, and politics, going back no farther than World War II, would require a book in its own right.

I have confined myself (with one exception) to the English language, and particularly to the United States and UK, and we have noticed profound differences between the nature of the fables and counter-fables in those two countries. One could analyze public management narratives in other economically advanced English-speaking countries, such as Canada, Australia, and New Zealand. Going farther afield would require more reliance on translations and on other writers' interpretations of cultures with which I am familiar at most as a tourist. For example, in my estimation, Egyptian Nobel laureate for literature Naguib Mahfouz's 1975 novel, *Respected Sir*, is a superbly written ironic tale of bureaucratic ambition, but I do not know enough about its social and literary context to locate it relative to Egyptian dominant or counter-fables, especially because the works of other Egyptian authors are not available in translation. Furthermore, the overthrow of Hosni Mubarak and prospects for democratization—unfolding as I write this chapter—would necessarily demand a reinterpretation of that novel.

Another direction for research using this methodology would be a book about narratives concerning contemporary private sector managers, also intended to identify dominant and counter-fables. The contexts for the various genres would be selected on the basis of industry sector and/ or managerial functions. While the research process itself would finalize the contexts to be studied and the texts to be used, the following is a first sketch of both:

- Narratives about the financial sector, particularly recent narratives emerging from the market crash of 2008–2009: (*Wall Street* (1987); *Wall Street: Money Never Sleeps* (2010); Charles Ferguson's documentary, *Inside Job* (2010); *Other People's Money* (1991); Caryl Churchill's 1987 play, *Serious Money*; Michael Lewis, *Liar's Poker* (1989); and *The Big Short* (2010); *Barbarians at the Gates* (1993); *The Rogue Trader* (1999)
- Narratives about entrepreneurship: *Startup.com* (2001); Tracy Kidder, *The Soul of A New Machine* (1991); *Tucker: The Man and his Dream* (1988); *Flash of Genius* (2008); Mezrich, *The Accidental Billionaires* (2010); and its film adaptation, *The Social Network* (2010)
- Narratives about the media industry: *Broadcast News* (1987), *Absence of Malice* (1981), *All the President's Men* (1976), *Citizen Kane* (1941), *Good Night and Good Luck* (2005)
- Narratives about the excesses or social costs of business: McLean and Elkind, *Enron: The Smartest Guys in the Room* (2003 book and 2005 film), *Erin Brockovich* (2000), *The Insider* (1999), *The Corporation* (2003), *A Civil Action* (1998) *North Country* (2005), *Norma Rae* (1979)
- Narratives about people in sales or marketing: Arthur Miller, *Death of a Salesman* (1949); David Mamet, *Glengarry Glen Ross* (1984); *Mad Men*, (2007–2010), *The Boiler Room* (2000)
- Narratives about "office politics": *The Office* (BBC and other versions); David Lodge, *Nice Work* (1988); *Office Space* (1999); *Executive Suite* (1954); Sloan Wilson, *The Man in the Gray Flannel Suit* (1955); Joseph Heller, *Something Happened* (1966).

The length of this list, formulated without undertaking any extensive bibliographical research, makes clear the richness of the private sector management genre in contemporary British and American narratives.

In addition, or as an alternative, to studying authored narratives about public and/or private sector management, one could study narratives produced by practitioners. I have recently completed a study (Borins, 2011) applying narratological concepts to public management innovation in which I analyzed practitioner narratives describing the origins of a sample of 31 finalist and award-winning applications to the Harvard Kennedy School's Innovations in American Government Awards Program. The study characterizes a dominant fable of public management innovation and analyzes the differences among three different narratives generated by each application. Innovators are a particularly rewarding group to study, because innovation represents a process of organizational change that unfolds over time and readily produces narratives. But many other groups of practitioners have stories to tell.

Yet another fertile area for narratological inquiry and analysis would encompass how practitioners, both politicians and public servants, use narrative to engage, inspire, persuade, or "spin." Examples abound. Political candidates produce favorable narratives about their life histories and experiences and their campaigns disseminate critical or skeptical ones about their opponents. Politicians in power (or their spokespeople) expound self-validating narratives designed to demonstrate their effectiveness as negotiators or decision makers. Baker (2010a) recounted in detail President Obama's role in recent nuclear arms control negotiations with the Russian government. It is clear from the article that Obama's staff cooperated fully with the author in order to generate an account that demonstrated Obama's engagement and toughness, itself an attempt to identify with the dominant fable of U.S.–Soviet relations concerning nuclear weapons over the last half-century. Policy advocates wield narratives as strategic weapons, telling stories to support their own proposals and discredit those of their opponents. The popular discourse of politics and governance has increasingly become a clash of competing narratives. Researchers could compile and then analyze the narratives used by candidates in election campaigns or by competing advocates regarding a contentious policy issue. For example, in a political campaign, the narratives would include those each party provides (on its Web site, in its advertising, and in speeches and press releases) about its candidate and his or her opponent, about "where the country is headed," about relevant policy issues, and about representative personal case histories. Politicians and public servants use narratives because they believe narratives are effective at creating an emotional bond between the audience and the narrator's cause, but are they correct in their beliefs? It should be possible to design laboratory experiments to evaluate the reactions of audiences to, and hence persuasiveness of, various narrative messages and styles regarding a contentious policy issue.

I began this book with the belief that the explosion of interest in narrative in other fields of scholarship, as well as in the culture at large, represents an important social and intellectual phenomenon. Inspired by that belief, I have applied narrative analysis to several areas of public management scholarship. As the title of this chapter indicates, I view this as a story that is only beginning.

A Final Word: Ten Essential Narratives

The narratives in this book were selected from a much larger set primarily for their analytic value in defining dominant and counter-fables within my chosen public sector contexts. Unlike a parent, I feel no obligation to love them all equally, and over the months and years I've spent thinking and writing about them, I have developed clear favorites. I include them here, in order of their appearance in the book, in the hopes of encouraging readers who have not already encountered them to do so. (And with the additional hope that the analysis offered in the preceding chapters will add to the rewards of engaging with them.)

1. *Stand and Deliver*
Jaime Escalante was an ordinary man whose charisma came from his extraordinary enthusiasm for what he was teaching and his passionate commitment to his students. His teaching did not reward or encourage self-revelation, but it demanded mastery of abstract concepts and the self-discipline to meet externally imposed standards. *Stand and Deliver* remains the original, and best, transformational teacher narrative.

2. *Cheaters*
It succeeds both because of the intelligence with which it inverts the transformational teacher fable and because it poses the thought-provoking question of whether as competitive a society as the United States subtly encourages those with high aspirations to cheat. It thus serves as a fitting introduction to a different genre; namely, the many narratives about corruption in the corporate world.

3. *The Class*
The Class (Entre les Murs) challenges the transformational teacher fable by transposing it to a different culture and portraying a teacher who is well meaning and energetic but who makes mistakes in classroom management

that leave him on the verge of losing control over the class. Could he have handled the situation more effectively? Producing the film through improvisation by an ensemble that includes the students provides a variety of perspectives on the instructor's pedagogy.

4. *Yes Minister/Yes Prime Minister*
The rigor and cleverness of its application of public-choice principles to a wide variety of public policy and management questions is unparalleled. Its dazzling linguistic comedy—the grand arias of bureaucratese and double-speak—masks a serious exploration of the (mis)use of language in politics and governance. The two episodes of *Yes Prime Minister* discussed in Chapter 3, "The Ministerial Broadcast" and "The Smokescreen," are a good starting point.

5. Kazuo Ishiguro's *The Remains of the Day*
While the film adaptation is excellent, going back to the original novel is even better. The author's creation of Stevens' unique voice and his slow revelation of an unsettled and anxiety-provoking story are masterful. The novel paints a devastating portrait of the psychology of appeasement and raises profound questions regarding individual moral responsibility. The beauty of the writing only strengthens the seriousness of its inquiry.

6. *Advise and Consent*
By downplaying the heavy-handed anti-Communist perspective of Allen Drury, the author of the original novel, Otto Preminger's film adaptation poses important questions concerning the legitimacy of the means used to achieve desired political ends. Are character assassination, blackmail, and lying under oath ever justified? Preminger also pushed the censorship envelope of the early sixties by depicting a gay lifestyle (even though the film stigmatized homosexuality).

7. *The Candidate*
Jeremy Larner's screenplay subtly portrays the process by which a politician, responding to the pressure of his handlers, the expectations of the voters, and opportunity created by his own gifts appears to lose his soul. Or does he? A "period" morality tale that seems no less relevant today. Also, by running a pseudocampaign, the filmmakers, in what was in effect an early experiment in crowd sourcing, ceded a measure of influence over the film to the members of the public who chose to participate in the pseudocampaign.

8. *The Fog of War*

Errol Morris's sympathetic but probing questions lead Robert McNamara to overturn the received wisdom regarding the Cuban Missile Crisis and to relive the trauma of Vietnam. We come to understand the extraordinary arc of McNamara's life story, but the moral questions of wartime leadership remain unresolved. A mesmerizing visual narrative and musical score create a documentary that is elegant, unsettling, and profoundly moving.

9. *The West Wing*

Wish-fulfillment of the highest order: Who doesn't want to watch seven seasons of a president who has a vision for the nation, who is a thoughtful and careful decision maker, and who has established a culture in which his brilliant and dedicated West Wing staff are not afraid to speak what they see as the truth to power? However stylized the Sorkin-speak dialogue with its much-parodied "walk and talks," the series' intelligent scripts and astute plotting replicate the frenetic pace of the actual West Wing, with a continuing stream of crises and issues to be managed. Of its 154 episodes, I recommend: season 1, episode 9 ("The Short List") about the choice of a nominee for the Supreme Court; season 1, episode 14 ("Take this Sabbath Day") about capital punishment; season 1, episode 19 ("Let Bartlet be Bartlet") about difficulty advancing the president's agenda; season 3, episode 8 ("The Women of Qumar") about issues management and compromising one's ideals; and season 7, episode 7 ("The Debate"), which presents an intelligent and thoughtful debate between the Democratic and Republican nominees to succeed President Bartlet (filmed live with two appealing and intelligent actors in top form).

10. *Twelve Angry Men*

Rightly considered a classic as both play and movie, *Twelve Angry Men* builds its tension through heated deliberation in a claustrophobic jury room. While Juror Number 8 (the architect, portrayed by Henry Fonda) heroically leads the jury to its verdict, the crime is not solved, inviting viewers to deliberate on their own about the guilt or innocence of the accused and perhaps to contemplate the subjective nature of every explanatory narrative.

References

Adams, J. (1993). *Yes Prime Minister:* The ministerial broadcast (Jonathan Lynn & Anthony Jay): Social reality and comic realism in popular television drama (pp. 62–85). In George W. Brandt (Ed.), *British Television Drama in the 1980s.* Cambridge, UK: Cambridge University Press.

Allison, G. (1971). *Essence of decision: Explaining the Cuban missile crisis.* Boston: Little, Brown.

Allison, G., & Zelikow, P. (1999). *Essence of decision: Explaining the Cuban missile crisis* (2nd ed.). New York: Addison Wesley Longman.

Alvarez, J., & Merchan, C. (1992). The role of narrative fiction in the development of imagination for action. *International Studies of Management and Organization, 22*(3), 27–45.

Angell, R. (2004, January 19). Late Review. *The New Yorker,* p. 87.

Armstrong, D. (1992). *Managing by storying around: A new method of leadership.* New York: Doubleday Currency.

Asimow, M. (2007). *12 Angry Men:* A revisionist view. *Chicago-Kent Law Review, 82*(2), 711–716.

Augustine, N., & Adelman, K. (1999). *Shakespeare in charge: The bard's guide to leading and succeeding on the business stage.* New York: Hyperion.

Axelrod, A. (2009). *Winston Churchill, CEO: 25 lessons for bold business leaders.* New York: Sterling.

Babcock, B., & Sassoubre, T. (2007). Deliberation in *12 Angry Men. Chicago-Kent Law Review, 82*(2), 633–642.

Badaracco, J. (2006). *Questions of character: Illuminating the heart of leadership through literature.* Boston: Harvard Business School Press.

Bagehot, W. (2001). *The English constitution.* Cambridge, UK: Cambridge University Press.

Governing Fables: Learning from Public Sector Narratives, pages 265–277

Baker, P. (2010a, March 27). Twists and turns on way to arms pact with Russia. *The New York Times*. Retrieved May 5, 2011 from http://www.nytimes.com/2010/03/27/world/europe/27start.html?ref=peterbaker

Baker, P. (2010b, August 11). The first wave of weary aides heads for the exits. *The New York Times*. Retrieved May 5, 2011 from http://www.nytimes.com/2010/08/12/us/politics/12memo.html?ref=peterbaker

Bal, M. (1997). *Narratology: Introduction to the theory of narrative* (2nd ed.). Toronto: University of Toronto Press.

Begaudeau, F. (2006). *Entre les murs*. (L. Asher,Trans.) Paris: Gallimard. *The class*. (2009). New York: Seven Stories Press.

Bellow, S. (1965, April 4). Mind over chatter. *Book Week*, p. 2.

Bennett, A. (2004). *The history boys*. New York: Faber and Faber.

Blair, T. (2010). *A journey: My political life*. New York: Knopf.

Borins, S. (1988). Public choice: "Yes Minister" made it popular, but does winning a Nobel prize make it true? *Canadian Public Administration, 31*(1), 12–26.

Borins, S. (1998). *Innovating with integrity: How local heroes are transforming American government*. Washington, DC: Georgetown University Press.

Borins, S. (2006). The challenge of innovating in government (2nd ed.). *IBM Foundation for the Business of Government*. Retrieved July 14, 2010, from http://www.businessofgovernment.org/sites/default/files/BorinsInnovatingInGov.pdf

Borins, S. (2010). Strategic planning from Robert McNamara to Gov 2.0. *Public Administration Review, 70*(supp. 1), S220–S221.

Borins, S. (2011). Making narrative count: A narratological approach to public management innovation. *Journal of Public Administration Research and Theory*, doi: 10.1093/jopart/muq088.

Borins, S., Kernaghan, K., Brown, D., Bontis, N., Thompson, F., & Perri 6 (2007). *Digital state at the leading edge*. Toronto: University of Toronto Press.

Brawer, R. (1998). *Fictions of business: Insights on management from great literature*. New York: Wiley.

Brown, M., & Rossi, R. (1995, April 16). No easy answers found in scandals at Steinmetz. *Chicago Sun-Times*, p. 19.

Bulman, R. (2005). *Hollywood goes to high school: Cinema, schools, and American culture*. New York: Worth Publishers.

Burgess, A. (1965). Powers that be. *Encounter, 24*, 71–76.

Burnett, D. G. (2001). *A trial by jury*. New York: Knopf.

Burnett, D. G. (2007). Foreword. *Chicago-Kent Law Review, 82*(2), 551–556.

Burns, R. (2007). A jury between fact and norm. *Chicago-Kent Law Review, 82*(2), 643–662.

Campbell, A. (2009, March 24). Was I offended by this brutal spinmeister? No. I was bored [Review of the motion picture *In the Loop*]. *The Guardian*. Retrieved January 6, 2011, from http://www.guardian.co.uk/commentisfree/2009/mar/24/in-the-loop-alastair-campbell

Canby, V. (1972, June 30). Candidate, a comedy about the state of politics, opens [Review of the motion picture *The Candidate*]. *The New York Times*, p. 25.

Canby, V. (1989, June 2). Shaking up a boys' school with poetry [Review of the motion picture *Dead Poets Society*]. *The New York Times*, p. AR1.

Carroll, J. (2009, July 13). McNamara and our nuclear madness. *The Boston Globe*. Retrieved May 5, 2011 from http://www.boston.com/bostonglobe/ editorial_opinion/oped/articles/2009/07/13/mcnamara_and_our_ nuclear_madness/

Center for Media and Public Affairs. (2003). Changing images of government in TV entertainment. *Public Voices, 6*(2), 70–72.

Chambers, S. (2003). Dialogue, deliberation, and discourse: The far-reaching politics of The West Wing. In P. Rollins & J. O'Connor (Eds.), *The West Wing: The American presidency as television drama* (pp. 83–100). Syracuse, NY: Syracuse University Press.

Champoux, J. (2001a). *Management: Using film to visualize principles and practices.* Cincinnati, OH: South-Western College Publishing.

Champoux, J. (2001b). *Organizational behaviour: Using film to visualize principles and practices.* Cincinnati, OH: South-Western College Publishing.

Chase, A. (2003). Elections and party politics. In P. Rollins (Ed.), *The Columbia companion to American history on film* (pp. 527–533). New York: Columbia University Press.

Christensen, T., & Haas, P. (2005). *Projecting politics: Political messages in American film.* Armonk, NY: M. E. Sharpe.

Churchill, C. (1987). *Serious money.* London: Methuen.

Churchill, W. (1938, October 5). Speech to the House of Commons. Retrieved May 5, 2011 from http://hansard.millbanksystems.com/commons/1938/ oct/05/policy-of-his-majestys-government#S5CV0339P0_19381005_ HOC_218

Churchill, W. (1939, September 3). Speech to the House of Commons. Retrieved May 5, 2011 from http://hansard.millbanksystems.com/commons/1939/ sep/03/prime-ministers-announcement#S5CV0351P0_19390903_ HOC_38

Churchill, W. (1940a, May 13). Speech to the House of Commons. Retrieved May 5, 2011 from http://hansard.millbanksystems.com/commons/1940/ may/13/his-majestys-government-1

Churchill, W. (1940b, June 4). Speech to the House of Commons. Retrieved May 5, 2011 from http://hansard.millbanksystems.com/commons/1940/ jun/04/war-situation

Clemens, J., & Wolff, M. (1999). *Movies to manage by: Lessons in leadership from great films.* Chicago: Contemporary Books.

Cohen, C. (1998). Using narrative fiction within management education. *Management Learning, 29*(2), 165–181.

Cohen, P. (2010, April 1). Next big thing in English: Knowing they know that you know. *The New York Times*, p. C1.

Corrigan, P. (1999). *Shakespeare on management: Leadership lessons for today's managers*. London: Kogan Page.

Cowley, P. (2006, October 6). Politics for morons. *Times Higher Education*. Retrieved January 6, 2011, from http://www.timeshighereducation.co.uk/story.asp?storyCode=205839&sectioncode=26

Coyne, M. (2008). *Hollywood goes to Washington: American politics on screen*. London: Reaktion Books.

Crawley, M. (2006). *Mr. Sorkin goes to Washington: Shaping the president on television's The West Wing*. Jefferson, NC: McFarland and Company.

Crile, G. (2003). *Charlie Wilson's war*. New York: Grove Press.

Crossman, R. (1972). *The myths of cabinet government*. Cambridge, MA: Harvard University Press.

Crossman, R. (1975). *The diaries of a cabinet minister* (Vol. 1). New York: Holt Rinehart Winston.

Crossman, R. (1977). *The diaries of a cabinet minister* (Vol. 3). New York: Holt Rinehart Winston.

Crowther, B. (1949, November 9). *All the King's Men*, Columbia film based on the novel by Warren, at Victoria [Review of the motioin picture *All the King's Men*]. *The New York Times*, p. 37.

Crowther, B. (1958, October 24). Spencer Tracy in "The Last Hurrah"; Portrays Skeffington; John Ford directs [Review of the motioin picture *The Last Hurrah*]. *The New York Times*, p. 40.

Czarniawska-Joerges, B., & Guillet de Montoux, P. (1994). Introduction: Management beyond case and cliché. In B. Czarniawska-Joerges & P. Guillet de Montoux (Eds.), *Good novels, better management: Reading organizational realities* (pp. 1–16). Chur, Switzerland: Harwood Academic Publishers.

Dargis, M. (2006, August 11). In "Half Nelson" a student knows a teacher's secret [Review of the motioin picture *Half Nelson*]. *The New York Times*, p. AR1.

Dargis, M. (2007, January 5). To Ms. with love, in a seething Los Angeles. *The New York Times*, p. AR1.

Dargis, M. (2008, September 28). Learning to be the future of France [Review of the motion picture *Enre les murs*]. *The New York Times*, p. AR1.

Dalyell, T. (1989). *Dick Crossman: A portrait*. London: Weidenfeld and Nicholson.

Denning, S. (2001). *The springboard: How storytelling ignites action in knowledge-era organizations*. Burlington, MA: Elsevier.

Denning, S. (2005). *The leader's guide to storytelling: Mastering the art and discipline of business narrative*. San Francisco: Jossey-Bass.

Denning, S. (2007). *The secret language of leadership: How leaders inspire action through narrative*. San Francisco: Jossey-Bass.

Dobbs, M. (1989). *House of cards*. London: Fontana.

Dobbs, M. (2003). *Never surrender*. London: Harper Collins.

Dobbs, M. (2008). *One minute to midnight: Kennedy, Khrushchev, and Castro on the brink of nuclear war.* New York: A. A. Knopf.

Dodge, J., Ospina, S., & Foldy, E. (2005). Integrating rigor and relevance in public administration scholarship: The contribution of narrative inquiry. *Public Administration Review, 65*(3), 286–300.

Downs, A. (1967). *Inside bureaucracy.* Boston: Little, Brown.

Drury, A. (1961). *Advise and consent.* New York: Pocket Books.

Dubnick, M. (2000). Movies and morals: Energizing ethical thinking among professionals. *Journal of Public Affairs Education, 6*(3), 147–160.

Ebert, R. (1989, June 9). [Review of the motion picture *Dead Poets Society*]. *Chicago Sun-Times.* Retrieved May 5, 2011 from http://rogerebert.suntimes.com/apps/pbcs.dll/article?AID=/19890609/REVIEWS/906090301/1023

Ebert, R. (1993, November 5). [Review of the motion picture *The Remains of the Day*]. *Chicago Sun-Times.* Retrieved May 5, 2011 from http://rogerebert.suntimes.com/apps/pbcs.dll/article?AID=/19931105/REVIEWS/311050304/

Ebert, R. (1998, May 22). [Review of the motion picture *Bulworth*]. *Chicago Sun-Times.* Retrieved May 5, 2011 from http://rogerebert.suntimes.com/apps/pbcs.dll/article?AID=/19980522/REVIEWS/805220301/1023

Ebert, R. (2002, September 29). [Review of the motion picture *12 Angry Men*]. *Chicago Sun-Times.* Retrieved May 5, 2011 from http://rogerebert.suntimes.com/apps/pbcs.dll/article?AID=/20020929/REVIEWS08/209290301/1023

Ebert, R. (2004, January 23). [Review of the motion picture *The Fog of War*]. *Chicago Sun-Times.* Retrieved May 5, 2011 from http://rogerebert.suntimes.com/apps/pbcs.dll/article?AID=%2F20040123%2FREVIEWS%2F401230302%2F1023

Elliott, S. (1993, January 10). Hollywood's pet: Schoolteachers. *The New York Times.* Retrieved May 5, 2011 from http://www.nytimes.com/1993/01/10/education/hollywood-s-pet-schoolteachers.html?scp=1&sq=elliott+hollywood%27s+pet&st=nyt

Emerson, J. (1989). *Dead Poets Society.* www.cinepad.com.

Erikson, E. (1980). *Identity and the life cycle.* New York: Norton.

Erikson, E. (1985). *The life cycle completed.* New York: Norton.

Feeney, F. X. (2006). *A fisher of kings: Steven Zaillian dramatizes destiny and the stuff of dreams.* Retrieved February 24, 2011, from http://www.wga.org/writtenby/writtenbysub.aspx?id=2229

Foldy, E., Goldman, L., & Ospina, S. (2008). Sensegiving and the role of cognitive shifts in the work of leadership. *The Leadership Quarterly, 19*(4), 514–529.

Foote, D. (2009). *Relentless pursuit: A year in the trenches with teach for America.* New York: Vintage Books.

Freedland, J. (2008, February 21). From West Wing to the real thing. *The Guardian.* Retrieved February 25, 2011, from http://www.guardian.co.uk/world/2008/feb/21/barackobama.uselections2008

Freedom Writers, & Gruwell, E. (1999). *The freedom writers diary.* New York: Doubleday.

Garber, M. (2008). *Shakespeare and modern culture.* New York: Pantheon Books.

Ganz, M. (2008). *What is public narrative?* Unpublished paper.

Gianos, P. (1999). *Politics and politicians in American film.* New York: Praeger.

Giglio, E. (2005). *Here's looking at you: Hollywood, film, and politics* (2nd ed.). New York: Peter Lang.

Gill, A. A. (2006, October 8). The hammy house of Horrocks. *The Sunday Times.* Retrieved January 6, 2011, from http://entertainment.timesonline.co.uk/tol/arts_and_entertainment/article659916.ece

Gladwell, M. (2006). *Blink: The power of thinking without thinking.* Boston: Back Bay Books.

Goodsell, C., & Murray, N. (1995). Prologue: Building new bridges. In C. Goodsell & N. Murray (Eds.), *Public administration illuminated and inspired by the arts* (pp. 3–24). Westport, CT: Praeger.

Gordon, T. (2000). *Parent effectiveness training: The proven program for raising responsible children.* New York: Three Rivers Press.

Gottschall, J., & Wilson, D. S. (2005). Introduction: Literature—A last frontier in human evolutionary studies. In J. Gottschall & D. Wilson (Eds.), *The literary animal: Evolution and the nature of narrative* (pp. xvii–xxvi). Evanston: IL: Northwestern University Press.

Graver, L. (1989, October 8). What the butler saw. *The New York Times Book Review,* p. 7.

Groen, R. (1989, June 2). "Dead Poets" script well-versed in formula [Review of the motion picture *Dead Poets Society*]. *The Globe and Mail,* p. D1.

Groen, R. (2007, January 5). Familiar tale can't make the grade. *The Globe and Mail,* p. R7.

Gruwell, E. (2007). *Teach with your heart: Lessons I learned from the Freedom Writers.* New York: Doubleday.

Halperin, J. (1983). *C. P. Snow: An oral biography.* New York: St. Martin's Press.

Hay, B. (2007). Charades: Religious allegory in 12 Angry Men. *Chicago-Kent Law Review, 82*(2), 811–862.

Hayward, S. (2006). *Cinema studies: The key concepts* (3rd ed.). London: Routledge.

Hegedus, C. (2004). *Filmmaker introduction to The War Room* (DVD re-release) Los Angeles, CA: Focus Features.

Heilman, R. (2001). The great-teacher myth. *The American Scholar, 60*(3), 417–423.

Heller, J. (1966). *Something happened.* New York: Dell.

Higgins, S., & Striegel, C. (1999). *Movies for leaders: Management lessons from all-time great movies.* Spokane, WA: New Media Ventures.

Holzer, M. (1997). Communicating administrative issues through creative forms. In J. Garnett & A. Kouzmin (Eds.), *Handbook of administrative communication* (pp. 203–225). New York: Marcel Dekker.

Holzer, M., Morris, K., & Ludwin, W. (1979). *Literature in bureaucracy: Readings in administrative fiction.* Wayne, NJ: Avery Publishing Group.

Holzer, M., & Slater, L. (1995). Insights from bureaucracy into film: Visualizing stereotypes. In C. Goodsell & N. Murray (Eds.), *Public administration illuminated and inspired by the arts* (pp. 75–90). Westport, CT: Praeger.

Iannucci, A. (2005, April 19). Interview with Armando Iannucci, Chris Langham, and Peter Capaldi. *BBC Four.* Retrieved January 6, 2011, from http://www.bbc.co.uk/print/bbcfour/thickofit/armando-iannucci.shtml

Iannucci, A., Armstrong, J., Blackwell, S., Martin, I., & Roche, T. (2007). *The Thick of It: The scripts.* London: Hodder and Stoughton.

Illiash, I. (2004). Waldo revisited or genesis of the idea of looking at administration through the prism of the arts. *Public Voices, 7*(2), 63–72.

Ishiguro, K. (1989). *The remains of the day.* London: Penguin.

Ishiguro, K. (2005). *Never let me go.* New York: A. A. Knopf.

James, C. (1977, March 31). On Richard Crossman. *New York Review of Books.* Retrieved January 6, 2011, from http://www.clivejames.com/pieces/Hercules/Crossman

James, C. (1989, June 11). Growing up is hard to put in focus [Review of the motion picture *Dead Poets Society*]. *The New York Times,* p. AR2.

Jenkins, R. (2001). *Churchill: A biography.* New York: Penguin.

Jesness, J. (2002). *Stand and Deliver* revisited. *Reason.* Retrieved November 22, 2007, from http://www.reason.com/news/show/28479.html

Johnson, D. (1995a, March 31). Chicago's "Cinderella team" scholars are suspected of cheating. *New York Times,* p. A14.

Johnson, D. (1995b, April 13). Academic competitors at a Chicago school now admit cheating. *New York Times,* p. A18.

Johnson, D. (2000, May 16). Cheaters learned a lesson, sort of. *The New York Times.* Retrieved May 5, 2011 from http://www.nytimes.com/2000/05/16/us/cheaters-final-response-so-what.html?ref=dirkjohnson

Johnson, L. (1992). *My posse don't do homework.* [published after 1995 as *Dangerous minds.*] New York: St. Martin's

Jurkiewicz, C., & Giacalone, R. (2000). Through the lens clearly: Using films to demonstrate ethical decision-making in the public service. *Journal of Public Affairs Education, 6*(4), 257–266.

Just, R. (2003). Cerebral vortex: How Aaron Sorkin, the brains behind TV's smartest show, got the last laugh. *The American Prospect.* Retrieved June 10, 2010, from http://www.prospect.org/cs/articles?article=cerebral_vortex

Kammeraad-Campbell, S. (2005). *Doc: The story of Dennis Littky and his fight for a better school.* Alexandria, VA: Association for Supervision and Curriculum Development.

Kaplan, F. (2003, December 19). The evasions of Robert McNamara: What's true and what's a lie in The Fog of War? *Slate.* Retrieved May 4, 2011 from http://www.slate.com/id/2092916/

Kaplan, F. (2004, October 10). Truth stranger than "Strangelove." *The New York Times,* p. AR21.

Kennedy, J. F. (1940). *Why England slept.* New York: Wilfred Funk.

Kennedy, R. (1969). *Thirteen days: A memoir of the Cuban missile crisis.* New York: Norton.

Kidder, T. (1981). *The soul of a new machine.* New York: Random House.

Kirby, T. (2007, February 10). Ian Richardson, the PM who couldn't possibly comment, dies aged 72. *The Independent.* Retrieved January 6, 2011, from http://www.independent.co.uk/news/media/ian-richardson-the-pm-who-couldnt-possibly-comment-dies-aged-72-435815.html

Kroll, M. (1995). The administrator-viewer reviewed through film. In C. Goodsell & N. Murray (Eds.), *Public administration illuminated and inspired by the arts* (pp. 91–106). Westport, CT: Praeger.

Landsman, S. (2007). Mad about 12 Angry Men. *Chicago-Kent Law Review, 82*(2), 748–758.

Lane, A. (2009, July 27). Gray skies. *The New Yorker,* pp. 78–79.

Larner, J. (1988, October 23). Politics catches up to "The Candidate." *The New York Times,* p. E23.

Larner, J. (2001, March 18). Film: Shaping words into an Oscar: Six writers who did. *The New York Times,* p. AR6.

Lee, M., & Paddock, S. (2001). Strange but true tales from Hollywood: The bureaucrat as movie hero. *Public Administration and Management: An Interactive Journal, 6*(4), 166–194.

Levine, M. (2003). The West Wing (NBC) and the west wing (DC): Myth and reality in television's portrayal of the White House. In P. Rollins & J. O'Connor. *The West Wing: The American presidency as television drama* (pp. 42–62). Syracuse, NY: Syracuse University Press.

Levine, M. (2005). Myth and reality in the Hollywood campaign film: Primary Colors (1998) and The War Room (1994). In P. Rollins & J. O'Connor (Eds.), *Hollywood's White House: The American presidency in film and history* (pp. 288–308). Lexington, KY: University Press of Kentucky.

Lewis, M. (1989). *Liar's poker.* New York: W. W. Norton.

Lewis, M. (2010). *The big short: Inside the doomsday machine.* New York: W. W. Norton.

Lichter, S. R., Lichter, L., & Amundson, D. (2000). Government goes down the tube: Images of government in TV entertainment, 1955–98. *Press/Politics, 5*(2), 96–103.

Lim, D. (2008, September 21). French school as democracy and stage. *The New York Times,* p. AR11.

Liptak, A. (2004, October 17). Trial by actors. *The New York Times,* p. AR7.

Littky, D., & Grabelle, S. (2004). *The big picture: Education is everyone's business.* Alexandria, VA: Association for Supervision and Curriculum Development.

Lodge, D. (1988). *Nice work.* London: Penguin.

Lukacs, J. (1999). *Five days in London: May 1940.* New Haven, CT: Yale University Press.

Lumet, S. (1995). *Making movies.* New York: A. A. Knopf.

Lynn, J., & Jay, A. (1986). *Yes Prime Minister: The diaries of the Right Hon. James Hacker* (Vol. 1). London: BBC.

Mamet, D. (1984). *Glengarry Glen Ross.* New York: Grove Press.

Marder, N. (Ed.). (2007a). Symposium: The 50th anniversary of 12 Angry Men. *Chicago-Kent Law Review, 82*(2), 551–901.

Marder, N. (2007b). The banality of evil: A portrayal in 12 Angry Men. *The Chicago-Kent Law Review, 82*(2), 887–902.

Maslin, J. (1998, May 15). White bread senator turns homeboy [Review of the motion picture *Bulworth*]. *The New York Times.* Retrieved May 5, 2011 from http://www.nytimes.com/1998/05/15/movies/film-review-white-bread-senator-turns-homeboy.html?scp=1&sq=maslin+white+bread+senator+turns+homeboy&st=nyt

Matthews, J. (1988). *Escalante: The best teacher in America.* New York: Henry Holt.

May, E. (2001). Thirteen days in 145 minutes. *The American Prospect, 12*(1), 34–35.

Maynard-Moody, S., & Musheno, M. (2003). *Cops, teachers, counselors: Stories from the front lines of public service.* Ann Arbor: University of Michigan Press.

McAdams, D. (2006). *The redemptive self: Stories Americans live by.* New York: Oxford.

McKee, R. (1997). *Story: Substance, structure, style, and the principles of screenwriting.* New York: Harper Collins.

McKinley, M. (2006). *Hockey: A people's history.* Toronto: McClelland and Stewart.

McLean, B., & Elkind, P. (2003). *The smartest guys in the room: The amazing rise and scandalous fall of Enron.* New York: Penguin.

McNamara, R., & VanDeMark, B. (1995). *In retrospect: The tragedy and lessons of Vietnam.* New York: Vintage.

McSwite, O. C. (2002). Narrative in literature, film, video, and painting: Theoretical and practical considerations of their relevance to public administration. *Public Voices, 5*(1), 89–98.

Mezrich, B. (2010). *The accidental billionaires.* New York: Anchor.

Miller, A. (1949). *Death of a salesman.* New York: Viking.

Moore, M. (1995). *Creating public value: Strategic management in government.* Cambridge, MA: Harvard University Press.

Morris, E. (2008a, April 3). Play it Again, Sam (Re-enactments, Part One). *Errol Morris Blog—NYTime.com.* Retrieved May 5, 2011 from http://opinionator.blogs.nytimes.com/2008/04/03/play-it-again-sam-re-enactments-part-one/

Morris, E. (2008b, April 10). Play it Again, Sam (Re-enactments, Part Two). *Errol Morris Blog—NYTime.com.* Retrieved May 5, 2011 from http://opinionator

.blogs.nytimes.com/2008/04/10/play-it-again-sam-re-enactments-part-two/

Morris, E. (2009, July 7). McNamara in context. *The New York Times.* Retrieved May 5, 2011 from http://opinionator.blogs.nytimes.com/2009/07/07/mcnamara-in-context/?scp=2&sq=morris++mcnamara+in+context&st=nyt

Moretti, F. (2005). *Graphs, maps, trees: Abstract models for literary history.* London: Verso.

Mullin, C. (1982). *A very British coup.* London: Hodder and Stoughton.

Mullin, C. (2006, March 7). When the threat of a coup seemed more than fiction. *The Guardian.* Retrieved January 6, 2011, from http://www.guardian.co.uk/politics/2006/mar/07/past.comment/print

Munton, D., & Welch, D. (2007). *The Cuban missile crisis; A concise history.* New York: Oxford.

Neustadt, R. (1980). *Presidential power: The politics of leadership from FDR to Carter.* New York: Wiley.

New Leaders for New Schools. (2009). *Finalist application to the Innovations in American Government awards program.* Cambridge, MA: Harvard Kennedy School, Ash Center for Democratic Governance and Innovation.

Nussbaum, M. (1995). *Poetic justice: The literary imagination and public life.* Boston: Beacon.

Olson, L. (2007). *Troublesome young men: The rebels who brought Churchill to power and helped save England.* New York: Random House.

Ospina, S., & Dodge, J. (2005a). Its about time: Catching method up to meaning—The usefulness of narrative inquiry in public administration research. *Public Administration Review, 65*(2), 143–157.

Ospina, S., & Dodge, J. (2005b). Narrative inquiry and the search for connectedness: Practitioners and Academics developing public administration scholarship. *Public Administration Review, 65*(4), 400–423.

Ospina, S., & Foldy, E. (2010). Building bridges from the margins: The work of leadership in social change organizations. *The Leadership Quarterly, 21*(2), 291–307.

Papke, D. (2007). 12 Angry Men is not an archetype: Reflections on the jury in contemporary popular culture. *Chicago-Kent Law Review, 82*(2), 735–748.

Parry-Giles, T., & Parry-Giles, S. (2006). *The prime-time presidency: The West Wing and US nationalism.* Urbana: University of Illinois Press.

Pautz, M., & Roselle, L. (2009). Are they ready for their close-up? Civil servants and their portrayal in contemporary American cinema. *Public Voices, 11*(1), 8–32.

Peters, T., & Waterman, R. (1982). *In search of excellence: Lessons from America's best-run companies.* New York: HarperCollins.

Phillips, N. (1995). Telling organizational tales: On the role of narrative fiction in the study of organizations. *Organization Studies, 16*(4), 625–649.

Podhoretz, J. (2003). The liberal imagination. In P. Rollins & J. O'Connor (Eds.), *The West Wing: The American presidency as television drama* (pp. 222–231). Syracuse, NY: Syracuse University Press.

Pompper, D. (2003). The West Wing: White House narratives that journalism cannot tell. In P. Rollins & J. O'Connor (Eds.), *The West Wing: The American presidency as television drama* (pp. 17–31). Syracuse, NY: Syracuse University Press.

Posner, R. (1988). *Law and literature: A misunderstood relation.* Cambridge, MA: Harvard University Press.

Posner, R. (1998). *Law and literature: Revised and enlarged edition.* Cambridge, MA: Harvard University Press.

Posner, R.(2009). *Law and literature* (3rd ed.). Cambridge, MA: Harvard University Press.

Prince, G. (2003). *A dictionary of narratology* (Rev. ed.). Lincoln: University of Nebraska Press.

Propp, V. (1968). *Morphology of the folktale* (2nd ed., L. Scott, Trans.). Austin: University of Texas Press.

Puffer, S. (1991). *Managerial insights from literature.* Boston: PWS-Kent Publishing Company.

Ramanathan, S. (1978). *The novels of C. P. Snow.* London: Macmillan.

Rawls, J. (1971). *A theory of justice.* Cambridge, MA: Harvard University Press.

Rees, J. (2010, February 17). Yes Prime Minister on stage. *The Daily Telegraph.* Retrieved January 26, 2011, from http://www.telegraph.co.uk/culture/theatre/theatre-features/7258497/Yes-Prime-Minister-on-stage.html

Reissman, C. (2008). *Narrative methods for the social sciences.* Thousand Oaks, CA: Sage Publications.

Ringle, K. (2001, February 4). "Thirteen Days" embellishes crisis roles. *Washington Post,* p. 20.

Ritter, J., & Sneed, M. (1995, March 24). Steinmetz decathlon title pulled: Team vows to fight decision in court. *Chicago Sun-Times,* p. 6.

Roazen, P. (1976). Erik H. Erikson: The power and limits of a vision. New York: Free Press.

Roe, E. (1994). *Narrative policy analysis: Theory and practice.* Durham, NC: Duke University Press.

Rollins, P., & O'Connor, J. (2003). *The West Wing: The American presidency as television drama.* Syracuse, NY: Syracuse University Press.

Rose, R. (2006). *Twelve angry men.* New York: Penguin Classics.

Rossi, R., Sneed, M., & Brown, M. (1995, April 12). We didn't cheat: They had us fooled: Three students admit cheating in decathlon. *Chicago Sun-Times,* p. 1.

Sarat, A. (2007). Fathers in law: Violence and reason in 12 Angry Men. *Chicago-Kent Law Review, 82*(2), 863–886.

Savoie, D. (2007). *Court government and the collapse of accountability in Canada and the United Kingdom.* Toronto: University of Toronto Press.

Scott, A. O. (2009, July 24). War of words, misspoken and spun [Review of the motion picture *In the Loop*]. *The New York Times*, p. AR1.

Shafritz, J. (1999). *Shakespeare on management: Wise business counsel from the bard.* New York: Harper Business.

Simmons, A. (2001). *The story factor: Inspiration, influence, and persuasion through the art of storytelling.* New York: Basic Books.

Simmons, A. (2007). *Whoever tells the best story wins: How to use your own stories to communicate with power and impact.* New York: American Management Association.

Slingerland, E. (2008). *What science offers the humanities: Integrating body and culture.* Cambridge, UK: Cambridge University Press.

Smith, G. (2003). The left takes back the flag: The Steadicam, the snippet, and the song in The West Wing's "In Excelcis Deo." In P. Rollins & J. O'Connor (Eds.), *The West Wing: The American presidency as television drama* (pp. 125–135). Syracuse, NY: Syracuse University Press.

Sneed, M., & Rodriguez, A. (1995, March 26). Steinmetz admits cheating in '94: Coach gave out answers, principal says. *Chicago Sun-Times*, p. 1.

Snow, C. P. (1975). *Trollope: His life and art.* London: Macmillan.

Snow, C. P. (1984). *Corridors of power.* Harmondsworth, UK: Penguin.

Snow, P. (1982). *Stranger and brother: A portrait of C. P. Snow.* London: Macmillan.

Sorensen, T. (1963). *Decision-making in the White House: The olive branch or the arrows.* New York: Columbia University Press.

Sorkin, A. (2000, September 27). *Interview with Terence Smith on NewsHour with Jim Lehrer.* Retrieved June 10, 2010, from http://www.pbs.org/newshour/media/west_wing/sorkin.html

Sorkin, A. (2002, October 2). *Interview with Charley Rose.* Retrieved June 10, 2010, from http://www.charlierose.com/view/interview/2351

Taylor, C. (1998, March 20). Standing for nothing. [Review of the motion picture *Primary Colors*]. *Salon.com.* Retrieved February 24, 2011, from http://www.salon.com/entertainment/movies/1998/03/20primary.html?CP=SAL&DN=110

Theakston, K. (2003). Richard Crossman: The diaries of a cabinet minister. *Public Policy and Administration, 18*(4), 20–40.

Travers, P. (2006, September 21). [Review of the motion picture *All the King's Men*]. *Rolling Stone.* Retrieved May 5, 2011 from http://www.rollingstone.com/movies/reviews/all-the-kings-men-20060921

Vest, J. (2003). From The American President to The West Wing: A Scriptwriter's Perspective. In P. Rollins & J. O'Connor (Eds.), *The West Wing: The American presidency as television drama* (pp. 136–156). Syracuse, NY: Syracuse University Press.

Vidmar, N., Beale, S., Chemerinsky, E., & Coleman, J. (2007). Was he guilty as charged? An alternative narrative based on the circumstantial evidence about 12 Angry Men. *Chicago-Kent Law Review, 82*(2), 691–710.

Waldo, D. (1968). *The novelist on organization and administration: An inquiry into the relationship between two worlds.* Berkeley: University of California, Berkeley Institute of Governmental Studies.

Warren, R. (1946). *All the king's men.* New York: Harcourt, Brace.

Weisselberg, C. (2007). Good film, bad Jury. *Chicago-Kent Law Review, 82*(2), 717–734.

Whitney, J., & Packer, T. (2000). *Power plays: Shakespeare's lessons in leadership and management.* New York: Simon and Schuster.

Wilson, H. (1978, January 5). A desire to educate. *The Listener,* 4–7.

Wilson, S. (1955). *The man in the gray flannel suit.* Cambridge, MA: Da Capo Press.

Winerip, M. (2010, July 11). A chosen few are teaching for America. *The New York Times.* Retrieved May 5, 2011 from http://www.nytimes.com/2010/07/12/education/12winerip.html?scp=2&sq=winerip+chosen+few+are+teaching+for+america&st=nyt

Youngs, I. (2007, February 9). Richardson's rule in House of Cards. *BBC News.* Retrieved January 6, 2011, from http://news.bbc.co.uk/2/hi/entertainment/6346897.stm

About the Author

Sandford Borins is a Professor of Strategic Management at the University of Toronto. He is also a Research Fellow at the Ash Center for Democratic Governance and Innovation. He has been a visiting professor at the Harvard Kennedy School, Goldman School of Public Policy at the University of California at Berkeley, and a Scholar-in-Residence in the Ontario Cabinet Office.

Professor Borins is well known for his scholarship in the areas of narrative, innovation, and public management reform. He is the author of numerous articles as well as eight books, including *Innovations in Government: Research, Recognition, and Replication* (Brookings, 2008), *Digital State at the Leading Edge* (University of Toronto Press, 2007), *"If you build it..." Business, Government, and Ontario's Electronic Toll Highway* (University of Toronto Press, 2005), *Political Management in Canada*, co-authored with Allan Blakeney, former premier of Saskatchewan (University of Toronto Press, 1998), *Innovating with Integrity: How Local Heroes are Transforming American Government* (Georgetown University Press, 1998), and *The Language of the Skies: The Bilingual Air Traffic Control Conflict in Canada* (McGill-Queens University Press, 1983).

He did his undergraduate studies at Harvard, where he graduated magna cum laude, was elected to Phi Beta Kappa, and received a Woodrow Wilson Fellowship. He then took a Master in Public Policy at the Kennedy School of Government and received his PhD in economics at Harvard.

Governing Fables: Learning from Public Sector Narratives, page 279
Copyright © 2011 by Information Age Publishing
All rights of reproduction in any form reserved.

Index

A

active listening, 221

Adams, J., 79

administrative novels, 18–19

Advise and Consent, 148–50, 151–2, 159, 172, 251, 263; fable structure of, 244 table 8.2, 246; as polyphonic, 149, 254

All the King's Men, 139–41, 143, 145, 172, 173; fable structure of, 244 table 8.2, 245

Allison, Graham: *Essence of Decision*, 24, 181, 182, 189–94, 201, 208, 237, 243–4, 254

Allison, Graham, and Philip Zelikow, 177–8, 181, 189–94, 199, 209, 210

Altman, Robert, 175n. 7

Alvarez, J., and C. Merchan, 12

The Amazing Mrs. Pritchard, 23–4, 66, 86, 88–93, 96, 172, 251; fable structure of, 241 table 8.1, 243

American jury narratives, 5, 25, 213–38; as citizens' stories, 216; as 'frontline' fables, 213; juries and cabinets as analogous, 216; juries compared to other public sector tribunals, 235–6; juries as unique decision-making body, 215–16, 235; Juror 8 in *Twelve Angry Men*, 217, 218, 219, 220, 221–7, 229, 231, 236, 237, 238, 238n. 2, 244 table 8.2, 246, 255, 264; management

lessons derived from, 236–8; *The Runaway Jury* (Grisham), 216; *A Trial by Jury* (Burnett), 25, 213–15, 227–35, 236, 244 table 8.2, 245, 255; *A Trial by Jury* and Burnett's managerial behavior, 231, 235, 237–8; *A Trial by Jury* and polyphony, 233; *A Trial by Jury* and use of the first person, 228; *Twelve Angry Men* (Rose), 25, 214–15, 216, 216–27, 228, 230, 232, 236, 237, 238, 244 table 8.2, 245, 246, 255, 264; *Twelve Angry Men* as classic management text, 219; *Twelve Angry Men* and the word 'listen,' 218, 221–7; use of storytelling in, 255

American narratives of educational reform, 5, 10, 27–60, 213, 240, 248, 252–3, 256; 'based on a true story' narratives, 23, 29, 30, 35–8, 43, 60; *Cheaters* as counter-fable, 30, 39–44, 45, 55, 56, 61n. 3, 240, 254, 262; *The Class (Entre les Murs)* as counter-fable, 48–51, 55, 56, 240, 262–3; compared to American political fables, 247; counter-fables, 23, 29–30, 38–51, 55, 65–6, 240; *Dangerous Minds* as transformational teacher narrative, 30, 31–3, 34–5, 36–7, 49, 55; *Dead Poets Society* as counter-fable, 30, 46–8, 55, 240; fable

25, 165, 253–4; and Dobbs's historical novels dealing with Churchill, 133n. 5; and *Essence of Decision*, 189, 192, 194; and *The Fog of War*, 24–5, 206, 254; intranarrative vs. internarrative, 8, 253; and Morgan's Blair narratives, 99–100, 254; and *One Minute to Midnight*, 187; public sector narratives as multivoiced, 253–4, 258; and *Thirteen Days*, 200; and *A Trial by Jury*, 233, 235; and *Twelve Angry Men*, 221; and *The West Wing*, 165, 169; and *Yes Prime Minister*, 254

Pompper, D., 170

Posner, Richard, 19–21, 26n. 5, 213, 217, 218

Preminger, Otto, 148, 149, 263

Presidential Power, 191

Primary Colors, 145–7, 172; fable structure of, 244 table 8.2, 246–7

Prince, G., 5, 11, 145, 198

Propp, Vladimir, 7–8

public-choice theory, 10, 249; and American political fables, 246; and British narratives of government, 137–8, 173, 241; defined, 75–6; and *The Distinguished Gentleman*, 141, 245; and *Inside Bureaucracy*, 101–2n. 9; and *The West Wing*, 178; and *Yes Minister*, 4, 23, 75–6, 79, 98, 101–2n. 9, 263

public management: literature on images of politicians and public servants, 13–14; literature on narrative and, 3–4, 10–21, 255; literature on narrative as research methodology, 17–18; 'management lessons from film and literature' literature, 14–16, 258–9; narrative used in courses on, 4, 11–12, 23; narrative as research object and methodology of, 1–25; and the 'narrative turn,' 8, 17; relationship between managerial content and narrative form, 3, 25, 239–40; storytelling as management tool, 16–17, 237–8, 240, 255–8; work narratives of public servants, 2. *See also* frontline public servants; public sector narratives

public sector narratives: administrative novels, 18–21; American jury narratives, 5, 25, 213–38 (*see also separate heading*); American narratives of educational reform, 5, 10, 23, 27–60,

240, 248, 252–3, 256 (*see also separate heading*); American political fables, 24, 67, 135–73, 243–7 (*see also separate heading*); axes of organizational and individual outcomes in, 8–10; British narratives of government, 5, 23–4, 63–100, 240–3 (*see also separate heading*); British narratives of leadership, 24, 103–32, 240–3 (*see also separate heading*); classification of, 5, 8–10, 17, 54–6, 138, 240–8; Cuban Missile Crisis narratives, 177–211, 243–4 (*see also separate heading*); cumulative model of responsible public sector leadership generated from, 25, 240, 248–53; and directions for future research, 258–62; dominant fables vs. counter-fables, 7–8, 10, 18, 240–8, 258, 259, 260 (*see also under individual public sector narratives*); fables of organizational decline or renewal, 8–10, 55 table 2.1, 241 table 8.1, 244 table 8.2, 245–6; leadership lessons derived from Churchillian narratives, 24, 116–18; list of subgenres, 5; list of ten essential narratives, 262–4; management lessons derived from American jury narratives, 236–8, 248; management lessons derived from American narratives of educational reform, 56–7, 248; management lessons derived from British narratives of government, 97–100, 248; management lessons derived from Cuban Missile Crisis narratives, 178, 186, 188–9, 205, 208–11, 248; as multivoiced, 243–4, 258; narratives concerning contemporary private sector managers, 260; and questions of form, 253–4; role of scandal in, 251–2; structural comparisons among, 247–8; tension between public and private motivations in, 22; types of texts, 23, 253; use of storytelling in, 255

Puffer, S., 11

Q

Quayle, Dan, 155, 157

The Queen, 24, 66–7, 94, 95, 98–9

R

Ramanathan, S., 68, 100n. 2